"From the first pages of this book, I felt moved by the honest self-biography of Claude Steiner, put together in a beautifully co-creative edition by Keith Tudor, who himself contributes a number of chapters and also integrates chapters written by other colleagues. Some of the contributors review and critique different aspects of Claude's contributions to transactional analysis, while others share their own experiences of Claude's passionate interest for radical psychiatry, which inspired his life and work. I found this book very interesting, being eager to continue reading till the end. Through this book readers will also learn about and understand the influence that Claude had, not least in the evolution of transactional analysis in Latin America – he himself was fluent in Spanish and able to speak like a native, and, indeed, most of his books and many of his articles have been translated into Spanish. It is very interesting to understand how the life story of famous authors in psychology influenced their theories, either consciously or unconsciously. For Claude, beyond his own family history, the influence of Eric Berne as his mentor was decisive in his life, as well as the sociopolitical context of the San Francisco Bay area in the 1960s. This is an extraordinary book; one that provides the background to understanding the life and work of a great man, as well as the transgenerational script of transactional analysis itself, through at least three generations."

Gloria Noriega, *Winner of the Eric Berne Memorial Award 2008, Teaching and Supervising Transactional Analyst, Mexico City, Mexico*

"My gratitude to Keith for bringing together this excellent volume. Claude had a rare ability to talk to many different audiences while never compromising his essential political values. Relating the different pieces of his legacy to the varied voices collected here gives us a portrait of Claude infused with his commitment to cooperation and his talent for relationship."

Beth Roy, *San Francisco, USA*

"I am excited that Keith Tudor has invested such a huge amount of time and energy to put this great book together to make the challenging ideas of the emotional activist Claude Steiner about power, love, and emotional literacy known to a broader audience. The theory and practice of emotional literacy have had a great positive influence on my professional life as a psychotherapist working with couples and groups as well as on my personal relationships. Keith Tudor's book will provide a stimulus for engagement with and intensive discussion concerning these important concepts and Claude Steiner's life and work."

Anne Kohlhaas-Reith, *Medical Doctor, Teaching and Supervising Transactional Analyst, Waldkirch, Germany*

"Structurally, this work is fascinating. There are thematic seams that thicken and then narrow throughout the book, and Steiner's voice is (unexpectedly) intensified through the interpolations of other voices. The best way to see one colour is to contrast it with others, and in a sense, that is what the editor has achieved here. The biographical (and autobiographical) material on Steiner is obviously part of a

mosaic that combines with his ideas and perspectives. This approach works exceptionally well. Like all mosaics, up close it can appear fragmented, but there is a definite method in the organisation of those fragments, and that shines through clearly. This is a daring piece of work, and the most evocative book of someone's life I have read for some time. Professor Keith Tudor and his fellow-travellers have served up an extraordinary rendition of an even more extraordinary individual. Claude Steiner features prominently in this book, both directly in his own words, and refracted through the recollections of those who encountered this unique individual. The enormously diverse perspectives that are offered on Steiner's life and work achieve – through skilful editorial alchemy – a lasting impression of an author, activist, psychiatrist, and above all, someone who ceaselessly explored what it meant to be all too human."

Professor Paul Moon, *Auckland University of Technology, New Zealand*

"While providing us with many authors' plentiful reviews of his work in transactional analysis, radical therapy, emotional literacy, power, and other important areas of human behavior, what is extraordinary about this book is how my colleague Claude, following his dictum of "no lies", candidly and unabashedly reveals to the reader his "Confessions of a Psychomechanic" in many intimate aspects of his life. Not only does the reader get excellent summaries of Claude's timeless contributions from various authors, but also interspersed among them are autobiographical details, such as his death with dignity, that humanize both him and his legacy."

Leonard Campos, *PhD, Sacramento, USA*

Claude Steiner, Emotional Activist

This book describes the life and work of Claude Michel Steiner, a close colleague and friend of Eric Berne, the founder of transactional analysis. Steiner was an early and influential transactional analyst, an exponent of radical psychiatry, and the founder of emotional literacy. Steiner also contributed a number of theories and concepts to the psychological literature.

The book comprises edited excerpts from his unpublished autobiography, "Confessions of a Psychomechanic", alongside commentaries and critical essays from colleagues on his major contributions to the fields of psychology, transactional analysis, radical therapy, and emotional literacy. Topics covered include script theory and the theory of strokes, recognition hunger, radical therapy, and the concept of power, and emotional literacy and love. In assessing Steiner's various contributions, the book also identifies central themes in his work and life and considers the autobiographical nature of theory.

This unique collection demonstrates not only the range of Steiner's insights but also his importance to the wider field and will be essential reading for practitioners and trainees alike.

Keith Tudor is a Certified Transactional Analyst and a Teaching and Supervising Transactional Analyst, accredited by the International Transactional Analysis Association. He has been involved in transactional analysis for over 30 years and is the author of some 80 publications on the subject, including three books.

Claude Steiner, Emotional Activist

The Life and Work of Claude Michel Steiner

Edited by Keith Tudor

LONDON AND NEW YORK

First published 2020
by Routledge
2 Park Square, Milton Park, Abingdon, Oxon OX14 4RN

and by Routledge
52 Vanderbilt Avenue, New York, NY 10017

Routledge is an imprint of the Taylor & Francis Group, an Informa business

© 2020 selection and editorial matter, Keith Tudor; individual chapters, the contributors

The right of Keith Tudor to be identified as the author of the editorial material, and of the authors for their individual chapters, has been asserted in accordance with sections 77 and 78 of the Copyright, Designs and Patents Act 1988.

All rights reserved. No part of this book may be reprinted or reproduced or utilised in any form or by any electronic, mechanical, or other means, now known or hereafter invented, including photocopying and recording, or in any information storage or retrieval system, without permission in writing from the publishers.

Trademark notice: Product or corporate names may be trademarks or registered trademarks, and are used only for identification and explanation without intent to infringe.

British Library Cataloguing-in-Publication Data
A catalogue record for this book is available from the British Library

Library of Congress Cataloging-in-Publication Data
Names: Tudor, Keith, 1955- editor.
Title: The life and work of Claude Steiner : emotional activist / edited by Keith Tudor.
Description: Abingdon, Oxon ; New York, NY : Routledge, 2020. | Includes bibliographical references and index.
Identifiers: LCCN 2019043769 | ISBN 9780367188801 (hbk) | ISBN 9780367188818 (pbk) | ISBN 9780429198977 (ebk)
Subjects: LCSH: Steiner, Claude, 1935- | Psychologists–United States–Biography. | Transactional analysis–United States–Biography. | Political activists–United States–Biography.
Classification: LCC BF109.S74 L54 2020 | DDC 150.92 [B]–dc23
LC record available at https://lccn.loc.gov/2019043769

ISBN: 978-0-367-18880-1 (hbk)
ISBN: 978-0-367-18881-8 (pbk)
ISBN: 978-0-429-19897-7 (ebk)

Typeset in Times New Roman
by Swales & Willis, Exeter, Devon, UK

Printed and bound in Great Britain by
TJ International Ltd, Padstow, Cornwall

Contents

Contributors		x
Foreword		xiv
Introduction		1
KEITH TUDOR		

UNO
Identifying the legacy   7

1   Claude Michel Steiner: his life and work   9
KEITH TUDOR

2   Claude Michel Steiner: an annotated bibliography   27
KEITH TUDOR

DOS
Scripts   55

3   Confessions of a psychomechanic: excerpts on script   57
CLAUDE STEINER

4   Attribution and alienation: reflections on
Claude Steiner's script theory   66
WILLIAM F. CORNELL

TRES
Strokes   81

5   Confessions of a psychomechanic: excerpts on strokes   83
CLAUDE STEINER

6   On strokes   89
DEEPAK DHANANJAYA

viii *Contents*

CUATRO
Radical psychiatry 103

7 **Confessions of a psychomechanic: excerpts on radical psychiatry** 105
CLAUDE STEINER

8 **Radical therapy: from the first decade onwards** 116
BECKY JENKINS, ELLEN MORRISON, AND ROBERT SCHWEBEL

9 **Radical therapy: the fifth decade** 131
LUIGI (GINO) ALTHÖFER AND V. RIESENFELD

CINCO
Power 145

10 **Confessions of a psychomechanic: excerpts on power** 147
CLAUDE STEINER

11 **On power** 155
LUIGI (GINO) ALTHÖFER AND KEITH TUDOR

SEIS
Emotional literacy 173

12 **Confessions of a psychomechanic: excerpts on emotional literacy** 175
CLAUDE STEINER

13 **On emotional literacy** 182
HARTMUT OBERDIECK

SIETE
Love 201

14 **Confessions of a psychomechanic: excerpts on love and sex** 203
CLAUDE STEINER

15 **Love is the answer** 210
KAREN MINIKIN

OCHO
Reflecting on the legacy 221

16 **A final confession from the psychomechanic: on games** 223
CLAUDE STEINER WITH KEITH TUDOR

17 **Claude Michel Steiner: death, life, and legacy** 228
KEITH TUDOR

References 250
Index 264

Contributors

Keith Tudor is a Certified Transactional Analyst and a Teaching and Supervising Transactional Analyst (both in the field of psychotherapy). He was drawn to transactional analysis (TA) partly because of its radical psychiatry tradition, and has been involved in TA for over 30 years. He is the author of over 80 publications on TA, including three books. He is Professor of Psychotherapy at Auckland University of Technology, Aotearoa New Zealand, where for the past four years he was also Head of the School of Public Health & Psychosocial Studies. He is also Visiting Associate Professor at the Univerza na Primorskem (University of Primorska), Slovenia, Honorary Senior Research Fellow at the University of Roehampton, London, and Honorary Fellow of The Critical Institute.

Luigi Althöfer, known as Gino, was born in 1973 in West Germany. He was involved in squatting, left-alternative community projects, political activism, and was prosecuted for non-compliance of conscription until his late twenties. He came in contact with Radikale Therapie (RT) in a men's group in 1999 and has been contributing to the dissemination of RT since 2002. He is a graduate social worker, legal guardian, mediator, Transactional Analysis counsellor, psychotherapist, member of the RT Instructors' Collective (RT-Starter*innen-Kollektiv, RTSK). In 2011, Gino received an award from the German TA organization (DGTA) for his diploma thesis on "Radikale Therapie and its Methodological Substantiation through Transactional Analysis and Co-Counseling". He first encountered Claude in 2008 and is thankful for the time he subsequently spent with him in Berkeley and Ukiah. Gino lives in Berlin within a family of four, including his two children. His email address is: gino@radikale-therapie.de.

William F. Cornell, MA, TSTA-P, has maintained an independent practice of psychotherapy, consultation, and training for more than 40 years. He introduced and edited *The Healer's Bent: Solitude and Dialogue in the Clinical Encounter*, the collected papers of James T. McLaughlin (Routledge, 2005), and *Intimacy and Separateness in Psychoanalysis*, the collected papers of Warren Poland (Routledge, 2017). Bill is the author of *Explorations in Transactional Analysis: The Meech Lake Papers* (TA Press, 2008), *Somatic Experience in Psychoanalysis and Psychotherapy: In the Expressive Language of the Living* (Routledge,

Contributors xi

2015), *Self-Examination in Psychoanalysis and Psychotherapy: Countertransference and Subjectivity in Clinical Practice* (Routledge, 2018), *At the Interface of Transactional Analysis, Psychoanalysis, and Body Psychotherapy: Clinical and Theoretical Perspectives* (Routledge, 2018), *Une Vie Pour Etre Soi* (A Life to be Oneself) (Payot, 2015), and a co-author and editor of *Into TA: A Comprehensive Textbook* (Karnac, 2016), as well as numerous articles and book chapters. He was a co-editor of the *Transactional Analysis Journal* (2003–2018) and is now the editor of the Routledge book series, "Innovations in Transactional Analysis". Bill was the recipient of the Eric Berne Memorial Award in 2010 for his contribution to the relational and somatic organisation of the child ego state, and the European Association for Transactional Analysis Gold Medal in 2015 for his commitment to supporting the dissemination of TA in scientific literature, academia, and wider professional communities.

Deepak Dhananjaya is a Certified Transactional Analyst in Psychotherapy (CTA-P), Psychotherapist, Agile Coach and a Leadership coach (ACC-ICF). He has a private practice and runs an organisation development and transformation organisation, AgileSattva Consulting in Bangalore, India. He is an engineer and has earned a Master's degree in Sexuality and Sexual Counselling. He works in the area of sexuality, focusing on helping clients accept their own sexuality, building support systems that can help them experience inclusion and developing safe behaviours. In Bangalore he works with groups, families, and individuals. His work is deeply influenced by transactional analysis, and he has developed an interest in deepening and integrating relational psychotherapy principles in his practice. He is currently Managing Editor of the *South Asian Journal of Transactional Analysis*, the e-journal of the South Asian Association of Transactional Analysis, and is Vice President (Development) of the International Transactional Analysis Association. Deepak believes in compassionate activism.

Becky Jenkins was born in 1937 in Brooklyn, New York, and returned to San Francisco when she was two years old. Her parents were famous West Coast artists, Dorothea Lange and Maynard Dixon, and were both politically active: her mother worked for the Works Progress Administration and the Writer's Project in New York, and her father worked in the East Coast Labor Movement. Becky had a tumultuous childhood and, after being placed in a boarding school, she had the good fortune of being included in her father's new family when she was eight years old. She attended public schools in San Francisco (SF) at the height of America's McCarthy witch hunt, and, during her adolescence, was active in various political groups fighting for civil rights and against the Korean War. While studying at SF State University, she was a primary organizer of the emerging student movement. Having completed a BA in Theater Arts, and after a variety of jobs, she began receiving therapy from a young interesting-sounding TA therapist in the East Bay: Claude Steiner. He soon recruited her and others, including Bob Schwebel, to become part of the emerging radical psychiatry movement. Bob and Becky began to run groups supervised by Claude and working in a collective of others who

xii   *Contributors*

were interested in this new approach. Since those early days she has conducted many groups, done innumerable mediations, seen individuals, and trained others to be radical therapists – over the last almost 50 years. Her practice is somewhat diminished now that she is an "old lady", but she continues happily to run several groups, to see people individually or over the phone when called for, and to conduct mediations at her home in San Francisco.

Karen Minikin, MSc CTA(P) TSTA(P), is a Teaching and Supervising Transactional Analyst with a clinical and supervision practice in Devon and West Somerset. She teaches psychotherapy at a number of training institutes within the UK and Europe and has presented at national and international conferences. She is interested in the conscious and unconscious dynamics of power, politics, and relational dynamics across all fields of transactional analysis, though her writing focuses on the psychotherapy field. Previously, she edited the race and culture column for the *Counselling and Psychotherapy Journal* (the journal of the British Association of Counselling and Psychotherapy) and has contributed a chapter on the **subject** in *Relational Transactional Analysis: Principles in Practice*, edited by Heather Fowlie and Charlotte Sills (Karnac, 2011), and (with Keith Tudor) on gender psychopolitics in *Transactional Analysis in Contemporary Psychotherapy*, edited by Richard Erskine (Karnac, 2015). She has also contributed articles to journals, including the *Transactional Analysis Journal*.

Ellen Morrison, Licensed Clinical Social Worker, professional facilitator and artist, lives with her wife in Berkeley, California and deeply enjoys being close to the coastline. Growing up in communities centred around political action, Ellen carries forward a social justice lens informed by being a white, queer woman, with Swedish immigrant heritage, in an inter-racial marriage. Focused on equitable relationships, she brings attention to the analysis of power as a core element of interpersonal and social change and is grateful to her radical therapy training for giving her this foundation. This body of work is truly at the heart of her life's work. In her extensive work in the field of community mental health as well as with intercultural and interracial relationships, she weaves together diverse practices helpful to navigating the complexities of human behaviour and interrupting cycles of trauma and oppression. Ellen currently has a psychotherapy, mediation, and consultation practice committed to centralizing racial justice and collective liberation.

Hartmut Oberdieck is a Clinical Transactional Analyst, Senior Teacher of Emotional Competence, physician, and a specialist in psychotherapeutic medicine. After nearly 30 years of clinical leadership (including 12 years in a drug treatment facility in Berlin and more than 16 years as chief medical officer and deputy chief physician in a psychosomatic clinic in the Allgäu, Germany), he works in his own practice offering psychotherapy, supervision, and further education. For more than 30 years, he has been working on the concept of emotional competence, which he learned from Claude Steiner. Claude and he enjoyed a close collegial relationship for many years, in addition to which he had a deep friendship with him. From June

2010 to October 2016, he was chief executive officer of the German Association for Emotional Competence.

V. Riesenfeld grew up in Berlin (Germany) in very poor and unstable conditions with a single mother. V's life can best be described as a patchwork in which there are often simultaneities and atypical sequences. So the parenting (three children) and training (electrician, nurse*) came early, the high school graduation late. In the course of this "work of art" V. has been employed as a factory worker, student, graduate sociologist, political educator, DJ*, techno/houseclub owner (as part of a collective), gender researcher, systemic therapist, and mediator, work and skills V. has provided for people and groups for donations. V. has lived in shared apartments and occupied house projects, in a marriage, with children, and as a single person. Today V. lives alone in a small apartment, but extends feelers into a commune with a common economy. V. had first contact with Radical Therapy (RT) in 2003. V. has been involved in the dissemination of RT since 2015 and is a member of the RT-Instructors-Collective in Germany.* (An explanation of Riesenfeld's use of asterisks can be found in the note on p.144.)

Robert Schwebel grew up in a loving and politically progressive family in New York. More good luck: As an undergraduate he studied with Jean Piaget for nine months in Geneva, Switzerland and was taught the Piagetian interview method because they needed an English speaker for a study. More good luck: At the end of his first year in graduate school, he met Claude Steiner and became part of the original Radical Psychiatry Collective. In 1976 he received a PhD from the University of California, Berkeley. In 1981 he moved to Tucson, Arizona where he directed a public funded drug-counselling programme, wrote several books, and started The Seven Challenges Program (www.sevenchallenges.com), a continuation and expansion of radical psychiatry and of Claude's work in transactional analysis with regard to alcohol and other drugs. More good luck: he met and married a wonderful Mexican woman named Claudia. They are happily married with two grown sons.

Foreword

For as long as I can remember, my Dad would tell me that he was going to live to be 100. He said that Eric Berne's example had convinced him that he could determine the length of his own life. Because my Dad was so often right about his theories, I wholeheartedly believed him. We envisioned that he would be giving world lecture tours, writing books filled with new ideas, and playing with his great grandchildren up to the day he died on January 6, 2035.

While my Dad was often right, he sometimes was disastrously wrong. We lost him 18 years earlier than we expected. The last chapter of his biography, about his gradual and tragic dying from prostate cancer and Parkinson's disease, is yet to be written. While he never got to see any of his grandchildren married, and he never got to go on the next trip to Peru or vote in the next election, his last day with us was like a lifetime of healing. He made apologies and shared intimate words of love with each of us individually, and a lifetime of lessons ("Don't let perfection be the enemy of the good") and coming to peace. His penultimate words "I'm so lucky" and his ultimate words "Love is the answer" are with us always.

This biography is a tremendous gift to my father's legacy. On behalf of my family I want to express our deep gratitude to Keith for writing this biography, and to all the colleagues who contributed.

There were so many people that Dad loved, deeply, that he couldn't tell us about them all. We just knew that there were many people in his life that mattered the world to him, and with all of us he loved to have discussions about life and to talk for hours about true feelings. We knew he loved entire countries, like Nicaragua and Mexico. We knew he loved Paris, the city of his birth. There are stories and people that are not in this book: about his best friend Charlie Rappeleye, and his oldest friend David Geisinger. That's the way it was with Dad: there was always more to learn about and from him – and this book demonstrates that this is still the case.

Someday, we (Claude's family and close colleagues) hope to establish the Claude Steiner Library at the "Healing Center" where he lived on his 180-acre Round Mountain Ranch in Ukiah, northern California. We hope to restore the ranch to its original beautiful idyllic state and to have non-profit retreats there to further his legacy. Our hope is that this book will make that dream possible so that many more chapters, articles, and books are written!

Mimi Doohan (née Steiner)

Introduction

Keith Tudor

I first came across Claude Steiner in 1977 when I was introduced to his – and others' – work on radical psychiatry. I was studying social work and specifically interested in its radical praxis, so the critique offered by the radical psychiatrists, psychologists, and other workers in the field of mental health of the psychiatric and, more broadly, health and social care systems was informative, influential, and exciting. During this training (1977–1979), whilst on a community work placement, I was introduced to Claude's work on scripts and strokes. Later, in 1985, when I came to consider in which modality of psychotherapy I wanted to train, the radical psychiatry tradition informed my choice of transactional analysis (TA). By then, Claude's work on emotional literacy had been published (Steiner, 1984b); I was living in a collective house which was informed by our knowledge of TA, and we used emotional literacy to facilitate and enhance our relationships with each other and to inform our collective approach to domestic life including sharing finances and childcare.

I didn't actually meet Claude in person, however, until nearly 30 years later, in 2005, when we met at the International Transactional Analysis Association's (ITAA) Annual Conference, which, that year, was held in Edinburgh, UK. I was speaking on a panel on the subject of relational ethics (see Cornell et al., 2006), at the end of which Claude articulated his disagreement with some of us and, specifically, with Richard Erskine, Graeme Summers, and myself about our model of ego states – or, more precisely, our understanding of Berne's models of ego states (see Erskine, 1988; Summers & Tudor, 2000; Tudor, 2003). As the panel session was about to finish, I offered to meet Claude later to discuss our differences and/or disagreements. When the two of us actually met up, I noticed a certain sadness in and about him on which I commented, as a result of which we had much more of a personal than theoretical conversation, which, it transpired, forged the basis of our subsequent relationship, both intellectual and personal. Following the conference, we established a correspondence and communication (by phone, email, and later Skype) which endured until his death in 2017.

In 2008 I invited him to Sheffield, in the UK (where I was then living) to run a workshop on TA, during which he stayed in my house, met my family, and we had the opportunity to deepen our relationship. One of my enduring and endearing memories of this visit was of Claude reading *The Warm Fuzzy Tale* (Steiner,

1977d) to my daughter, Esther, then aged eight, as she sat on his knee. He was also very kind to my niece, Toni, who, at the time, was somewhat starstruck by meeting Claude! At one point during the visit, during an early morning walk in the local park, we had a very animated conversation about models of ego states, including what Berne had written and what he had said, a conversation which resulted in me conducting a close textual analysis of *Transactional Analysis in Psychotherapy* (Berne, 1961/1975a) in a review article which was published a few years later (Tudor, 2010; also see Steiner, 1998b). It was also during that visit that we realised the autobiographical nature of our differences: Claude's first training was as a mechanic (see Chapters 3 and 17), mine as a philosopher (my first degree was in philosophy and theology). During the visit, Toni took a picture of the two of us, which I sent to Claude, a copy of which he subsequently returned to me with the addition of two speech bubbles inserted to indicate him thinking (about me) "philosopher", no doubt with some suitable epithet, and me thinking (about him), equally epithetically, "mechanic"! (see Figure I.1).[1]

Claude and I had a number of differences and disagreements: about the definition and nature of ego states, and of integration; about the significance of the inconsistencies in Berne's writings, and his (Claude's) insistence that the oral tradition (including his personal knowledge of Berne) took precedence over the written tradition (as in what Berne actually wrote); about organisational aspects of TA; about some of his personal and professional conduct, past and present; and about his social or "political politics" (see Chapter 11).[2] Notwithstanding all this – and, indeed, in large part precisely *because* we could and did disagree robustly about all of this – we got on, and, more than that, had a lot of respect for each other. One of the qualities and, indeed, a practice that Claude credited Eric Berne as having taught him was "the value of intellectual generosity that seeks only an open-minded, intelligent response" (Steiner, 2004, p. 2), and I certainly experienced that with Claude.[3] Also, we did agree about a number of things and, not least, the original radicalism of TA, and I certainly came to appreciate his perspective on psychomechanics.

Figure I.1 Claude and Keith, Sheffield, 2008

Introduction 3

In 2010 we ran a workshop together, in Manchester, UK, during which we again articulated some disagreements but also demonstrated our respect and love for each other, a dynamic that appeared to have a powerful impact on some of the participants.

This book began its life, appropriately enough, in Claude's house in Berkeley, California. I was visiting Claude a few days before the ITAA World Conference which was being held in San Francisco in August 2014. Some years earlier, in 2007, a TA conference had been organised and held, also in San Francisco, on the subject of "Cooperation & Power", to which Claude had not been invited. Whilst I appreciate that Claude was not an easy person to deal with and, during the course of his career in and association with TA, he had upset a lot of people (see Chapters 3, 13, and 16), nevertheless, given his contribution to these specific subjects, I considered that his exclusion from this particular conference had been a significant personal and organisational discount of Claude and his work (see Chapter 16). When I learned that the 2014 ITAA Conference was being held in San Francisco, I was determined to honour Claude's work and legacy in his home city, and so discussed with him the possibility of him running a workshop there. As by then he was experiencing significant health problems (prostate cancer, and the early onset of Parkinson's disease), this was complicated, and so we came up with the solution that we would run the workshop together on the basis that, if he was well enough, he'd be there, and, if he wasn't, he wouldn't. In the event he was; the workshop was attended by nearly a third of the conference delegates, and was very successful (Steiner & Tudor, 2014). During this visit I initiated some conversations about his work and legacy and, given my experience of writing and editing, told him that I was interested in writing a book about him and his work. He was pleased and offered his full cooperation.

We maintained contact over the next two years, during which his health deteriorated significantly, and so I was not surprised when, early in 2016, I received an invitation to attend a workshop with him which, in a separate email to me, he described as his "last hurrah". Of course, I took up the invitation and attended the workshop, to which he had invited a number of colleagues (from Germany, Spain, and the United States), who represented his interests and contribution to TA, radical psychiatry, and emotional literacy (for a discussion of the relationship between which, see Chapters 1 and 17). The workshop took place at his ranch, the Round Mountain Ranch, just outside Ukiah, northern California, during 8–10 July that year. During this time I was fortunate not only to be able to experience him in action again, and for the last time, but also to meet colleagues from outside TA who were interested in these other aspects of Claude's contributions. These included:

- Becky Jenkins, Shelby Morgan, and Joshua Walker, and, later, Shelby Morgan, Ellen Morrison, and Bill Shields, representing Claude's involvement in radical psychiatry and, later, emotional literacy;
- Hartmut Oberdieck and Verena Kuhnen, representing Claude's work on emotional literacy;

4 Keith Tudor

- A group of younger, German colleagues – Gino (Luigi) Althöfer, Thies Diestelkamp, Andy Hecchler, Ulrike Liebsch, Barbara Magistry, Viola Niehoff, and Jess Ward – who had been inspired both by Claude's work in radical psychiatry and by Hogie Wyckoff's development of radical therapy and problem-solving groups; and
- Agustín Devós, Claude's protégé and Spanish publisher (Figure I.2).

Outside the workshop, I was fortunate to be able to spend time with Claude and some of his closest colleagues. The discussions we – specifically, Hartmut, Agustín, and myself – were able to have with him were not only informative and useful to me, but also, I know, helpful to Claude. We were also able to look after him (as much as he would let us); we cooked, laughed, and cried together; and had some great conversations and arguments. At one point during this visit, when Agustín, Hartmut, and I were enjoying a particularly robust discussion with each other, Claude commented: "This is just the right amount of adrenaline and aggression to keep me going!" (personal communication, 10 July 2016). Sadly, no amount of adrenaline, aggression, love, or will could keep him going beyond 9 January 2017, but, as he also commented wryly (personal communication, 11 July 2016): "If you're going to be a hippy environmentalist, then you have to accept death when it's time" – which he did (see Chapter 17).

Figure I.2 Claude's last workshop, Ukiah, California, July 2016

Introduction 5

The workshop was hosted by Claude's immediate family, specifically his daughter Mimi Doolan and son-in-law Jim Doolan, and his son Eric Steiner; and I was also able to get to know them and, specifically, to begin to talk especially with Claude and Mimi about his literary estate and legacy. In that albeit relatively brief time, I forged new relationships – especially with Becky, Gino, Hartmut, Mimi, Shelby, and Agustín – for which I am most grateful.

Finally, during that visit, I was also able to spend some time with Claude back in Berkeley, and to see him in person for what turned out to be the last time (on 21 July, 2016). During this visit, I recorded some conversations with Claude, some excerpts from which appear in the book (in Chapter 16), and which also informed the design, process, structure, philosophy, and production of this book – for further details of which, as well as a fuller introduction to the nature and structure of the book, see Chapter 1.

Acknowledgements (Stroke City)[4]

To paraphrase the famous maxim, it takes a village to raise a book, especially a book of this nature which brings together both Claude's own work and that of a number of contributors, including those for whom English is not their first language. So, my acknowledgements and profound thanks go:

- To Claude himself for supporting this project and trusting me with his work. In one of my last conversations with him, in July 2016, he said: "I know you'll do a good job in representing my work", which was not only a sign of his confidence but also a lovely stroke.
- To Claude's family, and especially Mimi, Eric, and Denali, for their support for and cooperation with this project. I have worked most closely with Mimi over some three years, and have also appreciated her confidence and honest feedback about the book as it emerged, changed, and was finalised. I also thank Matthew Doohan, Mimi's son, and Claude's grandson for his permission to reproduce the words of the song "Look Deep into My Eyes" (Doohan, 2016) which he wrote for Claude.
- To the contributors – Luigi (Gino) Althöfer, Bill Cornell, Deepak Dhananjaya, Becky Jenkins, Karen Minikin, Ellen Morrison, Hartmut Oberdiek, V. Riesenfeld, and Robert (Bob) Schwebel – both for their fine contributions and for their patience as the project grew, changed, was delayed, and changed again.
- To the translators – Tul'si (Tuesday) Bhambry for her fine and timely translation and editing of Chapter 9, and Brigitte Viljoen for her help with Chapter 13.
- To various people who have helped with different aspects of the background research involved in the book – Agustín Devós for curating the website devoted to Claude's work (www.emotional-literacy.org/category/claude-steiner/) on which a number of Claude's articles and notes are available (see Chapter 2); Gino (again) with regard to the literature on radical psychiatry, radical therapy, and propaganda; and Robin Fryer for her search of old copies of *The Script* (1997–2002) for both articles by and photographs of Claude.

6 Keith Tudor

- To various people involved in the production – Karen Begg for her editorial assistance, especially with the Bibliography (Chapter 2) and the References; Louise Embleton Tudor, Professor Paul Moon, and Isabelle Sherrard for their close reading and peer review of the whole book; Leonard Campos, Anne Kolhaas-Reith, Paul Moon, Gloria Noriega, and Beth Roy for their generous endorsements; Russell George at Routledge and Tom Cole at Swales & Willis for guiding the project through production; and N. J. Fox at Swales & Willis for his close copy-editing.
- To my family – Louise, Saul, and Esther – and, with regard to this book, especially Esther, not only as she has fond memories of Claude's visit (as noted above) but also, as someone who likes making cocktails, and in honour of Claude's favourite drink, provided for the author/editor and two readers of the manuscript, some tequila sunrises and sunsets along the way!

Notes

1 Claude's apparent antipathy of philosophers and philosophy is somewhat contradicted by his own extensive reading and understanding of certain philosophers, represented most clearly in his "Notes for Philosophers" in his book *Emotional Literacy: Intelligence with a Heart* (Steiner, 2003c) in which he discusses the contribution of a number of philosophers, including Socrates, Plato, St. Augustine, Kant, Nietzsche, and Foucault, to the subject of love, lying and honesty, truth, violence, "the dark side", and abuse.
2 For instance, in the 2016 US primary elections, he supported Hilary Clinton rather than Bernie Sanders.
3 Although Claude's thrift (see Chapter 3) could, at times, appear as a certain meanness, he was intellectually very generous, for instance, in sharing a lot of his work and ideas through his website, an updated version of which can be found at: www.emotional-literacy.org.
4 That these acknowledgements are strokes or recognitions for the people concerned is itself an acknowledgement of the practice that Claude and other early radical psychiatrists and transactional analysts adopted as a way of counteracting (or "trashing") the stroke economy (Steiner, 1974a) (also see Chapters 5 and 6), and of promoting the cultivation of "our inborn loving capacities" (Steiner, 2003c, p. 57).

UNO

Identifying the legacy

1 Claude Michel Steiner

His life and work

Keith Tudor

This chapter sets the scene for the rest of the book by briefly introducing Claude Michel Steiner and his work, including that which lies beyond the scope of this book. It discusses the nature of the book, including the concept of confession, and its structure, which interleaves Claude's own words about his life with those of others, that is, colleagues who offer some commentary on his theoretical contributions. Together with Chapter 2 and Chapters 16 and 17, this chapter forms a pair of double bookends which frame the material in between: this first chapter focuses on introducing, scoping, and contextualising Claude's work, while the following chapter comprises an annotated bibliography of his work; in the last part of the book, Chapter 16 offers some reflections from Claude himself, while Chapter 17 comprises my reflections on his legacy, including his life and death.

Claude Michel Steiner

Claude Steiner was a mechanic, psychologist, transactional analyst, political activist, radical psychiatrist, and the founding exponent of emotional literacy, as well as a husband (twice) and partner (twice), a father (of three children), and a grandfather (to six grandchildren) (Figure 1.1).

He was the author of 13 books and numerous articles (all of which are listed in Chapter 2). As seven chapters of this book comprise Claude's life story in his own words, I don't summarise it here, but by way of introducing him and his achievements (and as he doesn't do this himself in his autobiography), I offer some key dates which pertain to his life and work (Table 1.1).

Claude was a man of many parts and, as his daughter, Mimi, puts it in her Foreword to this book, there was always more to learn about him. For instance, not everyone who knew Claude was aware of the fact that he made huge contributions to three specific areas: transactional analysis (TA), both generically and in developing specific theory and practice; radical psychiatry (RP) (similarly); and emotional literacy (EmLit), which, arguably, is itself a specific development from TA and RP. Although he presented himself in this way – see for instance his acknowledgements in his last book *The Heart of the Matter* (Steiner, 2009) – not everyone in these different fields and communities was – or is – necessarily aware of the extent

10 *Keith Tudor*

Figure 1.1 La Familia (from left to right): Eric (son), Julian (nephew), Claude, Miguel (brother), Mimi (daughter), Kati (sister), Allyson (niece), and Darca (partner), Santa Rosa, *c.*1978

Table 1.1 Key dates in Claude Steiner's life

1935	Born on 6 January in Paris, France to Valerie and Wilhelm Steiner
1937	His sister Kati is born (also in Paris)
1939–1946	Lives in Spain
1944	His brother Miguel is born, in Madrid, Spain
1946–1952	Lives in Mexico City and Cuernavaca, Mexico
1952–1954	Lives in Santa Monica, California, USA
1954	Graduates with an AA[1] in Physics, Santa Monica City College, Santa Monica, California
1954–1960	Lives in the San Francisco Bay Area, California
1956	Marries Ursula Cohen
1957	Meets Eric Berne
	Graduates with a BA Psychology, University of California, Berkeley
1959	Graduates with an MA in Child Development, University of California, Berkeley
1960–1965	Lives in Ann Arbor, Michigan
1962	His daughter Mimi is born
1964	His son Eric is born
1965	Graduates with a PhD in Clinical Psychology, University of Michigan, Ann Arbor
1965–2016	Lives in the San Francisco Bay Area, and Ukiah, California
1965–1970	Becomes a Staff Psychologist, Center for Special Problems, San Francisco
1967	Obtains his California Psychologist License, California
From 1969	Becomes a Teaching Member, International Transactional Analysis Association

1969	Claude and Ursula divorce[2]
	Meets Hogie Wyckoff
1970	Eric Berne dies
From 1970	Commences private practice, offering group and individual psychotherapy, Berkeley and Ukiah
1971	Receives the Eric Berne Scientific Award (for the script matrix)
	Publishes *Games Alcoholics Play* (with an introduction written by Eric Berne) Publishes *TA Made Simple*
1974	Publishes *Scripts People Live*
1975	Publishes an edited book *Readings in Radical Psychiatry*
1976	Separates from Hogie Wyckoff[3]
	Begins relationship with Darca Nicholson
	Publishes (with Carmen Kerr) an edited book *Beyond Scripts and Games by Eric Berne*
	Buys Round Mountain Ranch, Ukiah, California
1977	Publishes *The Warm Fuzzy Tale*
1979	Publishes *Healing Alcoholism*
1980	His daughter Denali Nicholson is born.
	Receives the Eric Berne Scientific Award (for the stroke economy)
	Publishes *A Manual on Cooperation*
	Publishes *The Other Side of Power*
1983	Begins relationship with Adriane Rainer[4]
1986	Publishes *When a Man Loves a Woman*
1989–1994	Is the Senior Editor, *Propaganda Review*
1989	Separates (finally) from Darca Nicholson
	Separates from Adriane
	Begins relationship with Jude Hall
1992	His first grandchild Matthew is born (to Mimi and Jim)
1994	His second grandchild Bella is born (to Mimi and Jim)
	Marries Jude Hall
1997	Publishes (with Paul Berry) *Achieving Emotional Literacy*
2000	His third grandchild Alex is born (to Eric and Vicki)
2003	His fourth grandchild Mariel is born (to Eric and Vicki)
2005	His fifth grandchild Adric is born (to Denali and Carl)
2008	Publishes (online) *Excellence in Aging for Men*
2009	His sixth grandchild Dylan is born (to Denali and Carl)
	Publishes *The Heart of the Matter*
2016, July	Conducts his last workshop, at his Round Mountain Ranch, Ukiah
2017	Dies on 9 January, in Ukiah

of his contribution to the other two fields. Indeed part of my motivation for designing and editing this book in the way I have is precisely to acknowledge and present the extent of Claude's contributions (summarised in Table 1.2).

Claude of course had his own views about his ideas, the development of his ideas, the relationship between different aspects of his work, and his legacy. When I met him for the last time on 17 July 2016, he gave me a piece of paper on which he'd written down what he thought had been his "10 Top Ideas" (see Figure 1.2.

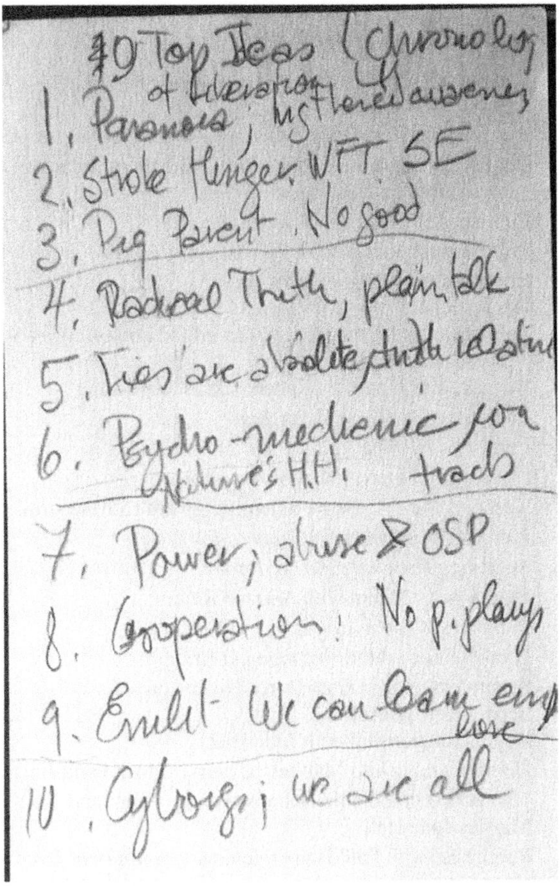

12   *Keith Tudor*

Figure 1.2 Claude's "10 Top Ideas", July 2016

When I discussed my concept for the structure of the book with Claude, which was to interleave his reflections with those of others, he said that he wanted it to represent what he considered to be the key concepts or new ideas that he had contributed to the field of psychology (and hence the list), although, while claiming these as significant, he also acknowledged that "these ideas, none of them are really new: they're all adaptations of old ideas" (Claude Steiner, personal communication, July 2016). Nevertheless, he defined these as follows (in chronological order):

1.   Regarding **paranoia** – specifically the reframing of paranoia as meaning "heightened awareness" (Steiner, 1973d), and the use of the phrase "paranoid fantasy" in emotional literacy (Steiner, 1984b), based on intuition (see Chapter 12). In claiming this contribution, Claude also acknowledged the influence of

His life and work 13

R. D. Laing (1960, 1969, 1972), whom he had met and interviewed in 1975 (Steiner & Meigham, 1975).

2. Regarding **stroke hunger** – specifically the identification of stroke hunger. However, as stroke hunger is another way of expressing recognition hunger as identified by Berne (1970/1973), I don't view this as a new contribution as much as his work on the stroke economy (Steiner, 1971f) which was new and for which he won the Eric Berne Scientific Award in 1971.

3. Regarding the Parent ego state – specifically the identification of the "**Pig Parent**" (Wyckoff & Steiner, 1971; Steiner, 1978e, 1979d, 1988e), the significance of which is discussed in Chapter 10).

4. Regarding transactions – his insistence on **radical truth** and plain talking, the prime examples of which are his autobiographical work (Steiner, 2008a, 2017) which is excerpted in this present work (in Chapters 3, 5, 7, 10, 12, 14, and 16), the significance of which is also discussed in this chapter and Chapter 17).

5. Regarding his definition of **lies** as absolute, compared with truth being relative (see Steiner, 2003c). I would view this as part of the previous contribution and not as a separate "top" idea.

6. Regarding the person and role of the therapist – his view of the therapist as a **psycho-mechanic**, which is represented throughout his *Confessions* (of which more below, and in Chapter 17).

7. Regarding **power** – a concept about which Claude wrote extensively (see Steiner, 1975e, 1975f, 1981e, 1987, 1988d, 1992, 1998a) and which is the subject of Chapters 10 and 11 and also discussed in Chapters 4, 6, 8, 9, 13, and 15.

8. Regarding practice – specifically **cooperation** and what he and the early radical psychiatrists referred to as the cooperative contract, i.e., no lies, no rescues, and no power plays (see, for example, Steiner, 1974a, 1975a, 1980a, and Chapters 10 and 17).

9. Regarding transactions and emotions – specifically his work on **emotional literacy** (Steiner, 1984a, 1984b, 1988b, 1992, 1996, 2003c; Steiner & Perry, 1997), which is the subject of Chapters 12 and 13.

10. Regarding human nature in the context of the information age – that is, his view that we are all **cyborgs**, about which he had written as early as 1998 (Steiner, 1998a).

While it was almost inevitable that we would disagree about aspects of his work and their relative significance (see Introduction), I had Claude's full support for this project and, in one of the last conversations I had with him (in July 2016), he said: "I know you'll do a good job in representing my work." I can only hope that I have.

Of course, neither the list above nor, indeed, this book represents all of Claude's work, which also includes:

• TA – in addition to his award-winning work on scripts (see Chapters 3 and 4) and strokes (see Chapters 5 and 6), Claude made a consistent contribution to TA theory and practice, from an article describing an early research experiment

14   *Keith Tudor*

(published in 1962) to a report on a conference he attended in Lima, Peru (published in 2015). In TA circles, Claude would usually introduce himself by saying that he was a disciple of Eric Berne – and he took (t)his discipleship very seriously, writing a lot over the years about what he viewed as the distinct contribution of TA (and of Berne) (for references to which see also Chapter 17).

- RP – Claude was central to the development of radical psychiatry and later radical therapy (RT) and was variously involved in three magazines promoting radical approaches to therapy: *The Radical Therapist* (1970–1971), *Issues in Radical Therapy*, *Issues in Radical Therapy & Cooperative Power*, and *Issues in Cooperation and Power* (1973–1981), and a second iteration of *Issues in Radical Therapy* (from 1982). He was a member of a number of RP collectives, both practising and training others. In addition to writing about RP itself (see Chapters 7, 8, and 9) and power (see Chapters 10 and 11), he wrote numerous articles about different aspects of RP, broadly from 1970 to 1988 (which are listed in the next chapter and many of which are cited in Chapter 17).[5]

- Research – Claude was passionate about research. Indeed, it was at Berne's instigation that Claude went to the University of Michigan (1960–1965) to study and complete his doctorate (see Steiner, 2013) on the subject of attention cathexis (Steiner, 1965).[6] Berne's motivation in encouraging Claude to undertake doctoral research was at least in part to lend weight to his emerging approach, a motivation which Claude drew on in advancing an agenda of research within TA over many years. As early as 1962 Claude was named as Director of Research for the San Francisco Social Psychiatry Seminars, and, some years later, within the International Transactional Analysis Association, he took up the position of Vice President of Research and Innovation (2001–2003).

- Alcohol studies – in the late 1960s, Claude undertook some important work in the field of alcoholism, applying Berne's game theory to games alcoholics played (Steiner, 1969c, 1971b) and, against the current wisdom of the time, which was heavily influenced by Alcoholics Anonymous, argued that people could be cured of alcoholism without having to stop drinking alcohol.

- Propaganda and information – in his biographical description in an unpublished paper titled *Surfing the Info-wave* (Steiner, 1992), Claude described himself as "a specialist on the impact of the information age in human psychology … He turned his attention to the issues of deceptive and mass communication a decade ago" (p. 3). In his interview with Anne Kohlhaas-Reith (conducted in December 1989 and December 1990), Claude acknowledged that he hadn't had a single new idea in TA or radical psychiatry in the previous ten years, but that his new ideas were in propaganda, deceptive communication, and the new information order. At the end of the interview he suggests:

> just as there is stroke hunger, there is information hunger, and just as there is stroke scarcity and a stroke economy there's information scarcity and an information economy. And just as there are warm fuzzies and

plastic fuzzies and cold pricklies there is true, valid, information, and there is false information, there is junk information, a major capitalist enterprise. And that people will take any information if they can't get good information.

(Kohlhaas-Reith & Steiner, 1991, p. 24)

- Technology – Claude was an early adopter of technology and, as Vice President Internet (2004–2007), stated that "My aim is to make full use of information technology to bring transactional analysis into the public's awareness" (Steiner, 2005b, p. 4). He also wrote about the information age, especially with regard to emotions (1992, 1997, 1999a, 1999b, 2000e, 2009). Claude's interest in technology and mechanics dates back to his childhood (Figure 1.3). As he himself comments in his *Confessions*:

  I have on my desk another significant photograph of myself, perhaps five years old, attentively looking at some gadget while applying a screwdriver to it. Also taken by my father this picture is prophetic for, as long as I can remember, I have been a tinkerer, using my hands and fingers to wield tools, a creative fixer, an assembler, a designer and inventor of useful electrical, mechanical and psychological devices: a dual light switch, an automatic door closer, a permission encounter exercise, an experiential practice to learn to love.

Figure 1.3 Claude, c.1940

16   *Keith Tudor*

- Emotional literacy – although Claude wrote the first article on emotional literacy, a term he credited to Nancy Graham (see Steiner, 2003c) in 1984 (published in the *Transactional Analysis Journal*), the antecedents of EmLit theory and practice may be found both in TA and RP. In addition to writing specifically about EmLit (see Chapters 12 and 13), he went on to write about love (see Chapters 14 and 15), emotional intelligence, ageing, emotional awareness, and dying.
- … and much more …

Based on my own reading of Claude's work, as well as my conversations with him, Table 1.2 brings all this together, noting (and providing citations for): (a) his main theoretical contributions, as well as his "top 10 ideas"; (b) where these fit within his three main fields of TA, RP, and EmLit; and (c) where these contributions are represented and discussed in this book.

The nature and structure of the book

In the course of planning and editing the book (over three years), a number of colleagues and friends referred to it as my "biography" of Claude, in response to which I often wanted to correct them and say "Oh no, it isn't!". However, I came to realise that in some ways it is – and in others ways it isn't! Although I was always clear about the overall structure – of interleaving Claude's own words about his life and work with those of others – as I come to the end of this process (Introductions and introductory chapters are always the last to be written), I am clearer about the nature of the book. As I see it, the book comprises three elements, layers, and methodologies:

- The first is autobiographical – and is represented by excerpts from an unpublished autobiography that Claude wrote about his life and work. The original was written in an unexpurgated, confessional style, based on his method of "plain talk" – which is implied in the TA principle of open communication, and is embodied in the practice of emotional literacy – and on a methodology or philosophy of radical truth. This aspect of the book is, I would say, psychobiographical (see Schultz, 2005) and, specifically, autopsychobiographical (see Young, 2008a, 2008b).
- The second is a review and is represented by seven chapters on what I have identified as Claude's six major contributions, that is, to script theory; to the theory of strokes, and specifically the stroke economy; to RP and therapy; to concepts of power and how to work with it; the development of EmLit; and to ideas about love. These chapters, written at my invitation by colleagues with specific interests in those subjects and areas, offer a review of Claude's respective theoretical contributions, and, in some cases, applications and developments of his work. Thus, this aspect of the book represents a (more or less) critical literature review of Claude's work in these areas, based on different

Table 1.2 Claude Steiner's theoretical contributions and their associations with TA, RP, and EmLit, sourced from his Bibliography (Chapter 2)

Theoretical contributions	Claude's "top 10 ideas" (as identified by him, in 2016)	TA	RP	EmLit	Represented in this book
Transactional analysis (generic) (numerous articles and four books 1966–2015)		x			
Script (Steiner, 1966,[7] 1967a, 1972b, 1974a)		x	x		Chapters 3 and 4
The treatment of alcoholism (Steiner, 1967b, 1968a, 1969a, 1969c, 1971b, 1979b)		x			
Games (Steiner, 1968a, 1969a, 1971b, 2000a)		x			
Permission (Steiner, 1968a, 1968b; Steiner, 1971b)		x		x	
Potency (Steiner, 1968b; 1971b)		x			
RP (generic) (numerous publications and three books 1972–1981, and Roy & Steiner, 1988; Steiner, 2001b)	Paranoia[8]		x		Chapters 7–9
Contracts (Steiner & Cassidy, 1969; Steiner, 1974a, 1975a)		x	x	x	
Warm fuzzies (Steiner, 1970, 1977d)		x		x	
The stroke economy,[9] strokes, and stroke-centred TA (Steiner, 1971f, 1975k, 1981a, 2000b, 2003a, 2007)	Stroke hunger[10]	x	x		Chapters 5 and 6
The Pig Parent (Wyckoff & Steiner, 1971; Steiner, 1978c, 1979d)	Pig Parent[11]	x	x		Chapter 10
About Eric Berne (Steiner, 1971a, 2004, 2005c, 2010; see also Kohlhaas-Reith & Steiner, 1991)		x			
	Radical truth, plain talk[12]			x	Chapter 12
	Lies (and truth)			x	Chapter 12

(*Continued*)

Table 1.2 (Cont.)

Theoretical contributions	Claude's "top 10 ideas" (as identified by him, in 2016)	TA	RP	EmLit	Represented in this book
	Psycho-mechanic[13]	x	x	x	Chapters 3, 5, 7, 10, 12, 14, and 16
Cooperation (a number of publications 1973–1979, 1980a; Steiner & Roy, 1988)	Cooperation (no power plays)		x		Chapter 10
Power (Steiner, 1975e, 1975f, 1981e, 1987, 1988d, 1992, 1998a)	Power, (and its) abuse[14]		x		Chapters 10 and 11
EmLit and emotional intelligence (Steiner, 1984a, 1984b, 1988b, 1992, 1996, 2003c, 2005a, 2016; Steiner with Perry, 1997)	Emotional literacy			x	Chapters 12 and 13
Love (various chapters in Wyckoff, 1976; Steiner, 1986, 1995b, 2000d, 2007, 2009)				x	Chapters 14 and 15
Propaganda (Steiner, six publications 1988–1989)					Chapter 11
Cyberpsychology (the information age, the internet (Steiner, 1997, 1998a, 1999a, 1999b, 2000e, 2001a, 2009)	Cyborgs (we are all)				
Apology (Steiner, 2000a)		x			
Research (a number of articles 2001–2009)		x			

His life and work 19

theoretical critiques: psychoanalytic (Chapter 4), cultural (Chapter 6), structural (Chapters 8, 9, and 11), and gender (Chapter 15).

- The third is an appraisal and is represented by my own research into and critical commentary on Claude's work, and, to some extent, his life.[15] These chapters are informed by ideas about scoping reviews (Wilson, Lavis, & Guta, 2012), and by the principles of the cooperative contact advocated by Claude and others involved in radical psychiatry (see Steiner, 1980a), and which I discuss further below. This aspect of the book represents a critical appraisal of Claude's work, which looks both backwards and forwards.

Here I elaborate these elements and introduce the book in more detail.

Autobiography, confession, and editing

Each of the following parts of the book is introduced by a chapter that contains some autobiographical material which I have excerpted from Claude's own writing – the main one which he titled *Confessions of a Psycho-Mechanic* (and dated 2008), and a second, shorter piece which he titled *CS at 80* (which he started in April 2015 and in which he made his last entry in 2017) – full versions of which he gave me, with permission to use.[16] Remarkably, he sent me the last version of *CS at 80* on the day before he died with the following email (dated 7 January 2017, 7.22 a.m.):

> Here are the last writings …
> My thanks for doing this
> Fuzzies
> Claude

Claude introduced his own *Confessions* by referring to those of the 18th-century Swiss/French philosopher, Jean-Jacques Rousseau, who, in his *Confessions*, pledged:

> to present my fellow-mortals with a man in all the integrity of nature; and this man shall be myself.
> … I will present myself … and loudly proclaim, thus have I acted; these were my thoughts; such was I. With equal freedom and veracity have I related what was laudable or wicked, I have concealed no crimes, added no virtues; and if I have sometimes introduced superfluous ornament, it was merely to occupy a void occasioned by defect of memory: I may have supposed that certain, which I only knew to be probable, but have never asserted as truth, a conscious falsehood. Such as I was, I have declared myself; sometimes vile and despicable, at others, virtuous, generous and sublime [Rousseau, 1782/2017].

(Steiner, 2008a)[17]

20   *Keith Tudor*

To this, referring to his own *Confessions*, Claude added:

> that not only have I not said anything [here] that I knew to be false but I also did not fail to mention whatever I remembered to be true and important, in other words: The truth, the whole truth and nothing but the truth, to the best of my ability and so help me God.
>
> I hope to illustrate that in spite of the all-too-human failings of my life I managed to be a good and effective healer. Since I am probably no better or worse a person than the average therapist, this text could be of comfort (cold or warm) to those who seek to be healed or those who seek to heal. In the end it is *Vis Medicatrix Naturae*, Nature's ever present and relentless healing hand – a fact that Jean-Jacques Rousseau was fully aware of, and extensively referred to – that makes the difference.[18]

> (ibid, 2008a)

I was interested to draw on Claude's *Confessions* because, for a long time, I have been interested in the idea that all theory is autobiographical (see Valéry, 1957; Shlien, 1989/2003), and so was delighted – and appreciative – to have the opportunity to present both the autobiographical, that is, that written from Claude's experience and perspective, as well as the biographical, in the sense that, in offering critical review and appraisal of Claude's work, the contributors to this volume are, arguably, also offering some critical view of Claude himself. At the same time, there is an idea about a poetic or literary identity separate from the identity of the person. This is encapsulated in the phase "*Je est un autre*" (I is an other/ someone else), coined by the French poet Arthur Rimbaud (1971/1958). In this sense, the author is distinct from his or her work, and the task is to separate the "I" in a piece of work or writing from the identity of the author, and of the statement – and hence the linguistic device using the third-person singular form of the verb to describe the first person pronoun. This perspective has, for example, influenced the approach of Bob Dylan to his work and public persona (see Dylan, 2004; Thomas, 2017). If we think about this in terms of Berne's (1962) criteria for the diagnosis of ego states (personality), we might say that the autobiographical represents the historical and phenomenological diagnosis (or self-knowing), while the biographical represents the behavioural and social diagnosis (i.e., the view from others). My aim in interleaving Claude's voice with those of others is in order to present both the man and his ideas, as well as the interrelationship between them, on which I offer some reflections in the final chapter. In order to maximise this connection, I gave each of the contributors a copy of the chapter I had edited from Claude's *Confessions*, so that it could inform their work and they could refer to it (which most have done explicitly). In undertaking this task, we are perhaps representing the views of another songwriter, and a friend of Claude's, Jackson Browne (1967/1973) when he wrote: "Let your voice ring back my memory | Sing my songs to me."

On the basis of his own writings, represented here in the excerpts from his *Confessions* and *CS at 80*, it is clear that Claude valued honesty and, for all his faults,

His life and work   21

was honest – with and about himself, as well as with and about others. As the reader will see, some of the comments Claude makes about himself in his *Confessions* do not paint a pretty or flattering picture; they do, however, form part of an honest account of him as a person – and, again, I offer some reflections on this in the final chapter.

Being given an unpublished and unexpurgated autobiography is, of course, not only a great privilege, it is also a great responsibility, and one about which I had to think carefully. In deciding what to use, I held two things in mind. Firstly, I was clear that this book was and is not the edited autobiography of Claude Steiner (which would – and may indeed – be another project);[19] this is, rather, a book about (what I consider to be) his major contributions. So, with this in mind, I have selected passages from his *Confessions* that were relevant to the six areas represented. In fact, the passages selected from the *Confessions* and *CS at 80* and reproduced here (in Chapters 3, 5, 7, 10, 12, and 14), a total of just over 24,000 words, represent only about a quarter of the total word count of those two documents. Secondly, I was aware that the *Confessions* were not originally written for publication; Claude's idea to publish them came later,[20] and he never planned to publish *CS at 80* (though, as I have noted, he did give permission to use it). As I and others have acknowledged, Claude was very honest both about himself and others, but at times this honesty could be hurtful. So, in planning, discussing, designing, and editing this book, I have adopted the slogans of the cooperative contract from RP, that is "No power plays, no lies, no Rescues" (see Steiner, 1978a), with the addition of "no hurts", in that I have edited the selected passages from Claude's *Confessions* and *CS at 80* bearing in mind not only his own wishes, but also a mindfulness for the people to whom he refers. In undertaking this, I have been guided not only by conversations and correspondence with Claude, but also by his own reflections in a coda to the *Confessions*:

> Writing this … has been a surprisingly emotional enterprise. Sadness as I saw where I missed human opportunities, guilt as I recognized things I should and should not have done, pride at my accomplishments, happiness and dread when I recovered long forgotten memories, and awe about how much has happened and had been forgotten in my life. I was fearful that what I was taking such pains to write could not be published or that, if I published it, I would suffer or make others suffer.
>
> (Steiner, 2008a)

In maintaining this undertaking since Claude's death, I have been particularly guided by Mimi Doohan (née Steiner), his daughter and literary executor, to whom I again offer my heartfelt thanks and appreciation for her engagement and cooperation with this project.

Finally, with regard to Claude's *Confessions* (and the few passages from *CS at 80* that I have included), I have edited them [using square brackets] in terms of sense, language, and context by including citations, some explanatory footnotes, and, where possible, dates (as Claude didn't date any of his entries in the *Confessions* or

22 Keith Tudor

give much of an indication of the dates or times to which he was referring). I have retained the original directness of style, the US English spelling and punctuation, and, of course, their confessional quality.

The six areas of Claude's contributions

The structure of the book reflects six main areas in which (I think) Claude contributed to the field of psychotherapy and, more broadly, psychology and self-help, that is, with regard to (life) scripts, strokes, RP or therapy, power, emotional literacy, and love, the order of which reflects the chronological development of these ideas.

Each subsequent part, which are titled in Spanish in acknowledgement of Claude's first language, focuses on each of these six areas and, as noted, is introduced by a chapter comprising excepts from Claude's own writing from the *Confessions*. These are followed in each part by a chapter – and in the case of RP, two chapters – that provide(s) a critical review of Claude's work in that particular area.

In Dos, following Chapter 3, which comprises excerpts from Claude's *Confessions* that focus on his own life script, about which he reflected in some detail, from cradle to grave, in Chapter 4 Bill Cornell offers a critical review of Claude's work on scripts, a review which both acknowledges Claude's contribution to this aspect of TA theory and takes issue with some of the ways in which Claude concretised some of what Bill sees as Berne's original contributions. Bill is a leading figure in TA, a prolific writer and editor – and disagreed with Claude as much if not more than I did! Claude and Bill clashed on a number of occasions; nevertheless, Bill was the perfect choice to write this chapter and I am particularly appreciative of his continued engagement with Claude.

In Tres, following Chapter 5, which comprises those aspects of his *Confessions* that refer to strokes, in Chapter 6, Deepak Dhananjaya reviews Claude's work in this area, specifically Steiner (1971ff, 2003a). In doing so, Deepak offers a development of stroke theory from the perspective of two-person psychology (Stark, 1999), and of his own cultural context in India, specifically with regard to the Cultural Parent (Drego, 1983) and his own work with people who identify and are viewed as representing a sexual minority. Further examples of work with the stroke economy also appear in Chapter 5. In many ways, Deepak represents the next generation of transactional analysts, that is, those who knew Claude more through his writing than through direct contact with him. I am delighted to have Deepak's voice in these pages; he has taken forward some of Claude's ideas, especially with regard to culture. This, for me and others, is part of a broader project that questions the hegemony of Western psychology and its claims to universalism, and, for example, considers whether and, if so, how TA, with its roots in American empiricism as well as existentialism, can be applied to other cultural contexts.

In Cuarto, following Chapter 7, which comprises Claude's own reflections on RP, there are two chapters on the development of these ideas. In Chapter 8, Becky Jenkins, Ellen Morrison, and Robert Schwebel offer their personal accounts of the history of RP, including their differences with some of the developments of this aspect of Claude's work. I was determined to honour the work of this original

His life and work 23

Collective and so am particularly delighted and appreciative that Becky and Robert agreed to reflect on old times, and Ellen on more recent times. After the workshop in Ukiah, I had the good fortune to get to know Becky and to meet others (Shelby Morgan, Beth Roy, and Bill Shields) and to talk radical, gender, race, class, environmental, and indigenous politics, then and now. At the workshop in Ukiah, I also met Luigi (Gino) Althöfer and a number of other younger, radical therapists from Germany (see Introduction);[21] and, the following year, in 2017, I made the opportunity to meet and spend a couple of days with members of the Berlin group of radical therapists, in Berlin, Germany, during which we exchanged ideas about RT, RP, and TA. Gino and V. are two of this group of young(er) radical therapists based in Berlin, and of a broader movement in Germany which traces its lineage from members of the original group in San Francisco as well as from Hogie Wyckoff's own work on cooperation and problem-solving (Wyckoff, 1975b, 1977, 1980) and problem-solving (Wyckoff, 1977, 1980). During both the workshop in Ukiah and the workshop in Berlin, I was struck by the different groups holding different – and sometimes differing – aspects of the legacy of RP and RT and so I was also keen to include the voices of colleagues practising RT after some five decades of RP and RT.

In Cinco, following Chapter 10, which comprises Claude's own reflections on power, in Chapter 11, Gino and I review Claude's writings on power. When I first met Gino at the Ukiah workshop, I was immediately drawn to him as a person, as well as to his extensive interest in and knowledge of the literature of RP and RT, especially that on alienation and power. We spent some time together at that workshop and have subsequently kept in touch, and when I visited Berlin I stayed with him and his family. I am delighted to have engaged with him in this project – and look forward to future collaboration.

In Seis, following Chapter 12, which comprises those parts of the *Confessions* in which Claude reflects on the development of the theory and practice of EmLit, in Chapter 13, Hartmut Oberdieck reviews Claude's writings on this subject, and the current state of the EmLit movement. I first met Hartmut also at the Ukiah workshop: we got on, enjoyed each other's company, and had a lot of fun. Since then we have maintained contact, and, not least, were both involved in negotiating and organising the workshop about Claude at the International Transactional Analysis Association (ITAA) World Conference in Berlin in 2017. Hartmut has been centrally involved in the development of EmLit in Germany (and, indeed, in Europe), and I am delighted that he, too, has been willing to engage in and support this project.

In Siete, following Chapter 14, which comprises excepts from the *Confessions* that focus on the subject of love, about which Claude had a lot to say both personally and, increasingly, theoretically, in Chapter 15 Karen Minikin reviews his writing on love, specifically Steiner (1986, 2000d, 2009). Significantly, Claude's last words, as reported by his daughter, Mimi (see Introduction and Chapter 17), were "I'm so lucky" and "Love is the answer".[22] I first met Karen in 2003 when she was a student at the Metanoia Institute in London. Since the completion of her clinical training, she has gone on to become a Teaching and Supervising Transactional Analyst (Psychotherapy), and is a close colleague and friend. Karen is developing

24   *Keith Tudor*

her own relational perspective to RP, and I am very appreciative of her relational lens on Claude's ideas about love.

In terms of overall editing, as this book is about Claude's work, and there are many references to it from each of the contributing authors, as well as myself, I have combined the references from each chapter into one list of References. Although this is a little unusual in an edited book, I think it also brings the book together as a whole – and saves paper, regarding which I am sure that, as a "hippy environmentalist" (see Introduction), Claude would have approved!

The bookends

In my experience, books change as they progress from initial conception through various stages of gestation until publication – and this book is no exception. Although the basic concept and structure has remained constant, the details – the choice and number of Claude's contributions, the number of chapters and contributors, the overall structure and design, and the nature of the reflective chapters – have all changed, and what you, the reader, are now reading is (at least) the seventh version of the original one! As part of this, I decided to offer what I conceptualise as two double bookends to the six parts to frame the overall project of presenting Claude's life and work.

The first bookend forms Uno comprising two chapters, the first of which is this current one in which the focus is or has been on presenting an overview or scoping review of Claude's work and to introduce the thesis and structure of the book. This is followed, somewhat unusually, by a Chapter which comprises an annotated bibliography of Claude's work. I say "unusually" as such lists are usually placed in – one might say relegated to – an appendix and, for a while (in previous drafts of the book) this was also the case in this book. However, and somewhat latterly, I decided that if the theme of this part was that of identifying the legacy, then Claude's bibliography should be and is appropriately placed here.

The second bookend is Ocho which also comprises two chapters. The first comprises excerpts from Claude's *Confessions*, and from a last conversation he and I had. Interestingly, in his *Confessions*, Claude wrote comparatively little about games, and so, when I spoke to him in July 2016, in what was to be our last meeting and recorded conversation, I asked him about this, and have included his response in this chapter. Apart from the poignancy of this occasion, I think the excerpt is remarkable, though not unusual, for Claude's honesty as he clearly reflects on the games he played and links this "game-playing" to his script (see Chapter 3). The second chapter in this part and the concluding chapter in the book offers a critical appraisal of Claude's legacy.

In my last face-to-face conversation with Claude, during which we discussed what he viewed as his contributions and this book, he said: "I really appreciate your interest in my work". Then, with what was a familiar twinkle in his eyes, he added, "I guess that makes me interesting!" We both laughed. It was a lovely, spontaneous moment in what was a poignant last meeting. In this spirit, I hope that this introductory chapter has set the scene for what I hope is an interesting book about an interesting man.

Notes

1 An undergraduate "Associate" degree.
2 Ursula died in 2016.
3 Hogie died in 2002.
4 In his *Confessions* (Chapter 3), Claude notes that Darca left him in 1983.
5 Claude is sometimes, mistakenly, referred to as the founder or originator of RP. It was in fact founded by a group of people (see Chapters 7, 8, and 9), and, although Claude wrote a lot about RP (see Chapter 2), a number of others contributed to RP praxis and to the development of ideas that went into articles that appeared under Claude's name. In her introduction to a collection of papers from the second decade of RP, Beth Roy (1988a) put this well and honestly: "While his [Claude's] contribution was substantial, nonetheless the ideas he presented had been the product of collective experience thinking. However carefully he gave others credit, his name on the spine of the book nonetheless mystified the collective nature of the work" (p. 3).
6 In his *Confessions*, Claude acknowledges that his interest in the subject of attention cathexis (a Freudian concept), which today would be diagnosed as Attention Deficit Disorder, was "due probably to my own pathological fixations" (Steiner, 2008a). He goes on to say that "in emulation of my intellectual models – Einstein and Berne – I was very motivated to develop and test innovative hypotheses", describing that "when my daughter Mimi was born, in emulation of the famous 'Skinner box', I built a contraption with a baby car seat in which I could observe her eye movements in response to different visual and auditory stimuli. I had been studying the writings of Piaget on synaesthesia, the blending of the perceptions of different senses and in fact observed that Mimi noticed different things with her eyes depending on what she was hearing".
7 For his work on which Claude received the Eric Berne Memorial Award in 1971.
8 I have placed paranoia here in the context of RP as Claude himself placed this as his first "top idea" (and before his work on stroke hunger), and, as noted in the text, as it was influenced by Claude's reading of R. D. Laing. The earliest reference I can find to his use of the concept is in a letter Claude wrote to *Issues in Radical Therapy* (Steiner, 1973e). Later, the checking out and acknowledgement of paranoid fantasies became a key concept in EmLit.
9 For his work on which Claude received the Eric Berne Memorial Award in 1980.
10 In his own note on this Claude cites his work on *The Warm Fuzzy Tale* (Steiner, 1977d) and the stroke economy (Steiner, 1971c).
11 Claude himself placed this third in his "top ideas" as this had been developed in RP some years before he wrote it up with regard to TA. The earliest reference I have found to this – and thanks again to Gino Althöfer for his help with tracking this down – is in an article on alienation by Hogie Wyckoff and Claude Steiner, published in *Issues in Radical Therapy* (Wyckoff & Steiner, 1971), in which they write: "Parental and societal injunctions are eventually incorporated by the person in the form of the 'Pig Parent' which, like a chronic implant in the brain, controls people's behavior according to an oppressive scheme" (p. 4).
12 In his own note on this, Claude placed this and his next two contributions – on lies and (being a) psycho-mechanic – before his work on power and cooperation.
13 Although his *Confessions* are dated 2008.
14 In his own notes on this Claude cites his work on *The Other Side of Power* (Steiner, 1981e).
15 I say, to some extent, as I and most of the contributors to this book make some comments on Claude's life – as he presented it in his *Confessions*. Claude himself was critical of some colleagues and, in particular, Helena Hargaden, who he (Claude) considered interpreted Berne's behaviour and motivations inappropriately (see Hargaden, 2003b, 2005; Steiner, 2003e, 2003f, 2006d). I discussed this with Claude and disagreed with him about this: I think he was overly defensive and protective of his mentor's reputation

26 *Keith Tudor*

and overly agressive towards colleagues who were raising – and who continue to raise – important questions about Berne's life and work and the implications of this for TA history, theory, and practice. With regard to this present work, I am clear – and was clear with Claude – that, while I was not so interested in interpreting him, by wanting his *Confessions* (or, at least, excerpts from them) in the public domain, he was opening himself, his reputation, and legacy up to comments, commentary, and critique.

16 A complete, edited version of Claude's *Confessions* will be published by Mimi Doolan.

17 This quotation, from the Project Gutenberg eBook edition of Rousseau's *Confessions*, is slightly different from the one that Claude quotes, but, given that Claude was not writing for publication, and in the interest of consistency and accessibility, I have updated this quotation, citation, and reference (as well as others).

18 In referring to *vis medicatrix naturae*, Claude is echoing the phrase Eric Berne used to describe one of his three therapeutic slogans (Berne, 1966b).

19 As this book went to press, Mimi was planning to publish a relatively complete version of the *Confessions* which would be presented in chronological order.

20 I would say in 2008, when he referred to his *Confessions* as "this book".

21 Following the workshop in Ukiah, members of the original RP Collective (in San Francisco) invited members of the Berlin RT group to a day workshop in San Francisco (which took place in July 2016) in which both groups exchanged ideas about five decades of radical therapy.

22 Interestingly, in his "Last word" of his last published book, *The Heart of the Matter* (Steiner, 2009), Claude wrote: "Ever powerful in human affairs, love alone has not been equal to the redemptive task. [However, t]eamed with information, love, I believe, is still the answer. Love is the answer" (p. 237).

2 Claude Michel Steiner

An annotated bibliography

Keith Tudor

This list of Claude Steiner's publications is based on the one he published on his own website, with additions as a result of further research, which have more than doubled the original list. This present list includes all Claude's known published work, including poems and DVDs, as well as articles that he originally posted on his own website, which have been transferred to the Claude Steiner Archivos (www.emotional-literacy.org/category/claude-steiner/), now curated by Agustín Devós; for the purposes of this bibliography, I have only included those articles posted on this website which have not been published elsewhere. Finally, this list excludes oral presentations (speeches, workshops, etc.) where there was no written paper, as well as personal and professional correspondence, some of the latter of which may be found in the Eric Berne Archives at the University of California (www.ericbernearchives.org/). The bibliography is annotated in that I provide explanatory notes to entries; I have also cross-referenced the dates of subsequent versions as well as translations of original publications.

Every effort has been made to ensure that this bibliography is as complete as possible, and, to this end, I am especially grateful to: Luigi (Gino) Althöfer for putting me on to Claude's work on propaganda and for checking back issues of *The Radical Therapist* (1970–1972), *Issues in Radical Therapy* (1973–1979), *Issues in Radical Therapy & Cooperative Power* (1979), and *Issues in Cooperation & Power* (1980–1981); Robin Fryer for reading through those back issues of *The Script* that are not yet available online; Karen Begg for her thorough editorial assistance; and a number of colleagues who checked the details of translations, namely Niels Bagge, Agustín Devós, and Laurie Hawkes and members of the Practiciens en Analyse Transactionnelle Facebook Group. The bibliography is presented in chronological order from 1962 to 2019 (and includes the chapters from Claude's *Confessions* in this book), a chronology that is also maintained, as far as possible, within each year; a line separates the publications within a year where the month of publication is not known. This bibliography, as well as any updates to it, will also be posted on the website www.emotional-literacy.org.

Claude himself edited a book of Berne's own writing, with Carmen Kerr, entitled *Beyond Scripts and Games* (Steiner & Kerr, 1977), in which they included a complete bibliography of Berne's writing. In his conclusion to that book, Claude wrote the following:

28 *Keith Tudor*

It is our hope that having read this collection of Eric Berne's writings the reader will have a well-rounded understanding of his contribution. Some readers will wish to read on. We believe that those who do should go to the original sources. Either way we hope to have managed to present Eric Berne fairly and completely. Eric Berne's contribution goes far beyond what could possibly be included in an anthology of this sort. His writings were only part of his work.

(Steiner, 1977a, p. 371)

It seems appropriate to introduce this bibliography of Claude Steiner's writings with this reflection, hope, and acknowledgement – which I echo.

1962
October
1. Steiner, C. (1962). "No exit" revisited. *Transactional Analysis Bulletin, 1*(4), 36.

1965
Summer
2. Steiner, C. M. (1965). *An investigation of Freud's attention cathexis theory in the context of a concept formation task.* A dissertation submitted in partial requirement for the degree of Doctor of Philosophy, University of Michigan, Ann Arbor, Michigan, USA.[1]

1966
April
3. Steiner, C. (1966). Script and counterscript. *Transactional Analysis Bulletin, 5*(18), 133–135.

July
4. Steiner, C. (Ed.). (1966). Script Analysis [Section]: *Transactional Analysis Bulletin, 5*(19).
5. Steiner, C. (1966). Introductory remarks. *Transactional Analysis Bulletin, 5*(19), 150–151.

1967
April
6. Steiner, C. (1967). A script checklist. *Transactional Analysis Bulletin, 6*(22), 38–39, 56.

July
7. Steiner, C. (1967). The treatment of alcoholism. *Transactional Analysis Bulletin, 6*(23), 69–71.

October
8. Perls, F., & Steiner, C. (1967). Gestalt therapy and TA. *Transactional Analysis Bulletin, 6*(24), 93–94.

1968
January

9. Steiner, C. (1968). The alcoholic game. *Transactional Analysis Bulletin*, *7*(25), 6–16.

July

10. Steiner, C. (1968). Transactional analysis as a treatment philosophy. *Transactional Analysis Bulletin*, *7*(27), 61–64.

October

11. Steiner, C., with Steiner, U. (1968). Permission classes. *Transactional Analysis Bulletin*, *7*(28), 89.

1969
April

12. Steiner, C. M., & Cassidy, W. (1969). Therapeutic contracts in group treatment. *Transactional Analysis Bulletin*, *8*(30), 29–31.

June

13. Steiner, C. (1968). What are transsexuals and transvestites? In E. Berne *A layman's guide to psychiatry and psychoanalysis* (pp. 254–255). London, UK: Deutsch.

Summer

14. Steiner, C. (1969). *Radical psychiatry manifesto*. Retrieved from www.emotional-literacy.org/radical-psychiatry-manifesto/#more-187.[2]

October

15. Berne, E., Harris, T., & Steiner, C. (1969). Writing for publication. *Transactional Analysis Bulletin*, *8*(32), 88–89.
16. Steiner, C. (1969). Alcoholism. *Transactional Analysis Bulletin*, *8*(32), 96–97.

---

17. Steiner, C. (1969). The alcoholic game. *Quarterly Journal of Studies on Alcohol*, *30*(4), 920–938.

1970
July

18. Steiner, C. (1970). RAP Center Training Manual. *The Radical Therapist*, *1*(2).

October

19. Steiner, C. M. (1970). A fairytale. *Transactional Analysis Bulletin*, *9*(36), 146–149.
20. Dusay, J. M., Karpman, S., Steiner, C., & Cheney, W. D. (1970). Editorial policy of the TAB. *Transactional Analysis Bulletin*, *9*(36), 156–157.

30 *Keith Tudor*

1971
January
21. Steiner, C. (1971). Radical psychiatry: Principles. *The Radical Therapist*, *1*(5).
22. Steiner, C. M. (1971). A little boy's dream. *Transactional Analysis Journal*, *1*(1), 46–48.

March
23. Steiner, C. (1971). Radical psychiatry and movement groups. *The Radical Therapist*, *1*(6).

April
24. Dusay, J. M., Ernst, F. H., Everts, K. V., Groder, M. G., Karpman, S. B., Selinger, Z., & Steiner, C. (1971). Editorial policy of the TAJ. *Transactional Analysis Journal*, *1*(2), 45.[3]

July
25. Steiner, C. M. (Ed.). (1971). Strokes [Special issue]. *Transactional Analysis Journal*, *1*(3).
26. Steiner, C. M. (1971). Editorial. Strokes [Special issue]. *Transactional Analysis Journal*, *1*(3), 7–8.
27. Steiner, C. M. (1971). The stroke economy. Strokes [Special issue]. *Transactional Analysis Journal*, *1*(3), 9–15.

October
28. Conrad, F., Fort, J. & Steiner, C. M. (1971). Attitudes of mental health professionals toward homosexuality and its treatment. *Psychological Reports*, *29*, 347–350.
29. Steiner, C. (1971). Radical psychiatry manifesto. Berkeley [Special issue]. *The Radical Therapist*, *2*(3), 2. (Original work written 1969 [i.e., #14])
30. Steiner, C. (1971). Radical psychiatry: Principles. Berkeley [Special issue]. *The Radical Therapist*, *2*(3), 3. (Original work published 1971 [#21])
31. Steiner, C. (1971). Radical psychiatry: History. Berkeley [Special issue]. *The Radical Therapist*, *2*(3), 3.
32. Wyckoff, H., & Steiner, C. (1971). Alienation. Berkeley [Special issue]. *The Radical Therapist*, *2*(3), 4.
33. Steiner, C. (1971). A fuzzy tale. Berkeley [Special issue]. *The Radical Therapist*, *2*(3), 5. (Original work published 1970 [#19])
34. Steiner, C. (1971). Stroke economy. Berkeley [Special issue]. *The Radical Therapist*, *2*(3), 6–7. (Original work published 1971 [#27])
35. Steiner, C. (1971). Contractual problem solving groups. Berkeley [Special issue]. *The Radical Therapist*, *2*(3), 13.
36. Steiner, C. (1971). Radical psychiatry and movement groups [Special issue]. *The Radical Therapist*, *2*(3), 18. (Original work published 1971 [#23])
37. Steiner, C. (1971). Teaching radical psychiatry. Berkeley [Special issue]. *The Radical Therapist*, *2*(3), 23–25.

An annotated bibliography 31

38. Steiner, C. (1971). 2001 A.D. Berkeley [Special issue]. *The Radical Therapist, 2*(3).

---

39. Steiner, C. (1971). *Games alcoholics play: The analysis of life scripts.* New York, NY: Grove Press.[4]
40. Steiner, C. (1971). Radical psychiatry: Principles. In The Radical Therapist Collective *The radical therapist* (J. Agel, Producer; pp. 3–7). New York, NY: Ballantine. (Original work published 1971 [#21])[5]
41. Steiner, C. (1971). Radical psychiatry and movement groups. In The Radical Therapist Collective *The radical therapist* (J. Agel, Producer; pp. 18–26). New York, NY: Ballantine. (Original work published 1971 [#23])[6]
42. Steiner, C. (1971). Radical psychiatry manifesto. In The Radical Therapist Collective *The radical therapist* (J. Agel, Producer; pp. 280–282). New York, NY: Ballantine. (Original work published 1971 [#29])[7]
43. Steiner, C. (1971). *TA made simple: Ego states, games, scripts and "the fuzzy tale".* Berkeley, CA: TA Simple.
44. Steiner, C. M., & Dusay, J. (1971). Transactional analysis in groups. In H. I. Kaplan & B. J. Sadock (Eds.), *Comprehensive group psychotherapy* (pp. 195–204). Baltimore, MD: Williams & Wilkins.

1972
January
45. Steiner, C. M. (1972). 1971 Eric Berne Memorial Scientific Award Lecture. *Transactional Analysis Journal, 2*(1), 34–37.

April
46. Steiner, C. M. (1972). Scripts revisited. *Transactional Analysis Journal, 2*(2), 83–86.

Summer
47. Steiner, C. (1972). My insides were once a safe place. In J. Marcus (Ed.), *Poem-maker soul-healer* (p. 6). Berkeley, CA: Radical Psychiatry Community Press.
48. Steiner, C. (1972). Poems to Hogie. In J. Marcus (Ed.), *Poem-maker soul-healer* (p. 18). Berkeley, CA: Radical Psychiatry Community Press.
49. Steiner, C. (1972). Two love poems. In J. Marcus (Ed.), *Poem-maker soul-healer* (p. 18). Berkeley, CA: Radical Psychiatry Community Press.

---

50. Steiner, C. (1972) *If I do my thing* [poem].[8]
51. Steiner, C. M. (1972). Radical psychiatry. In H. M. Ruitenbeek (Ed.), *Going crazy: The radical therapy of R. D. Laing and others.* New York: Bantam Books.

1973
January
52. Steiner, C. (1973, January). [Open] Letter to a brother: Reflections on men's liberation. *Issues in Radical Therapy, 1*(1), 15–18.

Keith Tudor

Spring

53. Steiner, C. (1973, Spring). Inside TA or I'm OK, you're OK (but what about them?). *Issues in Radical Therapy*, *1*(2), 3–7.

54. Steiner, C. M. (1973, Spring). Radical psychiatry manifesto. *Issues in Radical Therapy*, *1*(2), p. 24. (Original work published 1971 [#29])[9]

Summer

55. Steiner, C. M. (1973, Summer). Cooperation. *Issues in Radical Therapy*, *1*(3), 7.

Autumn

56. Steiner, C. (1973, Autumn). The rescue triangle. *Issues in Radical Therapy*, *1*(4), 20–24.

57. Steiner, C. (1973, Autumn). Coupleism. *Issues in Radical Therapy*, *1*(4), 31–32.

58. Steiner, C. (1973, Autumn). Letter to the editor [regarding TA and attack therapy]. *Issues in Radical Therapy*, *1*(4), 34.

---

59. Berne, E., Steiner, C. M., & Dusay, J. M. (1973). Transactional analysis. In M. Ratibor-Ray, & M. Jurjevich (Eds.), *Direct psychotherapy: 28 American originals* (pp. 370–393). Coral Gables, FL: University of Miami Press.

1974
Winter

60. Issues in Radical Therapy Collective. (1973/1974, Winter). Radical therapy and body politics [Editorial]. Wilhelm Reich and body politics, Part I [Special issue]. *Issues in Radical Therapy*, *2*(1), 3.[10]

Spring

61. Issues in Radical Therapy Collective. (1974, Spring). Editorial. Wilhelm Reich and body politics, Part II [Special issue]. *Issues in Radical Therapy*, *2*(2), 3.[11]

62. Steiner, C. (1974, Spring). Wilhelm Reich: A defeated revolutionary. *Issues in Radical Therapy*, *2*(2), 10–11.

Summer

63. Steiner, C. (1974, Summer). We are all outlaws. *Issues in Radical Therapy*, *2*(3), 26–28.

Autumn

64. Issues in Radical Therapy Collective. (1974, Autumn). Editorial. Cooperation [Special issue]. *Issues in Radical Therapy*, *2*(4), 3.[12]

---

65. Dusay, J., & Steiner, C. (1974). Transactional analysis in groups. In H. Kaplan & B. Sadock (Eds.), *New models for group therapy*. New York, NY: Jason Aronson.

An annotated bibliography 33

66. Steiner, C. (1974). *Scripts people live: Transactional analysis of life scripts.* New York, NY: Grove Press.[13,14]

1975
Winter

67. Issues in Radical Therapy Collective. (1975, Winter). Editorial. Sex and the Left [Special issue]. *Issues in Radical Therapy, 3*(1), 3.[15]
68. Steiner, C. (1975, Winter). [The] Expanding shrink. *Issues in Radical Therapy, 3*(1), 26–27.

June

69. Steiner, C. (1975, June). [Letter to the editor.] *The Script, 4,* 7.[16]

Summer

70. Steiner, C. (1975, Summer). Editorial. *Issues in Radical Therapy, 3*(3), 3.
71. Steiner, C. (1975, Summer). Power: Part I. *Issues in Radical Therapy, 3*(3), 7–12.
72. Steiner, C. (1975, Summer). Expanding shrink. *Issues in Radical Therapy, 3*(3), 24.

Fall

73. Steiner, C., with Meigham, S. (1975, Fall). An interview with R. D. Laing. *Issues in Radical Therapy, 3*(4), 3–9.
74. Steiner, C. (1975, Fall). [Review of book *Against our will* by S. Brownmiller]. *Issues in Radical Therapy, 3*(4), 17.
75. Steiner, C. (1975, Fall). Working cooperatively. *Issues in Radical Therapy, 3*(4), 22–25.

Winter

76. Steiner, C. (1975, Winter). Editorial. Power [Special issue]. *Issues in Radical Therapy, 4*(1), 3.
77. Steiner, C. (1975, Winter). Power: Part II. *Issues in Radical Therapy, 4*(1), 20–22.

78. Steiner, C. (Ed.). (1975). *Readings in radical psychiatry.* New York, NY: Grove Press.[17]
79. Steiner, C. (1975). Manifesto. In C. Steiner (Ed.), *Readings in radical psychiatry* (pp. 9–16). New York, NY: Grove Press. (Original work published 1971 [#29])[18]
80. Steiner, C., & Wyckoff, H. (1975). Alienation. In C. Steiner (Ed.), *Readings in radical psychiatry* (p. 17–27). New York, NY: Grove Press. (Original work published 1971 [#32])
81. Steiner, C. (1975). The stroke economy. In C. Steiner (Ed.), *Readings in radical psychiatry* (pp. 28–43). New York, NY: Grove Press. (Original work published 1971 [#27])[19]

34   *Keith Tudor*

82. Steiner, C. (1975). Teaching radical psychiatry. In C. Steiner (Ed.), *Readings in radical psychiatry* (pp. 55–70). New York, NY: Grove Press. (Original work published 1971 [#37])

83. Steiner, C. (1975). Contractual problem solving groups. In C. Steiner (Ed.), *Readings in radical psychiatry* (pp. 73–79). New York, NY: Grove Press. (Original work published 1971 [#35])

84. Steiner, C. (1975). Radical psychiatry history. In C. Steiner (Ed.), *Readings in radical psychiatry* (p. 142–147). New York, NY: Grove Press. (Original work published 1971 [#31])

85. Members of the Radical Psychiatry Center (1975). An analysis of the structure of the Berkeley Radical Psychiatry Center. In C. Steiner (Ed.), *Readings in radical psychiatry* (pp. 148–155). New York, NY: Grove Press.[20]

86. Members of the Radical Psychiatry Center (1975). A working contract for group leaders at the Berkeley Radical Psychiatry Center. In C. Steiner (Ed.), *Readings in radical psychiatry* (pp. 156–158). New York, NY: Grove Press.[14]

87. Members of the Radical Psychiatry Center (1975). An analysis of the political values of the Berkeley Radical Psychiatry Center. In C. Steiner (Ed.), *Readings in radical psychiatry* (pp. 159–161). New York, NY: Grove Press.[14]

88. Steiner, C. (1975). Radical psychiatry and movement groups. In C. Steiner (Ed.), *Readings in radical psychiatry* (pp. 172–183). New York, NY: Grove Press. (Original work published 1971 [#23])[21]

1976
January

89. Steiner, C. M. (1976). Socially responsible therapy: Reflections on "the female juvenile delinquent". *Transactional Analysis Journal, 6*(1), 11–14.

Spring

90. Issues in Radical Therapy Collective. (1976, Spring). Editorial discussion. Food and health [Special issue]. *Issues in Radical Therapy, 4*(2), 22.[22]

April

91. Steiner, C. (1976). *Op doop spoor: Transactionele analyse van levenss-cripten* [Scripts people live: Transactional analysis of life scripts] (M. Janssen, Trans.). Amsterdam, The Netherlands: Uitgeverij Bert Bakker. (Original work published 1974 [#66])

Summer

92. Steiner, C. M. (1976, Summer). Cooperative living. *Issues in Radical Therapy, 4*(3), 8–11.

July

93. Steiner, C. M. (1976). Book review? Reply. *Transactional Analysis Journal, 6*(3), 332–333.

An annotated bibliography   35

94. Steiner, C. M. (1976). *Alcoholismo: Una aplicacion practica del Analisis Transaccional* [Alcoholism: A practical application of transactional analysis]. Mexico City, Mexico: Editorial V. Siglos. (Original work published 1971 [#39])
95. Steiner, C. (1976). Cooperation. In H. Wyckoff (Ed.), *Love, therapy and politics: Issues in radical therapy – The first year* (pp. 28–42). New York, NY: Grove Press. (Original work published 1973 [#55])
96. Steiner, C. (1976). Rescue. In H. Wyckoff (Ed.), *Love, therapy and politics: Issues in radical therapy – The first year* (pp. 43–63). New York, NY: Grove Press.
97. Steiner, C. (1976). Coupleism. In H. Wyckoff (Ed.), *Love, therapy and politics: Issues in radical therapy – The first year* (pp. 127–135). New York, NY: Grove Press. (Original work published 1973 [#57])
98. Steiner, C. (1976). Open letter to a brother: Some reflections on men's liberation. In H. Wyckoff (Ed.), *Love, therapy and politics: Issues in radical therapy – The first year* (pp. 161–179). New York, NY: Grove Press. (Original work published 1973 [#52])
99. Steiner, C. (1976). Inside TA. In H. Wyckoff (Ed.), *Love, therapy and politics: Issues in radical therapy – The first year* (pp. 139–162). New York, NY: Grove Press. (Original work published 1973 [#53])
100. Steiner, C. M. (1976). *Os papeis que vivemos na vida; Analise transacional de nossas interpretacoes cotidianas* [*The roles we live in life: The transactional analysis of our daily interpretations*]. Rio de Janeiro, Brazil: Artenova. (Original work published 1974 [#66])

1977
January
101. Steiner, C. (1977). *The original warm fuzzy tale: A fairytale* (J-A. Dick, Illustrator). Rolling Hills Estate, CA: Jalmar Press.[23]

Winter
102. Steiner, C. (1977, Winter). Cooperative meetings. *Issues in Radical Therapy, 17*, 11.

Spring
103. Steiner, C. (1977, Spring). Wilhelm Reich: A defeated revolutionary. Fourth anniversary [Special] issue. *Issues in Radical Therapy, 18*, 8–9. (Original work published 1974 [#62])
104. Steiner, C. (1977, Spring). We are all outlaws. Fourth anniversary [Special] issue. *Issues in Radical Therapy, 18*, 30–31. (Original work published 1974 [#63])

Summer
105. Steiner, C. (1977, Summer). The principles revised. *Issues in Radical Therapy, 19*, 12–14.[24]

36 *Keith Tudor*

Fall

106. Steiner, C. (1977, Fall). Feminism for men. *Issues in Radical Therapy, 20,* 3–10.

---

107. Steiner, C. M., & Kerr, C. (Eds.). (1977). *Beyond games and scripts by Eric Berne: Selections from his major writings.* New York, NY: Grove Press.

108. Steiner, C. (1977). Introduction. In C. M. Steiner & C. Kerr (Eds.) *Beyond games and scripts by Eric Berne: Selections from his major writings* (pp. 3–4). New York, NY: Grove Press.

109. Steiner, C. (1977). Introduction [to part on ego states]. In C. M. Steiner & C. Kerr (Eds.) *Beyond games and scripts* (pp. 21–25). New York, NY: Grove Press.

110. Steiner, C. (1977). Introduction [to part on scripts]. In C. M. Steiner & C. Kerr (Eds.) *Beyond games and scripts by Eric Berne: Selections from his major writings* (pp. 135–136). New York, NY: Grove Press.

111. Steiner, C. (1977). Introduction [to part on group dynamics]. In C. M. Steiner & C. Kerr (Eds.) *Beyond games and scripts by Eric Berne: Selections from his major writings* (pp. 313–314). New York, NY: Grove Press.

112. Steiner, C. (1977). Conclusion. In C. M. Steiner & C. Kerr (Eds.) *Beyond games and scripts by Eric Berne: Selections from his major writings* (p. 371). New York, NY: Grove Press.

1978
Winter

113. Steiner, C. (1978, Winter). Back at the Ranch. *Issues in Radical Therapy, 21,* 28–29.

Spring

114. Steiner, C. (1978, Spring). Feminism for men, Part II. *Issues in Radical Therapy, 22,* 3–9.

April

115. Steiner, C. (1978, April). [Letter to the editor (Members Forum)].[25] *The Script, 7*(4), 4.

Summer

116. Steiner, C. M. (1978, Summer). The Pig Parent. *Issues in Radical Therapy, 23,* 5–11.

Fall

117. Steiner, C. (1978, Fall). Living visions: The Cooperative Healing Center, *Issues in Radical Therapy, 24,* 9.

1979
January

118. Steiner, C. M. (1979). The Pig Parent. *Transactional Analysis Journal, 9*(1), 26–37.

An annotated bibliography 37

Spring
119. Steiner, C. (1979, Spring). Radical psychiatry; Once again with feeling. *Issues in Radical Therapy, 25*, 26–30.

Fall
120. Steiner, C. (1979, Fall). Editorial. Cooperation [Special issue]. *Issues in Radical Therapy & Cooperative Power, 27*, 3.
121. Steiner, C. (1979, Fall). Cooperation [Special issue]. *Issues in Radical Therapy & Cooperative Power, 27*, 4–17. (Original work published 1973 [#55])[26]

Winter
122. Steiner, C. (1979, Winter). Editorial. *Issues in Radical Therapy & Cooperative Power, 28*, 3.

---

123. Steiner, C. M. (1979). *Healing alcoholism.* New York, NY: Grove Press.[27,28]
124. Steiner, C. M. (1979). *Nog eentje dan een: Psychotreapeutische behandeling van alcoholisme* [One more than one: The psychotherapeutic treatment of alcoholism] (R. Markveldt, Trans.). Amsterdam, The Netherlands: Uitgeverij Bert Bakker. (Original work published 1971[#39])
125. Steiner, C. M. (1979). Überarbeitete Prinzipien der radikalen Psychiatry [Revised principles of radical psychiatry]. *Psychologie und Gesellschaftskritik [Psychology and Social Criticism], 3*, 241–248. (Original work published 1977 [#105])

1980
June
126. Steiner, C. (1980, June). The human potential movement and transformation: A conversation with George Leonard. *The Script, 10*(5), 1–3.

July
127. Steiner, C. (1980). *A manual on cooperation.* Berkeley, CA: Issues in Cooperation and Power.[29]

Summer
128. Steiner, C. (1980, Summer). Editorial. *Issues in Cooperation and Power, 2*, 3.

Fall
129. Jenkins, B., & Steiner, C. (1980, Fall). Mediations. *Issues in Cooperation and Power, 3*, 4–11, 15–22.

Winter
130. Steiner, C. (1980, Winter). Editorial. Self-blame: Pig. *Issues in Cooperation and Power, 4*, 3.

38 Keith Tudor

1981
January

131. Steiner, C. M. (1981). *The other side of power: How to become powerful without being power-hungry.* New York: NY: Grove Press.[30]

132. Steiner, C. M. (1981). Acceptance statement from Claude Steiner on co-winning the Eric Berne Memorial Scientific Award for the stroke economy. *Transactional Analysis Journal, 11*(1), 6–9.

Spring

133. Steiner, C. (1981, Spring). Monogamy, non-monogamy, and omnigamy. *Issues in Cooperation and Power, 5,* 4–6, 8–11, 13–15, 18–19, 21–23.

May

134. Steiner, C. M. (1981). Radical psychiatry. In R. Corsini (Ed.), *Handbook of innovative psychotherapies* (pp. 724–735). New York, NY: Wiley & Sons.

Fall

135. Steiner, C. (1981, Fall). Omnigamy in Iowa. *Issues in Cooperation and Power, 7,* 18–25.

---

136. Steiner, C. M. (1981). *Alkoholist spel; Analys av livsmonster* [Games alcoholics play: The analysis of life scripts] Stockholm, Sweden: Studentlitteratur. (Original work published 1971[#39])

137. Steiner, C. M. (1981). *A quoi jouent les alcoholiques: Un nouvelle approche de l'analyse transactionelle* [Games alcoholics play: A new approach to transactional analysis]. Monaco City, Monaco: Epi Editeurs. (Original work published 1971[#39])

1982
Autumn

---

138. Steiner, C. M. (1982). *Wie man Lebenspläne verändert: Die Arbeit mit Skripts in der Transaktionsanalyse* [How to change life plans: Working with scripts in transactional analysis] (S. Mitzlaff, Trans.). Padeborn, Germany: Junferman. (Original work published 1974 [#66])

1983
October

139. Körner, H., Steiner, C. (1983). *Die Schmusegeschichte* [The cuddle-story]. In H. Körner (Ed.), *Die Farben der Wirklichkeit. Ein Märchenbuch* [The colours of reality. A book of fairytales] (pp. 89–93). Fellbach, Germany: Lucy Körner Verlag. (Original work published 1977 [#101])[31]

---

140. Mendelson, B., Steiner, C., & Sipe, R. (1982): Dialogue. *Issues in Radical Therapy, 10*(3), pp. 6–7, 60–61.[32]

1984
Spring

141. Steiner, C. (1984). Creating an ecology for emotional literacy. *Issues in Radical Therapy, 11*(2), 6–9, 49–52.

May

142. Steiner, C. M. (1984). *Le conte chaud et doux des chaudoudoux* [*The warm fuzzy tale*] (F. Paul-Cavaliier, Trans.). Paris, France: InterEditions. (Original work published 1971 [#101])[33]

July

143. Steiner, C. M. (1984). Emotional literacy. *Transactional Analysis Journal, 14*(3), 162–173.

144. Steiner, C. M. (1984). *O outro lado do poder: Como tornar-se poderoso sem ter sede de poder* [*The other side of power: How to become powerful without thirsting for power*]. Sao Paolo, Brazil: Nobel. (Original work published 1981 [#131])

1985
July

145. Steiner, C. (1985, July). Claude Steiner speaks out on US involvement in Nicaragua [Members Forum]. *The Script, 15*(5), 5.

146. Steiner, C. (1985). *Principles of radical psychiatry (1985 revision).* Retrieved from www.emotional-literacy.org/principles-radical-psychiatry-1985-revision/.

1986

147. Steiner, C. M. (1986). *When a man loves a woman.* New York, NY: Grove Press.[34]
148. Steiner, C. M. (1986). *Macht ohne Ausbeutung: Zur Ökologie zwischenmenschlicher Beziehungen* [Power without exploitation: Regarding the ecology of interpersonal relationships] (S. Mitzlaff, Trans.). Paderborn, Germany: Junfermann. (Original work published 1981 [#131])

1987
April

149. Steiner, C. (1987, April). TA formation. *The Script, 17*(3), 1, 4–5.[35]

July

150. Steiner, C. M. (1987). The seven sources of power: An alternative to authority. *Transactional Analysis Journal, 17*(3), 102–104.

40   *Keith Tudor*

1988
Summer

151. Steiner, C., & Rappleye, C. (1988, Summer). Jacques Ellul: Quirky trailblazer of propaganda theory. *Propaganda Review, 2,* 29–33.

August

152. Steiner, C., & Roy, B. (Eds.). (1988). *Radical psychiatry: The second decade.* Self-published manuscript available from www.radikale-therapie.de/DL/TSD.pdf.
153. Steiner, C. (1988). Power. In C. Steiner, & B. Roy (Eds.), *Radical psychiatry: The second decade* (pp. 9–10). Self-published manuscript available from www.radikale-therapie.de/DL/TSD.pdf.
154. Steiner, C., & Roy, B. (1988). Cooperation. In C. Steiner, & B. Roy (Eds.), *Radical psychiatry: The second decade* (pp. 44–46). Self-published manuscript available from www.radikale-therapie.de/DL/TSD.pdf. (Original work published 1976 [#95])[36]
155. Steiner, C. (1988). The Pig Parent. In C. Steiner, & B. Roy (Eds.), *Radical psychiatry: The second decade* (pp. 47–58). Self-published manuscript available from www.radikale-therapie.de/DL/TSD.pdf. (Original work published 1978 [#116] and 1979 [#118])
156. Steiner, C. (1988). Emotional literacy. In C. Steiner, & B. Roy (Eds.), *Radical psychiatry: The second decade* (pp. 77–90). Self-published manuscript available from www.radikale-therapie.de/DL/TSD.pdf. (Original work published 1984 [#143])
157. Jenkins, B., & Steiner, C. (1988). Mediation. In C. Steiner, & B. Roy (Eds.), *Radical psychiatry: The second decade* (pp. 107–120). Self-published manuscript available from www.radikale-therapie.de/DL/TSD.pdf. (Original work published 1980 [#129])

Winter

158. Steiner, C. (1988, Winter). Brave New World Revisited, revisited. *Propaganda Review, 3,* 32–35.

December

159. Steiner, C. (1988, December). Global TA action projects encouraged. *The Script, 18*(9), 1, 7.

1989
Summer

160. Steiner, C. (Ed.). (1989, Summer). *Propaganda Review, 5.*
161. Steiner, C. (1989, Summer). Editorial. *Propaganda Review, 5,* 1
162. Steiner, C., & Rappleye. (1989, Summer). Propaganda is a conscious conspiracy, period. *Propaganda Review, 5,* 7, 10–11, 46.
163. Steiner, C. (1989, Summer). The PR wizard who stopped Alar: An interview with David Fenton. *Propaganda Review, 5,* 14–19.[37]

An annotated bibliography 41

1991
March
164. Steiner, C. M. (1991). *Los guiones que vivimos* [*Scripts people live*] (A. Devós, Trans). Barcelona, Spain: Kairós. (Original work published 1974 [#66])

June
165. Steiner, C., & Kohlhaas-Reith, A. (1991). *On the early years of transactional analysis: Eric Berne and his disciple Claude Steiner*. Manuscript available at www.ta-kohlhaas-reith.de/institut_publikationen.htm.

1992

166. Steiner, C. M. (1992). *Surfing the info-wave: Emotional literacy and personal power in the information age. How to live in the information-driven years without giving up your heart to the new machines*. Unpublished manuscript.

1993

167. Steiner, C. M. (1993). *Quando un homem ama uma mulher* [*When a man loves a woman*]. São Paolo, Brazil: Editora Gente. (Original work published 1986 [#147])

1995
January
168. Steiner, C. M. (1995). Thirty years of psychotherapy and transactional analysis in 1,500 words or less. *Transactional Analysis Journal, 25*(1), 83–86.[38]

October
169. Steiner, C. M. (1995) *L'autre face de pouvoir* [*The other side of power*] (G. Musnil-Smith, Trans.). Paris, France: Desclee de Brouwer. (Original work published 1981 [#131])

December
170. Steiner, C. (1995, December). The liberation of love and the emotions. *The Script, 25*(9), 1, 7.[39]

1996
January
171. Steiner, C. M. (1996). Emotional literacy training: The application of transactional analysis to the study of emotions. *Transactional Analysis Journal, 26*(1), 31–39.

April
172. Berne, E., Steiner, C. M. & Dusay, J. M. (1986). Transactional analysis. In J. E. Groves (Ed.), *Essential papers on short-term dynamic therapy* (pp. 149–170). New York: New York University Press.

42   *Keith Tudor*

173. Steiner, C. M. (1996). *Des scenarios et des hommes: Analyse transactionelle des scenarios de vie* [*Man and scripts: The transactional analysis of life scripts*] (C. Arsene, E. Leybold, C. Ramond, J. Turner, D. Verguin & I. Williams, Trans.). Paris, France: Desclee de Brouwer. (Original work published 1974 [#66])

1997
January
174. Steiner, C. M. (1997). Transactional analysis in the information age. *Transactional Analysis Journal, 27*(1), 15–23.[40]
175. Steiner, C. M., with Perry, P. (1997). *Achieving emotional literacy: A personal program to increase your emotional intelligence.* New York: Avon Books.[41]

March
176. Hamilton, L., & Steiner, C. (1997, March). Steiner to lead off Berne workshops.[42] *The Script, 27*(2), 1, 6.

177. Steiner, C. M., with Perry, P. (1997). *Emotionale Kompetenz* [*Emotional competence*] (S. Hornfeck, Trans.). München, Germany: Hanser. (Original work published 1997 [#175])

1998
March
178. Steiner, C., & Cornell, B. (1998, March). Transactional analysis and emotional literacy. *The Script,* 28(2), 1, 6.[43]

June
179. Steiner, C. (1998, May-June). [Letter to the editor.] *The Script, 28*(4), 5, 6.[44]

October
180. Steiner, C. M. (1998). [Letter to the Editor]. *Transactional Analysis Journal, 28*(4), 352–353.[45]
181. Steiner, C. M., with Perry, P. (1998). *L'ABC des emotions: Developper son intelligence emotionelle.* [*The ABC of emotions: Developing one's emotional intelligence*] (F. Olivier, Trans.). Paris, France: InterEditions. (Original work published 1997 [#175])

November
182. Steiner, C. M. (1998, November). [Letter to the editor].[46] *The Script, 28*(8), 6.

183. Steiner, C. M., with Perry, P. (1998). *Educacao emocional: Un programa personalizado para desenvolver sua inteligencia emocional.* [*Emotional*

education: A personalised programme to develop your emotional intelligence]. Rio de Janeiro, Brazil: Objetiva. (Original work published 1997 [#175])

184. Steiner, C. M., with Perry, P. (1998). *Emotioneel vaardig worden: Een persoonlijke cursus om emotioneel intelligent te worden [Becoming emotionally skilled: A personal course to become emotionally intelligent]* (S. Brinkman, Trans.). Amsterdam, The Netherlands: Uitgeverij De Arbeiderspers. (Original work published 1997 [#175])

185. Steiner, C. M., with Perry, P. (1998). *La educacion emocional [Emotional education]*. Buenos Aires, Argentina: Javier Vergara. (Original work published 1997 [#175])

186. Steiner, C. M., with Perry, P. (1998). *Lær at læse følelser: Og styrk din følelsesmæssige intelligens [Learn to read emotions: Strengthen your emotional intelligence]* (L. Rosenkvist, Trans.). Copenhagen, Denmark: Ashehoug Dansk Forlag. (Original work published 1997 [#175])

187. Steiner, C. (1998). *Cyber-psychology: Love, power and redemption in the age of information machines*. Unpublished manuscript.[47]

1999
January

188. Steiner, C. M. (1999). *Copioni di vita: Analisi transazionale dei copioni esistenziali [Life scripts: The transactional analysis of existential scripts]* (C. Chiaperotti, Trans.). Milano, Italy: Editizioni La Vita Felice. (Original work published 1974 [#66])

February

189. Steiner, C. M., with Perry, P. (1999). *L'Alfabeto delle emozioni [Achieving emotional literacy]* (L. S. Buosi, Trans.). Milano, Italy: Sperling and Kupfer. (Original work published 1997 [#175])

April

190. Steiner, C. (1999, April). The internet and the ITAA. *The Script, 29*(3), 2.

June

191. Steiner, C. (1999, May–June). Exponential opportunity [Net Connection column]. *The Script, 29*(4), 3.

July

192. Steiner, C. (1999, July). Prozac or face time: Internet or no internet? [Net Connection column]. *The Script, 29*(5), 3.

August

193. Steiner, C. (1999, August). E-style: The emotional wasteland [Net Connection column]. *The Script, 29*(6), 3.

44   Keith Tudor

October

194. Steiner, C. (1999, September–October). Denton Roberts honoured with living principles award. *The Script, 29*(7), 1, 7.

195. Steiner, C. (1999, September–October). Emotional excess on the internet [Net Connection column]. *The Script, 29*(7), 2.

---

196. Steiner, C. M., with Perry, P. (1999). [*Achieving emotional literacy*]. Morningstar Publishing Co. (Original work published 1997 [#175])

2000

February

197. Steiner, C. (2000, January–February). Transactional analysis in the information age. *The Script, 30*(1), 1, 7.

March

198. Steiner, C., & Rappleye, C. (2000, March). *Report from Central America; Following the US footprint across Mexico, Guatemala, El Salvador, Honduras, and Nicaragua (1986)*. Retrieved from www.emotional-literacy.org/report-central-america-following-us-footprint-across-mexico-guatemala-el-salvador-honduras-nicaragua-1986/.

April

199. Steiner, C. M. (2000). Apology: The transactional analysis of a fundamental exchange. *Transactional Analysis Journal, 30*(2), 145–149.

July

200. Steiner, C. (2000, July). Games and the stroke economy. *The Script, 30*(5), 1–2.

October

201. Steiner, C. M. (2000). [Letter to the Editor.] *Transactional Analysis Journal, 30*(4), 305.[48]

202. Steiner, C. (2000, October). *The meming of love: Invention of the human heart*. Keynote lecture given at the 3rd Adolescence Health Conference at the Royal College of Physicians, London, UK.[49]

---

203. Steiner, C. M. (2000). [*The warm fuzzy tale*.] Tokyo, Japan: Tuttle-Mory Agency. (Original work published 1971 [#101])[50]

2001

February

204. Steiner, C. M. (2001, January–February). Science and transactional analysis. *The Script, 31*(1), 8.

205. Steiner, C. M. (2001). Radical psychiatry. In R. Corsini (Ed.), *Handbook of innovative psychotherapies* (2nd Ed.; pp. 578–586). New York, NY: Wiley & Sons. (Original work published 1981 [#134])

An annotated bibliography 45

June

206. Steiner, C. M. (2001, May–June). Nowhere to hide: Feelings on the internet. *The Script, 31*(4), 3.

July

207. Steiner, C. M. (2001, July). Finding correlates to flights of fancy. *The Script, 31*(5), 1, 7.

December

208. Steiner, C. M. (2001, December). New research supports the efficacy of the internet. *The Script, 31*(9), 1–2.

—————

209. Steiner, C. M. (2001). [*The warm fuzzy tale.*] Cuilin, China: Guanxi Normal University Press. (Original work published 1971 [#101])[51]

2002
January

210. Steiner, C. M. (2002). The Adult: Once again, with feeling. *Transactional Analysis Journal, 32*(1), 62–65.

February

211. Steiner, C. (2002, January–February). [Letter to the Editor (Members' Forum: Thoughts on Ted Novey's latest research).] *The Script, 32*(1), 7.[52]

July

212. Steiner, C. (2002, July). Platform. *The Script, 32*(5), 5.[53]

December

213. Steiner, C. (2002, December). The development of transactional analysis theory and practice: A brief history. *The Script, 32*(9), 3.

2003
April

214. Steiner, C. M., & Tilney, T. (Eds.). (2003). Core Concepts [Special Issue]. *Transactional Analysis Journal, 33*(2).

215. Steiner, C. M. (2003). Letter from the Guest Editor. Core Concepts [Special Issue]. *Transactional Analysis Journal, 33*(2), 111–114.

216. Steiner, C. M. (2003). Core concepts of a stroke-centered transactional analysis. *Transactional Analysis Journal, 33*(2), 178–181.

217. Steiner, C. M., Campos, L., Drego, P., Joines, V., Ligabue, S., Noriega, G., Roberts, D., & Said, E. (2003). A compilation of core concepts. *Transactional Analysis Journal, 33*(2), 182–191.

218. Steiner, C. M. (2003). A response to Loria. *Transactional Analysis Journal, 33*(2), 201–202.

46 *Keith Tudor*

June

219. Steiner, C. (2003, May–June). Corroborating research sought [Research File]. *The Script, 33*(4), 3.

July

220. Steiner, C. (2003, July). Developing a research portfolio [Research File]. *The Script, 33*(5), 2.

August

221. Steiner, C. (2003, August). Theoretical musings [Research File]. *The Script, 33*(6), 3.

222. Steiner, C. (2003, August). [Letter to the Editor: Response to Hargaden's speech about Berne (Members' Forum).] *The Script, 33*(6), 5.

October

223. Steiner, C. (2003, September–October). [Letter to the Editor (Members' Forum).] *The Script 33*(7), 6.[54]

224. Steiner, C. M. (2003). [Letter to the Editor.] *Transactional Analysis Journal, 33*(4), 361–363.

November

225. Steiner, C. M. (2003). *Emotional intelligence with a heart.* Fawnskin, CA: Personhood Press.[55]

2004
June

226. Steiner, C. (2004, May–June). Understanding the enigma of Eric Berne [After He Said Hello (Ed., P. Levin)], *The Script 34*(4), 2.

November

227. Novey, T., & Steiner, C. (2003, November). Novey research shows effectiveness of transactional analysts. *The Script 34*(4), 3.

———

228. Steiner, C. M. (2004). [Healing alcoholism]. St Petersburg, Russia: Prime Evronak. (Original work published 1979 [**#123**])

229. Steiner, C. M. (2004). [The other side of power]. St Petersburg, Russia: Prime Evronak. (Original work published 1981 [**#131**])**2005**

January

230. Steiner, C. M. (2005). [Letter to the Editor]. *Transactional Analysis Journal, 35*(1), 92–93.[56]

March

231. Steiner, C. (2005, March). Transactional analysis: An elegant theory and practice. *The Script, 35*(2), 4–5.

An annotated bibliography 47

April

232. Steiner, C. (2005, April). Introducing members of the ITAA Board of Trustees: Claude Steiner, Vice President of Internet. _The Script, 35_(3), 4.

233. Steiner, C. M., & Novellino, M. (2005). Theoretical diversity: A debate about TA and psychoanalysis. _Transactional Analysis Journal, 35_(2), 110–118.

November

234. Steiner, C. (2005, November). [Letter: Steiner to Berne (Members' Forum).] _The Script, 35_(8), 5.

---

235. Steiner, C. (2005). _Emotional literacy_ [DVD]. Ipswich, UK: Concord Media.

2006
January

236. Steiner, C. M. (2006). [Letter to the Editor], _Transactional Analysis Journal, 36_(1), 70.[57]

July

237. Steiner, C. (2006, July). Games and lovelessness. _The Script, 36_(5), 1–2.

October

238. Steiner, C. M. (2006). Transactional analysis and psychoanalysis: Writing styles. _Transactional Analysis Journal, 36_(4), 330–334.

December

239. Steiner, C. (2006, December). Quo vadis transactional analysis? Change and trust. _The Script, 36_(9), 1, 6–7.[58]

2007
January

240. Steiner, C. M. (2007). Response to an article by Ken Woods "Regarding the stroking school of transactional analysis". _Transactional Analysis Journal, 37_(1).

April

241. Steiner, C. M. (2007). [Letter to the Editor]. _Transactional Analysis Journal, 37_(2), 176–177.[59]

October

242. Steiner, C. M. (2007). Stroking: What's love got to do with it? _Transactional Analysis Journal, 37_(4), 307–310.

243. James, M., English, F., Steiner, C., & Goulding, M. (2007). Master therapists [DVD]. Available from the ITAA at www.itaa-net.org.

48   *Keith Tudor*

2008
Winter

244. Steiner, C. (2008, Winter). Honesty and respect. *Greater Good, 4*(3).

___

245. Steiner, C. M. (2008) *Confessions of a psycho-mechanic.* Unpublished manuscript.
246. Steiner, C. (2008). *Excellence in aging for men: Twelve strategies.* Privately circulated publication.[60]

2009
March

247. Steiner, C. M. (2009). *El otro lado del poder* [*The other side of power*]. Sevilla, Spain: Jeder Libros. (Original work published 1981 [#131])

April

248. Steiner, C. (2009, April). Introducing members of the ITTA Board of Trustees. *The Script, 39*(3), 4.[61]

June

249. Steiner, C. (2009, May–June). Further thoughts on research project: From Claude Steiner. *The Script, 39*(4), 1.**October**
250. Steiner, C. (2009, September–October). [Letter (Members' Forum: Debate on Novey research continues).] *The Script, 39*(7), 5.

___

251. Steiner, C. M. (2009). *The heart of the matter: Love, information and transactional analysis.* San Francisco, CA: TA Press.[62,63]
252. Steiner, C. M. (2009). *La favola dei caldomorbidi* [The warm fuzzy tale] (C. Chiesa & S. Ligabue, Trans.). Bologna, Italy: Artebambini. (Original work published 1971 [#101])[64]

2010
January

253. Steiner, C. M. (2011). *El corazón del asunto: Amor, informacion y analysis transaccional* [*The heart of the matter: Love, information and transactional analysis*] (A. Devós, Trans). Sevilla, Spain: Jeder Libros. (Original work published 2009 [#251])

February

254. Steiner, C. M. (2010). *Forget the unconscious: An essay.* Retrieved from www.emotional-literacy.org/forget-unconscious-essay/.

May

255. Steiner, C. M. (2010). *Five columns that appeared in the Japan TA Association News 2009–2010.* Retrieved from www.emotional-literacy.org/five-columns-appeared-japan-ta-association-news-2009-2010/.

October
256. Steiner, C. M. (2010). Eric Berne's politics: "The great pyramid". *Transactional Analysis Journal, 40*(3–4), 212–216.

Autumn
257. Steiner, C. (2010). Eric Berne: Remembering and looking forward. *The Psychotherapist, 46,* 6–7.

---

258. Steiner, C. M. (2010). *Le pouvoir du coer [The heart of the matter]*. Paris, France: Inter Editions. (Original work published 2009 [#251])

2011
November
259. Steiner, C. M. (2011). *Pleased to meet you, hope you guess my name: The inner critic.* Retrieved from www.emotional-literacy.org/pleased-meet-hope-guess-name-inner-critic/.

2012
May
260. Steiner, C. (2008). *Wake up! You're dying. Excellence in aging for men: Twelve strategies.* Retrieved from www.emotional-literacy.org/wake-youre-dying/.

October
261. Steiner, C. M. (2010). The OK position: Freedom, equality, and the pursuit of happiness. *Transactional Analysis Journal, 42*(4), 294–297.

2013
January
262. Steiner, C. M. (2013). *Cuando un hombre ama a una mujer [When a man loves a woman]* (A. Devós, Trans.). Barcelona, Spain: Jeder. (Original work published 1986 [#**147**])

March
263. Steiner, C. M. (2013, March). Becoming a writer. *The Script, 43*(3), 6–7.

April
264. Steiner, C. M., with Perry, P. (2013). *La educación emocional [Emotional education]*. Barcelona, Spain: Jeder. (Original work published 1997 [#175])

2015
December
265. Steiner, C. (2015, December). Lima's conference honors Berne's legacy. *The Script, 45*(12), 1–3.

50 *Keith Tudor*

2017
January

266. Steiner, C. M. (2017) *CS at 80*. Unpublished manuscript.

April

267. Berne, E., Karpman, S., Dusay, J., Steiner, C., Callaghan, V., Boyce, M., Everts, K., David, G., & Kline, A. (2017). Eric Berne's San Francisco seminar: A transcript (B. Cornell with M. Landaiche, Transcribers & Eds.). *The Script, 47*(4), 7–18. (Original work transcribed 1970)[65]

2019
September

268. Steiner, C. e Coautores. (2019). *Educação emocional o que o amor tem a ver com isso? Edição especial artigos Claude Steiner* [Emotional education or what's love got to do with it? The articles of Claude Steiner] (S. M. de Jesus, Ed.). Rio de Janeiro, Brazil: União Nacional dos Analistas Transacionais.

2020
January

269. Steiner, C. M. (2020). Confessions of a psychomechanic: Excerpts on scripts. In K. Tudor (Ed.), *Claude Steiner, emotional activist: The life and work of Claude Michel Steiner* (pp. **57–65**). London, UK: Routledge.

270. Steiner, C. M. (2020). Confessions of a psychomechanic: Excerpts on strokes. In K. Tudor (Ed.), *Claude Steiner, emotional activist: The life and work of Claude Michel Steiner* (pp. **83–88**). London, UK: Routledge.

271. Steiner, C. M. (2020). Confessions of a psychomechanic: Excerpts on radical psychiatry. In K. Tudor (Ed.), *Emotional Claude Steiner, emotional activist: The life and work of Claude Michel Steiner* (pp. **105–115**). London, UK: Routledge.

272. Steiner, C. M. (2020). Confessions of a psychomechanic: Excerpts on power. In K. Tudor (Ed.), *Claude Steiner, emotional activist: The life and work of Claude Michel Steiner* (pp. **147–154**). London, UK: Routledge.

273. Steiner, C. M. (2020). Confessions of a psychomechanic: Excerpts on emotional literacy. In K. Tudor (Ed.), *Claude Steiner, emotional activist: The life and work of Claude Michel Steiner* (pp. **175–181**). London, UK: Routledge.

274. Steiner, C. M. (2020). Confessions of a psychomechanic: Excerpts on love and sex. In K. Tudor (Ed.), *Claude Steiner, emotional activist: The life and work of Claude Michel Steiner* (pp. **203–209**). London, UK: Routledge.

275. Steiner, C. M., & Tudor, K. (2020). A final confession from the psychomechanic: On games. In K. Tudor (Ed.), *Claude Steiner, emotional activist: The life and work of Claude Michel Steiner* (pp. **223–227**). London, UK: Routledge.

Notes

1 The doctoral committee for Claude's dissertation comprised Assistant Professor Edwin J. Martin, Dr Leslie D. Evans, Associate Professor Melvin Manis, Professor Edward L. Walker, and Dr Julius Wallner.

An annotated bibliography 51

2 The date of this first manifesto is taken from a note on the chapter in *Readings in Radical Psychiatry* (Steiner, 1975d, p. 6); in his *Confessions*, Claude dates this as 1970 (see p. 110).
3 This policy statement was reproduced in subsequent issues of the *TAJ*.
4 This book was translated into Spanish (1976) (#94), Dutch (1979) (#124), Swedish (1981) (#136), and French (1981) (#137).
5 See also #30.
6 See also #36.
7 See also #14.
8 This appears to have been published as a flyer for the Radical Psychiatry Summer Institute which that year was held in Berkeley 3–6 August. The poem can be found in the article "Emotional literacy training: The application of transactional analysis to the study of emotions" [#171] (Steiner, 1996, p. 33), in a couple of his books, and at www.emotional-literacy.org/i-do-my-thing-and-you-do-your-thing/.
9 See also #14 and #42.
10 As noted in this issue, the IRT Collective comprised Rick De Golia, Joy Marcus, Claude Steiner, and Hogie Wyckoff.
11 A footnote to this editorial acknowledges that "the editorial was initially framed by Joy Marcus and the final product is the result of a cooperative effort by all of us" (p. 3), a note that reflected the collective and cooperative spirit – and practice – of the Collective. (The IRT Collective remained the same as for the previous issue.)
12 A footnote to this editorial acknowledges that "this editorial was drafted by Claude Steiner from ideas contributed and organized by the IRT Collective" (p. 3).
13 Two chapters in this book – on "Sex role scripting in men and women" and "Banal scripts of women – were written by Hogie Wyckoff.
14 This book was translated into Dutch (1976 [#91]), Portuguese (1976 [#100]), German (1982 [#138]), Spanish (1991 [#164]), French (1996 [#173]), and Italian (1999 [#188]).
15 A footnote to this editorial is: "This editorial was drafted by Michael Votichenko and Sara Winter from ideas contributed and organized by the IRT Collective" (p. 3) which, at that point, comprised Joy Marcus, Bob Schwebel, Claude Steiner, Michael Votichenko, Sara Winter, and Hogie Wyckoff.
16 The letter concerned changes in ITAA election procedures and formalising his existing role which he described as "that of the grumbling sourpuss watchdog of abuses in TA and the enhancer and encourager of its scientific and educational uses" (Steiner, 1975c, p. 7). In owning this role, Claude referred to what Berne (1972/1975) called "the evangelical position" (p. 91), i.e., I'm OK, You're OK, They?
17 Although Claude was clearly credited as the editor of this book, in the bibliography of *Scripts People Live* the book appears as edited by Joy Marcus, Claude Steiner, and Hogie Wyckoff; moreover, while on the spine of the book *Readings ...* Claude is credited as the editor, the cover describes the book as "An anthology by Claude Steiner, Hogie Wyckoff, Daniel Goldstine, Peter Lariviere, Robert Schwebel, Joy Marcus and members of the Radical Psychiatry Center", a discrepancy that supports the point made by Beth Roy about mystification (see Chapter 1, p. 25, endnote 5).
18 See also #14, #42 and #54.
19 See also #34.
20 The principal authors of this chapter are identified as Anita Friedman, Claude Steiner, and Hogie Wyckoff.
21 See also #36 and #41.
22 This discussion involved Anthony Eschbach, Judy Mull, Darca Nicholson, Claude Steiner, Michael Votichenko, Sara Winter, and Hogie Wyckoff.
23 This book was translated into French (1984 [#142]), Japanese (2000 [#203]), Chinese (2001 [#209]), and Italian (2009 [#252]).
24 These were translated into German (1979 [#125]).
25 This letter concerned the ITAA's stance towards those states (of the United States of America) that had not ratified the Equal Rights Amendment in the USA.

52 *Keith Tudor*

26 See also #95.

27 In his Acknowledgements to this book, Claude makes the point that it is a completely new work, and distinct from his earlier book on *Games Alcoholics Play* (Steiner, 1971 [#39]). In his Preface, he acknowledges a certain dissatisfaction with his previous book on the subject, and its tone, and that he had learnt a great deal more about alcoholism since he wrote his previous book on the subject. He also makes an interesting distinction between the two books, i.e., that, while *Games Alcoholics Play* was written for professionals and (he hoped) made sense to alcoholics, *Healing Alcoholism* was written for the alcoholic and his or her social circle and (he hoped) made sense to professionals. He also reflects on himself:

> My own life over the past 10 years reflects the changes which this book has undergone. I am less brash and cocksure, and hopefully wiser. I no longer call the people I work for "my patients" nor do I call myself or invite them to call me "Dr Steiner". I have smoked marijuana, take my share of LSD and other hallucinogens and drink a very moderate amount, every so often: mostly beer and an occasional margarita when dining out. On the other hand, I have stopped smoking cigarettes and have drastically cut down my consumption of coffee, sugar, beef and other red meats. I enjoy getting high and have noticed the subtle differences in quality and duration of the intoxicating effects of different drugs.

Once a staunch defender of marijuana safe drug, I have come to realise that it, too, has its problem; more subtle not as damaging as alcohol, but nonetheless real (Steiner, 1979b, pp. 14–15).

28 This book was translated into Russian (2004 [#228]).

29 In an acknowledgement that appears at the end of this booklet, Claude notes the fact that "the material covered in these pages is the result of many years of theory building combined with daily practice in the radical psychiatry community" (Steiner, 1980a, p. 47), and specifically acknowledges Bob Schwebel, Hogie Wyckoff, Sandy Spiker, and Shelby Morgan.

30 This book was translated into Portuguese (1984 [#144]), German (1986 [#148]), French (1995 [#169]), Russian (2004 [#229]), and Spanish (2009) (#247).

31 See also #19.

32 This article concerned Marxism, dialectics, and radical therapy.

33 See also #19.

34 This book was translated into Portuguese (1993 [#167]) and Spanish (2013 [#262]).

35 In this article, Claude offers a critique of TA training practices and of "mean-spirited diagnosis".

36 See also #55, 121, and 127.

37 Three more issues of *Propaganda Review* were produced before the final issue which was published in 1991, but it is unlcear whether Claude was involved in those issues.

38 An updated version of this article was also published in *The Heart of the Matter* (Steiner, 2009) (as an Appendix: Notes for Psychotherapists).

39 This article is the text of the Eric Berne symposium given by Claude at the San Francisco Major International TA Conference, held in San Francisco in 1995.

40 A version of this article was also published in *The Heart of the Matter* (Steiner, 2009) (Chapter 13).

41 This book was translated into German (1997 [#177]), French (1998 [#181]), Portuguese (1998 [#183]), Dutch (1998 [#184]), Spanish (1998 [#185]), Danish (1998 [#186]), Italian (1999 [#189]), and Chinese (1999 [#196]).

42 An interview with Claude Steiner regarding an upcoming training workshop with four presenters: Claude, Fanita English, Steve Karpman, and Jack Dusay.

43 This was an interview with Claude Steiner about his new book, Berne, and the development of TA theory and technique as related to emotional literacy.

An annotated bibliography   53

44 This letter concerned integrative transactional analysis and differences between Ted Novey, and Richard Erskine and Rebecca Trautmann, and between Claude and Erskine and Trautmann.

45 This letter was written in response to an article on motivation and stroke theory written by Isabella D'Amore (1997).

46 This letter was published under the heading "Steiner and Erskine/Trautmann dialogue continues".

47 The table, contents, and summary of this book are available online at www.emotional-literacy.org/category/no-category/page/3/.

48 This letter was written in reponse to a letter from Mavis Klein (2000) which, in turn, was written in repsonse to Claude's article on "Apology" (Steiner, 2000).

49 This paper was published on Claude's own website in July 2007 (see www.emotional-literacy.org/meming-love-invention-human-heart/); he also published an edited version in *The Heart of the Matter* (Steiner, 2009) (as Chapter 2).

50 See also #19.

51 See also #19.

52 This was written in response to Ken Woods's letter regarding Ted Novey's research using methods and data from consumer reports.

53 This is Claude's candidate's statement for the position of ITAA President-Elect.

54 This letter was a continuation of the debate about Helena Hargaden's article in *The Script* (Hargaden, 2003).

55 By all accounts, Claude was not particularly happy with *Achieving Emotional Literacy* (Steiner with Perry, 1997), and, in the preface to *Emotional Intelligence with a Heart*, (Steiner, 2003c) wrote that: "[This] book is longer and more elaborate, and it incorporates feedback originated by the original book. It integrates information from readers and clients, what I have gleaned from other books on emotional intelligence, from evolutionary psychology and neuroscience, and from what I have learned in my personal life over the last years" (p. x).

56 This was written in response to (and in support of) Graham Barnes's article "Homosexuality in the first three decades of transactional analysis" (Barnes, 2004).

57 This was written in response to editorial comments made by Helen Hargaden introducing a special themed issue of the *Transactional Analysis Journal* on TA and psychoanalysis (Hargaden, 2005), and generally critiquing the influence of relational psychoanalytic thinking in TA.

58 This was an edited version of the speech Claude gave at the World TA Conference in Istanbul on 29 July 2006.

59 This was written in response to an article by Ken Woods "Regarding the stroking school of transactional analysis" (Woods, 2007).

60 The table of contents and introduction is available at: www.emotional-literacy.org/wake-youre-dying/.

61 Claude had just been appointed Vice President of Internet.

62 In the "Acknowledgements" to this book, Claude wrote that the book was originally meant to be a collection of his papers and, as such, "a legacy piece" (Steiner, 2009, p. vii). In the end he collected papers that he thought were of significance, rearranged them and edited them. As he himself put it, somewhat poignantly as this turned out to be his last published book: "anyone who has followed my ideas will see that they are all here, in one place, clarified to the maximum extent possible, while keeping the material readable" (ibid., p. vii).

63 This book was published in French (2010) (#258) and Spanish (2011) (#263).

64 See also #19.

65 As an audio tape originally transcribed and edited by Claude.

DOS
Scripts

3 Confessions of a psychomechanic

Excerpts on script

Claude Steiner

I first saw the light on January 6, 1935, half Jewish, half gentile, during the glory days of the Third Reich, in a small Paris hospital within walking distance of the Eiffel tower. It was a hard birth but I was evidently not the worse for wear. On the other hand, for all the years of my life, on my birthday, my mother reminded me, usually in a long-distance call, with an audibly rueful smile, how brutal her 28 hour labor had been.

…

My parents probably were not ready to have children when I arrived. They seemed to be quietly involved in the social life of Paris because my earliest memories are of being left alone at night. Of the remembrances that I have from that period, one is deeply etched in my mind. I woke up in a high walled crib in the maid's room at #4 Ville Eugene Manuel, several floors above my parent's apartment in Neuilly sur-Seine. I remember the bare walls and the smell of the chamber pot which the maid used, and I remember crying and being very sad. My parents were evidently out and so was the maid.

How genuine that memory is may be in question but not in doubt is the fact, confirmed by my aunt Hedi, my mother's sister who was in Paris from the day of my birth, is that my parents neglected me from the start. For instance, they failed, initially, to register my birth so that I don't have a proper birth certificate, which caused me serious legal difficulties later on. Whether their failure to circumcise me was a sign of neglect or foresight is not clear. Child neglect was the rule rather than the exception those days. In my case the failure to circumcise me was a good thing as were other, later, aspects of their neglect. The other vivid memory of neglect, years later, is that of a boarding house in the French countryside where my parents took me to visit and then, without warning, left me. I was so upset about this abandonment that I developed a high fever. They were summoned and had to interrupt their plans in order to pick me up. I never forgave them for that and I guilt tripped my mother about it throughout my childhood and adolescence.

There is a photograph that has informed my life's narrative; a beautiful shot, taken from slightly above, showing the back of my head on my mother's bare breasts as she appeared to feed me. Unfortunately, it seems that this image was just that: an image, a photo-op. My father was a photographer, fond of women's bodies, especially my mother's, whose luscious breasts they both probably wished

58   *Claude Steiner*

to preserve from the effects of breast-feeding. That image misled me into believing that I had been breast-fed. Decades later aunt Hedi, who became a guardian angel of sorts, confirmed that I had not been. In fact, I was so frustrated in my needs to suckle on a breast that I sucked my thumb right up to my teenage years.

…

What I also did not know and only learned the day of my mother's funeral is how deep my father's aversion against me may have been or eventually became. As I idly and disconsolately rummaged through her room after returning from the cemetery, I found among the family photographs arrayed on her dresser a framed picture of me, taken by my father, in which I am looking away from the camera with a forbidding frown. Along the right margin he had written, in German, DER ANTICHRIST. For a man who had become a fervent, fundamentalist, born again Christian, follower of Oral Roberts, this was a shocking and damning attribution.

My mother died at age 88 in Cuernavaca, state of Morelos a one-hour drive West from Mexico City. The morning after the funeral my father sought me out on the lush lawn of his estate (a large main house and several "bungalows" in a walled-in compound, the size of a small city block which he had designed and the building of which he had meticulously supervised) and cornered me into an angry confrontation. He was 90 and I was 58.

I had been visited in my bungalow by a young Mexican friend and her cousin and after she left I stayed up writing for many hours. My father knew I had a female visitor and had seen my light well after midnight. He made vague accusations that I was having sex with Claudia, who he suspected to be my lover, all through the night of my mother's interment. When I explained that I had been writing through the night he dismissed the notion with a wave of the hand and went back to an earlier controversy demanding that I find out my blood type. "Why do you want my blood type?" I asked. "Because I want to know once and for all if you are my son. Your mother had a three-year relationship with a man when you were born." I was stunned and could only say "It's none of your business what my blood type is," and he, in a fury, his dentures clacking loosely in his mouth, shouted "OK then get out of my house. I never want to see you here again."

…

When my parents met, they were both free thinkers, nudists, socialists and body culture devotees. He was charming, extremely handsome and well-proportioned and athletic and famous for his skill at dancing the Viennese Waltz. She was aware of having a fabulous body but was self-conscious of her Jewish nose which she artfully hid whenever possible. She, a Jewish princess whose self-image was a blend of Marlene Dietrich and Isadora Duncan; he a rough, sexy, Polish peasant.

…

I would say that Ursula [Claude's first wife] and I were well matched in our dysfunctionality and deserving of, as well as lucky to have found, each other. In Transactional Analysis terms we had matching scripts; life patterns that fit into each other like two puzzle pieces. I needed sex and female affection, which she gave me, and she needed sanity and security, which I provided. As long as we filled each other's needs we functioned better together than separately. As to the quality

Excerpts on script 59

of our love making it was of the classic, one-minute variety. If she ever had an orgasm in the 13 years of our relationship, I was not aware of it.

...

So, from my mother I got her intellectual curiosity and avid reading, her self-deprecating humor and frugality. From my father I got mechanical skills and inventiveness as well as the desire to persuade and make a difference. From both I got their dumb luck. On the bad side I acquired significant traces of my mother's emotional coolness, stinginess and paranoid pettiness and of my father's Bible-thumping fanaticism, anger and dominance, and from both a self-centered sense of entitlement. I do feel some empathy for my father's passionate and frustrated love for my mother, the thwarting of his Christian beliefs and the dismissal by her, her friends and his family.

My mother loved me but did not overtly express it and my father who loved her madly was proportionately jealous and competitive with me. Both led disturbed and disturbing sexual lives. To say that these facts affected my path would be an understatement. It's also probably correct to say that they did the best they could, given their background and the circumstances fate threw them into.

...

While in Mexico we lived in the capital for two years, then moved to Guadalajara, a provincial capital, for two years and then returned to Mexico City. Two more years later, in 1952, I left for the US. Six years is not a long time relatively speaking but in my memory those six years rank in importance with several, much longer eras in my life. The fact that my life in Mexico coincided with my adolescence and all of its hormonal implications has left an indelible mark in my heart. Emotionally, Mexico was and is my mother country: Mi Patria.

...

I don't think that my preoccupation with women especially women's breasts and the thumb sucking that preceded the more creative self-amusement period, was exclusively the result of not being breast-fed. It seems that the interest in the female breast is inbred and common to all human males and probably females ... But interest is different from obsession, and it was the obsessive part, which migrated from breasts to thumb to masturbation and eventually to the sexual fixation that fueled my relationships with women. I do believe that my love and sex addiction – in Twelve Step language – must have its origins in the fact that my mother was severely handicapped as a love-giver.

...

It should be no surprise, given what I have revealed about myself so far, that I left my adolescence with a great need for a fatherly man on one hand and an openly loving woman on the other. Eventually my pressing quest for love and sex, in classically Freudian manner, was the sublimated motivation for my career choice and psychological research and pursuits. Under its powerful influence I wrote a best-selling fairy tale [Steiner, 1977d], developed the theory of the stroke economy [1971c] and designed an emotional literacy training theory and program [1984b, 1996]. Let me now go back in time and pick up another important and perhaps more wholesome thread in my life.

60   *Claude Steiner*

...

Thrift is a feature of my character which I have had a life long struggle with; I see myself as a prudent, frugal spender, when it comes to expending money on services, I prefer to do it myself. I have never hired a regular gardener or maid to clean up after me. Consequently, I am seen by some as a financial, and, by extension, an emotional cheapskate: problems I eventually recognized as being real and which I have endeavored to correct over many years.

...

My father got on the phone and after some harsh words he hissed in German: "Das leben wird dir das genick brechen" (Life will break your neck) the last words I heard from him as I went on my Odyssey.

Undisturbed by my father's curse, I hung up the phone and climbed on the bus for the three-day ride north.

...

Over the years Hedi had several other opportunities to take care of me and while not always as oblivious as this time I never realized the level of protection that she had extended over me, until many years later when she was close to death.

...

Actually, I wasn't such a great catch as I was deranged in my own way. I have often wondered how on Earth anyone was able to tolerate, let alone love the insufferable character that I seemed to be. My Mexico City adolescence friend, Pau Cortes, recalls our interesting conversations and that we had a good friendship. He remembers me as an "enterprising and active young man," always with some money in my pocket from my tinkering enterprises. He admired that I could read the color codes on electronic resistors and that I was funny and always available for a good time. According to my graduate school friend Roger Strauss, I wore a certain narcissistic charm on my sleeve that got me by, at least at first. Eventually a number of people decided that they were through with me as was the case with Teddy Kompanyetz who shunned me after I thoughtlessly parked Ursula at his mother's house in Los Angeles after she got an abortion, and Iden Goodman who after years of friendship in Ann Arbor and Berkeley told me, point blank, that he did not want to be my friend anymore.

Others stuck it out, presumably (I am told) because they could see that I was funny, affectionate, intelligent and at bottom, a good person. A person from the 1970s – Ron Levaco, a friend to this day, says:

> There was always the problem of you being self-absorbed and not listening but on the other hand you were always open and available, you didn't give up, always came back. You were generous with your time and labor and helpful beyond the call of duty and always available for a good conversation.

...

"No hay mal que por bien no venga" is my favorite proverb (There is no bad thing that does not a goodness bring).

...

Excerpts on script 61

He [Eric] appreciated my driving and even devoted a few lines to it in *Games People Play* his best-selling book (Berne 1964/1966a), where, in a discussion of awareness, he describes the "natural driver,"

> to whom driving is a congenial science and art. [As he makes his way swiftly and skilfully through the traffic, he] is at one with his vehicle ... he is very much aware of himself and his machine which he controls so well, and to that extent he is alive
>
> (pp. 179–180)

– a paean, I felt, to my Mexico City driving skills. When I asked him if that was a description of me, he, not fond of being emotionally cornered, answered with a sly smile "and others."

...

In 1969, in the midst of the anti-war rebellion and in the early days of the radical psychiatry movement [see Part Cuatro] I was a died-in-the-wool male chauvinist; suit and tie, horn-rimmed glasses-and-pipe psychologist living in Berkeley. What made me an especially dangerous species of man was that I fantasized myself to be an especially "liberated" male: I liked independent women who would fend for themselves and not require me to take care of them. I was a passionate lover free of sexual hang-ups and had never felt possessive jealousy, which I considered an un-liberated emotion. My idea of a liberated woman was someone who gave me all of her passion, tender affection and open-ended time and enjoyed but did not expect more than that in return.

...

All my life, sex has been the gateway to my relationships with women. After Ursula I met Hogie and we had sex the very first time together, seven years later Hogie left me and I went to Darca with whom my first meaningful contact was sexual. Seven years later when Darca left me Adriane and I had sex the first time we went out and, seven years after that Jude and I made love the first time we got together after Adriane left. And every one of these important women in my life, except Ursula who was 21 – my same age – were about 25 years old when I met them while my age advanced steadily.

...

It should be no surprise that my work as psychologist was fueled by my emotional needs for affection and human contact. Anyone in the clinical area of psychology who claims to be motivated by pure scientific goals untrammeled by personal agendas is probably kidding him or herself though I suppose there are exceptions to the rule. In any case I was not.

...

Life scripts

I mentioned that Eric Berne's theory involved the proposition that people's lives were programmed in early life by a dramatic script which people read from, as on a

62   *Claude Steiner*

stage. This overarching life narrative is "decided" early in life and is fueled, maintained, kept alive by daily, dysfunctional, transactional sequences he called games. These interpersonal games keep the script alive and moving forward.

If a person has a life-long script of depression ending in suicide he keeps the script moving forward by playing depressive games such as "Kick me," "Schlemiel," "Why don't you yes but" which constantly reinforce the depressive basis of the script. Another person with a script of violence possibly ending in homicide will keep the script moving forward by games like "Now I've got you, you SoB," "Uproar," or, again, "Kick Me" which keep anger and violence alive. The games people play are varied and different but they all have one thing in common: they contain the three basic roles, Rescuer, Persecutor and Victim which are pursued in an endless merry-go-round of painful emotions and harmful behavior [see Berne, 1964/1966; Karpman, 1968].

How and why do children decide that their lives will follow a certain course? As intelligent sentient beings children seek explanations for the world they live in. As they look around they see examples, hear and read stories, receive advice, rewards and punishment and eventually create a narrative scheme that explains and rationalizes their predicaments and defines their opportunities. These narratives can be simple as in "I'll never be happy" or complicated "My life will be like Spider Man's." They can be positive as in "I will marry, have many children and die surrounded by loved ones," or it can be negative as in "I will be forever betrayed and die alone and in despair." When the narrative is negative it can be tragic as in suicide, murder or mortal accident or it can be banal as in lifelong depression. In the case of depression, for example, the script fueled by years of daily depressive games and each game in turn reinforces the validity of the script's existential position. "Life is hell and then you die."

The idea is that later life is complexly prefigured in earlier life in every case, as it was in mine. I was born and grew up in an ambiguously supportive world. My material needs were taken care of and I was left to fend for myself. My needs for love were not answered and I was needy but did not know of what. I had an active mind and fantasy life fed by voracious reading. I sought out stories of carnal love, which excited me in mysterious ways and soon saw myself involved in the conquest of female companions to feed my hunger. I felt betrayed by my parents and fastened on a fairy tale – The Pied Piper of Hamelin – that supplied me with a narrative which I then followed in a surprisingly literal manner as I will explain later.

How long will you live? A script decision

After Berne died, I wrote *Scripts People Live* [Steiner, 1974a]. In an introduction recalling Berne's life I ventured the notion that he had been under a strictly timed script to die of a broken heart. I based this on his frequent references to scripted death in his last years, especially in his posthumously published book *What Do You Say after You Say Hello?* [Berne, 1972/1975b]. His mother had died at age sixty of heart attack, a fact that he referred to frequently. He had a heart condition and he had a notoriously heart-breaking history in his relationships with women.

Excerpts on script 63

All of this led me to the conclusion that his early death was prefigured and therefore unnecessary. Some years later, when research showed that heart disease was closely related to hereditary factors, I had occasion to wonder whether I had made a rash statement that I needed to retract. But soon after, further research showed that people at risk of heart attack are less likely to have one and are more likely to recover if they do have one, when they live in a supportive, affectionate, stroke filled environment. So, my supposition, that he had a broken heart script became tenable.

When, after his first heart attack, Hogie and I visited Berne in his hospital bed in Carmel on a Sunday afternoon we found him correcting the galleys of *What Do You Say after You Say Hello?* Even though the book was full of references to scripted death he expected to recover and we spoke about future plans. I naively wondered if it would be a good idea if I moved to Carmel for a few weeks to look after him and Hogie climbed on his bed and hugged him and promised to "teach him about women and feminism" after he recovered ... We were both cheered by the visit, as he seemed to be.

Next morning after a good night's sleep he had his second massive, and this time fatal heart attack. I was utterly shocked and spent the next week in my study editing the hundreds of hours of seminar recordings that I had taped into an eight-hour tape. He was buried on July and his family closed ranks around him and pointedly did not invite anyone in the TA organization. I watched the funeral from a distance and when everyone had gone I approached the grave with Hogie and cried my heart out wetting the ground with my tears.

As I examined Berne's life I realized that I too, in my late thirties, had constructed a narrative scheme for my life which was programmed to end with the XX century and that my daily life was geared to support that outcome. Shocked by Berne's unexpected, but by him esoterically predicted death, I resolved at that time that I would break whatever script I was operating under, stop playing the games that supported it and endeavor to live to be one hundred years old. I put that pledge in writing in *Scripts People Live* [1974a] and that book, still in print, has been translated into seven languages so at this point I feel a responsibility to perform on that pledge. My method, at age seventy: Live every day as if it was the last one and plan to be alive for the next ten thousand.

...

Recognition

This incident [one in which Claude did not support his eldest daughter, Mimi, emotionally] illuminates one of the important family generational issues in my family. My father was of the opinion that a father's job is to point out to his children, especially the first-born son, what is defective about them. When I complained about his absolute lack of appreciation of me and my life, he ridiculed me telling me, essentially, to grow up. Even after getting my PhD and publishing my first book he continued to fail to show any appreciation of my accomplishments but instead insisted in criticizing me mercilessly.

64 *Claude Steiner*

Eventually I had enough. I had been advising clients whose parents were relentlessly critical of them and generating constant depression in them with their negative attitude, to deny them access to them. One person in particular showed up to the group deeply depressed every Monday; when we realized that he made a routine, Sunday evening phone call to his mother who never failed to denigrate him, I asked him to stop calling her which he did with great difficulty but very good results. Hogie encouraged me to do the same so I let my father know in a letter that unless he was willing to openly state that he respected my profession and my friends I would not be willing to spend time or even see him anymore.

He dismissed my request as ridiculous, but I was serious and stuck to my guns; one time he came to my house unannounced all the way from Mexico and when I realized who was at the door I hid in a closet while Hogie went to the door and told him I was not there. He was furious and called her a liar, but she was not impressed. Eventually, my mother and aunt entreated me to relent but I insisted and after almost three years of banishment he asked to see me for he had something important to tell me. He came to my house sat down in front of me and said: "I respect your profession and friends. So is that what you wanted?"

I was dumbfounded as I did not expect such a calloused response. He even followed up with a mind-boggling letter of hypocritical praise down to my, by him hitherto hated moustache. But he had done what I asked and I, rather confused by the developments, relented. That was the last time that he gave me any overt recognition.

While my father was bitterly critical, my mother's attitude was different even though she did not make a big point of it; she was proud of my academic and authorial accomplishments, carefully read every one of my books. When I graduated, she bought me an expensive, automatic gold Bulova watch while my father didn't even congratulate me. Recognition has been a life-long issue for me; in fact, I have a fervent wish that motivates me to be famous enough to be remembered for all times in psychiatric, soul-healing history. As I explained before, my life narrative (or script, in transactional analysis terms) was informed by the tale of the Pied Piper of Hamelin who failed to get recognition for his deeds; the result no doubt of the fact that my father refused to acknowledge any of my accomplishments – my degrees, my books, my career, my friends – as long as he lived.

Sadly, it seems that I passed portions of that narrative down to Mimi [Claude's eldest daughter], who in similar fashion, though in a far less toxic version has failed to get open recognition of her accomplishments from me not because I disapproved of her in any way but because recognition is something I don't handle very well as a giver or as a recipient. That is why I wasn't able to respond in the obvious way to the question: "Are you proud of Mimi?"

For all of her life, Mimi who adored me and probably still does has been performing amazing deeds, partially I'm sure to make me proud, and, somehow, I have been unable to respond in the appropriate proud way. Her accomplishments, taken for granted, seem to reinforce instead, the self-serving feeling that I must be a good father after all; that I must have done something right. I have to confess that

I have obviously been the victim of the most transparent of defense mechanisms where Mimi is concerned, [i.e.] denial …

The oblivious, unflappable tendency in me has divided us from each other and kept me from beholding the real Mimi. I see a beautiful strong, Earth Mother woman and fail to see the very intense feelings expressed in her face; whether she is feeling happy and loving, or unhappy with the conviction that she is being neglected or deprived.

For a while Mimi was deeply angry at me about [certain] childhood experiences and my cavalier treatment of them and convinced that I owed her a profound apology. By this I assumed she meant that parents are responsible for what happens on their watch. I know I have not been sufficiently proactive, have been lazy even, and taken refuge too often in my near-psychotic optimism. Denali, my second daughter with whom I did not have these problems, has urged me to take this matter on as a deeply important project and, in my own energy-efficient fashion. I have begun to do so, with good results, though perhaps with more patience and at a slower pace – once again trusting that time and nature's healing hand will do what haste cannot accomplish – than some observers might be able to comprehend.

CS at 80 (starting April 2015)

[With regard to his relationship with his wife, Jude.] Luckily I am able to distinguish my Pig's toxic narrative (betrayal, abandonment, utter loneliness, first degree power plays, destruction, revenge; the same old script) from the more rational but not lacking in strong emotions of sadness and fear, of doing the math and applying the wisdom-drenched conclusion which is that I have to relax, be patient and tolerant and see how this plays out while hoping that, while this is madness but OK, it will abate as nothing ever stays the same and could go my way or not, but is not under my control.

4 Attribution and alienation
Reflections on Claude Steiner's script theory

William F. Cornell

> The script matrix showed the parents above and the child below, thus realistically representing a dimension that goes beyond the transactional into the realm of power or the relative capacity of the players to affect each other (with the offspring at an obvious disadvantage). One of the most common and damaging scripts, which is largely shared by most people and is therefore taken for granted, is the script of powerlessness and its mirror image, authoritarianism.
> (Steiner, 1987, p. 102)

Claude and Eric: at the beginning

In the introduction to his classic text on script theory, *Scripts People Live*, Claude Steiner (1974a) offers an extended, personal, and at times conflicted reflection on the life, the then recent death, and script of his beloved mentor, Eric Berne. Claude's introductory essay is both a homage to Berne and an act of bereavement

Figure 4.1 Claude and the script matrix

in the face of Berne's death at the young age of 60 when his development of transactional analysis (TA) was still underway.

As I read Claude's account in his personal memoir, *Confessions of a Psychomechanic*, of his father's unrelenting criticism, I imagined the profound impact that Berne's appreciation and praise of Claude's intelligence must have had upon him. Claude describes his father's attitude:

> My father was of the opinion that a father's job is to point out to his children, especially the first-born son, what is defective about them. When I complained about his absolute lack of appreciation of me and my life he ridiculed me telling me, essentially, to grow up. Even after getting my PhD and publishing my first book he continued to fail to show any appreciation of my accomplishments but instead insisted in criticizing me mercilessly.
>
> (*Confessions* [in this book], p. 63)

Berne (1972/1975) offers a startling contrast in his forthright appreciation of Claude's thinking in *What Do You Say after You Say Hello?*:

> The script matrix in its present form was devised by Dr. Claude M. Steiner ... In my estimation, its value cannot be overestimated ... It is such an important invention that, without detracting from Dr. Steiner's perceptiveness, ingenuity, and creativity, I would like to claim a part of it.
>
> (p. 297, n. 2)

It is likely no accident that recognition and the stroke economy (Steiner, 1971f) became central to Claude's approach to TA theory and practice (Steiner, 2003a).

Claude vividly captures Berne's working attitude evident both in his writings and in the ways he guided the San Francisco Social Psychiatry Seminars: "He did everything he could to insure that during working hours of scientific meetings his and others' Adults were fully alert and maximally capable of performing their tasks" (Steiner, 1974a, p. 15).

Claude casts Berne's devotion to the centrality of the Adult ego state as a reflection of Berne's deep identification with his physician father as well as an expression of Berne's script, which severely limited his capacity to receive love and concern. Here both the life-enhancing and life-limiting aspects of Berne's script become evident as Claude observed that "in the early period of TA (1955–1965), Berne subtly and unwittingly discouraged us from studying strokes, intimacy and scripts" (p. 18). Claude speaks directly to the tragic aspects of Berne's script, observing that he was not receptive to caring concern and concluding:

> The injunctions concerning strokes which kept his script operative and his heart aching went unchallenged. The distance he kept from those who loved him, and whom he loved, including myself, prevented us from comforting him; he slipped out of our lives.
>
> (p. 19)

68 William F. Cornell

Figure 4.2 Claude receiving the Eric Berne Scientific Award (for the script matrix), 1971

Claude's introduction further offers a fascinating discussion of Berne's continuing involvement with psychoanalysis through to the end of his life, even as he became famous for his development of TA. He notes that even as Berne's writing came to increasingly center on script theory, he continued to practice individual sessions on the couch, during which he did script analysis. This was an area of considerable tension between Berne, Steiner, and other members of the San Francisco Social Psychiatry Seminar, as evidenced in a seminar tape Claude published after Berne's death, subsequently transcribed and published in *The Script* newsletter published by the International Transactional Analysis Association (ITAA) (Berne et al., 1968/2017).

As Claude was describing Berne's resistance to care, he wrote, "When he required psychotherapy he did not work in a group or consult a transactional analyst but worked with a psychoanalyst in individual psychotherapy" (p. 18). This would seem to have been the area of greatest tension and divergence between Claude and Eric, as Claude's emphasis in theory and practice moved increasingly into group and political realms and his identification with radical psychiatry (The Radical Therapist Collective, 1971; Steiner, 1975i), which I suspect deepened significantly after Berne's death.

A brief overview of Steiner's early writings on script

Eric Berne introduced the idea of script in his very first book elucidating TA theory (Berne, 1961/1975a), but it was Steiner – influenced to a great degree by his efforts to understand the hamartic scripts in his work with alcoholics and addicts (Steiner, 1968a, 1971b, 1979b) – who delineated a more complete model of the dynamics of script formation, described the function of counterscript, and created the script matrix (Steiner, 1966). In this article, "Script and Counterscript," he stressed that for a therapist invested in avoiding a tragic ending, it was crucial to distinguish between an apparent "cure" and a retreat to counterscript. He stressed, "structurally, script and counterscript are Parental precipitates, and therefore superficially indistinguishable, but closer scrutiny reveals important differences" (ibid., p. 133). The script matrix mapped those differences and dynamics. Steiner's earliest writings on script, including the script checklist (Steiner, 1967a), were published in the *Transactional Analysis Bulletin*.

The year 1972 saw an issue of the *Transactional Analysis Journal* (*TAJ*) devoted to script theory, with Steiner being invited to write a "Special Editorial Comment" that he entitled, "Scripts Revisited" (Steiner, 1972b), in which he addressed the state of the art following Berne's death. In this article we can see Steiner's identification with Berne, as he places emphasis on the scientific aspects of script theory, arguing "simplicity and parsimony are criteria for science" (ibid., p. 83). While that statement might have been an accurate rendering of the attitude of the natural sciences at that time, we have an abundance of experience now that suggests that the human sciences are a bit more complex. Simplicity may destroy nuance and imagination – and for all of my admiration of the radical psychiatry movement, I would find it hard to signify their theories as "scientific." In his reflections, Steiner identifies a shift in his own attention from the diagnostic focus of the script checklist and matrix as being "of an archeological nature" (ibid., p. 86) devoted to the understanding of the origins of script to his growing interest in the identifying "the fundamental therapeutic dimensions in TA" (ibid., p. 86). The processes of therapy and the functions of the therapist became central in Steiner's subsequent writing.

In his editorial reflections, Steiner discusses how TA theory will develop and confronts the emerging competitiveness among many theorists. He writes, "it is obvious, however, that whatever does become added to transactional analysis will have to be published in this *Journal* as the minimum first step" (Steiner, 1972b, p. 86). There is an irony here, in that his editorial is the last formal writing about script theory he made in the pages of the *TAJ*. His future contributions were to be many, but the body of his thinking was published in a series of books rather than the journal. For many years he maintained a conflicted and often contentious relationship with the ITAA and the diversity of developments within TA theory (see,

70   *William F. Cornell*

for instance, Steiner, 2003d). His subsequent contributions to the *TAJ* were focused primarily on bringing politics into TA and on the politics of TA.

In *Scripts People Live*, Steiner (1974a) presents his most comprehensive account of his script theory, elaborating the script checklist and the script matrix as key tools for understanding and treating the script. He identifies three basic script patterns: lovelessness, mindlessness, and joylessness, placing the dynamics of power at the heart of his model:

> The power of parents to influence their children – the power to mold them, the power to make them do things and prevent them from doing things – according to their wishes is an aspect of a more general capacity which all human beings have, the capacity for witchcraft. The analysis of witchcraft is a sub-heading of transactional analysis in that it deals with the analysis of covert or ulterior messages and their effect and power.
>
> (p. 64)

His sensitivity to power was reflected in such language as the Pig Parent and Witch messages, characteristic of the social revolutionary attitudes of the late 1960s and 1970s (Cooper, 1968; The Radical Therapist Collective, 1971), terms that are seldom used today. The dynamics of power remained at the heart of his work in TA (Steiner, 1975e, 1975f, 1981e, 1987).

In the remainder of this chapter, I will focus on two aspects of Steiner's understanding of script formation and its treatment: attribution and alienation, which I think have been under-theorized in TA.

Attribution

It can be said that, for Steiner, a child's script is, in its essence, created and enforced by the parents, serving parental needs far more than the healthy developmental needs of the child arguing that "restrictive injunctions and attributions are passed on to children in order to satisfy or comfort parents" (Steiner, 1974a, p. 59). While the notion of script injunctions is common throughout the TA theories of script, what I want to emphasize here is Steiner's attention to attributions, an important, additional perspective that has been largely overlooked in subsequent TA literature. In a discussion of script theory in the contemporary textbook of TA, *Into TA*, Cornell, de Graaf, Newton, and Thunnissen (2016) bring attention to the place of attribution in script formation, adding that attributions are not only said *to* the child directly, but also *about* the child to others, adding additional pressure for adaptation.

Steiner suggests that while injunctions instruct a child in what *not* to be or do, attributions are equally important communications that tell children who they *are* and what *to do*. He casts attributions as central to tragic scripts. In *Scripts People Live*, he quotes at length from R. D. Laing's (1972) *The Politics of the Family* to illustrate the process and power of attributions, suggesting that Laing's book is "essential to the understanding of scripts" (Steiner, 1974a, p. 62). It is certainly

Attribution and alienation 71

not coincidental that Steiner developed his understanding of script working with alcoholics and addicts, whom he saw as suffering from third degree scripts, while Laing developed his central ideas in working with those diagnosed as schizo-phrenic. Both client populations are among those most severely pathologized and marginalized and whose lives show the evidence of the damaging consequences of familial and social control.

In taking up the meaning and impact of attribution, I want to contrast Steiner's conceptualization with that of Laing. Steiner (ibid.) elaborates the influence of attributions by introducing the language and imagery of witchcraft:

> It is important to realize that bad witchcraft in the form of attribution is often used for the recipient's "own good" as judged by the witch; any attribution, no matter how good it looks or sounds, can be bad for the recipient.
>
> (p. 66)

He goes on to argue that "the exercise of power over people for the purpose of harming them seems to have two basic sources" (ibid., p. 66) which he describes as reactions to physical and psychological scarcity and to defenses against feelings of worthlessness or of being not OK. Steiner draws on the socio-political writings of Reich (1942/1961, 1945/1962) and Marcuse (1962) to further elaborate his ideas of social and familial power:

> Thus Marcuse and Wilhelm Reich connect the social and psychological manipulation of human beings by human beings surrounding them – including the family – with an oppressive social order. The following theory about the stroke economy is a similar effort in which it will be proposed that the free exchange of strokes which is equally a human capacity, a human propensity, and a human right has been artificially controlled for the purpose of rearing human beings who will behave in a way which is desirable to a larger social "good," though not necessarily best for the people themselves.
>
> (Steiner, 1974a, p. 112)

Steiner goes on to elaborate his ideas about the stroke economy, drawn from Reich's (1951/1971, 1972) "sex-pol" Marxist writings of the 1930s, placing it at the heart of his therapeutic process. Steiner's appropriation of Reich's writings are strik-ingly superficial and uncannily similar to his attitude toward Berne's continued regard for psychoanalysis. Reich's sex-pol writings were an effort to synthesize Marxist theory with psychoanalysis while arguing that Marxist thought and polit-ical movements needed to be reshaped by psychoanalytic and characterological perspectives: "The scope of human and social problems is far deeper and broader than Marxist economics encompasses. Time marches on, and political movements remain sitting on one spot" (Reich, 1951/1971, p. ix).

Here, to my mind, we come up against the style and limits of Steiner's concep-tualizations. His perspective tends to the concrete. He seems to reject any poten-tial value of psychoanalytic thinking, setting aside the psychoanalytic discourses

72   *William F. Cornell*

that were essential elements in the work of authors whose work he drew upon, including Berne, first and foremost, as well as other influences such as Marcuse, Reich, and Laing. He does write of covert communication as in game theory and script formation, but there is no articulated theory of unconscious dynamics or transferential/countertransferential pressures. His emphasis is on the deadening and warping impact of external forces. There is little evocation in his writing of the power of the unconscious, of self-destructive forces within the individual, or of the power and creativity of internal realities and subjectivity. This emphasis on external oppression as the primary source of psychological dysfunction is further elaborated in the work carried out by Steiner and his colleagues in the radical psychiatry movement. I think it has been this kind of concreteness in Steiner's models that has resulted in his script theory becoming less influential as TA has evolved.

Steiner's concreteness can be seen in an interchange with Berne during the San Francisco seminar mentioned earlier. Berne, who was discussing the place of transference and psychoanalytic interpretations within the practice of TA, argued that "you cannot cure the patient until you've analyzed the transference resistance" (in Berne et al., 1968/2017, p. 9). A lively, quite heated discussion ensued over the handling of transference in TA with Steiner arguing, "a TA therapist would say, 'Oh, don't give me that. I'm not your father.' A psychoanalyst would get to the edge of his chair and start scratching with his pencil" (pp. 11–12). Berne replied:

> The difference is you say, uhh, "The world in which your Child lives is still the world in which your father is going to bugger you, and so your Child is afraid of me. So let's talk about that." You don't say, "Knock it off," any more than you would say to a child who is afraid of bears in the bedroom, "Knock it off." You would say, "What bear?" or something. Whatever you would say, you don't say, "Knock it off" to a 4-year-old who's scared of bears.
>
> (p. 12)

In contrast to Steiner, Laing (1969), while equally immersed in the aggressive social and professional critique undertaken by the anti-psychiatry movement in England (Boyer, 1971; Laing & Cooper, 1964), was grounded in British psychoanalysis. Laing elaborated his psychoanalytic training within an existential-phenomenological perspective (see Beveridge, 2011), which he characterized as an "attempt to reconstruct the patient's way of being himself in the world, although, in the therapeutic relationship, the focus may be on the patient's way of being-with-me" (Laing, 1969, p. 24). Reading Laing (1972) on attribution is strikingly different from Steiner (1974a):

> As images of ghostly relations under the operation of projection, we induce others, and are ourselves induced, to *embody* them: to enact, unbeknown to ourselves, a shadow play, as images of images of images … of the dead, who have in their turn embodied and enacted such dramas projected upon them, and induced in them, by those before them … In a hypnotic (or similar) context,

Attribution and alienation 73

one does not tell him what *to be*, but tells him what he is. Such *attributions*, in context, are many times more powerful than orders (or other forms of coercion or persuasion).

(Laing, 1972, p. 78)

One's inner world, as described by Laing, while influenced – and perhaps maimed – by parental and social forces, were also alive, fluid, and creative:

> "Internalization" means to map "outer" onto "inner". It entails the transference of a group of relations constituting a set … from one modality of experience to others: namely from perception to imagination, memory, dreams. We perceive something in our waking life; we remember it; then we forget it; we dream something with different content but similar structure; we remember the dream but not the original perception. From this and other kinds of internalization, some patterns recur in our reveries, dreams, imagination, fantasy.
>
> (p. 7)

Laing's use of internalization can easily be seen as another term for the process of script formation: a map, a matrix of internalized beliefs, attributions, and injunctions, but Laing's internal maps are far more complex and active than those theorized by Steiner in his development of the script matrix.

I think of how often when I have been sitting with my adolescent clients and their parents to hear a parent say ever so matter-of-factly, "He's never been interested in anyone but himself"; "She's just never had what it takes"; "I could tell from the day she was born, she'd be impossible to satisfy"; "I always knew there was something wrong with her"; "He is always smiling, so I just can't understand why he's depressed"; or "It all became clear when our priest explained that he was possessed at birth." These are messages delivered as statements of reality. As I read the passage from Laing that I quoted above, I vividly recalled a phone conversation with a client's mother who was in intensive care. My client had been estranged from her mother for many years but upon hearing that she was critically ill decided to go to the hospital and see her. I agreed to call her at the hospital to add a voice of support. Her mother answered the bedside phone (this was long before cell phones), and I asked to talk with her daughter. "Which daughter? I have two stupid daughters." I named my client. "Why do you want to talk to *her*?" came a belligerent reply. I said I was a friend and knew this was a difficult trip, so I was calling to see how she was doing. "She doesn't have any friends," was the mother's reply. This brief interchange truly conveys the power of attribution, here from a mother who might well have been on her death bed. My client had had a life time of these statements of "fact." It took us many years to undo the deep internalization of these messages, often acted out in her personal and professional relationships as compelling, "paranoid" projections, leaving her all too often alone and isolated. I have no idea what "ghostly relations" haunted my client's mother, but I do know how long it took the two of us to put those ghost-driven attributions to rest and open new ways of her seeing herself and others.

74   *William F. Cornell*

While Laing never underestimated the psychic violence so often carried out in family and medical/psychiatric systems, he does not lose sight of the enormous active, creative, and disturbing forces of the unconscious aspects of our inner lives. Steiner made important use of Laing's accounts of attributions, but he seemed unable or unwilling to make use of the more subtle, inner-directed aspects of Laing's writing.

Alienation

A central focus on power returns again in Steiner's (1979b) elucidation of aliena-tion as "a condition in which people are estranged from their powers" (p. 95). The concept of alienation, drawn largely from the Marxist tradition (Steiner & Wyck-off, 1975), is foundational in the radical psychiatry movement in which Steiner was a key figure. Radical psychiatry was an effort to wrench the practice of psychiatry as a healing art from the control of medicine, arguing that "*Psychiatry is a political activity*. Persons who avail themselves of psychiatric aid are invariably in the midst of power-structured relationships with one or more other human beings" (Steiner, 1975b, p. 9, emphasis in original). The movement sought to change psychiatry "radically, that is, 'at the root'" (p. 9).

In his 1969 "Manifesto" outlining the basic tenets of the movement, Steiner declares, "PSYCHIATRIC DISTURBANCE IS EQUIVALENT WITH ALIEN-ATION WHICH IS THE RESULT OF MYSTIFIED OPPRESSION" (Steiner, 1969/1975d, p. 5, original emphasis). He describes alienation in this way: "Alien-ation is a feeling within a person that he is not part of the human species, that she is dead or that everyone is dead, that he does not deserve to live, or that someone wishes her to die" (ibid., p. 11).

Here is an evocation of alienation that closely mirrors that used by Laing to convey the lived experience of schizoid and schizophrenic individuals. If one has the feeling (or perception/conviction) that "I am not part of the human species" or that "someone wishes me dead," does this mean that a person inhabited by these ideas is schizophrenic? Laing (1960) would argue that this profound sense of alienation is fundamental to the schizoid experience of a "divided self." While Steiner's conceptualization of alienation was rooted in the work of Marx, Reich (1945/1962, 1972), and Marcuse (1962), Laing's was informed by existentialism and psychoanalysis, thereby bringing much more attention to a client's living, internal experience. Beveridge (2011), who gained access to Laing's unpublished papers, provides a striking account of the depth of Laing's immersion in existential and phenomenological authors that laid the foundation for the work for which he was to become both famous and infamous. Beveridge cites an unpublished speech on "Existential Analysis," given by Laing to the Royal Medical Psychological Association in 1960, in which he argues,

> one of its basic intentions is to discard any preoccupations which prevent one seeing the individual patient in the light of his own existence. That is, it attempts to understand the patient's complaints in his terms, as well as in our terms.
>
> (p. 137)

Attribution and alienation 75

In the opening pages of *The Divided Self*, Laing (1960) refers to the influences of Kierkegaard, Jaspers, Heidegger, Sartre, Binswanger, and Tillich on his thinking, and citing May, Angel and Ellenberg (1958) and Boss (1963). Laing (1960) writes about a patient who describes himself as an "unreal man," who says he "has been pretending for years to have been a real person but can maintain the deception no longer" (p. 38). Reflecting upon this state of deep alienation, Laing observes:

> the person whom we call "schizoid" feels both more exposed, more vulnerable to others than we do, and more isolated. Thus a schizophrenic may say that he is made of glass, of such transparency and fragility that a look directed at him splinters him to bits and penetrates straight through him. We may suppose that precisely as such he experiences himself.
>
> (p. 38)

While Laing sought to understand and treat the deep vulnerabilities of the alienated, divided self, Steiner approached alienation as an enemy that needs to be attacked: *"The third principle of radical psychiatry is that all alienation is the result of oppression about which the oppressed has been mystified or deceived* ... Oppression + Deception = Alienation [whereas] Oppression + Awareness = Anger" (Steiner, 1975h, pp. 11–12, original emphasis).

Steiner outlines the basic treatment formula for radical psychiatry as "Awareness + Contact = Action → Liberation" (ibid., p. 14), declaring unequivocally that "extended individual psychotherapy is an elitist, outmoded, as well as non-productive, form of psychiatric help" (Steiner, 1975d, p. 3). He argues that it is not possible to practice radical psychiatry within the context of individual psychotherapy, that "an individual cannot move against his oppression as an individual ... only action by groups of people who have become aware of how they are oppressed can lead to *liberation*" (Steiner, 1975h, p. 15, original emphasis). Here Steiner seems to be completely trashing the treatment model developed by Berne, who saw the group phase of psychotherapy as the opportunity to expose games and develop social control before returning to individual psychotherapy on the couch for depth script analysis. It is worth noting that the client with whom I had such a warm telephone chat with her hospitalized mother worked with me in both group and individual formats. Her work in the group was essential to her being able to observe and experience her distrust of people in action (i.e., her games). However, it was in the crucible of our transference and countertransference relationship that she was able to resolve far deeper levels of her paranoid projections and the vulnerability those projections guarded against.

Here again, as with the foundation of his theory of script, the bad folks are all on the outside, the oppressors. The individual is held in the place of hapless victim.

Steiner and his radical psychiatry colleagues were hardly the first psychotherapists to address the power of alienation. Writing from his psychoanalytic/Marxist perspective, Fromm (1953/2010, 1955) spoke forcefully about the impact of alienation within economic, political, and religious contexts: "It is the fact that *man does not experience himself as an active bearer of his own powers and richness,*

76 *William F. Cornell*

but as an impoverished 'thing,' dependent on powers outside himself, unto whom he has projected his living substance" (p. 124, original emphasis). Fromm argues for the essential awareness and articulation of social factors in the promotion of mental health, but, at the same time, he does not cast those who suffer the effects of alienation as innocent, helpless victims. He addresses the complicity of the "alienated" with the "oppressors," confronting the trade off that many have made, forsaking their autonomy and responsibility for the illusions of comfort and security offered by the oppressors:

> How can a sensitive and alive person ever feel secure? Because of the very conditions of our existence, we cannot feel secure about anything ... The psychic task which a person can and must set for himself, *is not to feel secure, but to be able to tolerate insecurity, without panic and undue fear* ... Life, in its mental and spiritual aspects, is by necessity insecure and uncertain ... *Free man is by necessity insecure; thinking man is by necessity uncertain.*"
>
> (Fromm, 1955, p. 196, original emphasis)

Fromm's sentiments and argument foreshadow the emergence of the existential traditions emergent in Europe and then emerging in the United States. It was existentialism as much as psychoanalysis that shaped much of Laing's work, which he initially referred to as "existential analysis" (Beveridge, p. 135). Like Fromm, Laing understood and addressed the dialectical tension between social forces and individual responsibility. In an unpublished speech titled "Existential Analysis," given to the Royal Medical Psychological Association, he spoke to what it is to be a human being:

> It involves taking responsibility for whatever one chooses to do in whatever situations one is in. One is in the world, but one knows that one was not always in the world and that one will not always be in the world. As a result of these considerations a person has to decide how to live one's life.
>
> (Laing, 1960, quoted in Beveridge, p. 136)

Beveridge, who gained access to Laing's unpublished papers, provides a striking account of the depth of Laing's immersion in existential and phenomenological authors that laid the foundation for the work for which he was to become both famous and infamous.

Whether addressed in Marxist terms or existentialism, alienation was in the air in the late 1960s (Aptheker, 1965; Boss, 1963; May, 1967) and early 1970s (Boss, 1979; Johnson, 1973). None of these rich, and often provocative, writings are referenced in Steiner's work or of others in the radical psychiatry movement. His was an embrace of a position with the kind of concrete certainty that typified much of his work.

Writing more recently, Tudor (1997/2017) takes up the place of alienation in feminist, social, and psychological discourse, arguing that "there is a fundamental fault running through most attempts to deal with the interplay between Marxism

Attribution and alienation 77

and psychoanalysis ... and, alternatively, in using Marxism as a tool in developing theories relevant to psychotherapy" (p. 59). He argues for the development of "a new, living Marxism ... one which takes account of the economic, the political, *and* the psychological" (p. 59, original emphasis). Tudor takes up the ways in which various theoretical models address alienation and describes the centrality of "the social entity of the family" (p. 62) as a structure promoting, even demanding, alienation: "The family is not just an ideological construct but a lived experience for people, one which ... cannot be wholly separated from social and biological pressures and an internal (family system and individual) psychological dynamic" (p. 63). It is within the lived experience of the family – the rich and enduring cauldron of love, dependency, loyalty, conflict, and woundedness – that script is formed, and in that adaptive creation of a scripted self there lies a fundamental alienation of real self from false self.

One does not need a radical, leftist social critique (although it helps!) to see that the political and psychological impact of alienation are as alive today as they were in the 1960s and 1970s. Look only to the resurgence of racism in the United States, nationalism throughout the world, and depersonalized violence as manifestations of profound personal alienation to see that the acknowledgment of alienation is as relevant today as it was half a century ago. On a much more modest and personal scale, I think of the myriad of young, alienated male clients in their early thirties I see who wonder who they are and what they want from life, and men in their fifties looking back on lives in which they did everything "right" while they struggle with meaningless, loneliness, and depression.

Oppression and activism

There is much to be said and appreciated for the profoundly activist stance of the therapists in the radical psychiatry movement. Their work mirrored the massive group-centered movements among the Vietnam veterans learning (having to) care for themselves and the liberating forces of the black, women's, and gay liberation movements, fighting against marginalization, neglect, disempowerment, stigmatization. So, too, the human potential movement sought to overturn the basic premises implicit in many of the medical and classical psychoanalytic models of the time, in which the professional was the expert and the patient was the dysfunctional object of treatment. These movements were revolutionary and essential for professional and societal change – and ultimately insufficient.

Rereading the strident articles and manifestos of this era took me back to my own involvement with the neo-Reichian movement – which also strongly influenced the radical psychiatry therapists. I was entranced by Reich's political fury and his aggressive approach to psychotherapy. Reich conceived of his patients' defenses as the result of an "emotional plague" (1948) that was consuming mankind and saw the consequent defenses as forms of "armor" that had to be attacked and broken through. The pathological influence of parents, the social structure, and the forces of oppression were to be named and attacked by the wise and well-meaning therapist. The bad were on the outside, the good on the inside. Once the therapist had broken

78   *William F. Cornell*

through the armor, the client's natural potential for health, sexuality, and self-regulation emerged. The power was to be taken away from the environment and given over to the therapist in service to the client. It became clear to me and to many of my neo-Reichian colleagues that what was promised by the theory did not happen in actuality. The interruption of muscular armor and/or interpersonal games was somehow not a guarantee of growth and robust health. Steiner's writing about and approach to the treatment of script seriously minimized the self-perpetuating nature of script. An activist stance is not sufficient. Altering a client's stroke economy is not sufficient. Behavior change is often insufficient to foster an in-depth examination of one's self and to promote robust, enduring psychological and emotional growth.

Chinnock and Minikin (2015) return to Steiner's radical psychiatry writings on oppression and mystification, taking these ideas up so as to examine and challenge the potentially oppressive functions of the therapist and the therapy. They offer a thoughtful discussion of the dangers of a therapist's countertransference in imagining that he/she knows what is best for the client or become overly invested in their theories and presumptions as to what constitutes psychopathology. Such certainty "can be exposing and unnecessarily shaming to clients, particularly if it closes down a process rather than opens up a dialogue" (p. 146). They argue that "if the goal is to stop the game and encourage behavior change, both therapist and client may miss a deeper exploration of vulnerabilities that might shed light on active unconscious processes" (p. 146). They outline a process of "dilemma transactions" through which a therapist takes an accounting of the dilemma created by his/her countertransference and finding ways to bring the dilemma into the therapeutic dialogue so as to create an exploratory space – first within the therapist and then with the client. The inner lives of therapist and client alike are subject to examination and discussion.

Closing thoughts

Steiner wrote with great certainty and passion. As he was formulating his basic concepts in the 1970s, there were few in any systematic models of the therapeutic uses of the therapist's countertransference. He certainly evidenced no curiosity ("knock it off") for or credibility to Berne's attention to transference or continued use of some aspects of psychoanalytic theory or technique. I would take Steiner's attitude toward Berne's blending of TA and psychoanalysis as some indication of his own unexamined countertransference, which seems to have been enacted in the declarative certainty that characterizes much of his writing, as well as the delineation of treatment rules so often put forth in his work. TA has continued to evolve. The constructivist model of Allen and Allen (1997), the relational TA model of Hargaden and Sills (2002) and their colleagues (e.g., Fowlie & Sills, 2011), the co-creative model of Tudor and Summers (2014), and my own writing (Cornell, 2016, 2019; Cornell & Landaiche, 2006) place attention on the risks of therapeutic oppression and mystification inadvertently created through the therapist's unexamined countertransference or devotion to a favored theory. Steiner continued to practice, write, and teach throughout this evolution of TA, but so far as I know, this evolution of TA was not a source of self-examination or theoretical renewal

Attribution and alienation 79

for Steiner. For Steiner it seems that the causes of games and script, the forces of injunctions, attributions, alienation, and oppression, remained those of the outside acting upon and against the individual. The forces of one's own unconscious, of one's own distorted thinking and projections, and of personal vulnerabilities rarely seemed to occupy a place within Steiner's thinking.

Claude was a master at upsetting complacency. Claude and his radical psychiatry colleagues pushed transactional analysis into the real world turmoil of the 1970s. Claude loved to argue. He was not afraid to provoke. He was not at all hesitant to state his position, although reconsidering a position does not seem to have been a strong suit of his. I cannot help but wonder had his beloved mentor, Eric, lived longer, how might have Claude's deepening political involvement influenced Eric? Would Eric have been drawn out of his post-McCarthy era trauma (see Chapter 7) into the social unrest of the 1970s? Could Claude have come to appreciate, perhaps respect and even integrate, some of what Eric saw as of essential value to be found in psychoanalysis? In returning to a careful re-reading of Steiner's work in preparation for this chapter, I was taken back to my own foundational days in TA, filled with excitement, alive with a revolutionary spirit, and a hopefulness for the capacity of human beings to learn and change. My intent here is to underscore and elaborate some aspects of Steiner's theory of script that I think merit further recognition and development – and, in closing, I offer both a critique of his model of script and a heartfelt appreciation of his revolutionary spirit.

Figure 4.3 Claude and Bill, Istanbul, 2006

TRES
Strokes

5 Confessions of a psychomechanic

Excerpts on strokes

Claude Steiner

Berne had led the way by ascribing central importance to strokes which he defined [in the singular] as "a unit of recognition" [Berne, 1972/1975b, p. 447], but which we assumed were really positive touch and affection. I embarked on my "scientific" work with strokes which had, without a doubt, deep roots in my emotional needs.

During those years I led a double life. On Tuesday and Wednesdays – my San Francisco life – I was Eric Berne's right-hand man, posing as a buttoned-down psychologist and transactional analyst with a successful group and individual psychotherapy private practice, a wife, two children, a suburban home, a station wagon and a sports car, trying to fit in with the psychiatric establishment. The rest of the week – my Berkeley life – I was a rebel, a radical psychiatrist involved in anti-war and liberation activism, a hippy, a womanizer, a cult leader and a writer of revolutionary screed. In between these two lives, undisturbed but informed by both of them I carried on my psychotherapy practice.

…

My curiosity and needs regarding strokes, sexual or otherwise, was not deterred by Berne's clear dictum. I was convinced that physical and verbal strokes were essential to healing and I had concluded that most people who are depressed are depressed because of a lack of strokes. As a way of including Ursula in my work and to give her a chance to express her talents I deputized her to teach "Permission" classes to my clients (permissions to move, dance, sing, yell, touch, etc.) thereby isolating myself physically from them. Selected members of my groups met with Ursula and she would lead them in a variety of physical, dance, massage, touching exercises and they would report the results to me in the group sessions [Steiner & Steiner 1968a, 1968b].

Berne, in a rare foray into the Berserkeley wilderness attended one of these classes and extensively described the session in his last book, *What Do You Say after You Say Hello?* [Berne, 1972/1975b], with evident Child approval as he kept a watchful Adult and Parental eye in case "things went too far, i.e., got too sexy" [p. 372]. Speaking of himself as Dr. Q., he writes: "Dr Q attended permission class in order to find out how it felt and what he could learn" [ibid., p. 372. He continued:] "His Child did get slightly aroused but there was no need for the Parent to come out since his Adult was quite able to handle the situation" [p. 372].

At the same time, I began to teach a variety of, for lack of a better name, "Laboratories in Group Dynamics" at the Berkeley Free University in which, keeping in

84   Claude Steiner

mind Berne's injunction, I duly warned participants that this was not to be therapy and I was not to be their therapist. Most of our experiments such as hot tub encounter, group massages and nude meditations were one-time attempts, and eventually this line of inquiry settled on a group encounter activity, which I called "Trash the Stroke Economy" or "Stroke City" for short.

I was reading about Wilhelm Reich's life and work and participating in various personal bioenergetics and body therapies. I began to use what I had learned from the laboratories, permission classes and my own personal work with my clients, in optional monthly sessions, available free to all my group patients. I conducted these meetings in the commune's huge living room, which I had equipped with large mirrors and extra-large gym mats. In these two-hour or longer sessions, with eight to twelve clients and a couple of assistants, we practiced a variant of Reich's methods.

...

The Warm Fuzzy Tale

The notion that physical activity, touching, moving and emoting was an essential aspect of soul healing took a hold in my thinking. Another body-centered notion inspired by Wilhelm Reich came to me: that there was a conspiracy afoot to rob people of their strokes and health in order to make them consumers for the benefit of the capitalist establishment. These notions resulted in the writing of the *Warm Fuzzy Tale* [1977d].

Eric Berne was in the habit of writing short "Living Problems" under the pseudonym of Cyprian St. Cyr in the *Transactional Analysis Bulletin*, which he published quarterly. These short fables ending with a question were intended to present us with a challenging view of a human dilemma. While I was still married to Ursula and shamefully philandering, we fought incessantly as she became righteously jealous. Inspired by a desperate need for a Utopian escape, and emulating Eric [Berne, 1968], I wrote a short story which I named *A Fuzzy Tale*. Even though it took me only a couple of hours to write, it eventually became the most best-selling and widely distributed piece I have written.

...

Strokes

The story had as its premise Berne's dictum that people need recognition, which he called strokes "or [else] their spinal cords will shrivel up."[1] He based that view on the research of René Spitz in which it was shown that baby orphans that were kept in sterile environments died of central nervous system atrophy while those who were handled, even if roughly, had far better rates of survival [Spitz, 1945]. The name of the story was taken from a client of mine that had called his wife a "warm fuzzy." My original contribution here was the insight that people were living in a scarcity of positive strokes and were hungry for affection because of a greedy witch's curse.

I wrote the [original] story in 1969 [titled "A Fairytale"] and submitted it to Berne for publication in the *Bulletin*. He kept it on his desk for almost a year and, when he died, I assumed it would not get published, but then it turned out that he had planned to publish it after all and it appeared in the first *Transactional Analysis Bulletin* [published] after his death [Steiner, 1970]. I included it in *Scripts People Live* [1974a], and from there on it was copied and recopied for use in schools, summer camps and churches, sometimes with my permission, sometimes without it.

Once, at a party, I overheard a beautiful young woman talk about warm fuzzies to an eager interlocutor. Seeing an opening for conversation I exclaimed "Oh, have you heard about warm fuzzies?" She answered "Yeah, it's a really wonderful story." Proudly I said: "I know, I wrote it." She looked at me quizzically and said "Oh no! It was written by an American Indian." Dumbfounded and not knowing how to respond, I slithered away, derailed in what I had thought was the smooth beginning of a beautiful friendship.

Be that as it may, *The [Warm] Fuzzy Tale* was the intuitive predecessor of my later theory of the stroke economy, which eventually became the centerpiece of my work.

...

Figure 5.1 Claude and the Eric Berne Scientific Award (for the stroke economy), 1980

86   Claude Steiner

Hogie and I believed in this theory and proceeded to live it. We saw the personal problems of the world in terms of alienation, oppression and isolation. Hogie's interest was in gender alienation. She saw many of the problems of women as an example of oppression, mystified by sexist views and she took on our relationship as a feminist project. She taught me feminism at the most personal level; her view was that men exploited women with an unequal exchange of strokes and affection which was justified by sexist gender roles; women's nature was to be nurturing while men's role was to work hard and be nurtured. The result was an unequal exchange of love causing women to become dissatisfied, angry and feeling worthless and the eventual victims of depression. This view was written up in an important paper "The Stroke Economy in Women's Scripts" [Wyckoff, 1971] which was published in the *Transactional Analysis Journal*.

The stroke economy

Theory and reality were on a collision course. In the early 1970s I had been hungrily reading Wilhelm Reich's work on sexuality, orgasm and orgones and thought that I saw parallels between him and myself; Berne was trying to gain the kind of prominence that Freud had achieved with psychoanalysis and Reich was his favorite disciple. I was arguably Berne's favorite and, like Reich [was in relation to Freud], I was the political radical in Berne's circle.

The idea of the Stroke Economy originated from a conversation between Hogie and myself. We had just made love and I was hurriedly getting dressed. Hogie, naked in bed, was reading Wilhelm Reich's [1933/1975] *The Mass Psychology of Fascism*. "Claude listen to this!" she called out, "as you know Reich was considerably sexually obsessed. He writes about sex economy sociology." When she had my attention, she read from the book: "Sex-economic sociology … asks, *For what sociological reason does society suppress sexuality [and does the individual repress it]?*" [ibid. p. 24].

Moving down the page she read on: "In brief, the goal of sexual suppression is that of producing an individual who is adjusted to the authoritarian order and who will submit to it in spite of all misery and degradation" [p. 26], and further down the page "*The formation of the authoritarian structure takes place through the anchoring of sexual inhibition and sexual anxiety*" [ibid. p. 26, original emphasis].

Flipping the pages she went on: "Listen." She read, "Sexual repression … makes the mass individual passive and unpolitical" [ibid. p. 27], "youth as a result of sexual suppression, is sex-starved" [ibid. p. 27], and "*the [economically] suppressed individual … [thinks], feels and acts against his own material interests*" [ibid. p. 27, original emphasis]. I listened with half an ear and when she was done, not quite getting the point I asked "So?"

Hogie said: "Look! I think what he says about sexuality is really true about strokes." With a brilliant smile she continued [in her own words]:

> The police, the politicians, the establishment are trying to keep young people from loving each other, and cracking their heads when they disobey, take

Excerpts on strokes 87

drugs and make love. They are trying to enforce obedience by controlling the economy of strokes!

The proverbial light bulb went on in my head and I sat down on the bed. Why of course! According to Reich, the Nazis isolated the German youth from sexuality thereby causing a scarcity of sex – the sex economy – which generated their fanaticism and obeisance to Nazism. To Reich, "full body orgasm" was the antidote. But the true isolation was not from sex but from strokes and what we needed was a method to facilitate and liberate strokes, mutual recognition, love and affection as well as sex, rather than just liberating orgasm.

There actually was an economy of strokes, a pervasive stroke hunger that was being openly quenched by the flower children with their talk of love and their sexual acting out, facilitated by marihuana and LSD. No wonder, I reasoned, there were such bloody reprisals against the hippies and their leaders. They were disrupting the social order, inciting people to riot. What was going on in the streets were love riots in rebellion against love hunger and those we held responsible for it, the war and all other evils; the establishment.

...

Radical stroke economics

In our Radical Psychiatry work the notion of a Stroke Economy enforced by, and to benefit the establishment was a bull's eye. Stroke City was our political action response, a group situation where people could "trash the stroke economy" and in which we exposed and struggled with the mystified oppression of people's capacity to care for each other. In a group, to combat isolation, we developed awareness of how our loving capacities had been damaged and took action by giving and accepting strokes.

We had been conducting "Contact Raps" in the large living room of the RAP Center – open-ended discussion groups – and we added "Stroke City" three times a week. Stroke City was billed, in the style of the rebellious '60s, as a "liberated space for the revolutionary struggle against the internalized oppression of love" or "Trashing the Stroke Economy" for short. For two hours in the afternoon about 20 people could give strokes, accept strokes, ask for strokes, and even give themselves strokes in a safe, protected environment.

We created these meetings hoping to teach people contact skills, to open up and to exchange strokes freely in a competitive and harsh world. However, we soon observed a dramatic though not wholly unexpected side effect. Participants would often look around after some time and declare that they "loved everyone in the room." They would speak of pervasive feelings of love as they placed their hand over their hearts and they left these meetings with a light step and a happy, loving glow on their faces.

Participants spoke of loving feelings, of having an open heart, of a transcendent experience of affection, an oceanic feeling and so on. What had started as an exercise to practice how to be cooperative, mutually supportive and positive, turned out to be much more. It affected the participants' loving capacities in a powerful and heart-expanding way. It was then that we began to see, in practical rather than theoretical effects, the hitherto unexplored connection between contact, strokes and love. We realized that learning how to exchange positive strokes might have an effect on people's overall capacity to love.

Eventually it became clear, not surprisingly, that strokes and loving feelings are intimately related to each other. Why were we surprised? That's a good question. The answer is probably that we were afflicted by the common tendency to entertain all sorts of theories without expecting them to be proven in the real world. We spoke and wrote about contact, recognition, strokes and love but we did not think of love as something that could be affected by anything as practical as a stroke exercise or that loving was a skill that could actually be taught and unleashed from the imprisoned heart.

Our rather abstract radical psychiatry ideology began to take concrete shape in this work. Here was a real human potential-love-being alienated by the lies we had been told about it. Faithful to radical psychiatry theory we regained power over that human potential by becoming aware of the interpersonal transactions that made the alienation real and by acting against them within the protective environment of a group of like-minded people.

CS at 80 (starting April 2015)

Depression

I have always claimed that depression is the consequence of stroke hunger and this [present] situation demonstrates that vividly: the only thing that reliably lifts me is physical contact with Jude, to which I am addicted.

Note

1   This phrase is attributed to Berne and is clarified in Woollams and Brown's (1978) description of external strokes:

> The quest for strokes becomes a pursuit for attention, which enables a person to feel alive and energized. On the other hand, a lack of strokes leads to mental, emotional, and physical deterioration, or colloquially, "If you don't get enough strokes, your spinal cord will shrivel up" (p. 47).

6 On strokes

Deepak Dhananjaya

"Do you see me?" is a question that would pop up in my head frequently as a child. While I had a sense of seeing others, it was important for me to know that I was seen. I would do as I was told, and be a good boy. The formula that I computed in my head to be seen was "Just be the good boy now". I only realised the power of the answer to this question when I started my transactional analysis (TA) training. The concept of strokes, as originally identified by Eric Berne (in 1964), and developed by Claude Steiner in his work (1971f, 2003a) has provided an exploratory path for me to understand both my question and the answer, and hence my interest in contributing this chapter to this book. I discuss Claude Steiner's work on strokes, offering some critique as well as some extension of his ideas, informed not only by more recent theories in TA but also by a different cultural context, all of which are based on my own experiences and exploration.

In the first part of this Chapter I offer some brief remarks on the development of stroke theory, following which I discuss stroke-centred TA, strokes and their connection to brain and body, and the stroke economy in the Indian cultural context.[1]

The development of stroke theory

Berne (1964/1966a) defined stroke as a unit of social action. He based his theory on the research of Spitz which showed that baby orphans who were kept in sterile environments died of atrophy of the central nervous system while those who were handled, even roughly, had far better rates of survival. Berne stated that every infant needed physical strokes. As the infant develops, this exchange of physical strokes is limited, due to social constraints and constructs. Over time, the individual settles for any form of recognition, which is a way for an individual to know his/her existence in the world. Strokes are not given or received in isolation; rather they are experienced in relation to the other, and mediated by the wider context. This is one of the ways Berne emphasised the impact of relationship. Later, Berne (1964/1966a) developed the theory of games based on strokes.

90 *Deepak Dhananjaya*

As he himself acknowledges in his *Confessions*, Steiner was influenced by Reich's body-centred work:

> Another body-centered notion inspired by Wilhelm Reich came to me; that there was a conspiracy afoot to rob people of their strokes and health in order to make them consumers for the benefit of the capitalist establishment. These notions resulted in the writing of *The Warm Fuzzy Tale*.
>
> (*Confessions*, Chapter 5, p. 84)

This tale explains the way free exchange of strokes gets restricted in society. Through this tale, Steiner invited readers to reflect on their restrictions and start exchanging strokes. In this Steiner was influenced not only by Reich's work on the sex economy but also by his conversations with his then partner, Hogie Wyckoff, about sexual oppression in youth and its impact on them, whereby they become passive and unpolitical. Based on Hogie's suggestion regarding the parallels between sexual oppression and strokes, Steiner says:

> According to Reich, the Nazis isolated the German youth from sexuality thereby causing a scarcity of sex – the sex economy – which generated their fanaticism and obeisance to Nazism. To Reich "full body orgasm" was the antidote. But the true isolation was not from sex but from strokes and what we needed was a method to facilitate and liberate strokes, mutual recognition, love and affection as well as sex, rather than just liberating orgasm.
>
> (Chapter 5, p. 87)

The concept of the stroke economy, as developed by Steiner, explained the psychosocial context in which individuals restrict the exchange of the free flow of strokes. In response, he started a movement to trash the stroke economy and to enable people to exchange strokes freely, a practice he referred to as "Stroke City", whereby people in a group exchanged strokes with each other. The therapist's role in this was to facilitate this exchange so as to foster the exchange of authentic positive strokes, and to ensure that there was no exchange of plastic positive or negative strokes.

Stroke-centred TA

Later, and based on the theory of strokes, Steiner developed what he referred to as stroke-centred TA (Steiner, 2003a). This was, in part, his attempt to answer the question "What is transactional analysis?" by identifying a set of core concepts. In his paper "Core Concepts of a Stroke-centered Transactional Analysis" (Steiner, 2003a), he made connections between strokes and other concepts in TA in an attempt to summarise and organise TA concepts as a whole. In the article Steiner clusters a number of concepts and propositions under some general headings: the purpose and function of TA (concepts 1–3); motivational basis and strokes (concepts 4–6); transactions and ego states (concepts 7 and 8); interaction, power plays,

On strokes 91

and cooperation (concept 9); games, roles, and scripts (concepts 10–12); and the practice of TA (concepts 13–15).

Writing about motivation, Steiner (2003a) asserts:

- That "people need strokes to survive physically and psychologically [and that] stroke hunger is a form of information hunger" (p. 178). We know that script is formed as a result of the experiences the baby has with the environment. These experiences begin with the primary caregiver, usually the mother, and involves the exchange of strokes. The baby learns to survive in the environment based on these exchanges and experiences.
- That positive strokes are in "pervasive scarcity" (ibid., p. 178). See point made above regarding the sex economy and sexual oppression.
- That people will accept negative strokes rather than no strokes. In this case, the process of survival is an adaptation to the stroke economy which, in turn, influences the formation of the script. Thus, negative strokes are the foundation for the development of a person's script. One of my clients, Tara (not her real name), explained that her mother would beat her when she threw tantrums. On further enquiry, she revealed that she was the fifth child, and her mother hardly had time to attend to her. As a child, while her mother was busy, Tara would be left alone with her toys, and she was compliant with this; when she threw tantrums, she got punished by her mother, but at least got her attention for a while. Not surprisingly, Tara's survival strategy was to throw tantrums thereby continuing to get attention but by collecting negative strokes. She entered therapy to better her relationships with people in her life, and during therapy, she learnt to ask for strokes directly and authentically.

In his discussion of interaction, power plays, and cooperation Steiner draws a distinction between cooperation and competition: competition is transacted by the need for power while cooperation is free of power plays. I think the need to compete and not to compete arises from the "stroke needs" of the person. It is important for us to reflect on what drives power plays and what is the stroking profile in the system (environment) that demands power plays from individuals in order to survive. Moreover, I wonder if individuals can ever transact free of power plays? To me, it seems somewhat idealistic.

In the following group of concepts, Steiner links games, roles, and scripts, and makes two important points about strokes:

- That games are power plays for strokes; and
- That games are "habitual, dysfunctional patterns of stroke procurement, usually learned in the family early life, that undermine health and human potential". (Steiner, 2003a, p. 180)

Thus, healing is a process of learning about the structuring of healthy exchanges and building healthy sources of strokes.

92 *Deepak Dhananjaya*

Strokes, body, and brain

Interestingly, both Berne's and Steiner's contributions were influenced by work related to the body: Berne by Spitz's (1945) work on the impact of the deprivation of holding infants, and Steiner by Reich's (1942/1961) body-centric work. In my opinion, although the concepts of script and strokes both have their roots in an appreciation of the somatic, it is only scripts that have been discussed in this regard (see Childs-Gowell & Kinnaman, 1978; Cassius, 1980; Cornell, 1975; Ligabue, 1991), and that some time ago. In contemporary TA, both this history and the connection between strokes and the somatic is not emphasised, as a result of which our understanding of strokes has lost its potency and predominantly remains at the social and verbal level. Here, I attempt to revive this connection between strokes, the body, and the brain. I begin this by explaining the function of the brain that regulates the emotions; the theory of affect regulation; the connection between unexpressed strokes and the body; and, finally, I propose my own theory of the regulation of strokes in a therapeutic relationship that enables the individual to develop self-regulation.

The autonomic nervous system (ANS) of the human brain keeps the body in homeostasis (balance). Hill (2015) has explained affect as "somatic-based information signalling the arousal level of the vital organs. To regulate affect is to regulate the body" (p. 6). Affect regulation is controlled by the ANS. In normal conditions, there will be a gentle flow and rhythm between the sympathetic nervous system (which stimulates the body's fight or flight response to any potential threat) and the parasympathetic nervous system (the reasoning and calming system), which, together, maintains homeostasis in individuals with the result that they are able to self-regulate emotions. Hill (2015) connected the early unhealthy attachment styles identified by Ainsworth (1973) with the dysregulation in individuals who have faced trauma or pain in early infancy. This can be understood in terms of the Child ego state proposed by Hargaden and Sills (2002). An individual with an ability to self-regulate affect has a fully developed sense of self and stable internalised other (P_0). On reception of a high intensity stroke, they are able to regulate within themselves with the help of the stable other (P_0). In individuals with unhealthy attachment styles, there is a lack of this internalised stable other (P_0). As a grown-up adult, when they receive a high intensity stroke, there is dysregulation of affect, which is the manifestation of activation of the sympathetic nervous system. The memory of their early trauma kicks in, minimising their ability to activate the parasympathetic nervous system to regulate the effect caused by the stroke they received. This lack of ability to self-regulate indicates the lack of or an underdeveloped internalised stable other (P_0).

Hill (2015) explained that, in any relationship, affect is communicated implicitly through facial displays, rhythm, intonations, and stresses of speech, postures, and gestures: in other words, we are wired to understand each other's affects. The involuntary neurobiological matching is the way we experience the subjective experience of others. The exchange of affect is the way we decipher our subjective experience and others' subjective experiences.

On strokes   93

In order to understand such subjective experiences in relationships and in context, we have to consider the stroke economy (Steiner, 1971f). These subjective experiences can be altered or modified based on the stroke economy of the individuals and the culture to which they belong and/or live. For example, if it's culturally unacceptable to express anger to authority figures, our brains will be wired and our parasympathetic nervous systems trained to suppress expressions of anger and will adapt to the culturally acceptable expression; in this way, anger is suppressed. As per Reich's work, the body stores the affect that does not find an expression in the form of tensions in the muscles – which, in turn, become part of the regulation of the affect, and hence, body scripts and body scripting (Cassius, 1980). The expression is blocked due to the stroke economy that exists in the environment. Tensions in the muscles can be released through some of Reich's body-centric work, which involves tuning into the body's tensions, understanding them, and finding their expression. This should also involve understanding the blocks to the free flow of strokes that results in tensed muscles: these are non-verbal, non-cognitive strokes stored in the body. For example, the experience and grief of losing a person, fear, and anger are meant to be expressed as strokes or exchanges; when they are not, they get absorbed by the body and, as it were, settle in so they become part of that body. This expression (or non-expression) connects psychobiologically with the mind and gets regulated in the most appropriate form of adapting to the environment as summarised by the stroke economy (Steiner, 1971f):

- Don't give strokes you want to give.
- Don't ask for strokes you want.
- Don't accept strokes you want.
- Don't reject strokes you don't want.
- Don't give yourselves strokes.

As these operate as much at the unconscious level as the conscious level, it's often hard for the individual to understand this, and hence their experiences remain unexpressed or adapted.

As a therapist, I find this understanding of the connection between early attachment styles, affect regulation, and the body most useful. I apply the concept of holding, as proposed by Hargaden and Sills (2002), to clients who are lacking a stable internal other, so they can develop an internal stable other (P_0) (depicted in Figure 6.1). Slochower (1996; cited by Hargaden & Sills, 2002) described three major occasions when this type of holding is essential: (1) when the patient has regressed to total dependence; (2) when the patient's need for mirroring is absolute and anything other than affirmation and empathy would seem like an attack; and (3) when the patient is connected with rage and hate (in TA terms, P_1) and any attempt to explain or interpret could be experienced as punishing, rejecting, or irrelevant. When clients who lack potent P_0 receive a high intensity stroke from their environment (stimulus S1 in Figure 6.1), they feel dysregulated and experience distress. In analysing it structurally, we see that they are in distress (C_1), which triggers an internal regulating process. Since there is a lack of internal potency (P_0), the core

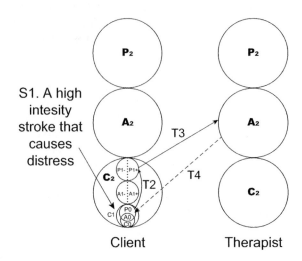

Figure 6.1 Relational stroke completion (RSC)

self (A_0) is underdeveloped, which makes it hard to self-regulate. This distressed self is walled off from the outside world, a retreat which is maintained by means of P_{1-} projections (transactions T2 and T3 in Figure 6.1).

In therapy sessions, therapists become the outside world for the client. In this process of regulating, therapists are often invited to approve or disapprove of the stroke(s) clients receive and, indeed, to give them reparative strokes; but if we do that, we take on the parental (and Parental) position. However, in and from this position, there is a danger that we reinforce their script or create a new experience, but one that initiates dependency. In this case, I propose "holding" to (and of) the dysregulated client, which enables them to internalise this experience to strengthen P_0 (T4 in Figure 6.1). Being with the client in their stroke experience helps them regulate their emotions and make meaning of it. I realise that in my journey towards two-person psychology (Stark, 1999), it is important for therapists to facilitate the client to make meaning of their experience through the therapeutic relationship. This phenomenon of being with the client is attunement (Schore, 1994, 2012) and a synchronicity of affect states. An attuned therapist is psychobiologically attuned to the client, which means that they are "in sync" with the subjective experience of the client (as distinct from pragmatic experience). This attunement is a form of dyadic regulation for the client, through which they viscerally experience empathy. This experience with the therapist over a period of time helps them to learn to regulate their hypo-arousal or hyper-arousal affect states within, thereby developing an internal stable other (P_0). I call this process relational stroke completion (RSC), as, in this process, the stroke received by the client is completed when they experience holding from the therapist, which internally influences strengthening of their P_0. In strengthening the P_0, the core self (A_0) strengthens.

I illustrate this with reference to my experience of working with a client, Jaya (not her real name, and with her permission), which compelled me to understand the connection between brain, body, and strokes. There was a point in therapy at which our relationship was in deep waters and needed help to survive. In my stroke economy, there is a restriction to reject strokes and to express anger. In Jaya's stroke economy, there was a restriction to express vulnerability or anger directly. We were both coloured by our respective stroke economies, as a result of which we created – and co-created – subjective experiences that made us walk on eggshells in the therapy room. Jaya would experience distress in the therapeutic relationship when there was any form of denial of a request; for instance, her request that we do a certain kind of bodywork (in which I am not trained). This would trigger her sympathetic nervous system to fight as she was unconsciously reminded of her earlier insecure attachment traumas that were stored in her body. She would express her distress in the form of anger towards me. I found myself adapting to the situation with her and other similar situations (and embodied in my parasympathetic nervous system) and confirmed by my stroke economy. With the help of supervision, I realised that my stroke economy was restricting me in being able to hold her anger towards me. I would feel being "Not a good enough therapist" triggering feeling OK. I needed to learn to be OK with her anger, to hold it, and to help Jaya make sense of it. The first step for me was to start acknowledging the anger that she had towards me and to be OK with being the "bad object". However, this wasn't sufficient; it was also important and necessary for me to help Jaya to develop the ability to self-regulate this anger. This was possible only when she was able to make the connection (with the help of her A_2) of her denial of her earlier trauma of abandonment and rejection. In this process, her parasympathetic nervous system started developing the ability to reflect on and reason regarding the denial of the requests she made in the therapeutic relationship. The denial triggered her distress; however, gradually, and as I was able to "hold" her in and to this, she was able to acknowledge it, express it appropriately, and regulate it within her, thereby restoring her OKness – and, importantly, her relational OKness. An important aspect of this was my openness to be the "bad object" at all levels (i.e., projected P_2, P_1, and P_0), to hold and help her make sense of her distress, and to help her develop an internal stable other (P_0). As at the time of writing, this work is still in progress, but I see that, together, we are able to co-create a subjective experience that is developing her internal stable other (P_0). This results in developing her sense of self A_0.

In this part of the Chapter I explore Steiner's (1971f) concept of the stoke economy in relation to Drego's (1983) concept of the Cultural Parent. In doing so, I challenge the ways proposed and practised to "trash" the stroke economy (Steiner, 1984a), and also discuss the stroke economy with regard to sexual minorities in the cultural context of India.

Trashing the stroke economy and the Cultural Parent

In his work on the stroke economy, Steiner (1974a) suggested that, in order to enable the free exchange of strokes, we need to trash the stroke economy (also see

96   *Deepak Dhananjaya*

Schwebel, 1975b; Wyckoff, 1975a). It is important to understand the definition of strokes and what comprises strokes. As we know, any form and unit of recognition (verbal, non-verbal, physical, action, etc.) is considered a stroke. However, these days the predominant form both of stroking and of trashing the stroke economy seems to be through verbal strokes. In this context, it is also important to consider the cultural aspect(s) of the individual and group we are addressing. There are cultures in which gestures (which are non-verbal) are an important way to recognise the other, such as bowing to, feeding, and spending time with the other. According to Drego (1983), these gestures are defined by the Cultural Parent in the individual and in the group, and represent an exchange of genuine strokes unless they are done as rituals for the sake of doing them, mechanically and, in that sense, without meaning. For instance, in India, the country to which I belong, we bow down and touch the feet of elders/teachers, which is a genuine expression of strokes towards the other person. For his/her part, the elder/teacher blesses the person bowing down, a gesture which is also a genuine expression of a stroke. This expression of strokes forms a part of many ceremonies and social gatherings, and has a huge impact in Indian culture(s). My argument here is that while trashing the stroke economy is good in countering the Critical Parent, we also need to account for the positive values and beliefs of the Cultural Parent. Finally, I would say that trashing the stroke economy is not an event, it's a continuous process. As practitioners, it is important to pause and reflect before we invite the client to trash her/his stroke economy.

The stroke economy and sexual minorities

The Cultural Parent has a strong influence on both individuals and groups.

Indian society was more accepting of sexual differences and sexual minorities during its precolonial period, evidence of which is available in the ancient monuments and sculptures in temples like Khajurao (in Madhya Pradesh). There were also mythical characters like Shikhandi (transgender) in one of our two major Sanskrit epics, the *Mahabharata*. However, since the colonisation of India by the British, we carry more of a legacy of alternative sexuality being regarded and treated as unnatural, and for much of our more recent history, homosexuality has been criminalised, under the Indian Penal Code (which was originally drafted in 1860 under British rule), which stated, under a section on "Unnatural offences" that:

> Whoever voluntarily has carnal intercourse against the order of nature with any man, woman or animal shall be punished with imprisonment for life, or with imprisonment of either description for a term which may extend to ten years, and shall also be liable to a fine.
>
> (Section 377)

Despite the fact that this Section was recently repealed by a historical judgment of the Indian Supreme Court (in September 2018) which, in effect, decriminalised homosexuality, homosexual alliances are still considered socially sinful and taboo; and individuals who identify themselves as homosexual or as part of any other sexual minority are shamed and ostracised, both physically and psychologically. In my journey of accepting my own sexual identity and working as a therapist with sexual minorities, I have experienced the deprivation of acceptance at the social level, both interpersonally and constitutionally, and at the psychological level (Dhananjaya, 2018), both for myself and as reported by my clients.

In this section, I conceptualise my experience with reference to the Cultural Parent (Drego, 1983) and to the theory of alienation from radical psychiatry (Wyckoff & Steiner, 1971; Steiner & Wyckoff, 1975; see also Chapters 7, 8, 9, and 11).

Firstly, in terms of ego states, this experience is explained as a model (Figure 6.2), which offers a representation of society that deals with difference(s). In it, I represent the Cultural Parent (Drego, 1983) as a container for society which functions by adapting to the norms of the Cultural Parent. In this sense I represent the negative Cultural Parent as a square, playing on the notions of straight and gay. Sexual minorities are alienated in society (represented, ideally, as an encompassing circle) by splitting off to form a "dark self" (which I refer to as dark in that it is in shadow). Any overt expression by sexual minorities attracts censure from society, which is one way in which society in general or subsets of that society adapt to this particular negative Cultural Parent. It is my view that this dark self develops a protective layer to cope with shame from the Cultural Parent, often doing so by presenting a square (or "straight") protective layer, skin, or front (represented by the square in Figure 6.2).

Secondly, I explain this through the formula from radical psychiatry that equates and describes alienation in terms of Oppression + Mystification + Isolation (Steiner, 1979c).

Oppression

In Indian society, due to the impact of the negative Cultural Parent, sexual minorities are oppressed and marginalised. Indian society finds it difficult to accept us due to negative Cultural Parent messages such as "It's a sin and not part of our culture",

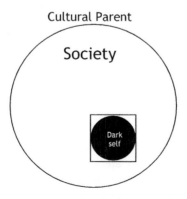

Figure 6.2 The dark self, as oppressed in society

98 *Deepak Dhananjaya*

"It's a disease which can be cured", "It will take you to hell", and so on, though, as noted, this oppression largely dates from and is a result of the colonial era in India. In my view, such messages are defensive, as if, in order to maintain and manage the OKness in society, the heterosexual majority splits off sexual minorities which, thereby, form what might be considered the "dark self" of society (Figure 6.2). Thus, society maintains its OKness (or conditional OKness) in a number of ways, including pathologising alternative sexualities. A substantial part of the oppressed believe that we are not OK, and feel ashamed about it. Most religious and cultural groups propagate that being anything other than heterosexual is unnatural and a sin, and thus instil isolation – and for those who feel or who contemplate being different, a fear of isolation. For the most part there is a lack of potent representation of sexual minority characters in the mainstream media; instead non-heteronormative people are represented as silly and impotent characters who are often bullied. This has influenced the feeling of "not OK" in the community. As a result, hiding one's sexual identity becomes a way of coping and leads to the development of the protective layer represented in Figure 6.2 precisely to avoid the potential shame from the Cultural Parent as represented by actual parents, family, relatives, friends, colleagues, and the rest.

Mystification

Such oppression has continued for years, and is supported by what the radical psychiatrists referred to as mystification, which I think of as a set of reasons that justify the power abuse perpetrated on its victims. In this case, we have been made to believe that there is a problem with us; that we are sick; and that, with treatment, we are curable. In the initial period of exploration of sexual identity, it is very common for sexual minorities to reach out to doctors for a cure, because they are of the strong belief that being attracted to the same sex is a disease, a belief that was true for me, too. Moreover, there are many doctors who have indicated that non-heteronormative sexuality and behaviour can be treated. The first question many lesbians and gay, bisexual, transgender, queer, and intersex (LGBTQI) people are asked when they come out (at least in India) is: "Have you consulted the doctor?" Many sexual minority people are single and this is treated as "normal"; "straight" people may think "How can a gay person have a partner?" "What is the need for them to marry?" However, often such questions and thoughts and the attitudes that belie them are not explicit, and such oppression is not in the awareness of the oppressors. Nevertheless the impact of such mystification is that oppression is not only internalised in the person but also in the system.

Isolation

People who identify as LGBTQI tend to feel isolated from society, and experience shame and guilt for being who we are. As a result, in India, as in other countries, within the dominant heteronormative culture, there is a hidden, secret culture that is formed by the sexual minority community. However, due to the oppression of and mystification about alternative sexualities, including internalised oppression, common responses to living in a secret culture include the lack of intimate relationships and engagement in covert promiscuous behaviours, as well as a pseudo-OKness, and pseudo-belongingness within the heteronormative community. In Figure 6.2, the "dark self" representing the sexual minority community that is split off in society, experiences a deep sense of shame and pain when in contact with the negative Cultural Parent and hence a need for a protective layer around the dark self. This protective layer comprises the adaptations the alternative community develops in order to cope with the negative Cultural Parent but, in making such adaptations, we tend to hide our identity, and lose our vitality and capacity to be who we really are. These adaptations often take the form of being in false/forced heterosexual relationships and forced marriages, adapting to the societal narrative of being not OK, and hiding genuine intimate relationships, and so on. In a nutshell, we adapt by denying our own sexual identities.

I represent the experience we as an alternative community have with society as it is mirrored intrapsychically for us as individuals in Figure 6.3.

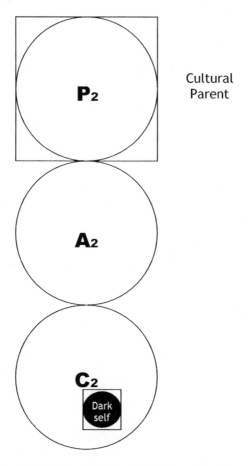

Figure 6.3 The dark self within the individual, hidden from the Cultural Parent

100 *Deepak Dhananjaya*

We can think of this dynamic as follows. The negative (and "square") Cultural Parent internally oppresses the needs of the Child to be attractive and attracted to be in a relationship with someone of the same sex or gender identity. That part of the Child triggers not OKness in the self. To restore OKness in the individual, that part is split off to form the "dark self" within the Child, which is hidden from the negative Cultural Parent. The "dark self" hides by creating a protective layer around it. This protective layer is a set of adaptations towards the negative Cultural Parent which take the form of denial of their own sexuality, the pretence of being in heterosexual relationships, unhealthy sexual behaviors, and so on.

The impact of alienation

The alienation that we sexual minorities experience at both the group level and the individual level is painful and difficult as it is expressed as a lack of strokes for the "dark self" again, with regard both to individuals and the group/community as a whole. Bearing in mind what we know about strokes and stroking, in order to survive, there is a need to stroke the "dark self". In response to the deprivation of strokes from heteronormative society, there are times in which people in the LGBTQI community settle for negative strokes, through promiscuity, unstable relationships, unsafe sexual practices, and so on. Berne explains that the most gratifying stroke is physical touch. We know that the sexual act including orgasms release hormones such as oxytocin, and endorphins which offer a natural pain-release. In my understanding and practice as a psychotherapist with sexual minorities, the instant and random sexual act is a way of relieving the pain of alienation and experiencing the most gratifying stroke, that of physical, body-to-body contact. Conceptually, the sexual act is one of the ways the dark self gets acknowledged, albeit temporarily. Such physical body strokes are like steroids, providing quick relief from the pain of alienation. It is, however, a temporary relief as, in this process, the dark self is not integrated with other parts of society and the self.

This alienation creates a stroke economy for the sexual minorities, and the stroking of the dark self of the individual and of society is restricted and constrained. In this context, I propose two additional rules of a restrictive stroke economy that are pertinent to sexual minorities:

- Don't show your sexual self. This extends the injunction "Don't be you" (Goulding & Goulding, 1976), and leads to the individual and/or group hiding their sexual desire and sexual activity, as exhibiting it attracts shame and alienation from society. Instead, the stroke economy rules that sexual minorities should keep their sexuality secret, and feel shameful about it.
- Don't be in intimate relationships. This extends the injunction "Don't be close" (Goulding & Goulding, 1979), and discourages the individual from having and enjoying intimacy in non-heterosexual relationships. As sexual minorities have fewer references in society to authentic, intimate, and non-heteronormative relationships, when sexual minority couples face difficulty in relationships, it can be easier to break up rather than to work through the difficulty.

This stroke economy of sexual minorities keeps them in a vicious cycle which both alienates the dark self from the whole self within the individual, and the dark self group from the "whole" society.

Trashing the stroke economy of sexual minorities

This oppression has continued over years and has become mystified. Currently in India, there is a beginning of a movement for fighting this oppression. In TA terms, I propose that the way to do this and accessing the "dark self" is by challenging the contaminated beliefs in the negative Cultural Parent. For any oppression to be broken, Steiner (1988d) suggested the following formula: "Contact + Awareness + Action = Liberation". Further, he explained that contact, awareness, and action are forms of power: awareness is the power of knowledge, contact is the power of people, and action is the power of aggressive behaviour (in the positive sense of aggression). Of course, power can be used both to oppress and to liberate (see Chapters 10 and 11). Drawing on the idea from the early days of radical psychiatry of "trashing" the stroke economy, I propose the following in order to trash the negative stroke economy by which sexual minorities are oppressed.

Contact

The power of contact with and between sexual minorities is important. In India this contact has been enabled by the decriminalisation of Section 377 of the Indian Penal Code (see above), which has provided at least constitutional acceptance of alternative sexual expression and identities (Dhananjaya, 2018). What we need now is social acceptance (Dhananjaya, 2018), including normalising alternative sexualities for instance by means of positive representations in the media. Empathic listening and positive responses to our (sexual minority) stories on the part of wider society can be a powerful tool in establishing contact. One such example of contact are various Pride events that happen in India.

Awareness

Information is power, and, for the most part, accurate information about sexual minorities is lacking in contemporary Indian society. Psycho-education on the topic of sexualities and sexual health could help the wider society to normalise alternative sexualities, and reduce the negative Cultural Parent.

Action

Gathering a collective voice that supports the rights of sexual minorities would be powerful in order to take action in fighting oppression. India witnessed one such collective force during the period of fighting for change in the law and the subsequent constitutional acceptance as many LGBTQI rights' organisations came together to lobby for this change. Apart from that, integrating people with

102 *Deepak Dhananjaya*

alternative sexual identities into social gatherings, mainstream media, schools, and at all levels of society would be a powerful act of inclusiveness.

Conclusion

My experience of writing this chapter was refreshing as I got to visit the concept of strokes, especially as developed by Claude Steiner. In the process, initially I also got caught up in my own cultural stroke economy which was specific to my negative Cultural Parent, but I was able to "trash" it by having conversations with Keith (the editor), my trainer, and my friends. As a result, the experience of writing this chapter has led to many relational stroke completions with many significant people in my life. Sharing my experiences of being a sexual minority with you as reader, I aim to experience a relational stroke completion that will lead to the integration of the remaining parts of my "dark self", and so I end this chapter by hoping that I have "seen" or offered some seeing of you and by asking myself "Do you see me?" I think so!

Note

1   I am grateful to Keith Tudor for providing me with this space to share with many accomplished authors, and for supporting my thinking and encouraging me to express my thoughts and find my voice as a writer. In writing this Chapter, I would like to acknowledge and thank my clients, Tara and Jaya (not their real names), who agreed that I could draw on their work with me; Karen Minikin, who introduced me to affect regulation theory and radical psychiatry; Kiran Shetty, the language editor who supported me; Prathitha Gangadharan, who attempted to enter my brain and help me express my thoughts in technical language; and my friends, who acted as sounding boards especially in challenging my thought process.

CUATRO

Radical psychiatry

7 Confessions of a psychomechanic

Excerpts on radical psychiatry

Claude Steiner

For years I wondered why he called himself The Great Pyramid until many years later I found that Berne had suffered persecution in the 1950s during the McCarthy era. He was investigated by the US House of Un-American Activities Committee, lost his job with the government and was interrogated over a period of several years and even had his passport rescinded. He had signed a petition circulated by prominent scientists calling for the government to stop politicizing scientific research. As long as I knew him I was puzzled by the fact that he refused to speak of politics at the [San Francisco Social Psychiatry] Seminars while at the same time he seemed to be a deeply political thinker. Perhaps this pyramid metaphor refers to his hard antipolitical exterior containing a secret liberal chamber deep within [see Steiner, 2010].

...

Evidently he was badly frightened by this experience for he seemed phobic of any political involvement; in therapy he denigrated political discourse or references to oppression (sexism, racism) as a pastime or game of "Ain't it Awful" and his suggested response to complaints of oppression was "OK, so what are you going to do about it?" A good suggestion, I thought, as I continued my political work and kept it away from him [see Steiner, 2010].

Wild therapy

I began these sessions by explaining the basis of the process – breathing – to the comfortably dressed group members lying on their backs, in bare feet:

> How we breathe has a lot to do with how much we feel and also perhaps how we feel. Breathing deeply has the effect of fanning your feelings like embers in a fire. Sometimes flames will break out into a roaring blaze; breathing will make feelings more vivid, and sometimes it will cut them loose into a roaring emotional fire.
>
> As you breathe more fully, you are going to inevitably have to make some noise. Don't hold it back. Make any noise that naturally, normally accompanies that kind of breathing for you. Opening up your throat as much as you can, breathe deeply, through your mouth. Don't worry about being foolish; say, express anything you feel with sounds, whether they are words, grunts,

106   Claude Steiner

laughter, sighs, curses or screams. Don't worry about obscenity, it's OK. I am inviting you to be visited by madness. Now let us begin.

After this point I instructed them to rapidly breathe, breathe, breathe. I encouraged whatever expressions naturally happened, modeling loud deep breathing, echoing and amplifying their utterances, letting them run through the flow of emotion that came to them.

Usually about one-third of the people had a powerful and meaningful emotional release; thrashing about, hitting the mat with hands and legs, cursing or crying. Some remained mostly silent and tripped out along with the others. A few found themselves completely shut down, cut off, alienated.

As the session proceeds, it feels a bit like a storm at sea. Feelings come in waves of deep sadness, pitiful pleading, wild anger, uncontrolled laughter, cursing and sobbing following one upon the other. After a period, which may vary between fifteen and forty-five minutes the emotional storm subsides, and everyone relaxes. The session leaves them with a feeling of liberation, rebirth or great joy. A sense of peace comes over the group. One by one they sit up, reclining on pillows, some leaning on each other comfortably and talk about what transpired. Invariably there is amazement at the intensity of the experience and questions as to how it happens that mere breathing can cause such emotional storms. Good question; exactly why it happens is not clear to me to this day, but the result is a rich, textured experience, and often leads to important insights about the person's emotions. The wrap-up discussion of the work is very important because without the emotional/cognitive integration at the end of the session, the experience can be just that; an experience, and fail to turn into a lasting change.

I demonstrated these sessions in groups of up to 30 participants at our Radical Therapy conferences. These sessions were very popular and received much praise from the participants. There were occasional instances of a person who, after experiencing emotional release, was not able to calm down at the end of the session. In those situations, my helpers and I stayed with the person until he or she recovered, usually within half an hour; never more than an hour.

Unfortunately, effective as this sort of work is, it is impossible to practice in the US any longer because of its wild nature and the strict ethical regulations regarding "boundaries" or any semblance of therapist–patient sexual behavior. It was clear to me in my groups how disruptive a sexually charged touch could be. Though I did touch my bodywork clients on occasion it was with a total devotion to keeping my contact non-sexual. When I did touch somebody, it was either a calming touch if I sensed that a person needed support, or a touch designed to draw attention and energy to a specific part of the body.

Today, if I wanted to practice any sort of body therapy, I would have to have a massage license and at least one other credible professional in attendance at all times to testify for my defense in case I was sued for sexual misconduct. In addition, this sort of work requires several assistants, a large sound proofed room to mask the screams and curses that often occurred especially when there was a large group.

The neighbors became a problem. When on occasion everybody let go at once these meetings had a realistic sound of Bedlam. I had installed a large greenhouse

Excerpts on radical psychiatry   107

with a hot tub attached to the front of the house and the noises from the tub, the sounds of loud orgasms emanating from the house as well as the monthly body work groups and the occasional party we threw got the neighbors in an uproar. They thought we were running some sort of a brothel and when the police started coming to our door it took a concerted neighborhood public relations campaign to calm things down.

With all these difficulties you might justifiably ask, why bother? What is so special about this sort of therapy that would justify the extra effort? At the time we accepted Reich's premise that people carried in their body the physical manifestations of their psychic conflicts; their pent-up emotions blocked by prohibitions about emotional expression. My observation certainly confirmed the blocking of feelings; the way people exploded into emotional outbursts and the salutary consequences of the release were unmistakable. People felt relieved, stronger, their spirits lifted and with a sense that something important had happened that often connected with their difficulties. Specifically, for alcoholics the bodywork experienced mimicked the elation and relaxation of drinking and suggested that alcohol wasn't necessary to achieve those effects.

The expanding shrink[1]

Even though *The Warm Fuzzy Tale* [1970, 1977d] had political overtones, I had not fully entered the political arena though my sympathies were squarely in the New Left corner. What political views and feelings I possessed had their roots in my first encounter with class issues many years earlier in Mexico.

In my childhood I was raised with maids to clean up after me. I took their presence for granted; everyone had maids. However, I was repulsed by my mother's treatments of them. She clearly thought they were stupid, lazy and next to worthless, and though she depended on them she had no respect for them and I found that appalling. I was interested in the maids because they were female, and I could see that they were not stupid but simply cowed or covertly angry. Given half a chance they were sweet and cheerful and I, in my 14-year-old adolescent libidinized state appreciated that.

Later, in college, my psychopathology class was taken to Napa State Mental Hospital where a series of "cases" were trotted out for demonstration purposes. A young woman diagnosed as catatonic was brought into the large classroom by a jaded psychiatrist who manipulated her limbs, which remained in whatever position he placed them in. This was supposed to be an example of waxy flexibility, a symptom of serious psychosis but to me, who noticed the tears in the patient's eyes; it was just an outrageous example of psychiatric insensitivity and abuse.

It took years for these core experiences to become significant. On a trip through Florida preceding the 1969 APA [American Psychiatric Association] Conference in Miami at which Berne, myself and others in TA were scheduled to make presentations, I was invited for dinner to the home of a psychiatrist … What I witnessed in the form of autocratic, patriarchal, power playing, denigrating, pathologizing treatment of this man's wife and "retarded" child reminded me of my mother's treatment of the maids. It was so repugnant that I was suddenly radicalized.

108   *Claude Steiner*

When we finally arrived at the convention hotel I was ripe for a new weltan-schauung [world view]. Overhead, in the blue Florida sky, as a message from the divinity, a plane dragged a Scientology banner that read "Psychiatry Kills." Inside a group of scruffy, bearded young men were handing out leaflets signed by the Radical Caucus of the American Psychiatric Association demanding that members of the APA immediately terminate all training and research affiliated with the military and called for the expulsion of voluntary military psychiatrists from APA membership. I eagerly took and read their eye-opening literature and when I returned to Berkeley from Florida I was loaded for bear.[2]

Radical psychiatry

In the Spring of 1969 I offered a course in Radical Psychiatry at the Berkeley Free University. One of the New Left's greatest innovations, the Free U offered courses parallel with the University of California. During the university's registration period, at the Free Church on Ellsworth and Parker Streets, anyone who wanted to teach a course posted a sign-up sheet explaining the course and the time it would meet. People signed up, and the teacher contacted the people who signed and let them know where the course was meeting. Voila! a free education; free in more than one way.

Since I was a psychologist and not a psychiatrist you might ask "Why Radical Psychiatry?" Let me explain: inspired by the young psychiatrists in Florida I had come to the conclusion that the medical profession had usurped the practice of soul healing (from the Greek psyche: soul, and iatreia; healing) to the great detriment of people's mental health. In the tradition of the students that had taken over the University of California's Chancellor's office and smoked the Chancellor's cigars with their feet on his desk, I meant to take possession of the hallowed edifice of medical psychiatry. Any one competent in soul healing was a psychiatrist, I claimed. Psychiatry was no longer the exclusive domain of physicians.

The description in the catalogue read:

> Briefly, the course deals with the manner in which establishment psychiatry promotes emotional disturbance and resists approaches which dilute its control even when they are helpful to people. We will discuss how medicine has usurped the practice of psychiatry (the art of healing the soul) and how the concepts of mental illness, unconsciousness, diagnostic categories and use of psychotropic drugs are devised to maintain control over psychiatric clients. The elitist and socially unjust nature of individual psychotherapy, the tyranny of non-contractual treatment and the hocus pocus of diagnostic projective psychological tests will be discussed. Decision, unawareness, descriptions of behavior will be offered as alternatives to disease, unconsciousness, diagnostic labels and individual therapy.

Despite the somewhat chaotic content of the announcement people signed up in droves and I was soon lecturing to large audiences about the abuses of psychiatry and the need for a whole new perspective on people's emotional and mental

Excerpts on radical psychiatry 109

difficulties. Thus began my career as a political speaker and lecturer. At first my lectures were just rants about psychiatry but eventually, as my point of view matured, I developed a set of well-ordered complaints as well as proposed solutions. I was so familiar with the subject that I required minimal notes and every lecture was different and therefore elicited a lot of interest as my audiences continued to grow.

Comrade in arms

Just as importantly she [Hogie] was a comrade in a revolutionary struggle. During this period of time [Claude met Hogie in 1969], in our many anti-Vietnam and Radical Psychiatry activities, we had opportunity to have political and personal disagreements at meetings with a number of different other activists.

A number of people joined our discussions, people that were concerned with patriarchy, egotism and hierarchies. They disdained Robert's "Rules of Order"[3] which they saw as an authoritarian regime and they wanted to operate by democratic consensus. This meant that every decision had to be unanimous which added a huge time burden on our deliberations. I thought of these people as lacking purpose or focus, spaced-out hippies who preferred talking endlessly to taking action. For some of them this was true but not for others. The latter, mostly women, were trying to bring their egalitarian ideas to our activities. Some of them were gay and among them were some who were separatists refusing to deal with men at all.

I tended to see all those women who were gay separatists as simply being man-haters. But some of them weren't, and simply found dealing with men too difficult; some of them decided that they didn't have to deal with men at all, no hard feelings. That was exactly the sort of man I was; my tendency in these situations was to take the lead, speak louder and oftener than everyone else in the group, to interrupt to push through, to override and to use the power plays and generally behave in the dominant, competitive manner that was second nature to an aggressive male in which I had been trained for all the years of my life.

Hogie became my constant companion at these meetings pressing her own views, trying to mitigate my outrageous behavior and defending me against attacks from people who saw me as a huge ego tripper. Often, after these meetings were over and both of us exhausted, she, doubly exhausted by the meeting's difficult agenda and from dealing with my problematic behavior, would turn on me and in no uncertain terms tell me how badly I had behaved and how necessary it was that I stop such behavior. Over the years I have encountered that problem repeatedly in meetings and I have gradually learned to behave more respectfully, to listen and to obey Hogie's wish that I "shut the fuck up."

The Radical Psychiatry Collective

When I met Hogie I had a full-time private individual and group transactional analysis psychotherapy practice. I had been with Eric Berne for a decade and from him I had learned my psychotherapy skills and professional ethics. I was a competent, fervent, young psychotherapist practicing a modern cutting-edge method. Hogie

110   *Claude Steiner*

had a degree in philosophy and added her Marxist perspective to which I added my therapy skills and inventiveness. Together we developed a theory and practice, based on the notion that the personal is inevitably political, which many people found interesting enough to join. Combining my transactional analysis and her feminism we started the Radical Psychiatry movement.

During 1969, myself, Hogie Wyckoff, Joy Marcus and a handful of other political activists formed the Radical Psychiatry Collective and joined the Berkeley Free Clinic, an organization started by a group of Vietnam paramedics and antiwar medical professionals to start a psychological counseling section, the Rap Center (Radical Approach to Psychiatry). We offered drug, welfare, and draft counseling services, group psychotherapy, and some individual one-to-one therapy to the young people who were crowding the streets of Berkeley. Many of these "street people" were involved in the student revolt and participated in the riots against the Vietnam War and in support of the People's Park revolt that took place in Berkeley during that period. A number of the young men wished to avoid the military draft and we helped any way we could. Over the next two years as we taught radical psychiatry and trained radical psychiatrists we refined our psychiatric theory and practice.

In September 1970, a coalition of feminist women, gay men, lesbians, and mental patients with the encouragement of the radical caucus within the APA organized to disrupt the American Psychiatric Association's conference meeting in San Francisco. We obtained the ID badge of a comrade psychiatrist and made two dozen copies of it, which we distributed to infiltrators who planned to disrupt the meeting with our message. Gay men kissed passionately during a presentation about how to help gay men change sexual orientation, mental patients distributed leaflets to the conference participants, Vietnam veterans heckled psychiatrists presenting their methods of dealing with young men who refused to serve for the war. I wrote the Radical Psychiatry Manifesto and nailed it (well, I taped it) to the doors of the convention hall.

The theory of alienation

A fundamental premise of our theory was that people have, by their nature, the potential of living in harmony with themselves, each other, and nature. To the extent that they fail, they are alienated. Some people become alienated from their hearts; their natural tendencies to love, appreciate, cooperate, and help each other and are literally starved for love affection and support. I was a textbook example of this sort of alienation, as Hogie kept reminding me.

Other people become alienated from their minds, their capacity to understand the facts and workings of the world, to predict the outcome of events, and to solve problems, in a thoughtful and orderly way. Confusion and utter terror of mental breakdown are the extreme form of this kind of alienation, which is often misdiagnosed as schizophrenia. Ursula was a heart-breaking example of this sort of alienation.

Finally, we become alienated from our bodies, that is, from healthy bodily response. We ignore our body's perceptions, and deal with dis-ease through drugs

Excerpts on radical psychiatry 111

that temporarily eradicate the symptoms of dysfunction. We develop dependency and addiction to foods and chemicals over which we have no control.

We become alienated from the creative and productive capacity of our hands; people's enjoyment of productive labor is lost. People resign themselves to being unhappy at work and seek pleasure through recreation. We come to feel that we are unproductive, bored, without goals in life, lazy, and worthless failures.

We had a simple formula:

ALIENATION = OPPRESSION + MYSTIFICATION + ISOLATION

Mystified oppression in isolation is the cause of alienation. Oppression is usually accompanied by some kind of explanation, which supposedly justifies it. Eventually people come to believe the lies that are used to justify the abuse they are subjected to. Instead of rebelling against abuse, people will blame themselves for their failures, accept them and assume that they are responsible for their own unhappiness.

Being isolated from others who are in similar circumstances, we are powerless to think through our problems or do anything about them.

Our second formula represents the reversal or the antidote to Alienation; power in the world:

POWER IN THE WORLD = CONTACT + AWARENESS + ACTION[4]

Awareness of the mechanisms of abuse in class oppression, racism, sexism, ageism, heterosexism, coupleism and the way they affect us.

Action with people's support is the way out of alienation and into empowerment. Action implies risk, and when a person takes risks, he or she may need protection from the fears and actual dangers that can result from that action.

Contact with others who are oppressed is essential for change. Potent protection in the form of actual alliances for physical or moral support is needed in effective action and are an essential aspect of contact.

We applied these ideas in our training and therapy sessions. We provided contact by practicing in groups in which we focused on the way in which racism, class prejudice, sexism, heterosexism, ageism and other forms of oppressive activity caused the emotional disturbance and symptoms that people suffered.

But awareness and contact were not enough. We supported some sort of action to deal with the problem. The combination of group support, awareness raising and action proved to be quite effective in mobilizing people into taking responsibility and being proactive in the solution of their problems.

Hogie and I believed in this theory and proceeded to live it. We saw the personal problems of the world in terms of alienation oppression and isolation. Hogie's interest was in gender alienation. She saw many of the problems of women as an example of oppression, mystified by sexist views and she took on our relationship as a feminist project. She taught me feminism at the most personal level; her view was that men exploited women with an unequal exchange of strokes and affection

112 *Claude Steiner*

which was justified by sexist gender roles; women's nature was to be nurturing while men's role was to work hard and be nurtured. The result was an unequal exchange of love causing women to become dissatisfied, angry and feeling worthless and the eventual victims of depression. This view was written up in an important paper "The Stroke Economy in Women's Scripts" which was published in the *Transactional Analysis Journal* [Wyckoff, 1971].

For my part it slowly began to dawn on me just how severely alienated I was from my emotions. As an example of this problem in our own lives, once when she had asked me, point blank, if I loved her, I tried to get around my incapacity to say so with the usual evasions "You know I love you" and "If I didn't love you I would not be here, would I?" or "Haven't I told you that I do already?" I was not able to openly express the feelings I had for Hogie. I was uncomfortable with them, was embarrassed by them and sought to minimize them.

But she kept asking: "Sure, but do you love me, say it!" As I continued to demur she eventually got furious at me. I like to say that she taught me feminism at the point of a bayonet; [at one point] she pushed me against the wall and ... snarled, between clenched teeth "Listen motherfucker. If you want any more of this, you better learn to say 'I love you' a lot better than that." In radical psychiatry terms she made us both aware of the oppressive stroke inequalities that I was imposing on her and she suggested an action and offered me her love (contact) in return. That made an impression on me because I was in fact fully in love with her. To the best of my feeble abilities I squeezed out "I gllooovyuuu." She looked at me squinting her eyes and then burst out laughing. After a few bedazzled seconds so did I and we fell into each other's arms.

I was in the grips of a typical male form of oppression; uptight, out of touch with my feelings, a depressive workaholic. When she was not mad at me Hogie was unendingly nurturing and sweet; she insisted that we go camping and hiking, that I "get into my body," that I talk about what I wanted and what I felt while at the same time she fed my ravenous sexual hunger. At first I didn't understand her; wasn't my sexuality proof that I was fully into my body? In response she handed me a book by Herbert Marcuse, *One Dimensional Man* [Marcuse, 1968] in which he makes the argument that men's sensuality and capacity to feel is reduced to their penis by the capitalist oppression of their labor and productivity, leaving the rest of the body clueless. I had to admit that there was merit to that description of me.

In addition to the People's Park revolt, in 1969, there was the drugs, sex and rock and roll "Summer of Love" in San Francisco. In July I traveled to Florida and for the first time heard the term "radical psychiatry" at the APA meeting. A few months later I started teaching a course on "radical psychiatry" at the Free U. My paper on alcoholic games appeared in the *Quarterly Journal on Alcoholism* [Steiner, 1969a]. Also in 1969, Hogie and I invented the stroke economy [published two years later (1971c)] and wrote the radical psychiatry "formulas" [see Marcus, LaRiviere, & Goldstine, 1971; Steiner, 1975e]; I wrote the "Radical Psychiatry Manifesto",[5] I finished my first book *Games Alcoholics Play* [Steiner, 1971b] and Ursula and I divorced.

In 1970 I started writing an "Expanding Shrink" advice column in the *Berkeley Tribe*, an alternative press weekly. We disrupted the San Francisco APA meeting,

Excerpts on radical psychiatry 113

Grove Press agreed to publish *Readings in Radical Psychiatry* [Steiner, 1975i], Eric Berne wrote the preface to my *Games Alcoholics Play* [Berne, 1971][6] and a few months later died of a heart attack.

Early in 1972 the Free Clinic without giving a reason or warning evicted us from their building on Haste Street. In July 1972 we bought the house on Webster Street next to the COOP market on Telegraph and Ashby and started the RAP Center. In October we launched the quarterly *Issues in Radical Therapy*. What an amazing time!

The views about strokes, cooperation, truthfulness, power plays and the Critical Parent that we developed in those years have been adopted by thousands of people across the world many of who don't even know their origins just like the many who use the phrase "warm and fuzzy" have no idea that I was the originator of that concept.

People are always calling my attention to incidents in the media in which some idea or other of mine is being used, especially the "warm and fuzzy" bit, with no credit given. My reaction is that it can't be helped and that on the other hand it gives me satisfaction that these ideas have permeated the culture to that degree. An even larger infusion of the popular culture has happened with Berne's concepts, which also permeate contemporary thinking at this time and are seldom if ever credited to him.

By 1974 the Radical Psychiatry Movement had a Manifesto, a quarterly journal, *Issues in Radical Therapy*, with 1200 subscribers, a book *Readings in Radical Psychiatry* [Steiner, 1975i] a communal house, a walk-in store front and building on Howe Street – the RAP Center – next to the COOP on Ashby and Telegraph, we attracted talented dedicated people like Joy Marcus, Becky Jenkins, Robert Schwebel, we trained radical psychiatrists and we traveled widely to teach our revolutionary point of view to eager audiences (see Figure 7.1).

We were hot, we were sexy, and we were radical. We were part of the new left: sex, drugs and rock and roll counterculture. We were devoted to stopping the Vietnam War and had seen the war end. We had seen Nixon resign in disgrace and we meant to liberate the US from the grip of the "establishment." We saw our liberating efforts spread from California across the world and Reagan was, permanently we thought, retired. We imagined we had won.

But as we reveled in our victories, things began to unravel. The RAP collective split into two warring factions,[7] Reagan was eventually elected president and the US march to the Right started in earnest. Some of the most vocal members of the New Left disgusted by what they saw as that movement's acquiescence to the "evil (Soviet) empire" became neo-conservatives. Thirty years later they steadily acquired center stage and finally were in possession of both houses of Congress and the Supreme Court. For the eight years of George W. Bush's presidency they ran the country with a thoroughly deceptive authoritarian and antidemocratic point of view.

But we had made progress; we established sizable beachheads and hopefully our time will come again. Those short two years, a relatively short period in my life left a clear impression on my work; that is, politics. Politics, not in the usual sense of

Figure 7.1 The Radical Psychiatry Collective, 1971

elections and government but in the sense of the personal being also political, and of the awareness of power relations and the love-centered sources of depression, the most common emotional ailment.

I first saw the error of this line of thinking when Martin Groder who briefly ran the Marion penitentiary special unit invited me to teach at his program. He was a brilliant, radical, transactional analysis prison psychiatrist who wanted me to bring my work to his population but when he heard me declare that his black charges were all political prisoners he looked at me in disbelief and called me a fool. Of course some of the black inmates were victims of racist persecution, he said, but the statement that they all were political prisoners was beyond the pale. That statement was in the spirit of similar such radical statements being made on the Left such as Susan Brownmiller's "All men oppress all women all the time" [Brownmiller, 1975] or Andrea Dworkin's "All [heterosexual] intercourse is rape" [Dworkin, 1987]; statements which appealed to us because they were at once outlandish and in some way true. The same theatrical overstatements supported our statement "All soul healers are psychiatrists" and the labeling ourselves radical psychiatrists.

Excerpts on radical psychiatry   115

This confusion is easier to understand when the police and government were persecuting us for smoking pot and putting our leaders in jail for years for the possession of a joint or even one marihuana seed in their cars. Because of the obvious lies that the government was telling about the war, the callous pursuit of untold deaths in Vietnam, the draconian marihuana laws, the police brutality, we came to see the government as entirely and hopelessly corrupt and felt duty bound to oppose it.

I liked to cast myself as an outlaw; at a certain point I came to feel that as a privileged white man I had the obligation to break unreasonable laws. I wrote an article for *Issues in Radical Therapy* "We are all outlaws" in which I cast our outlaw sexual behavior as a form of legitimate rebellion against establishment oppression of our humanity [Steiner, 1974b]. But equating myself in any way with the experience of hard-core criminality was just plain stupid no matter how intellectually appealing it might have been.

Notes

1   The title of a column that appeared in *Issues in Radical Therapy* in 1975, written by Claude.
2   This is a North American colloquial expression meaning to be fully prepared for any eventuality, especially a confrontation or challenge.
3   Robert's "Rules of Order" or "Robert's Rules" is the most widely used manual of parliamentary procedure in the United States. It was first published in 1876 by US Army officer Henry Martyn Robert, who adapted the rules and practice of the US Congress to the needs of non-legislative societies. Since then, ten subsequent editions have been published, the latest of which in 2011 (Robert, Robert, Robert, Evans, Honemann & Balch, 2011).
4   There were – and are – several versions and variations of this formula (see Marcus, LaRiviere & Goldstine, 1971, 1975; Steiner, 1975e; Members of the Radical Psychiatry Center, 1975; *Issues in Radical Therapy*, 1977; Steiner, 1979c; and p, 130 n1).
5   Published later – in 1971c, 1972a and 1975d.
6   Published posthumously.
7   For details of which, see Glen (1973), The Rough Times Staff (1973a), Marcus (1973) and Appendix: A résumé of the criticisms of radical psychiatry made by the New Radical Psychiatry Group (in Steiner, 1975i). The split (in 1971/1972) was between those who identified more with RP (and the politics of therapy), and those who went on to form the Rough Times Collective (Rough Times Staff, 1973) who were more focused on the therapy of politics, and rejected the liberalism of therapy. This split was healed (at least in name) some ten years later in 1982 when the two groups, who had edited *Issues in Radical Therapy*, *Issues in Radical Therapy* (*IRT*), and *Issues in Cooperation & Power* (1980–1981), and *Rough Times* and *State of Mind* (1972–1981), respectively, came together and edited *Issues in Radical Therapy* (from 1982). Althöfer, however, has questioned the extent of this healing as, on the basis of his analysis of the tables of contents of the respective journals, he has pointed out that "there was obviously a complete change of contributors. I can't see that two groups came together here. It seems that the Berkeley IRT Collective just gave up the IRT project" (personal [email] communication, 20 November 2019).

8 Radical therapy

From the first decade onwards

Becky Jenkins, Ellen Morrison, and Robert Schwebel

In 1970, American citizens were actively involved in the Civil Rights movement combatting racism, a movement that led to important progressive legislation and social change. At the same time, the women's movement was gaining great momentum and protesters across the nation were amassing influence to the point that they were a driving force to end the United States (US) war of aggression in South-East Asia. It was a hopeful time with positive change in the wind. This was the climate in the US that helped give rise to the radical psychiatry movement, originated and founded by Claude Steiner. In this chapter, we tell very personal stories of how the movement evolved, how Claude engaged us as individuals, and, specifically, how he worked as a masterful trainer and teacher.

Claude was a master therapist, a protégé of Eric Berne. He regularly attended the Transactional Analysis (TA) seminars in San Francisco (SF), and provided counseling services to people from his home office in Kensington, CA, just outside of Berkeley. He was developing a social consciousness in the late 1960s and making it part of his professional practice. These were the seeds from which radical psychiatry emerged. He worked with his friend, colleague, and lover, Hogie Wyckoff, to develop the original radical psychiatry formula: oppression + mystification = alienation, and its counterpart, as originally constructed: contact + awareness = liberation (see also Steiner, 1975e).[1] Gradually the theory emerged and Claude began to invite people he knew to join what was called The Radical Psychiatry Collective. Hogie was there from the beginning. Joy Marcus, a reporter from an alternative newspaper, *The Berkeley Tribe*, interviewed Claude for a story and was among the first invited. She, along with two of the authors of this chapter, Becky Jenkins and Robert Schwebel, were part of the original group that began the movement. Some of the others who participated at the beginning eventually left. Over the years, others were either invited to join or asked to join.

Before it all began, one of us (Becky Jenkins) was a client member in one of Claude's therapy groups and this became the foundation of her own training. Claude taught so much by demonstrating his work. Here is Becky's story, in brief:

Becky Jenkins's story
I'm a child of political radicals, Jews, labor leaders, and artists. My political activism started at a young age and included being arrested protesting at an

Radical therapy 117

historic demonstration against the House Un-American Activities Committee at San Francisco's City Hall in 1960. After a decade of studying dance and theater and working primarily for non-profit organizations to promote the arts, I was at a depressing standstill about what to do next. I had heard about Claude and joined his group. Transactional Analysis was helpful, although the details didn't interest me much. I did like that Claude's approach quickly provided tools that were simple and easy to use.

Several months into my work as a client with Claude he asked if I would be interested in training to be a therapist – he thought I "had talent." I was stunned. Years earlier, I had taken a course in Abnormal Psychology while struggling to decide my major area of study. I had been horrified. The medical model reigned supreme and everyone had to be diagnosed with a "sickness." I fled the field, majored in drama, and tried my hand in the arts. Time spent in New York cured me of any illusions about surviving my life as an artist. Claude's proposal was irresistible.

Claude taught and I learned by participation in his group, and then by following the poor man everywhere, absorbing it all. I was his apprentice in every sense of the word. I saw the advantages of people working in groups. Participants decided what they wanted to work on: made contracts to improve their lives (no psychiatrizing them – telling them what their problems were). People learned how to give critical feedback without trashing others and then were given permission to give strokes (positive compliments), the ever absent "commodity" in a highly competitive alienated culture that was making all of us "sick." It was magic. People felt better quickly, much better, once their isolation and loneliness was significantly reduced. I was observing Claude's groups and following him around asking him endless questions about why he intervened when he did, and why he said what he said.

Here is Robert's story, in brief, of how he began training with Claude:

Robert Schwebel's story
I also had an activist background, including participation in historic demonstrations during the 1960s, such as the Civil Right's March in Washington, DC, at which Martin Luther King gave his famous "I have a dream" speech. I had been part of the "siege of the Pentagon," now memorialized with iconic photos of young women putting flowers in the barrel of the soldier's rifles and in Norman Mailer's book: The Armies of the Night (Mailer, 1968).

In the summer of 1970, Claude was committed to teaching a class on "Radical Psychiatry" at the Free University of Berkeley. He had taught the class once before but said it was more like a rant than what it became on this occasion during the summer. I signed up for the class because I was a doctoral student in clinical psychology at the University of California at Berkeley, searching for a meaningful way to incorporate a progressive worldview into my work. Claude rolled out the newly-minted radical psychiatry formula at the first session and I decided to immediately incorporate it into my summer job working at a Veteran's Administration (VA) hospital.

There was a group activity during the first class. We got into small groups of seven and were asked to find something attractive in every person's face in our group. Shaken a bit, I didn't think this was possible. However, I was shocked that it was so easy. I'm not sure Claude even discussed strokes in this session, but his teaching strategy was to provide learning experiences. A few weeks later, I went up to Claude to thank him for the class, still in progress, and told him how I was applying what I learned at the VA. He said "I love people who take action" and invited me to join a radical psychiatry collective that was just forming. Shortly thereafter, he invited me to start observing his groups.

(Schwebel, 1975b)

It was at one of the early collective meetings that the two of us (Becky and Robert) met. We're not sure how we were paired to lead a group together, though we remain close friends some 50 years later. Joy Marcus and Hogie Wyckoff also started a group at this time. We were learning by observation of Claude's groups, which was the main way he taught. Another main way he taught was by facilitating a community of learners at the weekly collective meetings. A third way was by forming a community of activists working together. During this period of his life, Claude was seeing himself as a trainer of therapists.

Learning by observation and then participation

The two of us (Becky and Robert) agree that learning by observation of a master therapist is the key to good training. Claude had a great plan, which is an approach that we both have continued to this day. This is how it went. When you start observing a group, you do not actively participate for at least two good reasons: (1) you

Figure 8.1 Robert and Claude, Berkeley, 1976

Radical therapy 119

should focus on learning and not be distracted by the necessity of devising something to say and (2) you do not yet have much therapeutic skill. This allows for a relaxed learning environment. However, there was one other rule: you had to say at least one thing of a nurturing nature at every session so that you were a warm presence, rather than a distant outside observer. The two of us were given a prolonged period of time to observe our groups (many months) with Claude, without pressure to participate. Then, gradually we were invited to participate more fully. Eventually, we both became back-up resources to conduct the groups when Claude was out of town or unable to attend. We continued observing Claude for more than a year, long after we started our own group together.

Unfortunately, in the modern therapy era in the United States, people without much experience are rushed into leading groups before they are trained and prepared. They often revert to very structured psychosocial sessions or simply strive for a participatory discussion, a far cry from individualized, focused counseling as part of the group process. To us, from our background, the lack of training these days seems irresponsible to clients and more like throwing young therapists to the wolves than helping them gain skills.

We (Becky and Robert) both learned an enormous amount by watching the "master" work his craft. We would observe sessions and then talk about them with Claude afterwards before leaving. We saw how large problems could be broken into smaller pieces, how people could be marshaled to support one another, how focus could be directed to the person who was "working," one at a time, which was the approach of TA. We saw how time could be shared, modeling cooperation, so that everyone had an opportunity to work on their own issues as well as help solve the problems of others. We liked how Claude would reframe problems. He would listen to what clients said, follow their lead, and yet somehow manage to reframe an issue in a way that validated clients' experiences and empowered them to make changes. When he did this, we noted he slanted his head sideways, not trying to stay so narrowly focused on the details but digging in his mind to deeper issues that would resonate and form a theme about what was happening to, and within, the individual. He was not seeking to pigeon-hole anyone with a simplistic diagnosis, but rather looking for a way to connect the concerns and pain people were experiencing (the immediate issue) to the bigger issues (general patterns) that were disempowering them. We saw that people could define their own goals and structure the counseling process, without us resorting to diagnostic labels that would pigeon hole them.

Unfortunately, even up to the present time, therapists use diagnostic labels to explain the distress of individuals out of context of their life experiences. In order to get paid by insurers, they are forced to quickly issue a diagnostic label that places the locus of the problem entirely within the functioning of the individual's brain, overlooking all the social and situational causes of distress. Social injustices and trauma are swept away along with all the sad and difficult conditions and missed opportunities that people may have experienced in their lifetimes. The diagnostic labels assigned to individuals become part of a (their) medical record that follows them for life. Those of us influenced by Claude still hope we can do as

120 *Becky Jenkins et al.*

much as possible to bring back attention to the context of people's lives. Sadly, this perspective has been sacrificed for economic gain.

Part of the magic of our (Becky and Robert's) training experience was that Claude wanted innovative and progressive therapy ideas to spread as part of a movement. He wanted participation and brought us all together. At first, we were a small group, varying from six to eight or so. Claude, Hogie, Joy, and the two of us (Becky and Robert) were the core who stayed on, with others doing shorter stints. Eventually Beth Roy and then Shelby Morgan joined under Becky's tutelage and Darca Nicholson under Claude's tutelage. They also became part of the core group. Much attention was paid to sex roles in those early days and there was a strong feminist orientation. We called ourselves a collective and met diligently every week to discuss our work as therapists using this new practice and sharing new ideas, of which there were many. There was also enormous personal openness and vulnerability. In our personal lives we were experiencing exactly what the people in the groups we were leading were experiencing. We shared many of their problems. In our training collective, we would try out new ideas on ourselves and sometime serve as guinea pigs in personal experimentation. Claude used the TA group model in the collective, in which people could bring issues on which to work. Sometimes it would be about our therapy work and sometimes it would be personal. Sometimes it would be about our own interactions as a group. It was important to practice what we preached. What Claude developed at this time could be best described as a training strategy, rather than simply a teaching strategy.

Early in the history of our collective, Claude suggested we practice a technique for expressing resentments that he had learned years before at Askleipieion, a therapeutic community within the Federal Penitentiary at Marion, Illinois (Steiner, 1974a; see also Groder, 1977). The idea of the activity was to allow for the communication of held resentment that might otherwise remain unexpressed. This activity corresponded with the concept of "stamps" in TA. Practitioners of TA had noted that people would withhold their feelings of resentment until they had enough "saved" to justify an outburst of some sort. At that time in the US, big chain supermarkets that were replacing local grocery stores would give out sheets of small sticky stamps (like postage stamps) that you could lick and attach in a booklet they provided. When you had enough booklets, you could trade your saved stamps for a big prize, such as a toaster. Similarly, it was argued, some people saved their resentments so that they could "cash them in" with a big blowup. So, Claude suggested we should learn to express our "stamps" as they occurred and "clear the air" before we would conduct business in our collective meetings. He said, we should not simply launch into this like a free-for-all, but rather ask permission of one another to make sure the recipient was in a receptive state of mind. We would say, for example, "[person's name], I have a stamp for you. Can I say it?" If that person felt unable to handle a stamp at the time, they could respond, "No, not right now" and the exchange would be delayed. This was an early seed of what would later become Claude's emotional literacy program. Soon the term stamp was dropped and we would say a "held feeling" which reflected our understanding that it wasn't only anger and resentment that was withheld, but a variety of other feelings as well.

Radical therapy 121

Either at that same meeting or shortly thereafter, Claude built off his own classic statement that "paranoia is a heightened state of awareness." He said we should check out our paranoias (negative intuitions) about what others were thinking, feeling, or doing. He said "there is always a grain of truth in a paranoia" so when one person communicates concern with regard to a negative intuition, it is important that the recipient of the communication should first search for the validation before shifting focus and saying what wasn't true or something else, perhaps of a consoling nature. For example: "I have a paranoia that you are angry and have been avoiding me." The response: "Actually it is true that I was hurt when you didn't call or visit me when I was sick and have felt a little distant since then. But, I haven't been angry at you."

From this it is clear that Claude taught by personal engagement and experimentation. You have an idea and you first test it on yourself. Our collective agreed that we must be emotionally literate in order to do our work well and help others gain competency with the skills we teach. On a personal level, we all benefitted from this.

Claude, of course, is famous for the Warm Fuzzy story that has become part of American and worldwide culture (Steiner, 1977d). The concept of strokes originated within TA and is central to the idea of "game-playing", that is, people play games in order to get attention and "strokes." Claude also introduced the idea of the "stroke economy" (Steiner, 1971c), in which strokes are treated like money or currency – as if they were a limited commodity – and people would withhold or hoard their affection for one another, almost as if they were stored in a bank. Instead, he proposed we should exchange strokes freely. We have an unlimited amount of love and affection that will not run out. So, we started to incorporate the free exchange of strokes in all of our collective meetings. It was about this time, too, that Claude introduced the activity, "trashing the stroke economy" (Steiner, 1974a, for descriptions of which, also see Schwebel, 1975b; Wyckoff, 1975a). We used it among ourselves and then at the drop-in center, a free community service that we provided. With this activity, people were invited (1) to offer strokes; (2) to ask for strokes; (3) to turn down unwanted strokes, and (4) to brag (which means give oneself strokes). It is based on the idea that even within a small group, there is enough affection and good will so that everyone can feel satisfied. We can take care of ourselves individually and collectively.

The Radical Psychiatry Collective was a talent magnet and the two of us (Becky and Robert) who did not know each other had the good fortune of being paired as co-leaders of groups. We were immediately comfortable with one another, a perfect match with similar backgrounds and compatible personalities. We learned a lot from each other, which really was part of Claude's teaching methods – connecting people to learn together.

I [Robert] marveled at Becky's ability to see the core of an issue. Perhaps most of all, I appreciated how she taught me to bring passion to our work. I was in a graduate school setting, sterile enough in those days, horrific these days, with psychologists in training acting distant and remote; kind of like

122 *Becky Jenkins et al.*

make-believe-doctors wearing white coats. I loved to watch Becky. When there was an injustice in a group member's life, Becky called it out … and with passion. "This isn't right. You never should have been treated this way!" Then, she would explain. I adopted Becky's emphatic passion as did others and it really became part of the essence of radical psychiatry. Plus, Becky was a master in complimenting people in the group in a most genuine way.

I [Becky] appreciated that Robert was thoughtful and nurturing. He was way ahead of me in some of the informative events that helped shaped the emerging theory of "healing." Claude and Hogie talked about resisting power abuse, and at some point Robert proposed "cooperation" was what we were trying to obtain as the alternative. Formulating what we were striving for (not only a cooperative way to help heal people but also a way to live in a culture distorted by competition and personal gain over the wellbeing of the group) was an invaluable contribution to the practice and theory of radical psychiatry. He and I saw the importance of a positive vision of not only caring for one another but also of the common good. We must not only identify problems, but also promote positive solutions.

As we all worked to develop therapy skills, we always had the collective and importantly, Claude's guidance, when we needed help. Here's an example from Becky and Robert.

We were greenhorns when we first started working together in 1970. In one session we were having group members participate in the activity "Trash the stroke economy," which included an individual getting into the center of the room and giving oneself strokes or "bragging," as we called it. This aspect of the activity gives people an opportunity to break a taboo and publicly express pride in themselves. One day in a group the two of us were conducting, someone with a self-esteem issue asked if she could get in the middle of the room and brag. Sometimes when people do this exercise, they get dumbfounded and can't find the words. It turns out to be very hard for them. When this happens, group members help by giving strokes (compliments) that are true and honest. The idea is that the person in the middle may or may not feel positive about themselves but will at least believe that the other persons means what they say and will therefore repeat the strokes in front of the group. When our group member arose on that day in our session, she got in the middle of the room and went silent. You have to remember this is 1970s Berkeley, so we're all sitting on big pillows in the group room. The "bragger" stands in the middle. Well, our bragger was stuck and instead of helping her, one group member started hurling put downs and insults in a loud and booming voice. We don't remember the details (thankfully), but neither of us handled it well. We're not proud telling this story, but it was part of the training process.

We went to the collective meeting and reported the event. Claude explained that we are responsible for the safety of all group members and must learn to intervene. We agreed of course, but said we were blindsided by this very surprising and loud turn of events. Claude said, "This is what you do." He asked for one person to act as the "bragger" and another as the "insulter." Then as the insulter started with the put downs, Claude immediately jumped up from his pillow and placed himself squarely between the insulter and the bragger and forcefully and loudly said to the insulter: "Stop! You can't do this here." What a lesson for us. From that moment on, we became the protectors we needed to be in our groups. Many years later, one of us [Robert] wrote, inspired by that lesson, what he called the "safety rule" for group members in his program, a descendant of radical psychiatry, called The Seven Challenges: "You can't take information that you learn about an individual and deliberately use it to hurt them." Just as we would not allow physical bullying, we cannot allow emotional bullying.

Theory, practice, and growing influence

The Radical Psychiatry Collective had a strong feminist orientation; one that was inclusive of males who were in support of equality, and not abusive. It made sense as we explored sex roles that power distinctions and power abuses would be identified. Hogie eventually wrote a book about leading women's groups that discussed the scripts of girls and women (Wyckoff, 1980). Claude and Hogie figured prominently in beginning to talk about "power plays," how to identify them, and how to respond to them in powerful ways. This was an important contribution to the field of counseling and to understanding human interactions. It is still often overlooked and needs more attention so many years later. As we continued to discuss power plays, one of us (Robert) did a workshop for everyone on cooperation, and introduced this as the alternative to power plays. Claude was always open to new ideas and always gave people credit for their contributions. We have all been grateful for that. Soon after the workshop, Claude wrote about the rules for cooperative relationships, which became an important part of emotional literacy.

The next logical extension of the emotional work (strokes, expressing resentments and other feelings, and checking-out paranoias) was the development of a radical psychiatry approach to mediation. Claude introduced it and we believe we were the guinea pigs on this one. As usual, Claude taught us by showing it, even as the format was still developing. Whenever we had relationship problems, either among ourselves or in our personal lives, we would get a mediation. Claude would often turn to Becky for his own mediations. It was a simple process that continues to this day, with parties to a dispute expressing their emotions in disciplined "I statements" and stating their "paranoias" clearly. As the emotions are exposed, the underlying problems become evident. We all developed skill in the art of seeing what each party to a dispute could do to contribute to a cooperative and equitable solution to relationship problems. Claude was masterful at this. Then, participants would agree about how they could continue by working on their own part of the problem. Soon, we were conducting mediations in the community, not only for couples and families, but also for organizations. Becky and Claude wrote an article on mediation for *Issues in Cooperation and Power* (Jenkins & Steiner, 1980), and

124   *Becky Jenkins et al.*

Robert co-authored an article on the subject that was published in *Professional Psychology*, a journal of the American Psychological Association (Schwebel, Schwebel, & Schwebel, 1985). Through word of mouth, Becky built a huge reputation in the Bay Area for her work on mediation. She also trained Beth Roy who has continued in her own work to become a national and international figure in the mediation field (see Roy, 2014).

In the mid-1970s massage and body work modalities were beginning to take hold in the SF Bay area. Someone, we're not sure who it was but would guess Hogie or Claude, came to know Ann Kent Rush, who had written a popular book, *Getting Clear: Body Work for Women* (1973), gave us a cut rate, and as an entire group we received training in bodywork techniques. We personally benefitted from this work and began to incorporate the bodywork in some of our sessions. Eventually, prohibitions about touching clients really put a cloud over our efforts to incorporate a more holistic/physical component in our work. Working in this way was also made difficult because it required larger spaces and more personnel to do it safely. However, Darca Nicholson, who had become an important part of our collective, continued to work in the physical realm and became a very distinguished master of various aspects of bodywork and compiled her work in a book, *Body Matters* (Nicholson, 2007) (also see Chapter 6).

The other major way that Claude trained was in the context of community involvement, which involved some degree of communal living as well as the provision of services to the community. In the early 1970s, someone lent Claude money and he personally signed for the purchase of a house in Berkeley, which became the home of the Radical Psychiatry Drop-In Center. Every day we took turns in providing free group services on a drop-in basis that included counseling sessions and a variety of activities. Every day, there was an opportunity to participate in "trashing the stroke economy," an activity that was valued by the people who would drop in.

Claude taught many of his new ideas in workshops outside of the Bay Area. He was an original thinker and an inspirational speaker who always found an interesting way to present interesting ideas … and to demonstrate them. Claude also was an excellent writer, following Eric Berne's idea that writing should be "simple so that even an eight year old could understand it." All through these years with the collective, Claude also taught through his writing. Claude published several books and we began to become more of a movement with the launch, in January of 1973, of our own publication: *Issues in Radical Therapy* (*IRT*). Joy had journalism and production experience which helped get it started. IRT brought in a national and even international following, often all the way to our doorstep, because it was published from the house in which many of us (Robert included) lived. We were regularly surprised by our doorbell being rung by a reader from somewhere in the US or abroad.

As our reputation spread, the next logical step was to hold an annual conference, which we did for several years in the 1970s. The Bay Area people presented at the conference, but we also began to invite speakers from around the country who had been to Claude's workshops or were reading *IRT*. A lot of effort went in to planning these events, so much so, that we eventually discontinued the practice. However,

Radical therapy   125

the conventions were quite powerful and joyful experiences. During the first one, we were surprised by an apparent tone of discontent among participants on the first day. At first, we were taken aback (after all our hard effort), but Claude suggested we offer a period of time for the very large group to express their resentments and other feelings. We got helpful feedback from this experience and it cleared the air, as the negativity dissipated. We continued with the practice of giving participants an opportunity to express feelings on a regular basis at all the events. The problems of that first day at the conference never re-occurred.

During our first decade together we were calling ourselves radical psychiatrists. There was also an emerging radical therapy movement throughout the United States that consisted of progressive people who worked in the field and wanted to promote social justice. In the mid-1970s there was another publication called *The Radical Therapist* which had nothing to do with us. Our own group was unique in that we had a comprehensive model of practice, not just a set of important and good progressive ideas. However, in a first step toward becoming part of a bigger movement, our publication (newsletter/magazine) was launched with the title of *Issues in Radical Therapy*. Later in the 1980s, the name "radical psychiatry" was dropped completely and we, too, call ourselves radical therapists. It's not clear exactly how the name change evolved. It seemed like we shifted to a more general and recognizable name, which was easier to explain than calling our practice radical psychiatry.[2] We also had issues with psychiatry becoming less counseling oriented, and more directed to prescribing psychotropic drugs.

Reflecting back all these years, it is clear that Claude was both a trainer in skills and a teacher of ideas. His didactic teaching in the 1970s in Berkeley and San Francisco was very limited. The only formal course we know about was the one-time class at the Free University. Claude also continued to give workshops around the country and later around the world for people in the TA community and would incorporate his radical psychiatry work in them (see Steiner, 1975i, 1975j). These workshops were brief (two and a half days) and certain key skills would be demonstrated and practiced by participants whenever possible. Later, in the 1980s and beyond he started developing and teaching emotional literacy, which combined a didactic component with skills training and practice (see pp. 186–188). For a few of us in radical psychiatry in Berkeley and San Francisco, we were, in reality, Claude's apprentices. We got to observe a master therapist at work and listen to his insights day-by-day after sessions and week-by-week at our collective for countless years. As a result, we all eventually evolved into master therapists. This was the beginning of our small group evolving into a bigger movement. By the mid-1970s, Hogie Wycoff, Joy Marcus, and the two of us (Becky and Robert) began our own training groups composed of individuals from the Bay Area. Shortly thereafter, Beth Roy emerged as a leader and was training others alongside Becky.

It would be incomplete to talk about Claude as a teacher without talking about his fun-loving nature and his friendship. He wanted to start a movement. He wanted his ideas to be a part of something bigger. He generously taught us all and we all became friends. We dared to share our vulnerable feelings with one another and became a tight-knit group. He taught us to think big and encouraged us to connect with one another. We all grew as individuals because we all were getting insightful and powerful feedback from Claude and each other. Most of all, we remember the fun and the laughter and joy. This was part of his approach to teaching, and an important one. Sure, our work was serious, and we had issues with one another at times, but mostly it was a blast.

Dispersion and differences

In the early 1980s, Claude's interests began to shift and there were many changes in the operations of what had been radical psychiatry, which was now being called radical therapy (see also Chapter 9). Claude gradually phased out and stopped his clinical practice (except for occasional mediations and special meetings), started writing more about issues related to power – see, for example, his book, *The Other Side of Power* (Steiner, 1981e) – and then in earnest began organizing many of his contributions in terms of emotional literacy. He began to spend more of his time in Ukiah, California on the ranch, more distant from the SF Bay Area. Claude also traveled extensively doing workshops for TA groups in Europe and South America, and Australasia. The collective, with an ever-changing membership, began meeting less frequently, more like once a month.

Claude had already made an enormous contribution to the field of therapy. Included among his accomplishments was the development of an array of communication skills, practices, and protocols that he believed could be taught to a wider audience, not just to individuals in therapy. Over the next 20 years he refined his ideas further and organized this work into what he named emotional literacy (see Chapters 12 and 13). He prepared a teaching document that he would use, and others who were trained and certified by him could use. Instead of *training* counselors in the art of therapy, he wanted to *teach* people emotional literacy skills through the use of learning modules and psychosocial sessions at workshops. Claude taught the curriculum around the world. In a sense, it seems that the name "radical therapy" (formerly "radical psychiatry") has come to mean different things in different

Figure 8.2 Becky and Claude, Ukiah, July 2016

Radical therapy   127

locations. People who (1) were practicing therapy in ways that differ from how we were doing it in the SF Bay Area and (2) learned emotional literacy and incorporated it in their practices may have chosen and still choose to call themselves radical therapists. After all, Claude trained them. We assume(d) that other students who were or have been certified in emotional literacy simply incorporate the skills in their work or organizations. Some may be therapists and others not. So, in all, there has been some dispersion of the concept of what we now and still call radical therapy.

In 1981, one of us (Robert) moved to Tucson, Arizona where he incorporated radical psychiatry into his work. Joy Marcus withdrew from the collective. As the collective began to meet less frequently, the mantle for leading the radical therapy movement in the SF Bay Area was passed to Becky and Beth. Although the groups they trained were called collectives, they could more accurately be described as training groups. Sessions were structured much the same way as our original collective had been structured, using the same format. Trainees observed Becky and Beth's groups and mediation sessions, and they worked on issues during the training meetings. At this point, you could say that Claude had kind of passed the torch and turned his creation loose. Becky and Beth took up the mantle and developed a whole new cadre of skilled and smart therapists who became the core of radical therapy in the Bay Area. Claude would be invited and would readily come to offer his expertise to the training groups. Ellen Morrison, Shelby Morgan, JoAnn Costello, Carol Blecker, and others became the second wave, the next generation of radical therapists. To this day, Claude's radical therapy lives on in the Bay Area.

Because Claude had written *Games Alcoholics Play* (Steiner, 1971b) and *Healing Alcoholism* (Steiner, 1979b), the two of us (Becky and Robert) received many referrals from him to work with individuals with alcohol and other drug problems and so we developed some expertise in this area.

In January 1981, I (Robert) moved to Tucson, Arizona, where I became director of a community-based agency providing drug counseling services and in 1990 began developing The Seven Challenges Program (www.sevenchallenges.com), originally for adolescents and young adults with drug problems, and now for people of all ages. I basically incorporated all I learned from radical psychiatry into the program structure. The program is widely used across the United States, and now in Canada and in one site in Germany. It is used in about 500 different sites in 39 states in the US, including in counseling agencies, drug courts, residential treatment; public and private schools; wilderness programs; and juvenile justice settings. I consider it a direct descendant of radical psychiatry (and its TA heritage), incorporating: a focus on consideration of the social context of drug use behavior; holistic in that drug problems cannot be resolved in counseling without the entire context of life-counseling; consideration of the political in personal life; helping people with their distress with regard to drug use without stigma; use of a self-directed and self-empowering approach; giving clients choices (not just abstinence); the promotion of cooperative relationships; using radical therapy counseling skills and incorporating work on emotional literacy. In the footsteps of Claude, I have formed a group of colleagues that talks regularly, develops new ideas and strive for mastery level skills in counseling (see also Schwebel, 2018).

128 *Becky Jenkins et al.*

The two of us (Becky and Robert) attribute much of our own success to the lessons we learned from our teacher, Claude Steiner. Radical therapy also lives on the distinguished work that Beth Roy does worldwide in the field of mediation, and in Darca Nicholson's bodywork (Nicholson, 2007); Darca is a well-known provider of eclectic healing services in Northern California.

Radical therapy also lives on in the particular way that emotional literacy was taught and introduced in the SF Bay Area, which we describe below. We assume it was taught differently here because Claude introduced it to groups of people who had already been trained in many of the skills as participants in a radical therapy training group.

Radical therapy and emotional literacy in the 2000s – Ellen Morrison

This history of the introduction of emotional literacy to the Bay Area starts in 2005, when Beth and Becky developed a training group to teach radical therapy to members of their own therapy practices. I (Ellen Morrison) had been involved in the radical therapy community since 1999, initially as a member of a group and as a participant in a mediation, before being recruited for training. Beth and Becky recruited talent much as Claude had done with the original collective. My experience with radical therapy was personally transformative and deeply informed my professional path with an attention to the analysis of power as a core element of interpersonal and social change. I will share a bit of the history and experiences of my training group when Claude became involved with us. Many of us had met Claude as a visiting teacher to our group before October 2009 when he presented us with his writing and curriculum on emotional literacy and asked if we wanted to be certified. We collectively agreed it was a compelling direction for our training – the content was certainly familiar as the foundational skills of radical therapy. It offered the group an opportunity to expand our ability from leading mediations and groups to training others and sharing this information with a diverse audience. This option was liberating for the non-therapists in the group who felt working in this capacity was applicable to their responsibilities as classroom teachers, political organizers, or coaches.

In preparation for writing this section of this chapter, some of us from our training group met in September of 2018 to reflect on Claude as a teacher (2009–2017). In this discussion a consistent theme emerged that many in the group had experienced a similar tension while working with him: on the one hand we had great praise for the man and his work with respect for his leadership in the development of radical therapy. On the other hand, we had some confusion and irritation resulting from his separation of emotional literacy from radical therapy and, therefore, its radical roots. Claude had created and organized a body of theory and practice into a book containing a curriculum that he coined "emotional literacy," which he viewed as a modernization of radical therapy. Many of us trainees saw the tools as essentially the same ones that we were already using in radical therapy. We were concerned, though, that the formulation in terms of emotional literacy was narrowing and devoid of attention to the ways in which people's problems were the

Radical therapy 129

result of social forces that worked against them. This aspect of radical therapy, we felt, provided a valuable framework for personal and social change. In all candor, there were some rough edges as Claude entered an established group committed to a power analysis. Claude was challenged and we appreciated his humility and openness to the consistent dialogue and partnership of accountability with women and other men in the group as we confronted privilege and other power dynamics. Nevertheless, and despite our differing views on some matters, the whole group recalled our excitement about the possibility of expanding our radical therapy community by utilizing Claude's emotional literacy curriculum.

It was at this crossroads in our training that we entered a process of becoming certified as emotional literacy trainers and shifted our focus to create an integrated body of work in meaningful ways, including co-creating a curriculum and teaching a class for City College of San Francisco (CCSF), Labor and Community Studies Department (www.ccsf.edu). We were part of a course of study that provided members of San Francisco labor unions and other interested individuals with: a comprehensive introduction to the role and contributions of organized labor to American society; a thorough grounding in the rights of employees on the job; and a specialized training in the skills necessary to be an effective practitioner in the field of labor and industrial relations. The class was based on the concepts and skills of emotional literacy and how it could support conflict resolution in labor and community organizations, at work, and in personal relationships.

Each month, the core group simultaneously developed as trainers and worked on how to best make the information accessible to the student body of primarily community organizers, union shop stewards, and peer counselors. It was quite a collaboration: Bill Shields was the Department Chair and lead teacher who stewarded the institutional support; Carol Blecker, Shelby Morgan, and I taught classes and worked on the curriculum design and development; Roy Harrison, Joelle Ehre, and Joshua Walker attended classes, gave feedback, and supported the curriculum development. Claude, alongside Becky and Beth, transferred the knowledge we needed to be confident trainers.

Claude was instrumental in this training process as he led foundational training on the theory and practices of emotional literacy, rooted in TA (see Steiner, 1984b), that, when filtered through the lens of power, the training group recognized as radical therapy. We brought issues to work on to the training group and Claude would help facilitate skill development and coach us as we taught each other the skills. The training structure was familiar: we identified who had problem-solving to do and made time for emotional clearing that needed to happen. Claude taught some skills didactically, but mostly through interpersonal work. We ended with strokes. Claude had developed a curriculum or process for teaching the content of emotional literacy that resembled other things we did in our training group and maintained our supportive approach.

We remembered how Claude formulated his analysis quickly and how his swift and direct response consistently clarified and moved the work forward. For example, we all recalled his teaching of the "paranoia (intuition) – validation": he was leading our group in a mediation when he stopped the person offering the validation

130 *Becky Jenkins et al.*

mid-sentence and said, "Don't tell her what isn't true, tell her what is true. What is the grain of truth?" he insisted. The person struggled and Claude coached her in identifying the grain of truth. When done, she still wanted to say what wasn't true, a very strong inclination among people in general, but he said, "No need – the transaction is complete." We recalled leaving this teaching with more clarity about the value of practicing the skill of saying what is true first and foremost. This skill, in particular, is one of the more important contributions of radical therapy and it was Claude's willingness to stop what was happening and step in at the moment that brought the lesson home.

It was an exciting time. A body of work that is so dear to us was making its way into the hearts and minds of a diverse student body at CCSF (something we had not been able to do successfully as radical therapists because designating our work as "radical therapy" limited our audience). As training progressed, Claude acknowledged that radical therapy was the US version of "his work," as compared to how it was being utilized in places like Germany, Spain, and Latin America. Rather than being used primarily by TA therapists and in their therapeutic institutions, we were part of this body of knowledge taking hold in community-based work, and ultimately living on not only in the social workers, teachers, and trades-people in our group, but also the students who participated in this mentoring relationship being offered by the College.

Claude was an invaluable teacher and a member of our community and although the group's membership changed over time, the group met consistently up until Claude's death in 2017. The development of this class, and ultimately the emotional literacy curriculum, was a dynamic partnership that gave us all an opportunity to practice the skills we were learning. Each of us had a memory of caring deeply about Claude's feedback of our work and felt his striving for collaborative thought-partnerships throughout the training process – the curriculum and our utilization of the skills are strengthened because of our time with him. We are all grateful to him as teacher, mentor, and collaborator.

Notes

1   Robert notes that this was the original formula, which focused on liberation. Claude Steiner's (1975e) version of the formula of radical psychiatry was: Awareness + Contact = Action → Liberation. Robert notes that Joy Marcus contributed the addition of action, and that the arrow indicated progress toward liberation, rather than the achievement of liberation.
2   Claude discusses this in a chapter on "Radical psychiatry history" (Steiner, 1975g) in *Readings in Radical Psychiatry* (Steiner, 1975i).

9 Radical therapy
The fifth decade

Luigi (Gino) Althöfer and V. Riesenfeld

This chapter presents Radikale Therapie (radical therapy or RT) as an approach that has been practised in Germany since the mid-1980s. RT is a method of self-help group therapy conducted without professional therapists. The method operates within self-organised networks and is passed on free of charge by people who have experienced RT themselves. The therapeutic concept of RT is based on the theory and practice of radical psychiatry (RP) (see Chapter 7), with the addition of various working and support techniques from co-counselling (CC). Some elements of RT also have parallels with the concept of emotional literacy (EmLit) (see Chapters 12 and 13).

In the tradition of RP, the term "radical" identifies the conceptual focus of understanding and working on individual problems within their underlying social causes. The aim of the therapeutic work, therefore, is to free oneself from internalised oppression, to recognise new options for action, and to implement the corresponding decisions in everyday life. In this chapter, we first explain the methodological background and the history of RT, and, in doing so, also give an insight into the current practice of RT and the status of the RT movement in Germany today. Finally, we briefly summarise the central features of RT.[1]

Radical psychiatry

In 1969, Steiner wrote the "Radical Psychiatry Manifesto", which included a fundamental critique of the psychiatric system in the United States (US) and argued that the discipline of psychiatry was infiltrated by irrelevant medical concepts. For him, diagnoses and diagnostic methods were "meaningless mystifications" ("Radical Psychiatry Manifesto") as they obscured oppressive social structures as a significant cause of psychiatric disease. By remaining neutral in the context of oppression, psychiatry – particularly as it was practised in the public sector – had become an enforcer of the values and laws of the establishment (Steiner, 1975i). Other influences on RP include Marxist and feminist perspectives, articulated especially by Hogie Wyckoff. The RP groups considered and addressed personal problems and patterns in the context of alienation theory, expressed by the formula: Alienation = Oppression + Mystification + Isolation (Steiner, 1975e). The therapeutic work on personal issues was based on a liberation approach and summarised

132   Luigi (Gino) Althöfer and V. Riesenfeld

in a complementary formula: Liberation = Contact + Awareness + Action (Steiner, 1975e), by which the therapeutic work in such groups had an explicitly political dimension and also aimed to develop a way of coping with oppressive situations (see Wyckoff, 1975a, 1977).

Steiner and Wyckoff argued that individuals are socialised to develop certain "sex roles" and are affected by sex/gender-specific alienation phenomena due to different experiences of oppression (see Wyckoff, 1975a, 1975b). For these reasons, RT established women's* groups and men's* groups as well as "mixed groups" (concerning sex/gender), each led by therapists of the Radical Psychiatry Collective (see Steiner, 1974a, 1975i; Wyckoff, 1974, 1975b, 1977).

Claude Steiner was an early student of Eric Berne and eventually became a teaching member of the International Transactional Analysis Association (ITAA) in 1960. Within the RP movement, Steiner made strong links with and references to transactional analysis (TA). The 24-page booklet, *TA Made Simple* (Steiner, 1971e), served as a handout within the RP groups and networks. Therapeutic group work was carried out especially in problem-solving groups (PSGs) whose practice in the 1970s can be regarded as TA-based group therapy (see Wyckoff, 1970). Participants worked intensively with models of ego states, transactions, and games, in the form of the drama triangle (see Karpman, 1968). The Critical Parent ego state was named "The Pig" and "The Pig Parent", the latter of which was also used in TA. Therapeutic exercises such as "Off[ing] the Pig" (Wyckoff, 1975a) and "The Critical Parent Exercise" (Steiner, 2009) were developed. Drawing on contracts and the three Ps (permission, protection, and potency), people worked on individual influences and on resolving their scripts. On the social level, RT groups aimed at refraining from destructive psychological games among themselves and, instead, to enter into intimacy in their relationships with each other (see Wyckoff, 1970, 1977; Steiner, 1975i).

The essential elements of what later became EmLit were developed in the group work of RP. For example, already in the PSGs of the 1970s, the cooperative contract (no secrets and lies, no rescues, no powerplays) was the basis for cooperative collaboration. There were structures to check intuition or paranoid fantasies; to communicate unpleasant emotions regarding the behaviour of other group participants; and to exchange appreciation according to the five permissions to overcome the stroke economy (Steiner, 1971c) with its five prohibitions (see Wyckoff, 1977). Over time, the concept of EmLit developed as a separate approach (see Steiner, 1984b, 2003c, 2009; Steiner & Perry, 1997; and Chapters 12 and 13).

Co-counselling

Co-counselling (CC) (also referred to as re-evaluation counselling) is sometimes called "therapy without a therapist" (Berger, 1996). It is a self-help therapeutic technique developed by Harvey Jackins and Mary McCabe in Seattle, Washington, in the 1950s. CC is based on reciprocity and not on payment. As a rule, two people

Radical therapy 133

are involved in a CC session. Within the framework of an agreed time commitment, people alternately support each other. First, as part of a CC training, certain working and support techniques are learned. During a CC session, the co-counsellor first and foremost gives full attention to the person who is "working" (i.e., the client at that point), and may also offer specific interventions to assist the client's process. However, in each case, the primary responsibility for the therapeutic process lies with the person "working", that is, the client (see Ernst & Goodison, 1981; Evison & Horobin, 1990; Jackins, 1982, 1994; Risse & Willms, 2011).

According to the theory of CC, psychological problems are due to the limiting patterns of feeling, thinking, and behaviour that individuals develop as a result of unprocessed painful experiences. The aim of CC is to work on this pain from the safe position of the "here-and-now". A key assumption in CC is that clients discharge and release emotions thanks to physical expression through body and voice. The conscious and regular practice of such a cathartic process serves to liberate the person from states of tension and to clarify their thinking and feeling. This, in turn, enables them to carry out a re-evaluation of the original stressful circumstances and, finally, to detach from fixations on certain patterns. Thus, CC enables intensive, profound, and therapeutically effective work on the psychological level (see Jackins, 1982, 1994).

According to Ernst and Goodison (1981), Meulenbelt (1983), and Rowan (1987), CC combines the "personal" with the "political", as individual problems and patterns are also seen in the context of social causes; in a more recent book on the subject, Kaufmann and New (2004) explicitly refer to psychological suffering and internalised oppression.

In the early 1970s, Gail Pheterson worked as a Co-Counselling Trainer with Harvey Jackins and Mary McCabe and was active in the US in both RP and CC communities. In Pheterson's understanding, both methods were related in different ways to a political-personal analysis. She saw the two approaches as methodologically and politically compatible and complementary. In 1975, she linked the concept of problem-solving groups from RP with the theory and practice of co-counselling into a new group practice and collaborated with Lilliam Moed on multi-day workshops within the politically active feminist movement in the Netherlands (see Pheterson, 1978).

RT as a self-help therapy

In PSGs, an appropriately trained member of the RP Collective would guide group sessions and accompany problem-solving processes as a therapist. Pheterson and Moed, meanwhile, taught their workshop participants to assist each other with CC techniques. The premise was that the newly formed groups would continue to work together for a year without professional guidance and that participants would take turns leading group sessions (see Pheterson, 1978; van Mens-Verhulst & Waaldijk, 2008). The result was what Meulenbelt (1983) called "a new form of self-help therapy" (p. 107). These groups were referred to as FORT groups (Feminist Oefengroepen Radicale Therapy), which translates as feminist radical therapy exercise groups.

134   *Luigi (Gino) Althöfer and V. Riesenfeld*

The groups instructed by Pheterson and Moed eventually formed networks in the Netherlands. By 1978, there were about 40 FORT groups (Pheterson, 1978); the Netherlands are said to have had a "strong FORT movement" as early as 1976 (Rauch, Detlefsen, & Stoebbener, 1996, p. 3). Over time, many women* who had attended a FORT group for a year or more began to help disseminate FORT and instruct new groups. Their efforts partially benefitted from state subsidies, but women* also volunteered within the FORT movement (see van Mens-Verhulst & Waaldijk, 2008).

Wyckoff's work had a strong impact on the practice of FORT and in the late 1970s Wyckoff and Pheterson were in touch personally. In 1979, Wyckoff's *Solving Women's Problems* (1977) was published in the Netherlands under the title *Vrouwenpraatgroepen: Feminist Oefengroepen Radicale Therapy*, with the subtitle being a legible reference to the FORT groups already established in the Netherlands.

FORT and M*RT

In the Netherlands RT was initially practised only within women's* groups, but pro-feminist RT men's* groups, referred to as "Mannen[*] Radicale Therapy" (Men's* radical therapy or M*RT), began to emerge in the early 1980s. Both FORT and M*RT were based on the conviction that relationships between women* and men* are characterised by patriarchal power structures. Thus, in the FORT groups one important concern was to become aware of sex/gender-specific oppressive life circumstances and to develop an ability to resist them. The M*RT concept was based on F*ORT in terms of both theory and method, with a few conceptual changes.[2] These included the intention to develop an awareness of the privileges of masculinity and to foster responsible behaviour. The engagement with the privileges of masculinity was a key element of the M*RT introduction (described below); it filled a complete session during the second weekend and included an exercise in which participants examined these aspects with reference to their own personal lives (see Van Velden & Severijnen, 1985).

As Steiner, Wyckoff, and other radical psychiatrists have emphasised, an underlying assumption of both FORT and M*RT is that, over the course of their lives, women* and men* experience different injunctions and attributions, that they inevitably undergo distinct processes of adaptation and develop corresponding patterns of behaviour. One of many objectives of both FORT and M*RT has always been to foster awareness of having been socialised as male or female, and to allow participants to free themselves from self-limiting and socially destructive behaviours that result form this socialisation.

While it was considered fundamental that women* and men* should practise in separate groups, there was also a lively exchange between FORT and M*RT networks (see Rauch et al., 1996; Van Velden & Severijnen, 1985).

In the mid-1980s Dutch people with RT experience brought the method to what was then West Germany. The first German M*RT group became active in West Berlin in 1985; the first F[*]ORT group was set afloat the following year (see

Radical therapy 135

Rauch et al., 1996; Van Velden & Severijnen, 1985). At this time, the meaning of the acronym FORT in Germany was changed into "Frauen[*] Organisieren Radikale Therapie" (Women* organise radical therapy). Since then, numerous new RT groups have been set up in Germany, resulting in a lively RT movement of some 30 years standing, in which several hundred people have practised – and continue to practise – RT in regular groups as well as in various national meetings and networks.

Relation to sex/gender in the RT movement today

In Germany, RT is still often practised in male* and female* groups. The concepts of F*ORT and M*RT continue to be based on the idea that people are socialised according to a male–female binary model, that they experience sex/gender-specific attributions and injunctions, and are immersed in social power structures.

That said, the RT community is made up of people who represent a great variety of perceptions and ideas about sex and gender as well as related roles and identities. Some concepts of sex/gender rely on biological or esoteric models. Classical sex/gender role models are sometimes considered "natural" and individually experienced as "authentic" expressions of "femininity" or "masculinity". In this context we might ask to what extent individual groups are still aware of the original goal of fostering sensitivity about sex/gender roles, and in how far established ideas about masculinity and femininity are being reproduced within RT. It should also be noted that within M*RT each person is free to decide if they want to engage in a critical examination of their privileges and responsibility; the pro-feminist objective that was key to the original M*RT concept is at risk (see Tha'sa, 2000).

RT was initially practised more or less exclusively by cis-men and cis-women, that is, individuals who identify with the sex assigned to them at birth. RT groups remained inaccessible to transgender* people for a long time, failing to provide a setting that was safe enough. In recent years, transgender* people have become more vocal criticising this practice and the construction of sex as well as gender. This has led to a growing accessibility of existing F*ORT and M*RT structures. Over the last few years, moreover, RT groups emerged that describe themselves as all-gender, queer*, trans*, inter*, and non-binary*. Even the asterisk in F*ORT and M*RT is becoming more and more established.

Instruction of new RT groups

The instruction of a new group (also known as "RT-Start") takes place over two weekends (Friday to Sunday) with an interval of six to eight weeks. These two weekends provide room for a systematic induction into the theory and practice of RT, for therapeutic work on individual topics as well as for group dynamic processes. Between the two Start weekends, the group meets weekly without external guidance or facilitation. After the complete instruction the new group should be able to maintain the therapeutic setting independently.

136 Luigi (Gino) Althöfer and V. Riesenfeld

Finally, at the end of the second Start weekend, each person decides for or against a commitment to the new RT group and, if applicable, concludes a contract to participate for one year. At the same time, all members of the new RT group receive a written document summarising the background and principal rules of RT (Rauch et al., 1996; Van Velden & Severijnen, 1985).

The instruction of new RT groups is given by two or three people who themselves have participated in a regularly instructed RT group for at least one year – mostly much longer. In addition to their own RT experience, instructors need to have some in-depth knowledge of the backgrounds of RT, and the instruction process entails detailed preparation. Unfortunately, there is no guarantee that the instruction is given with a clear reference to the underlying procedures and backgrounds of RT. As a result, their potential remains unexploited in many groups. In our view, both the therapeutic and the political potency have been watered down in some cases.

Over the past 30 years the RT movement has given rise to different collectives working to ensure that the dissemination of RT was based on solid theoretical foundations. Since late 2015 an "RT-Starter*innen-Kollektiv" (RTSK; RT Instructors' Collective) has been active in Germany. At present (January 2020) it consists of nine people, among them the authors of this chapter.

Publications on RT

Through various publications by individuals associated with the RT movement, RT has been made known especially in socio-critical circles (see Althöfer, 2017; Baruch, Frühling, & Mono, 2015; Breitenbürger & Faber, 1996; Hillar & Frick, 1996; *Männerrundbrief*, 2000). At the same time, the concrete practice of RT is not explained explicitly anywhere: the M*RT and F*ORT scripts (Rauch et al., 1996; Van Velden & Severijnen, 1985) are restricted for use within the RT movement and remain unpublished. One of the reasons behind this decision was to prevent people from creating therapeutic settings without prior and well-founded instruction.

Framework for the self-organised therapy setting

After the second Start weekend, the size of an RT group is usually between ten and twelve people. The RT group meets weekly for three to four hours. The sessions are prepared and facilitated by participants in pairs, and they take turns with this responsibility.

Time

In RT, a conscious and transparent use of the resource of time is practised. At each moment of the session, one person has the clock in view and makes appropriate time announcements, according to agreements or basic rules. For some elements of the RT session, the same amount of time, to the exact second, is available to every person, whereby an "extension" can be granted, with the exact amount of extra time being transparent to the group. In this way, individual patterns – usually a tendency to take up a lot of space or very little – can be made transparent, and also be changed. As part of the individual working time, each person first announces how much time they wish to work on a topic; the pair who lead the session take responsibility for moderating the decision-making process on how the available time is ultimately shared, taking into consideration the needs and concerns of all group members. Thus, a cooperative attitude and process is practised as an alternative to competitive behaviour.

Mutual support

During the RT session the participants work with mutual support based on CC (see description above). Whenever someone takes time for therapeutic work, they ask another one for support for a concrete number of minutes.

Reference to the body

According to CC theory, the body is involved in therapeutic work as a carrier of emotions and painful experiences. RT also encourages participants to pay attention to their body in order to become more sensitive to its messages. All physical needs and expressions are explicitly allowed.

In different situations of the RT session the person who is working has eye contact with their support person, who usually stands opposite them. The working person remains standing, which allows feelings in the body to become more noticeable; various forms of physical relief (such as hopping, pounding, stretching, shaking, etc.) are also easier to perform. The supporting person is physically present, too, in that they usually hold the working person's hands and, at times, reflect their physical expression.

In RT groups, there is explicit permission for participants to be physically close to each other. While the group mostly sits on the floor or stands – both in a circle – participants often have physical contact with the neighbouring person and/or lean against each other. Such bodily contact often quickly develops into a normality, even in new groups, giving many a strong sense of comfort and safety within the group. At the same time, a person's preference not to have body contact is treated with respect.

Individual responsibility

Within the fixed structure of RT, each participant decides on the content and form of their therapeutic work. It is everyone's responsibility to formulate their own needs as well as their boundaries. Different tools are in place to allow every person to take care of their needs and to guard their boundaries in a practice of self-care. As part of the Start weekends, the roles of the drama triangle (see Karpman, 1968) are explained, in order to counteract possible game dynamics within RT groups, and to convey possible alternatives and exit strategies.

138   Luigi (Gino) Althöfer and V. Riesenfeld

Attention

Another aspect of RT – also based on CC is the balance between "free attention" for whatever is happening during the session and attention to oneself. Specifically, this means that every person in the room focuses their attention as much as possible on the process that is currently at the centre of the group's activities. This ensures that the person working can use the structured space without competition and receives a high level of attention from the group. At the same time, everybody directs a certain amount of attention to their own inner processes. If a participant's attention shifts strongly to their own thoughts, emotions, or impulses for action, they can, after a short consultation with the facilitating pair, and with the support of another person, carry out a short process that is referred to as "*Aufmerksamkeitsarbeitszeit*" (attention working time). This process allows a person's attention to the group's activity to be restored by relieving emotions, briefly expressing thoughts, and/or carrying out a short problem-solving action (such as closing a window or putting on a sweater). In this way, all individuals can practise being in constant touch with themselves and taking their needs seriously so that they, in turn, can refocus on the work of others.

Contracts

As in the problem-solving groups of RP, and in EmLit training groups, in RT the cooperative contract – no secrets, no lies, no rescues, no powerplays (see Steiner, 2009; Wyckoff, 1977) – is the basis of cooperation. In addition, RT insists on agreeing a group contract about regular and binding participation in the group. This also implies that each person assumes responsibility for organisational matters as well as for facilitating the RT sessions. The group contract creates clarity and strengthens confidence in the group right from the start. Moreover, in RT, as well as in the former PSGs, individual contacts with regard to self-defined therapeutic goals are being worked on.

Structure of the meetings

Since RT groups are not run by professional therapists, therapeutic group work is based on a clear structure with a differentiated set of rules. The two Start weekends ensure there is a common level of knowledge across the group. The decision to participate in the RT group includes an agreement on shared responsibility for the implementation of the structure and rules as defined by the concept of RT. This mutual commitment replaces the responsibility for and control over therapeutic processes and situations that, in other group therapy settings, falls to a professional leader.

The clearly defined (and time-limited) responsibilities and the regulated structure of the meetings create a secure framework for both the individual and interactive processes in RT. CC techniques as well as methods from RP, PSGs, and TA are integrated within the sessions (see Rauch et al., 1996; Van Velden & Severijnen, 1985).

Radical therapy   139

Check-in

At the beginning of the RT session, each person, one by one, gets a specific amount of time to explicitly focus their attention, to perceive current emotions and thoughts, and to briefly express these (hence the "check-in"). This makes individuals more aware of their current condition and creates transparency within the group about the focus on the "here-and-now".

Goods and news

Following the check-in, each person has the opportunity to focus, with support, on good and new events and developments in their life, to connect with associated positive emotions, to verbalise relevant effects; and, at the same time, to identify their contribution. The point is to ensure that RT is not only about working on distressing topics, but also about creating access to one's sense of joy and about celebrating one's personal development and life as a whole. This exercise strengthens confidence in personal resources and creates a joyful climate of mutual empathy within the group, which counterbalances self-devaluation and negative views of one's own life circumstances.

Working time

In each RT session, a block of time is provided for working on individual topics using co-counselling work and support techniques. This working time usually takes place in front of the group and with the assistance of another person. Every person can address distressing events, life circumstances, and behavioural patterns. According to CC, this also provides a targeted relief of certain emotions. During the Start weekends, participants learn about various models from TA; they are also guided through exercises in self-awareness so that every person in an RT group can systematically fall back on the methods in their working time. As a rule, participants are free to decide on their topics and methods of their working time, provided the general principles of RT are observed.

For instance, a person's working time offers an opportunity to identify the injunctions and attributions associated with difficult issues and to work on the resolution of "pig messages" using the concept of internalised oppression from RP ("the Pig") and the methods of CC. This is about developing new attitudes and permissions, making the appropriate decisions and tackling the difficulties related to their implementation. In line with RP's approach to liberation, a person's working time can help them break through isolation with regard to their own problems (contact) and the obfuscation of oppression (awareness), allowing them eventually to develop and implement problem-solving actions (see Althöfer, 2017).

140 *Luigi (Gino) Althöfer and V. Riesenfeld*

Table 9.1 Radical psychiatry and Radikale Therapie

Radical psychiatry	Radikale Therapie
(Paranoid) fantasies	*Gespinsterunde* (Round of [paranoid] fantasies)
Action/feeling statements	*Grollrunde* (Round of resentments)
Strokes	*Schmuserunde* (Round of strokes)

Fantasies, resentments, and strokes

Each RT session includes three more structural elements called "rounds": a round of checking out paranoid fantasies, a round of resentments, a round of strokes. These elements have their origins in the theory and practice of problem-solving groups from RP; they are also based on the concept of EmLit (see Table 9.1).

Each round has a specific purpose. In addition, the rounds all serve to foster clarity concerning the relationships within the group. In order to ensure a safe framework for the respective processes, RT specifies a number of rules pertaining to these rounds (they are described in the following paragraphs). Each participant pays attention to observing these rules themselves and, if necessary, the facilitating group members intervene.

"Gespinsterunde": *the round of (paranoid) fantasies*

This round offers an opportunity to check fantasies or intuitions that refer to another person in the group – for example about their perception, their thinking, their needs, their intentions. A "*Gespinst*" is to be verbalised clearly and the person addressed is to answer honestly. In this way it is especially possible to clarify "paranoid" fantasies which also burden the relationship with another participant.

In principle, the round of fantasies has the same purpose as similar exercises in PSGs or EmLit. Essentially, it is about training one's intuition and learning to let go of excessive fantasies (or paranoia), especially if the accurate part or aspect is confirmed and not denied. In terms of RP, this round aims to counteract the "alienation from the mind" (Steiner, 1981d) or, in TA terms, the "no mind script" (Steiner, 1974a).

In the PSG and EmLit trainings, the recipients of the fantasy usually respond with full sentences, as a result of which a moderated dialogue often develops. In RT, the recipient only gives a short answer: "Yes", "No", or "Partially".

PERSON A: "I have the fantasy that (in situation x) you were angry with me."
PERSON B: "Yes."

The focus here is on confirming (or not confirming) the "grain of truth" of and in the fantasy; this is why the pertinent part (not the inaccurate part) is formulated in a few words. If necessary, the person receiving the fantasy may ask the one who has initiated this process to reformulate their statement or to provide a

Radical therapy 141

concrete example. Likewise, having received the answer, the initiator may also further reformulate or specify their (paranoid) fantasy to come to a more satisfying clarification. There are a number of other rules or guidelines pertaining to the expression of and response to the "*Gespinst*" or fantasy. The highly ritualised process allows us to clarify the many threads of a single fantasy and helps us to avoid unnecessary discussion and justification(s) (see Rauch et al., 1996; Van Velden & Severijnen, 1985).

"Grollrunde": *the round of resentments*

During the "*Grollrunde*" unpleasant emotions regarding the behaviour of other group participants are made transparent and treated therapeutically. In order to have and maintain a safe frame, this doesn't happen anywhere else during the RT session. At the beginning of the *Grollrunde*, one of the two facilitators asks the group: "Who wants to take advantage of '*Grollschut*' [resentment protection]?", which means not being confronted with resentments in this session. Then one after another, including the facilitators themselves, participants answer with "yes" or "no".

According to CC, the *Grollrunde* is also an explicit space for discharging emotions, and by that to use anger in a therapeutically constructive manner. Here both participants have the personal support (as described above) of someone else. There is a clear structure to ensure the necessary protection for everybody. Different variants of the *Grollrunde* have been established in F*ORT and M*RT groups, as well as for reasons unrelated to the sex/gender division, but, despite the differences, the *Grollrunde* always includes the following questions and steps:

1. What was the situation? What did it trigger in me?
   This involves a brief and factual naming of the trigger situation or the concrete behaviour to which the resentment refers.
2. What did that trigger do for me?
   This involves naming and releasing the emotions that occurred in the context of the situation or that, in retrospect, become present once again.
3. From where do I know this?
   Here, the personal biography and the personal relationship to the underlying issue is worked out or named.
   In some groups (and especially M*RT groups), a fourth step follows:
4. What do I want for our relationship?
   This expresses a wish – regarding the relationship – that shouldn't be an appeal to the other person.

In conclusion, and depending on the particular group practice, the person who had the *Groll* states "I had a *Groll* for you" or "I got rid of my *Groll*", and the person on the receiving end of this work answers with "I heard your *Groll*". Then there is no more direct interaction in regard to this.

142 *Luigi (Gino) Althöfer and V. Riesenfeld*

The processing of a grievance is not about lengthy explanations, so in general three or four minutes are enough. In RT, the attitude is that a *Groll* is welcome as a gift, as it also serves to clarify the relationship, to keep contact free of unspoken emotions, to counteract a hardening in the relationship, thus enabling a higher degree of closeness.

As part of the *Grollrunde*, participants learn to perceive their emotional reactions to certain triggers more consciously and to understand them in the context of their own biographies. This allows them to come into contact with previous injuries and to treat them separately, beyond the *Grollrunde*.

"Schmuserunde": *the round of strokes*

At the end of each RT session, the *Schmuserunde* takes place. This element of RT is designed to break the rules of the stroke economy (see Steiner, 1971c, 1977d). In other words, the five prohibitions – don't give strokes you want to give; don't accept strokes you want; don't reject strokes you don't want; don't ask for strokes you want; don't give yourself strokes – are reversed into explicit permissions. Thus, essentially, this round is about giving strokes, accepting strokes, rejecting strokes, asking for strokes, and giving oneself strokes with the attention of the group. In RT, participants do not express polite gratitude for a stroke. Instead, they take a moment to decide whether it "tastes good" (acceptance) or "doesn't taste good" (rejection), which is then briefly verbalised. Thus, in terms of RP, this round aims to counteract the alienation from the heart, and in TA terms, counters the "no love" script as well as psychological games played to satisfy stroke hunger. The result of this closing round is that participants provide themselves and each other with recognition (strokes according to TA), learning and practising an unrestricted approach to appreciation – a practice they can then integrate into their lives.

The current state of the RT movement in Germany

Today RT groups exist throughout Germany. There have always been certain geographic accumulations, with most groups being based in Berlin. Over the years, RT as a form of therapy has evolved into a self-organised community of people who have practised and appreciated it, either on a temporary or a more long-term basis. Beyond the regular meetings of the individual RT groups, various multi-day nationwide meetings with up to 150 participants (including children) take place throughout the year.

Within the RT movement, there is no formal organisation to prevent concentration of power. Thus, there is – intentionally – no authority to establish binding guidelines. As a result, different practices in terms of session design and the scope, form, and content of the dissemination have been developed and practised over the years. Discussions on the theory and practice of RT are conducted on various occasions and in different constellations.

Many of the people within the RT movement are cis-gender, heterosexual, white, able-bodied; there have been occasions when people with other affiliations experienced discrimination within RT – which leads to the important question as to what mechanisms exist within the RT movement that exclude people and how these can be addressed.

Concluding remarks

Radikale Therapie has existed in Germany for more than 30 years as a non-commercial, self-organised approach and has always been passed on without financial interests by people who identify with the background of RT and have benefited from it themselves. Individual access to RT is free and unbureaucratic. Some alternative communal living projects have also been using RT elements in a non-therapeutic way for their group meetings (see Hillar & Frick, 1996).

Through a reference to RP, participants can examine and address the difficulties they face in their lives in the context of social conditions. RT groups provide many opportunities to work together to develop a shared sensitivity and awareness of oppression. Although RT, with its history and underlying theories, is a political, socio-critical approach, there is no guarantee that the correspondence between "the personal" and "the political" will be considered in individual practice. The structure of RT offers no fixed elements for analysing the influence of social conditions on the participants' individual issues. Generally speaking, moreover, individual decisions to thematise specific issues or not are also obviously influenced by their own position in society. Therefore, it is possible that existing power relations will not be perceived or indeed reflected in RT. In our view it could be a step forward if appropriate exercises were developed and integrated into the regular structure of RT.

Participants in RT groups tend to quickly lose their fear of strong emotions in themselves and others; together they develop a joy in exploring and expressing their emotions and in participating in the emotions of others. In RT, people learn to understand their own needs, to take responsibility for them, to acknowledge others' needs, and to take them seriously.

In RT, profound therapeutic processes are possible without professional therapists. For many participants this practice has a strong empowering effect. Against the background of mutual support, participants in RT groups not only experience themselves in the client role, but from the beginning they also experience being able to support others in working therapeutically on their personal issues. Moreover, shared leadership means that all participants assume responsibility for the group process. In this way, RT creates a therapeutic alliance at an eye-to eye level, and thus promotes mutuality and equality.

In general, the attitudes implemented in the structure and rules of RT lead to sustainable personal development and an expansion of the possibilities available to a person in the way they manage their life and relationships. Thus, RT ultimately also has an effect on the social environment of people who have integrated the RT experience in their lives.

144 *Luigi (Gino) Althöfer and V. Riesenfeld*

Notes

1 This chapter was translated from German, a language in which one word (*Geschlecht*) stands for both sex and gender. The authors see both sex and gender as cultural constructs, hence the English version mostly translates *Geschlecht* as "gender/sex". Furthermore, this translation maintains a strategy developed in the German-speaking feminist context to convey an "open space" for all gender identities, whether male, female, or genderqueer. This so-called "gender star" (*Gendersternchen*) is an asterisk (*) added to words – including supposedly unambiguous ones such as female*, man*, trans* and queer* – in an attempt to question the dominant binary norm of sex/gender and also to mark it visually. All references to persons of a given sex/gender pertain to persons who assign themselves to the respective sex/gender. Finally, the singular "they" is used even when the presumed sex/gender of a person is known, thus: "Every woman* in the group is free to work on their issues."

- Translator's note.

2 The distinction between FORT and F*ORT is as follows: FORT without an asterisk refers to the groups in the Netherlands where the "F" stands for "Feminists"; F*ORT with the asterisk or gender star (see endnote above) refers to the groups practiced in the Germany as the "F" here stands for "Frauen" (women*). Also, while the "O" in FORT stands for the Dutch word "Oefengroepen" (exercise groups), the "O" in F*ORT stands for the German word "organisieren" (organised).

CINCO
Power

10 Confessions of a psychomechanic

Excerpts on power

Claude Steiner

Following my mother-derived predilections, I had been working as a counselor at the Jewish Community Center Summer Camp of which I eventually became the Director. This is where I got my first taste of leadership and the power associated with it, and my success inspired me to pursue my mother's vocation as a teacher and people-person.

...

One thing I do remember that made a profound impression on me was a conversation in which I revealed that I fantasized pursuing, and having sex with other women. Andy [Claude's therapist at the time] remarked, rather casually: "Well you're a grown up, that's up to you" which I took as permission to have extramarital affairs. That simple statement had a very powerful effect on me as it cleared me of any inhibitions regarding infidelity that I might have had. The realization of my therapist's statement [of] power led me later to write about the potency of therapeutic permission and how forceful (beneficial or harmful) a therapist's assertions can be [Steiner, 1968b].

...

The Pig Parent

An essential part of this worldview was the concept of the Pig Parent, the internal enforcer of all of the oppressive behaviors with which people manipulated and messed each other up. We called it the Pig Parent in honor of the policemen that were bashing heads in the Berkeley and Oakland streets who we called "pigs."

We saw the "nuclear family" that dominated the American scene as the source of all troubles. Jerry Rubin had written a book called *Kill Your Parents*[1] and one of our slogans was "Detonate the nuclear family." We were being provocative with these pronouncements and there was immediate negative reaction by some about the Pig Parent terminology. When my mother first read about it, to my great shock, she thought I was referring to her. So, we began to call it internalized oppression, the Enemy or the Inner Critic, but we did believe that parental oppression was the source of much emotional difficulty and that it was the Critical Pig Parent (as opposed to the Nurturing Parent; both concepts derived from TA) that was largely to blame.

148 *Claude Steiner*

The Pig Parent stood for long distance control by means of internalized oppression, the way in which people incorporated all the oppressive messages in their lives and not only applied them to themselves but also to others.

The phenomenon we called the Pig, Internal Critic or Critical Parent has been called by as many names as the Devil himself;[2] low self-esteem, the enemy, self-hatred, stinking thinking, negative self-talk, catastrophic expectations, the punitive protector, internalized oppression, the harsh superego to name a few.

Every personality theory has recognized this near universal phenomenon; that inner voice that tells us, in whispers or shouts, in good times and bad, from childhood to old age, when we are doing well or when we are doing badly, over and over, that we are in some way not OK. This may not seem to be part of the typical personal awareness and some people hate to admit that it is an experience they have. But many are surprised, when the Critical Parent is explained, to find how widely it controls their lives and how in most cases people agree with these critical judgments.

The basic message of the Critical Parent is: "You Are Not OK!" Specifically:

You are bad (sinful, lazy, wicked, etc.)
You are ugly (ugly face, ugly body, etc.)
You are crazy (mentally, emotionally, irrational, out of control, etc.)
You are stupid (retarded, can't think straight, confused, etc.)
You are doomed (ill, hopeless, self-destructive, etc.)

All of this boils down to: you will not be loved and in the end, you will be excluded from the tribe. Being excluded from the tribe's warm womb, left out in the snow to die is a primal threat that is very effective in making sure that people remain under control. This is the way people have been kept in line for as long as we have been herd animals.

The Pig or Critical Parent starts in our past fed to us by important people in our lives whose critical assertions are eventually incorporated which is why we also called it internalized oppression in radical psychiatry. The inner voice of the Pig Parent presents itself as our friend, doing what it does only to help us. However the truth is that its constant presence in our life effectively diminishes it for most of us, ruins it for many others and undercuts our capacity to succeed and be productive for all of us. The good news is that, since it has an external source, we can remove it as an influence in our lives.

The Critical Parent's role in relation to strokes is to enforce the rules of the stroke Economy and to prevent people from loving themselves or each other.

In my own case over the years until I threw it over it interfered with me being able to give, but also to accept strokes. I literally heard a voice in my head; when someone was "overly" expressive in their loving feelings I would hear "Perhaps you should be careful; if you accept all this you may be expected to reciprocate somehow."

If I felt the desire to give strokes there were all sorts of voices; "You may seem too needy," "If you give now you may be committing to endless giving later,"

Excerpts on power 149

"You'll come across as a phony" or, ironically "Why did it take you so long to do this? You are a day late and a dollar short."

This is how the Pig Parent accomplishes its purpose; by telling us that what we feel is stupid, wicked, crazy or ill timed. It renders us unable to know what we feel and why. It prevents us from caring about or understanding how others feel and therefore prevents us from fully loving others or ourselves.

To a larger or lesser extent, some form of the Critical Parent plagues most of us. By the time, in my late fifties, that I rid myself of stroke economy messages I began to be subjected to negative old-age messages. Reinforced by television programs and ads that denigrate old age, that pesky voice in my head started to harass me on a wholly new venue; "You forgot again, you must be getting senile," or "No one is interested in your old-fashioned opinions," or bluntly "You are old and ugly." I am not alone in this; lately in the US, in addition to the pervasive ageist prejudice, self-hatred based on being ugly or fat, or any combination of the three, repeatedly emphasized by the media and advertisement, is becoming endemic.

These internal voices or points of view devalue us, interfere with our thinking and prevent us from acting in our own interest. The only way to counteract them is with loving strokes from others or from the internal antagonist of the Inner Critic, the Nurturing Parent; in the form of self-strokes.

Over the years our theory of cooperation and its components – No power plays, No lies, no Rescues, zero Pig Parent tolerance – was thoroughly tested and accepted. We took on the premise that, in order to fully live out our potential for health, love and mutual responsibility, it was necessary that we relate to each other without power plays and most importantly excluding the Critical Parent from our transactions. No power plays included no lies; not speaking untruth and not hiding the truth. That implied that we truthfully asked for everything we wanted and did only what we wanted to do and ignore the Critical Parent's attempts to influence us.

...

The Other Side of Power

Transactional Analysis as conceived by Berne focused on transactions between people but it did not pay particular attention to the relative power of the participants. But my nascent interest in politics especially politics in the personal realm forced me to pay attention to the power issues imbedded in transactions. Berne defined games as a sequence of transactions with a beginning, an end and a payoff. The payoff had several aspects, the most important of which were the procurement of strokes and the reiteration of existential positions. For instance, when Hogie and I played the game of "Uproar" we both got needed strokes. In addition, each one of us was reasserting our interlaced existential narratives; Hogie playing out her victimized underprivileged neediness, *vis-a-vis* my privileged, controlling, withholding. Every time we played Uproar, which we did regularly, we reinforced our and the other's existential positions.

However, the concept of games did not adequately consider the additional payoff of the power struggles that occur between people. During the late 70s I wrote my

150   *Claude Steiner*

third book, *The Other Side of Power* [Steiner, 1981e] in which I explored power, power abuse and the many controlling, competitive power plays that people use to get what they want. My interest in power abuse originated specifically in my relationship with Hogie and in the relationships between men and women; the power plays men used to abuse their power with women, prevent women from becoming powerful in their own right and also how women retaliated in this power struggle with their own guerrilla power plays.

In my analysis of power, I concluded that power was a good thing to have. In those days of reaction against wholesale power abuse, seeking power was considered politically incorrect; men were supposed to hold back their power and wound up castrating themselves. I argued that men's power was a good thing and while it should not be abused it should be used, shared and given up; a quaint notion regarded with suspicion by feminist women who were weary of men and did not believe that they would willingly give up anything, let alone power or the abuse of it.

I thought of myself as a feminist man; [a] feminist as Carmen defined feminism [i.e.,] loving women. I wrote a paper "Feminism for Men" [originally published in two articles: Steiner, 1977c, 1978b] in which I espoused the view that feminist men who loved women needed to keep their own power while doing everything in their power to facilitate women's power; allowing them to become powerful and equal, mostly by staying out of their way.

Power, which I defined as the capacity to produce desired change or prevent undesired change was a human potential, which came in a variety of forms. The form of power that everyone seemed to seek or reject was the power of control and we lived, I argued, in a society that was overrun by control, power plays and competition. I defined power plays as transactions that have the purpose of dominating another person; causing them to do something they don't want to do, or conversely preventing them from doing what they did want to do.

I argued that in addition to the power of Control there were six other sources of power – the other side of power – which were equally effective as control in bringing about change; centering, passion, love, communication, wisdom and transcendence. These six sources of power can be developed as an alternative to control.

Nothing influenced me as decisively regarding the control power issue – between men and women – as several role reversals, which I underwent with Hogie. One, which I write about in the book, was a date with Hogie in which at her suggestion we completely reversed roles with her playing a sexy aggressive male and me playing a compliant woman.

To make a long story short, during a couple of hours I sat in the passenger seat of my TR-4 exposed to her aggressive handling of the ride, walked down the sidewalk while she held my arm and stopped to window shop and decided when and which way to proceed and how to cross the street, had an increasingly uncomfortable meal in which she most graciously suggested the menu, ordered the meal and paid the bill. When she eventually led me to the bedroom, I was not able to muster an erection.

Excerpts on power   151

On another, this time unintended, role reversal when doing a workshop on power in Australia – where men are men and women are women – I was accosted by a couple of not too attractive women who competed over me and pressed me into dancing with them while I, out of stunned politeness, reluctantly went along. Similarly, a few years later during my break up with Hogie when I let on that I was looking for a partner I experienced being aggressively sexually pursued in a manner that reminded me of my own pursuits and suddenly, finally made my own abuses of power with women painfully clear.

My interest in power relations between men and women quickly generalized to all categories of oppressors and oppressed. Racism, class oppression, homophobia, ageism (the oppression of the young and old by the middle aged), coupleism (the oppression of singles by couples), oppression of the disabled by the temporarily able, of the fat by the thin, the sick by the healthy, the mentally ill by the sane and so on.

In those days of liberation ideology, a ditty written by Fritz Perls became the dominant prayer of the human potential movement:

> I do my thing, and you do your thing.
> I am not in this world to live up to your expectations
> And you are not in this world to live up to mine.
> You are you and I am I, if by chance we find each other, it's beautiful.
> If not, it can't be helped.
>
> [Perls, 1969]

I believe that with his poem, Perls was trying to help people rid themselves of the excessive and guilt-based demands that people often make on themselves and each other. However, what he wrote became vulgarized into a call for emotional and political irresponsibility. In essence, it supported the belief that we are not responsible for each other and for the oppression that affects others.

I was so disturbed by the misguided implications in Perls' poem that I wrote a response to it:

> If I do my thing and you do your thing
> And if we don't live up to each other's expectations
> We might live but the world will not survive.
> You are you, and I am I,
> and together, joining hands, not by chance,
> We will find each other beautiful.
> If not, we can't be helped.
>
> [Steiner, 2003a/2003c, p. 85][3]

With *The Other Side of Power* I found my political legs. As an alternative to power abuse and oppression I offered cooperation: instead of competing and power playing for what we need we could use a cooperative approach. Basically, the idea was that in order for people to be able to cooperate all that was needed was to prevent power plays, lying and Rescuing among them. This belief was based on

152 *Claude Steiner*

the premise that if we want something from another person we have two choices. We can try to force compliance with power plays or we can engage in a cooperative negotiation in which both of us ask for 100% of what we want and work for a mutually satisfactory outcome.

These ideas led to the cooperative contract that we decided would be the basis for our relationships:

No power plays. Ask for everything you want 100% of the time and don't do anything you don't want to do. Look out for and especially avoid lies and secrets, and Rescues.

At the same time that I was developing these ideas, Michel Foucault was examining power issues in the arena of mental illness but from a different perspective [Foucault, 2006]. He analyzed the way in which people who deviate from normality are made powerless and kept powerless. His investigations thoroughly supported our views regarding oppression and mystification.

This sort of discourse led inevitably to politics. Starting at a personal level it reached into abuse at the governmental and corporate level. It included the Vietnam war and Nixon's attempts to subvert the Constitution. Starting with feminism we became revolutionaries.

The Other Side of Power was translated into several languages but failed to make an impression in the United Sates. The political Right was beginning to take a hold and Reagan was elected president. In the past when I went on the radio and television to speak about my books there had been universal acceptance. Now I encountered hostility and invective by people who heard my message as an attack on the American way of life which it, in a way, was. The book did not do well in the US and quickly went out of print, but it is still in print in Germany and France and it was reissued in Russia in 2002 in an updated edition. Withal, I believe that it is my most important work.

...

Propaganda

My trips to Nicaragua were motivated by my liberal political interest in matters Latin American but also by my interest in power plays which led me to the subtlest of all psychological power plays; propaganda. Reagan's White House propaganda about Central America especially the revolutionary Sandinista government and the US funded counterrevolutionaries – the contras – was impressive and depressing. After returning from Nicaragua – my interest in propaganda heightened – I had the opportunity to join the editorial staff of the nascent *Propaganda Review* quarterly (see http://powerbase.info/index.php/Propaganda_Review). For the following two years I was deeply involved in the study of propaganda, writing for the PR and eventually, with Charles Rappleye, developed what we called a "wave theory of propaganda" which outlined the ebb and flow of propaganda's effectiveness the elements of which have since been repeatedly confirmed (Steiner & Rappleye, 1989).

Briefly this theory postulated that the success of propaganda is cyclic; if it is effective it builds irresistibly and manages to massively affect public opinion but

Excerpts on power 153

eventually, following a period of arrogance and hubris inevitably collapses, as it did with Hitler and Stalin, and in lesser catastrophes with Nixon, Reagan and George W. Bush. The inevitable collapse of propaganda no matter how successful it may once have been, depends, in some measure, on the effectiveness of the media to debunk its lies. After every propaganda collapse, the public is refractory to further manipulation for a period of time. And then the cycle repeats itself.

In the pursuit of the mysteries of propaganda's damnable successes I had also traveled to France where, with my bother Miguel as translator, I interviewed Jacques Ellul, a renowned Marxist/Christian philosopher of technique and propaganda, 80 years old at the time (Steiner & Rappleye, 1988). Returning to the US, in characteristic stubborn manner I pushed for publication of my interview and fell in heavy disfavor with Marcy Darnowsky, one of the original members of the group, who objected to Ellul's Christianity and rejection of communism. Eventually at an editorial meeting in my living room, Marcy faced the group with a choice: "It is either Claude or me." She complained about my style and attitude, but she seemed to have other more covert motives among which, I suspect, the fact that I had made a couple of subtle passes at her. In any case, to her consternation, the group refused to respond to her power play and so she left the group.

Largely on my initiative we planned a national propaganda conference "Propaganda and Postmodernism" for the Fall of 1989 which was a surprising success attracting about 200 people and various very interesting speakers from around the country. The magazine was doing very well, we even began to receive journalism awards and were planning a second conference "Propaganda After the (Berlin) Wall." but we weren't making ends meet and eventually the volunteers, one by one, burned out and fell by the wayside with Johan Carlisle who had been the magazine's tireless managing editor and desktop publisher, hanging on to the bitter end. After almost three years and eight issues, *Propaganda Review* shut its doors. While we were failing to raise any funds and going out of business, the American Right was feeding hundreds of millions of dollars into similar [though] conservative publications, conferences and think-tanks thereby allowing them to continue their work while we withered away. As we twisted in the wind and eventually expired, the Right was on the march, the first Iraq war was won, and the seeds were sown for the second, this time disastrous, superbly propagandized, eventually collapsed, neo-conservative debacle.

Notes

1 This wasn't a book but something Jerry Rubin said in a number of speeches, for instance, "Until you're prepared to kill your parents, you're not really prepared to change the country because our parents are our first oppressors." In 1970, Rubin addressed a meeting of 1,500 students at Kent State University (a month before the shootings on 4th May). The *Akron Beacon Journal* reported Rubin as saying:

> Until you people are prepared to kill your parents you aren't ready for the revolution ... The American school system will be ended in two years. We are going to bring it down. Quit being students. Become criminals. We have to disrupt every

154 *Claude Steiner*

situation and break every law … Do you people want a diploma or to take this school over and use it for your own purposes? … It's quiet here now but things are going to start again.

2 Claude wrote a piece about the inner critic titled "Pleased to meet you, hope you guess my name", published on his website (Steiner, 2011).

3 Claude wrote about responding to Perls' poem in 1972 but gave no specific reference to where this was published. He did reproduce it in his book *Emotional Literacy: Intelligence with a Heart* (Steiner, 2003a). Another colleague also responded to Perls' individualism with another poem:

> If I just do my thing and you do yours,
> We stand in danger of losing each other
> And ourselves.
> I am not in this world to live up to your expectations:
> But I am in this world to confirm you
> As a unique human being,
> And to be confirmed by you.
> We are fully ourselves only in relation to each other;
> The I detached from a thou
> Disintegrates.
> I do not find you by chance; I find you by an active life
> Of reaching out.
> Rather than passively letting things happen to me:
> I act intentionally to make them happen.
> I must begin with myself, true;
> But I must not end with myself:
> The truth begins with two.

(Tubbs, 1972, p. 5)

11 On power

Luigi (Gino) Althöfer and Keith Tudor

From a critical perspective on therapy and, not least, in radical psychiatry (RP) (see Chapters 8 and 9), the issue and question of power is of central concern; as Steiner (1988d) himself put it: "Power is at the core of the concepts of Radical Psychiatry" (p. 11). This perspective is not unique to RP, and, for example, was addressed by Guggenbühl-Craig (1971), a contemporary of Steiner and other radical psychiatrists. Nevertheless, Steiner placed power at the centre of his analysis, both transactional and social/political, and, in doing so, made a major contribution to thinking about power in psychotherapy, a contribution that has been recognised and acknowledged by other writers and practitioners who focus on power such as Totton (2000).

This chapter reviews and considers Claude Steiner's contributions to the concept of power, from his early writings on the subject in *Issues in Radical Therapy*, through the negative manifestation of oppressive power as the "Pig Parent" (Steiner, 1978e, 1979d), to his later work on *The Other Side of Power* (Steiner, 1981e), and identification of different sources of power (Steiner, 1981e, 1987). Although Claude's ideas about power developed and also changed over time and, therefore, in a certain, chronological order, in this review we consider his ideas in a different, logical sequence, that is from his ideas about power as control, including the abuse of power and power plays (the methodology and method of power), through his work on different sources of power (which represent a different ontology of power); through the analysis of power imbalances (the aetiology of power, as it were); to power and responsibility, including how this is manifested as therapeutic potency (i.e., a different method).

From the excerpts on power in Claude's own *Confessions* (in Chapter 10), we identify a number of themes – i.e., leadership and power; power and therapeutic potency; power and oppression and, specifically, internalised oppression; power and transactions; and cooperation – some of which we refer to in this chapter. Finally, as part of this review, we also offer some critique of his theories – Claude would have expected no less!

156 *Luigi (Gino) Althöfer and Keith Tudor*

Power as control

Steiner among others described power in terms of control over others, that is, "the capacity to cause people to do things" (Steiner, 1974a, p. 253) and – with reference to the science of physics – "as the capacity to overcome and move against the resistance of an opposing force" (Steiner, 1975e, p. 10). He gave examples of using not only physical power but also menacing behaviour over others, as well as using convincing arguments from an intellectual superior position, and attractiveness or personal magnetism as tools to control others. From a critical perspective, Steiner described the exploitative, abusive, and oppressive use of power, putting these phenomena in the context of the general values of capitalist society (Steiner, 1974a, 1981d, 1981e, 1988d, 2009). He analysed different forms and aspects of power plays (Steiner, 1974a, 1981e) and developed strategies to resist power plays, that is to avoid being controlled (Steiner, 1981e). In the alienation theory of RP the fact of oppression (as an abuse of power) is of essential importance and the aim of the therapeutic work is to get awareness about oppression and get into action against internalised as well as factual existing oppression (Steiner, 1981d, 1988d).

> My opinion is that power is, per se, good. We need power, we want power, we deserve power. But power also corrupts and in order to have power without abusing it and oppressing others, we need to understand for what it is, how it operates, how it is accumulated, how it is shared and how it is given up. We need to understand which expressions of power are harmful to ourselves and others and which are beneficial.
>
> (Steiner, 1975e, pp. 9–10)

Although, over some 50 years, Steiner critiqued the destructive use of power in terms of control, in his view "power can be good or bad depending on whether it is abused to oppress or mystify, or whether it is used to liberate" (Steiner, 1975e, p. 7).

In the context of power sources Steiner named the power of control explicitly as one of the seven sources of power (Steiner, 1988d, 2009), and described control primarily in a positive manner as a capacity to change things, and to resist oppression, as well as people having self-control with regard to their own bodies and behaviour. In any case, Steiner strictly rejected the use of control as an unethical domination of others, and recommended that people who are hungry for the power of control should consciously give up control and develop access to other personal power sources in order to make use of them and to live in a more cooperative and liberated way. He described the widespread aspiration for the power of control as a person's compensation for powerlessness in other respects or aspects of their life (Steiner, 1974a, 1981d, 1981e, 1988a, 2009). In the context of RP (Steiner 1975i, Steiner, 1981d) as well as in the context of transactional analysis (TA) (Steiner, 1974a), he identified powerlessness as an important reason for playing games, for instance, in terms of the roles in the drama triangle, of Persecutor, Rescuer, and Victim (Karpman, 1968).

Relational power

In the context of his work about scripts Steiner pointed out the phenomenon of destructive power dynamics inside families, especially the essential influence to the script-building process of children, who are, in different ways, in an inferior power position with regard to their parents, expressing this in the hierarchical diagram of the original script matrix (Steiner, 1966; Figure 11.1).

As he himself later reflected:

> The script matrix showed the parents above and the child below, thus realistically representing a dimension that goes beyond the transactional into the realm of power or the relative capacity of the players to affect each other (with the offspring at an obvious disadvantage). I saw clearly for the first time that the young child is in the classic position of the oppressed: not totally powerless, but one-down in relation to the parents who are one-up.
>
> (Steiner, 1988a, p. 20)

Steiner understood relational power not only as an issue between children and adults. In his view every relationship is shaped by a particular power relation, influenced by numerous aspects such as: who has what possibilities to express and take care of their own needs? Who has what options and to what extent are they (in)dependent from the other(s)? Based on this understanding, Steiner analysed what happens between people in terms of power, and focused on the goal of creating cooperative relationships. His interest in politics and, specifically,

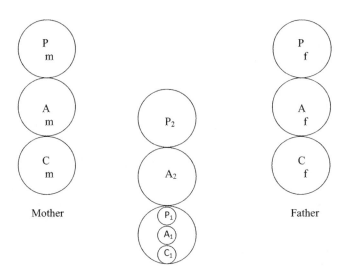

Figure 11.1 The script matrix (from Steiner, 1966)

158   *Luigi (Gino) Althöfer and Keith Tudor*

personal politics "forced me", as he put it, "to pay attention to the power issues imbedded [*sic*] in transactions" (*Confessions*, Chapter 10, p. 149), and, indeed, he went on to write that "every transaction has political consequences, every message has a meta-communication, a message about the message" (Steiner, 1981e, p. 171). Furthermore, Steiner brought to TA, which, generally, had a more individual(istic) view on relations, a more political dimension of structured and manifested power imbalances between individuals as well as in society at large.

Social imbalances of power

In Steiner's view, power imbalances are maintained by means of different social standings and/or power in the light of the position in relation to others, whether cultural, structural, and/or competitive. As Claude himself put it: "The acceptance of power imbalances and power abuses is drilled into us through hierarchies and competition, both of which are as American as apple pie" (Steiner, 1988d, p. 14). Moreover, Steiner emphasised the reality of a competitive world in which power is "unevenly distributed among people so that some have more and others have less" (Steiner, 1974a, p. 253). For example, he addressed the issues of "Male Supremacy in Psychiatry", "Class Analysis and Power", as well as "Power and Competition in the Movement" (Steiner, 1975e). Influenced no doubt by his reading of Karl Marx and Wilhelm Reich, and, more, by his exposure to some of the social movements of the 1960s and 1970s, especially feminism, as he put it:

> My interest in power relations between men and women quickly generalized to all categories of oppressors and oppressed. Racism, class oppression, homophobia, ageism (the oppression of the young and old by the middle aged), coupleism (the oppression of singles by couples), oppression of the disabled by the temporarily able, of the fat by the thin, the sick by the healthy, the mentally ill by the sane and so on.
>
> (Chapter 10, p. 151)

Manifestation of oppressive power: the Pig Parent

The abuse of relational power as well as power imbalances in society – in Steiner's view, and we agree – have various oppressive effects, in particular on those who deviate from certain social norms or people with structural disadvantages. As a consequence, at the psychological level this oppression leads to self-deprecation and, in TA terms, to the belief of being "not OK".

An important concept that Steiner and others in the RP movement developed was the "Pig Parent". As Steiner pointed out, "the Pig is the street name for the more academically and theoretically correct concept of Internalized Oppression" (Steiner, 1988e, p. 49). The concept of the Pig Parent was based on the TA concept of the Critical Parent. The difference between these two Parents

On power   159

is that the use of term "Pig Parent" acknowledged – and, we would argue, still acknowledges – the social dimension of power and, thus, focuses on the context of oppression:

> An essential part of this worldview was the concept of the Pig Parent, the internal enforcer of all of the oppressive behaviors with which people manipulated and messed each other up. We called it the Pig Parent in honor of the policemen that were bashing heads in the Berkeley and Oakland streets who we called "pigs." ... The Pig Parent stood for long distance control by means of internalized oppression, the way in which people incorporated all the oppressive messages in their lives and not only applied them to themselves but also to others.
>
> (Chapter 10, p. 147)

In the context of the RP movement, Steiner and others developed exercises to develop more awareness of the internal dialogue we have with the Pig Parent and thus to liberate ourselves from internalised oppression, a process also referred to as "offing the Pig" (see Rabenold 1988; Steiner, 1978e, 1988e, 2009; Wyckoff, 1975a).

Sources of power

Alongside his view of power as about control *over* another, Steiner was also developing a perspective about power as *for* everyone. Contrary to a number of theorists and commentators at the time, Steiner argued that power was a good thing to have; made a clear distinction between positive power and the abuse of power; and, therefore, between the desirability of power for good.

Still operating within the context of RP and its theory of alienation, Steiner developed different concepts of personal power sources. Especially in the early model of power sources, Steiner proposed that everybody should have as much power as possible and thus power has a positive meaning of capacities that ensure self-efficacy. As he put it:

> People are, by their nature, capable of living in harmony with themselves, each other, and their environment. To the extent that they succeed in this ideal, they feel, and are, powerful; to the extent that they fail, they are alienated.
>
> (Steiner, 1981d, p. 727)

In some of his writing on alienation, including the formula for alienation and liberation, Steiner referred to the opposite of alienation as "power" or "power in the world" instead of the more established term "liberation" (Roy, 1988c; Steiner, 1981d).

Steiner originally mentioned the sources of power in the RP literature to define and describe basic human potentials that people lose through alienation. Furthermore, he linked these ideas about sources of power and alienation and to the three

160   *Luigi (Gino) Althöfer and Keith Tudor*

basic life scripts of TA theory: loveless, mindless, and joyless. In later publications, Steiner named other categories of the power sources and, moreover, no longer linked them to alienation or to script theory. In this way, we think that the original overall context of the sources of power (with regard to alienation as well as to script theory) has been lost. Here we trace and comment on this development and the resulting theoretical inconsistency.

Four sources of power

In his chapter on "Radical Psychiatry" (Steiner, 1981d) for a *Handbook on Innovative Psychotherapies* (Corsini, 1981), Steiner denoted being "powerful" as referring to having access to certain human potential(s). He explicitly named four sources of power – "our hearts, our minds, our hands, and our bodies" (ibid., p. 727) – though, as he later explained that the body has a multiple meaning and includes our emotions, this may be taken as a fifth source. The (re)sources mentioned here in the context of alienation theory are viewed from an exclusively positive perspective and do not carry any negative connotation (Steiner, 1981d).

Steiner went on to describe how the power of people gets lost: "People's potentials are realized according to the conditions that they are born into and continue to find during their lives" (ibid., p. 727). In this context, the alienation theory developed by those involved in RP is of particular importance, that is, Alienation = Oppression + Mystification + Isolation (Steiner, 1981d).

Based on this theory of sources of power, Wyckoff and Steiner (1971) had already identified the four corresponding forms of alienation, that is, from the heart, mind, hands, and body, as a result of oppression (of the respective potentials), plus mystification (of the oppression), plus isolation (in respect of the outcome of the oppression and its mystification). Furthermore, Steiner had linked these ideas about alienation to script theory by assigning "the three basic life scripts" (Steiner, 1974a, p. 90) to the three forms of alienation (Steiner, 1981d; Steiner & Wyckoff, 1975), though he offered no script form that corresponds to alienation from hands (see Table 11.1).

Furthermore, in Steiner's theory, the three basic life scripts which, respectively, represent all forms of alienation, are also related to the personal power in the sense of control (see above). As Steiner (1974a) put it in his introduction to the banal scripting of powerlessness:

> Scripting robs people of their autonomy. The more thorough the scripting, the less control the person has over his [or her] life and the more he [or she] feels powerless. When feeling powerless people can't think, can't express themselves, can't work or study, can't enjoy themselves, can't stop smoking or drinking, can't wake up in the morning or go to sleep at night, can't cry or can't stop crying. Some people feel constantly utterly powerless; others only at certain times.
>
> (p. 146)

Table 11.1 Sources of power and their correlation to alienation and the three basic life scripts (based on Steiner, 1974a, 1981d; Steiner & Wyckoff, 1975)

Power source	Capacity	Form of alienation	Basic life scripts (types)	Underlying life script	Effects
Heart	To love	From love	Loveless		Depression
Mind	To think	From mind	Mindless		Madness
Body	To be in contact with one's body and emotions	From body and emotions	Joyless	Powerlessness	Addiction
Work	To be productive and creative in a satisfying way	From work	(No script defined)		Perceived senselessness of one's own work

Of course, every form of alienation, and, therefore, basic life script, is a manifestation of powerlessness. As Steiner himself put it, in one of his last books, *The Heart of the Matter*, "the ultimate manifestation of scarcity of human resources is the scarcity of power itself" (Steiner, 2009, p. 76), felt and expressed as powerlessness. According to Steiner, this lack of power in the sense of control causes people to play games, for instance, in the various roles of the drama triangle.

In the context of his commitment to radical psychiatry, Steiner focused more on the repressive conditions in society, while, in the context of TA, he focused more on the relational and internal process of the individual. However, in order to understand Steiner's contribution to RP and to TA, and, indeed, to emotional literacy (EmLit), we must appreciate that these different perspectives belong together (see also Chapter 17). In Steiner's understanding, script and scripting is always about alienation. As practitioners who identify with both traditions, we have found it both interesting and somewhat upsetting to realise how, in TA, script theory is taught without reference to its political underpinning. When we have discussed the interplay between RP and TA with the surviving members of the original RP group in San Francisco, they talk about having been taught and understanding the drama triangle (Karpman, 1971) as a political tool for confronting oppression and internalised oppression – and can't imagine how these aspects of TA theory can be taught without the politics. As Steiner put it, as early as 1971, "everything diagnosed psychiatrically, unless clearly organic in origin, is a form of alienation" (Steiner, 1971d, p. 5). Consequently, in the practice of RP, the stated aim was always to overcome alienation and to reclaim access to power.

From our point of view, Steiner's idea of the power sources, as a model for natural, human potentials, and their correlation to alienation and script theory, describe in a comprehensible and comprehensive way, what inherent (re)sources people have, as well as how they lose access to them under the primary influence of oppression. We welcome the underlying radical understanding of personality development and psychotherapy as well as the therapeutic aim to reclaim alienated power.

162 Luigi (Gino) Althöfer and Keith Tudor

Seven sources of power

In later publications and based on the Kundalini yoga concept of chakras, Steiner presented seven sources of power (Steiner, 1988d, 2003c, 2009; Steiner & Perry, 1997; also see Chapter 15), declaring as seven sources of "non-abusive" (Steiner, 2003c) or "heart-centered" (Steiner, 2009) power as an "alternative to authority" (Steiner, 1988d), thus (from Steiner & Perry, 1997):

1. Balance (referred to as "grounding" in Steiner, 1988d);
2. Passion;
3. Control;
4. Love;
5. Communication;
6. Information ("knowledge" in Steiner, 1988d);
7. Transcendence.

From 1988 Steiner changed the benchmark of the term "sources of power": "These seven power sources, of which control is just one, better represent the rainbow of options which is power than the colorless, unidimensional based solely on control" (Steiner, 1988d, p. 21). The sources mentioned here correspond neither to the forms of alienation, nor to the three basic forms of script. This model of power sources now stands more or less alone, separated from any theory of alienation and from script theory. The sources of power primarily illustrate a concept of different power aspects, which, according to yoga and to Steiner, people should develop and use in an appropriate way. Furthermore, the power sources no longer stand for generally positive potentials as in the earlier theory of power sources. Depending on the intensity of development, these power sources are now ascribed positive and negative effects (Steiner, 1988d, 2003c, 2009; Steiner & Perry, 1997). The goal is no longer to reclaim access to alienated power sources, but to reach a "happy medium" with regard to each power source (Steiner, 2003c, p. 213). Steiner's way of thinking about the potential and personality of human beings has fundamentally changed.

In this new schema, the fact that people lose access to their potentials through alienation is not considered to be a problem anymore. The problem now is viewed as being the under or over-development of potentials in terms of personality characteristics; and there is no longer any connection between the development of the power sources and the experience of oppression, mystification, or isolation. There is no analysis to explain under which concrete influences people develop and use their potentials and under which influences they do not; and there is no link to any therapeutic approach that addresses the use or development of these seven sources of power. We both had the good fortune to attend an invitational workshop (which all of us knew would be his last), which took place at his ranch in Ukiah, California, in July 2016. During the workshop, the participants had the opportunity to discuss a number of theoretical points with Claude, and, while we two each and both still draw on the concept of alienation, it was clear that Claude was less concerned about this – and, indeed, he said so explicitly.

Reflection on and critique of the seven sources of power

Given our continued and continuing interest in and valuing of the concept and reality of alienation and power, and, while recognising that the potentials of human beings can be considered and categorised in different ways, we identify four points of critique of the seven sources of power:

1. Conceptual. When anyone changes a theory, for instance, by adding to it, there are implications for other parts of that theory, as well as adjacent theories, in this case, of alienation (RP) and of script (TA). Thus, in order to maintain the integrity of the new theory, when Steiner changed the model (from four or five to seven sources of power), then, we think he should have also changed the forms of alienation and the types of script, accordingly. In this sense, we are critical of Steiner's lack of interest in the conceptual aspect of the theory of power, a lack of which is somewhat surprising given his comment about meta-communication (see above, p. 158).
2. Theoretical. Furthermore, we disagree with the way of thinking about the potential of human beings in the seven sources model. In our understanding, a power source in terms of a resource represents something fundamentally positive, although the fixation on a certain resource can be quite problematic in coping with life. However, there is no inevitable connection between the quantitative development of a resource and its fixation. Here different aspects are mixed in an undifferentiated way. To take one example, in the context of the power source of "Love", Steiner concluded: "If this power is overdeveloped, you will be a habitual Rescuer, driven to excessive sacrifices for others while neglecting yourself" (Steiner, 2003c, p. 214). We think it is somewhat abstruse to evaluate Rescuing as an overdevelopment of love!
3. Political. The seven sources model is completely apolitical. Steiner did not explain how the sources develop or are influenced or the psychological origins or political context(s) of these sources. In this respect, we consider the change of the model – from four or five sources based on a theory of alienation to seven sources based on a theory of chakras – as retrogressive, both psychologically and politically.
4. Practical. When discussing these sources and the model, Steiner, strangely, was not clear about their/its practical application. Neither RP nor EmLit, which also refer to these seven sources of power, discuss how to work therapeutically with these sources and, in that sense, the model has no practical relevance.

Cooperation as collective power

In addition to the four sources of power, Steiner (1981d) also named "collective power", which he described as "people's capacity to live, love, and work together" (p. 729). This, in effect, refers to different forms of cooperation which Steiner and others from the RP movement tried to practise and develop in various areas of their lives as a counter-model against individualism, competition, and power plays (see Steiner, 1980a).

164   *Luigi (Gino) Althöfer and Keith Tudor*

Promoting cooperation, some of the RP activists – as Claude and Hogie did – lived in social communities; practised free love in omnigamous relationships; worked and organised in collectives; and, in general, attempted to create relationships based on equality, honesty, and mutual consent. Drawing on his earlier work in TA on contracts, Steiner and others, including Hogie Wyckoff and Bob Schwebel (see Chapter 8) defined the cooperative contract as one which:

> specifically defines a relationship in which everyone has equal rights and which is free of (1) power plays, (2) lies and secrets, and (3) Rescues ... By not using power plays we mean that we do not coerce others into doing what they would not otherwise do.
>
> (Steiner, 1981d, p. 731)

Most people who worked with Claude saw this in action and, for all his faults, he was committed to cooperation (Steiner, 1973a, 1979a; Steiner & Roy, 1988), including cooperative meetings (Steiner, 1977a). He also wrote *A Manual on Cooperation* (Steiner, 1980a).

Power and responsibility

Depending on the respective constellation of relationship or situation, in Steiner's view, power is always related to a certain responsibility with regard to others. This means, in general, there is not only an imperative not to abuse power, but also to empower others to become more powerful themselves. As early as 1971, Steiner critiqued the classical (traditional) role of psychiatrists:

> psychiatry is a political activity. Persons who avail themselves of psychiatric aid are invariably in the midst of power-structured relationships with one or more other human beings. The psychiatrist has an influence in the power arrangements of these relationships. Psychiatrists pride themselves on being "neutral" in their professional dealings. However, when one person dominates or oppresses another, a neutral participant, especially when he is seen as an authority, becomes an enforcer of the domination and his lack of activity becomes essentially political and oppressive.
>
> (Steiner, 1971d, p. 3)

He was also critical of the fact that psychotherapists tended to ignore issues of power and, indeed, were trained to do so:

> Psychotherapists are trained to ignore the relative power of the persons that they work for. Generally speaking, power on other political considerations are considered to be irrelevant to the practice of psychiatry. This unawareness of power in psychotherapists prevents them from becoming aware of the abuses of power that occur between human beings and of the unhappiness these abuses cause. Acknowledging abuses of power would quickly lead

On power 165

most psychotherapists to the conclusion that as soul healers they must become advocates of those that are being oppressed rather than neutral observers who take no sides. As a consequence, because they would have to take sides with the powerless against the powerful, therapists are not too eager to become aware of such power factors.

(Steiner, 1974a, p. 254)

Revising this some 12 years later, Steiner (1988d) added that:

the people who indulge in power considerations are seen as "politically biased." As a consequence, psychotherapists tend to ignore what occurs in their consulting rooms when it has anything to do with the arrangements of power, especially the manner in which certain people, who have power over others, misuse it to their own advantage.

(p. 11)

This, in turn, meant that, as far as Steiner was concerned, "the power aspects of relationships have been ignored in transactional analysis as being of insufficient importance to be systemically mentioned" (Steiner, 1974a, p. 253), with the consequence that "in a routine transactional analysis of a relationship, the relative power of the individuals involved is not considered a relevant factor" (ibid., p. 253). This was why Steiner and other colleagues involved in RP introduced the concept and analysis of "power plays" (as a form of game) and to invite the cooperative contract of "no secrets and lies, no rescues and no power plays" (see Chapter 1, n. 5).

In 1981, Steiner commented that: "The task we as radical therapists set for ourselves is to aid people in reclaiming their alienated human powers" (Steiner, 1981d, p. 731). This for him included being aware of power issues and raising these issues in psychiatry, in therapy, and in other work such as mediation (see Jenkins & Steiner, 1988). Concerning the therapist's (or helper's) own power, he stated the value of transparency, instead of maintaining a mystifying power. Regarding relationships between adults and children he emphasised that children should be held powerlessness by permanently Rescuing them, because, as he put it: "Children who are trained as Victims grow up with varying degrees of disability or incapacitation" (Steiner, 1973e, p. 21).

The expression of the use of power with responsibility also found expression in Steiner's concept of therapeutic potency. He first used the word "potency" in an article on the treatment philosophy of TA to describe the therapist's positive use of power with clients (Steiner, 1968b). In doing so, he added the term "potency" to Crossman's (1966) concepts of "permission" and "protection", a taxonomy that subsequently became referred to as "the 3 Ps" of TA (for a history and analysis of which, see Tudor, 2016).

In his original article, Steiner (1968b) defined potency as "expressed in permission by the emphasis with which permission is given, and is exemplified in protection by the willingness of the therapist temporarily to carry the burden of

166 *Luigi (Gino) Althöfer and Keith Tudor*

the patient's panic when in an existential vacuum" (p. 63). He went on to assert that "it is an attribute which transactional analysts seek in their work" (p. 63), which involves a commitment to curing patients, with valid consideration, and a willingness to confront the patient at the impasse. Later, in his book *Games Alcoholics Play*, Steiner (1971b) summarised therapeutic potency as "the therapist's capacity to bring about a speedy cure" (p. 181), commenting that "the Potency of the therapist has to be commensurate with the potency of the injunction laid down by the parents of the patient" (ibid., p. 181). This echoes what Berne (1972/1975b) wrote about potency in the context of protection, that is, that the therapist should feel potent enough to deal with the patient's Parent and "the patient's Child must believe he [the therapist] is potent enough, to offer protection from the Parental wrath" (p. 374). However, whilst these ideas, from Steiner, Berne, and other transactional analysts, extolled the virtue and, indeed, necessity of the powerful therapist being able to direct the client/patient in their therapeutic work, they did not address the dangers of therapeutic potency. This is also linked with the other "P", that of permission. As Steiner reflects (in the previous chapter), his own therapist, Andy, apparently somewhat "casually" gave him permission to engage in extramarital affairs, a permission which Claude would presumably not have taken if his therapist had not also been somewhat potent and, thereby, influential.

These perspectives on therapeutic potency also extended outside the consulting room. As early as in the original "Manifesto" of RP, Steiner (1971c) had criticised the therapeutic neutrality of mental health professions – and professionals. Later, he argued that "by remaining 'neutral' in an oppressive situation, psychiatry, especially in the public sector, has become an enforcer of establishment values and laws" (Steiner, 1975d, p. 4).

These statements make clear that, from Steiner's point of view, mental health professionals, including psychotherapists, should:

1. Be aware of their own power or potency, and to be able to reflect on this and how they use and or misuse it;
2. Be able to analyse power dynamics and transactions in relationships, and to support their clients to develop their awareness about such dynamics;
3. Demystify the power of the therapist (see Roy 1988c); and
4. Be willing and able to comment and act on oppressive dynamics in the wider public mental health sector.

Power politics

In the 1980s Claude became very interested in the political abuse of power in terms of "mass communication", "media influence", "advertisement", and especially "propaganda". Between 1988 and 1991 he was a senior editor of the journal *Propaganda Review* (see Steiner, 1988a, 1989; Steiner & Rappleye, 1988, 1989), a socio-critical journal with regard to matters Latin American. While in some ways he

Figure 11.2 Some of Claude's books on power, propaganda, and the media

moved away from such interests as, in the 1990s, he focused more on the development of EmLit, he retained his interest in questions of power, propaganda, and the media: as we both know, Claude had a couple of metres of books on these subjects on his bookshelves in his house in Berkeley (see Figure 11.2).

From the beginning of radical psychiatry Steiner frequently referred to the aspect of power imbalances in society and wrote about issues like "Men's liberation" (1973d), "Coupleism" (1976b), and "Feminism for Men" (1977c, 1978b),

168   Luigi (Gino) Althöfer and Keith Tudor

and about men's role in patriarchy. In his last book *The Heart of the Matter*, Steiner (2009) wrote about himself:

> As a radical psychiatrist, I am interested in how children, old people, women, men, people of color, gays, poor – in fact everyone – is alienated from his or her power and potential. I am dedicated to exploring how the alienated can gain liberation and power in the world at the transactional, interpersonal level. I am also an emotional warrior, who, with emotional literacy training methods, struggles to free up people's emotional selves – including, of course, my own. Finally, the essence of my life's work and motivation has been liberating the human spirit from its shackles – instinctual, personal or institutional, while at the same time I have tried, in my way, to be free as well. That is why I can call myself, above all, a liberation psychologist.
>
> (pp. 18–19)

In the "Principles" of RP (Steiner, 1971d), Steiner stated that "psychiatry is a political activity" (p. 3). In this context, he catagorised "four types of psychotherapists" and described Eric Berne as one of the "Beta psychiatrist[s]" who are "conservative or liberal in their politics and radical in their methods" (ibid., 1971, p. 4). He wrote about TA and politics (Steiner, 1973c, 2009), and about what he viewed as Berne's "aversion" to politics and Berne's own personal politics (Steiner, 2009, 2010).

Right to the end of his life, Claude used to put the personal in the context of the political, though, over time, he focused much more on the personal aspects of the political and didn't elaborate the intrinsically political aspects, general social imbalances, or issues of structural oppression in society. Others of the first generation of the RP movement wrote with a stronger focus on such aspects, notably Beth Roy with regard to racism (Roy, 1988a) and Eleanor Smith with regard to disability (Smith 1988). By his own admission, both in writing and in conversation, Steiner – as a psychotherapist – was more interested in personal politics than in what we might distinguish as "political politics", and, indeed he himself acknowledged that his was a "liberal political interest" (Chapter 10, p. 152).

That Claude's politics or, at least, his radical politics, were predominantly personal was the result of the influence of feminism and, personally, especially that of Hogie Wyckoff, with whom he had a significant and loving relationship. Claude wrote – and also spoke – a lot about the importance of her personal influence on him. As he acknowledges in his *Confessions*, "my interest in power abuse originated specifically in my relationship with Hogie" (Chapter 10, p. 150). It is no accident that the majority of the published material in RP, including the Radical Therapist Collective (1971), Rough Times Staff (1973b), Steiner (1975i), and Wyckoff (1976), concerned gender politics. In some ways, this is one of the great strengths of RP as it explores and explains the personal manifestions of the dynamics of power: the personal is political, and political is personal. This approach also encompassed veterans (Schwebel, 1975b), gay and bisexual politics (Karakashian, 1976; Wyckoff, 1976), and fat liberation (Aldebaran, 1976).

On power 169

However, in our view this "bottom-up" approach to politics didn't go very far up; in other words, a number of the original radical psychiatrists/therapists didn't apply their analysis to other or wider matters and, rather, increasingly focused on therapy. Indeed, in the radical therapy community of the early 1970s there were some debates between those who identified more with the politics of therapy, and those who were more focused on the therapy of politics and rejected the liberalism of therapy (see Chapter 10).

From the late 1990s, and especially with regard to his work on EmLit, the political aspects were or became less evident. For example, the goals of most EmLit training were – and are – almost exclusively personal; although they can be linked to power and politics, they generally are not. Although the concept of EmLit was developed in the context and framework of radical psychiatry in the 1970s, the term "alienation" and its theory about oppression, mystification, and isolation seem not to have been of much importance in Claude's latest understanding of EmLit, a fact that some within the radical psychiatry movement openly critiqued (see Chapter 8).

In the last conference workshop Claude ran (with Keith) at the International Transactional Analysis Conference in San Francisco in 2014, in the context of encouraging people to take action, he kept saying: "It's a free country", a claim about which Keith and a number of others in the workshop challenged Claude on at the time. While he was quite radical in his personal politics, he was or had become quite conservative in his social or political politics, for example, supporting Hilary Clinton rather than Bernie Sanders in the 2016 US Democratic Party Presidential primaries. When visiting Claude in 2014, Keith asked him about indigenous politics and whether RP had developed any critique of this aspect of power dynamics between First Nations Americans and subsequent settlers and colonisers. This question was informed by Keith's interest in and bicultural engagement with Maori colleagues, friends, and clients in Aotearoa New Zealand (see Green & Tudor et al., 2014), and having found *Issues in Radical Therapy*, in which he found a couple of pictures that referred to indigenous struggles in the US: one, on the back page of *IRT 1*(2) (Spring 1973) with the slogan "Wounded Knee is not over". Claude shook his head, recalling that a native American guy had been in the group for a while, though not for long, and explained that, generally, they hadn't analysed what they hadn't experienced or weren't involved with.

In a conversation Gino had with Claude and his wife Jude Steiner-Hall in July 2015 about the loss of politics in emotional literacy (see also Chapter 8), Claude said explicitly that while he still "absolutely" believed in the theory of alienation (see the quotation from Steiner, 2009, on the previous page), he lost interest in thinking, talking, writing, and teaching about it some years ago: "I did it and I've done it." He confirmed this a year later (in July 2016), and, when we both attended his last gathering at his ranch in Ukiah, one of the sessions in which Claude didn't take part (albeit, partly due to his declining health) was that on "alienation" and the "sources of power". Nevertheless, we both did, and one result of that time we spent together, as well as subsequent exchanges, is this chapter.

Figure 11.3 Claude and Gino, Berkeley, 4 January, 2017

To summarise: we think that Claude's interest in power was more personal than political and more general than specific, but neither generalised nor systemic. Also, we know that, as time passed, he lost a certain relationship with his radical political roots and concerns or interests. While we respect and appreciate his work for its integrity and its consistency with the perspective that the personal is political, we also think that it lacks a more systemic and comprehensive analysis whereby the political is – and is made more – personal, and that, ultimately, this makes Steiner's analysis of power oppression somewhat limited. Of course, Claude never claimed to give an unlimited and complete analysis of anything. Knowing him as we did, he would probably say something like: "Yes, it's not perfect. I made what I made. You can do the rest."

Nevertheless, it is clear that, in the 1970s, Claude developed a life-long interest in power, which culminated in his book *The Other Side of Power* (Steiner, 1981e) with which, he reports, "I found my political legs" (Chapter 10, p. 151). However, while the book was translated into several languages, Steiner also comments that it was not as successful in the United States as his other books had been:

> In the past when I went on the radio and television to speak about my books there had been universal acceptance. Now I encountered hostility and invective by people who heard my message as an attack on the American way of life which it, in a way, was.
>
> (Chapter 10, p. 152)

Moreover, Steiner himself believed that it was his "most important work" (Chapter 10, p. 152), and in fact, within TA, and for a long time, Claude was one of only a few people who wrote and taught about power dynamics – and placed psychotherapy in a political context, which, we suggest, is one of the reasons why some of the TA community was somewhat sceptical about him.

Conclusion

In this chapter, we have addressed various aspects of Claude's work on power – and, perhaps, like Claude, we might emphasise that this is not a complete and conclusive account of it. Notwithstanding our criticism, we absolutely appreciate that, over a period of almost five decades, Claude repeatedly, although with varying focus and sometimes changing considerations, made reference to what for him was an important issue of power. We both came to know Claude as an extremely responsible and conscientious person, and we assume that this was partly due to his understanding of the responsible use of power, which was deeply rooted in his heart. We consider that his written discussions about power, sometimes as an explicit topic and at other times as a secondary topic in between the lines of other discussions, a valuable legacy; and hope that this chapter contributes to Claude's legacy on this subject, and acts as a resource for further exploration of the subject of power – in and beyond therapy – in its many facets.

SEIS

Emotional literacy

12 Confessions of a psychomechanic

Excerpts on emotional literacy

Claude Steiner

Paranoia's grain of truth

During that time [when Claude and Ursula were in Ann Arbour, 1960–1965] Ursula had become rightfully jealous of me to a paranoid degree. She imagined that my insistent erection was a radio tower sending coded messages to my many (at the time non-existent but certainly longed for) lovers. Ursula's behavior somehow fit in with my mother's paranoia. I had early observed that my mother suspected and at times accused people of hidden motives and while often incorrect about her suspicions regarding me, she was as often right as she was wrong. She accused me of a variety of motives; being interested in one of the maids, wanting to leave the house, expecting to get spending money, disagreeing with what she said. While I was incensed by the unfairness of her unproven assumptions and vehemently denied her accusations, I also noticed that they were more than occasionally correct.

Thirty years later when confronted with Ursula's extreme suspicions I saw that paranoia is generally based on a grain of truth, intuitively perceived and sometimes erroneously amplified. It was clear to me that Ursula's paranoid ideas, while overtly absurd, had a real, if small and hidden foundation. This is how I had my first original insight into an important aspect of the human mind: that "paranoia is heightened awareness," and that "there is a grain of truth to every paranoia."

This, it turns out, was not an entirely original insight; Sigmund Freud himself had [reputedly] remarked that the paranoid is never entirely mistaken. I suppose that in addition to reinventing the wheel, I added the practical concept that there is a grain of truth in every paranoia, which was the result of heightened attention and perception.

In graduate school, in spite of Freud's insight, I was being taught that paranoia was a matter of projection; paranoid people supposedly ascribed to others, motives of their own that they could not own up to, or even less convincingly, that paranoia was a symptom of latent homosexuality, a Freudian notion. However, my "heightened awareness" hypothesis was confirmed in case after case at the Veteran's hospital where I interned as a clinical psychologist, by patients who believed that they were being poisoned by the FBI, while they were forced to take massive doses of anti-psychotic chemicals with toxic side effects; patients that believed that they were the victims of a Jewish conspiracy while staff members (many Jewish)

176 *Claude Steiner*

made plans to transfer them to the VA [Veteran Association] system's backwaters; or patients who believed that the staff was having sexual orgies while the staff was in fact having sexual orgies and so on.

Later, I discovered R. D. Laing who, in his book *Politics of the Family* [Laing, 1969] showed how the denial – or as he called it the invalidation – of people's perceptions lead to a very understandable sort of mental invalidism or madness. Paranoids were maddened, I agreed, by having their intuitive perceptions routinely and roundly denied. This led me to an entirely novel way of seeing and dealing with paranoia. I believed that the kernel of truth of each paranoia needed to be validated and that wholesale denial of paranoia was a mistake, in fact destructive of a person's intuition, leading to mental confusion and inviting proliferation, rather than abatement, of paranoia. Search for, and validation of the grain of truth in every paranoia was a great method to still paranoia and incidentally, to develop intuition. Today, this notion is a vital aspect of Emotional Literacy training and the process of validating paranoia and intuition is – I teach – the way to develop empathic and intuitive skills.

As an example if a woman is having near psychotic delusions of persecution centered on her husband such as fear of being poisoned or murdered while he is having sex with every other woman in the neighborhood, my reaction instead of trying to talk or medicate her out of her clearly unrealistic delusions will be to let her tell what she has observed in his behavior that justifies her thinking. I then would listen to her story and see if something is going on with her husband that could be exaggerated into what she actually believes. Maybe he ogles and flirts with women he meets, maybe he encourages her to eat junk food because he no longer cares that she is becoming obese, and when confronted with her perceptions simply discounts them categorically. As a way of dealing with the paranoid aspect of her ideas I will suggest an alternative explanation for her perceptions without discounting them.

Radical truthfulness

We [radical psychiatrists] saw ourselves as codifiers of a new era of human potential. We sought to understand what would help people prosper and love together, cooperate and thrive while throwing off the shackles of bourgeois expectations. One indispensable aspect of that facilitation of our program was truthfulness. Being radically truthful including speaking truthfully about our feelings was a requisite of true cooperation.

Hogie insisted in complete honesty, not only not telling lies but also not keeping secrets. Without a pledge for complete honesty, she argued – no fake strokes, no acceptance of unwanted strokes – it was impossible to establish the mutual trust required to liberate people of their inhibitions to love; to give and accept strokes.

The subject matter of lying has been broached by many a theoretician and clinician and it's a thorny one. Everyone agrees that lying is bad and causes no end of trouble, but no one seems to want to recommend that people ought to stop; not even the Ten Commandments which as far as lying goes mentions only that we shall not

Excerpts on emotional literacy 177

bear false witness against our neighbor. The seven Catholic cardinal sins[1] do not include lying either.

Instead the belief seems to be that it is sometimes necessary to lie for people's good or that being totally honest can be cruel and even sadistic. In addition, there is the problem of lying to oneself. Even when we want to stop lying we never know if we are lying because of our capacity for self-deception.

We dealt with the problem of self-deception by defining lying as "saying something we consciously know not to be true or failing to reveal something that we consciously know is important." In other words, if lying is defined as a conscious activity, lying to oneself is not possible. Being truthful requires that we tell "the whole truth and nothing but the truth" as when we are required to swear, with hand on Bible, before testifying in court.

Regarding the cruelty of being truthful we added that the worst cruelty is a lie and that being truthful does not require being thoughtless or insensitive. Defined in this way the difference between being truthful and lying is simple, and equivocation is not possible. Of course, only the person knows if he or she is being truthful; cooperative truthfulness is an honor system. It is not possible in his system to say: "you are lying" to another; the only thing that can be reasonably said is: "Are you telling the truth?" or: "Are you telling me everything?" or: "I don't believe you, I think you are lying." Notice that in that last statement we are saying what we believe and not insisting that we are right in believing it.

This proposal – radical honesty – was something I was not entirely ready for. Here I must say – as if I have not, by now, confessed enough misdeeds – that I started my adult life as a petty liar and thief. Growing up in a series of corrupt cultures and observing my parents gave me the impression, as a child, that petty lies and thievery were part of everyday life and that one need only be clever enough not to be caught, to make it OK. I got my start as a petty thief at age 13 when I witnessed my mother stealing a small bag of pistachios at a newly installed Mexico supermarket where merchandise was for the first time openly displayed with no clerk to prevent pilfering. Impressed, I attempted to repeat the feat within days. I was caught and let go with a warning, which only caused me to refine my methods.

Petty dishonesty was a way of life in Mexico along with the monstrous dishonesty and theft of the Mexican Presidents whose plundering of the treasury was taken for granted and widely discussed, the only question being who stole more and by how many hundreds of millions. In addition the police routinely took bribes and politicians had whole families on the government payroll performing fictitious jobs, which provided their families with respectable middle class incomes. However, in Mexican morality, theft was OK only as long as it was from the government or some large corporation, never from a person, especially not a needy one.

The idea that a person should not lie in small self-seeking ways or filch small items simply did not occur to me until many years later when Hogie suggested, as part of our efforts to define cooperative behavior, that not lying was an essential aspect of cooperation. From my point of view – especially where matters of the heart and sexuality were concerned or in situations of enmity (all is fair in love and war) – lying was a practical necessity. Hogie, on the other hand, suggested the

178 *Claude Steiner*

concept of radical truth telling, that is, absolutely no lies of any sort, in any matter, at any level, except perhaps to protect oneself or others from certifiable harm.

My first reaction to this suggestion was the usual reaction I get from many people to this day. It did not make sense, I argued, it was too hard, and anyway being truthful can be a very cruel thing to do. However, it took me just a few minutes to realize how correct it was, and I took to it with more fervor than a reformed alcoholic takes to abstinence. This was difficult at first and I had a more than a few relapses, particularly since lying, in our new-found Gospel, included hiding what one believed or felt.

A saying I lived by: "Never let the truth stand in the way of a good story" was another difficult family tradition I had to overcome. I was known – as was my father – as an excellent raconteur and had developed a habit of elaborating my stories to levels akin to Munchausen syndrome – puzzling even to myself – supposedly for the entertainment value to my listeners.

From that day forward, I resolved that lies of commission or omission were absolutely harmful to the therapeutic process in particular, and to sanity in general; lying corrupts the mind of the liar and the person being lied to. This belief has deeply informed my therapeutic method. My firm resolution not to engage in any deception applied to my clients. I routinely informed any new client that I believed that anything short of full disclosure – any lies of omission or commission – would seriously impair any possible progress. In doing therapy for people who were in relationships, especially if married, I made it clear that I would not be willing to keep secrets from each other for them for more than a few weeks and would eventually pressure the lying party to come clean or discontinue therapy. At a time when psychotherapists were, by training, very coy in their questions I developed a method of direct – some said ruthless – questioning which was very effective in revealing the essence of people's life stories and moving the therapeutic process into realistic solutions.

As an example, when doing therapy with a couple, most therapists tiptoed or even avoided questions about the couple's sex life. By contrast, once I acquired the couple's confidence, I would ask point blank: "So, how is your sex life?" "How often?" "What is it like. What do you do?" "Do you come?" "How do you come?" and so on. In spite of how logical this approach was when I was being contracted to help a couple to get along, some of my colleagues found it hard to take, giving as a rationalization that such questions could be deeply embarrassing and traumatic. I did not find that to be the case; on the contrary I found people were quite willing to be explicit with me.

Over the years I have cleansed my life of lies and except for an occasional, I would argue, minor slip which I feel I must eventually reveal to those affected, I have discovered the great advantages of radical honesty. One advantage is not having to cover one's lies thereby freeing up large amounts of brain capacity for other matters. In fact, research evidence indicates that lying engages larger portions of the brain than being truthful.

However, and far more importantly, it is extremely difficult to build a relationship that is intimate, mutually supportive and reliable, while lying or keeping secrets. It may work for a while but eventually one or the other partner will discover one or more of the lies and feel betrayed and unable henceforth to trust the other. Suspicion, distance and even paranoia are the inevitable result. Most people enter into friendships and relationships assuming that they will not be lied to. Still very few make that assumption explicit by entering into truthfulness agreements. While this is common it is nevertheless unwise; a cooperative contract for truthfulness is a far better beginning for a lasting relationship.

Lying by those who govern is a commonplace which is incompatible with democracy yet at the turn of the millennium with the ascent of neo-conservative politicians in the US, lying was institutionalized on the basis of a belief that it is not possible to govern while being truthful. People need to be fed "noble lies" to appease them while what is really going on has to be kept hidden lest the foolishly oppose and vote against it. This is the belief of the disciples of Leo Strauss a mid-twentieth century philosopher who was the mentor of individuals like Dick Cheney, Donald Rumsfeld and Condoleeza Rice who held the levers of power of the Bush II administration.[2] The wholesale and conscious lying at all levels of Republican government that went on since George Bush usurped the presidency in 2000 caused potentially irreparable damage to the body politic, especially with the institution of the war on Iraq and the pretense that it is a war on terror when it was in fact a war for oil and a failed global power grab. Truth was on the retreat at that time and people are paying the consequences. How the citizenry of the US will deal with this problem remains to be seen. Clearly the rascals were thrown out by democratic vote, but is the damage to the collective mind repairable?

Rescuing

Lying was clearly a problem to deal with but there was another sort of errant behavior which was closely allied to lies and also needed to be addressed in cooperative relationships, and that is what Eric Berne termed Rescuing. Rescues, with a capital "R" should be distinguished from legitimate attempts to help – rescues, with a lower case "r." Rescues are a more complex form of lie.

I realized how often in a day I was tempted to do things I did not want to do and to lie about my feelings. As an example, because of my mechanic skills and the decrepit state of our vehicles I was often called upon when a car malfunctioned. Generally, I was glad to share my expertise but on occasion I would have preferred not to. Instead of saying "I don't want to take the time to fix your car just now" after ascertaining that it needed to have, say, a new master cylinder, I would lie and give a shallow excuse or worse I would grudgingly do the work. I was lying not just with my tongue but with my whole body; with my tongue because I was failing to speak the truth, namely that I didn't want to do what I was doing but also with my whole body when I crawled under the car I did the work when I really did not want to.

This created problems because in time I became resentful and grumpy, stopped being helpful with people's cars, failed to help people with doing their own work, cut myself out of the pleasure of being helpful, and so on. When we Rescue we

180   *Claude Steiner*

may not be fully aware of it, but our body knows, and that is why every Rescue leads to an eventual Persecution.

Not Rescuing, therefore, become part of the quest for radical truth. Like lies, Rescues are power plays; ways in which we manipulate others overtly or subtly. Bold face lies are the most overt; from there, lies of omission and Rescues become more and more subtle. The most subtle being not just when we Rescue people because we see them as impotent and incapable victims and don't believe they are capable of taking care of themselves and therefore need to be helped (even if they don't ask for it) but when we Rescue to create a sense of guilt and obligation in the Victim that we can use to manipulate him later.

One of the arguments most often advanced against honesty is that it often is a cover for emotional brutality. The example that comes up repeatedly has to do with physical appearance especially overweight ("Honey I cannot tell a lie, you are getting fat and turning me off"). Honesty in these situations can be brutal but does not need to be. The fact that the truth can hurt and that honesty can be used in a sadistic persecutory manner does not obviate its far more important advantages when exercised in a cooperative spirit and with a loving attitude. Not Rescuing or ceasing to Rescue is also often perceived as a form of emotional brutality or persecution which it can be, especially when habitual Rescuing is abruptly or angrily withdrawn.

Emotional literacy

As we developed these radical theories I used them in therapy and taught them in workshops on Radical Psychiatry, Power and Cooperation. In time I combined all of the transactional analysis and radical psychiatry insights into an Emotional Literacy Training program. The theory and practice of Emotional Literacy Training incorporates under one roof contracts, the analysis of transactions, strokes and the drama triangle stemming from TA on one hand, and on the other hand my theory of paranoia and intuition, *The Warm Fuzzy Tale* [Steiner, 1977d] and the stroke economy [1971f], the Critical Parent, power plays and cooperation.

I developed a pattern of teaching workshops in Europe for a month to six weeks every year, usually in the Fall, timed to end at Thanksgiving, my favorite holiday. I chose that time of the year because I discovered over the years that I suffered SAD (seasonal affective disorder) that began, as the days got shorter and usually ended with my birthday on the 6th of January. Taking an intense working trip in which I did about eight workshops in six weeks distracted me – made me oblivious – from the awareness of depression. By the time I recovered physically from these trips I had a few weeks before the solstice and then things began to look up again. Unfortunately, the effect of powering through my emotions in this manner, while effective in avoiding them, seemed to cause me to regularly come down with some other physical ailment, a bad back, a huge cold or flu, an eye infection, so I gave up this method of escaping depression. After a few years of experimentation, I found that having a full spectrum light coupled with a timer that went on in my bedroom at 5:30 in the AM to match a light cycle that resembles the summer pattern dealt with my sensitivity to the shortening of the daylight hours.

The way I dealt with my seasonal depressions might serve as an example of my general approach to solving people's emotional problems. I eschewed suggestions of long-term psychotherapy to get at deep conflicts, as well as the converse approach to "just get over it" or medicate it with antidepressants. Instead I chose a practical, empirical, conscious, Adult-centered, psycho-mechanic problem-solving approach which worked.

Notes

1 Gluttony (*gula*), lust (*luxuria, fornicatio*), avarice/greed (*avartitia*), pride/hubris (*superbia*), wrath (*ira*), envy (*invidia*), and sloth (*acedia*).
2 This appears somewhat overstated. There is no evidence that Strauss was a direct mentor to or of these specific individuals. Moreover, both Tarcov (1986) and Strauss Clay (2003) have addressed charges that Strauss's teaching fostered the neo-conservative foreign policy of the administration of George W. Bush (2001–2009).

13 On emotional literacy

Hartmut Oberdieck

Farewell

Claude accompanied me as a teacher and friend for over 32 years. In January 2017 he died after a long illness with his family at his favourite spot by the lake of his ranch in Ukiah. Claude took medical care to avoid enduring the unbearable effects of his advanced Parkinson's disease. He died as he lived: self-determined and free. His last words were: "I'm so lucky" and "Love is the answer".

I visited him in California in the summer of 2016, during which we had many personal conversations about life and death which were interrupted by breaks due to his exhaustion. Nevertheless, he invited old friends and companions from all over the world, one last time, to meet formally to discuss radical therapy, transactional analysis and "emotional competence" (here I use the literal translation of the German term), to exchange ideas and to get to know each other as in the old days. The free time was spent eating together, swimming in the lake and making music. In a large barn stood a formerly white grand piano and a set of drums, both of which had seen better times, and a guitar brought in by "Fat Dog", an old buddy of Claude from Berkeley, who runs a somewhat messy but extremely interesting guitar shop where, allegedly, the Rolling Stones have previously shopped.

There was an atmosphere of disorganised nostalgia, reminiscent of old hippie times, and it was quite unorthodox for a formal meeting, as it had often been with Claude. Despite his illness – as he was only able to attend meetings for a short time – his genius flashed again and again. Often we were just touched because the farewell was apparent.

First encounter and contact

My first encounter with Claude took place as part of my training as a transactional analyst (1979–1985) with his books: *Games Alcoholics Play* (Steiner, 1971b), *Scripts People Live* (Steiner, 1974a) and *The Other Side of Power* (Steiner, 1981e), which were among the first writings of his I read. I met him for the first time, personally late in 1984. After a three-month stay in the United States, I worked in Germany with other colleagues in a private practice that was transactionally oriented and, among others, came up with the idea of inviting Claude to a workshop on emotional competence.

On emotional literacy 183

I was tasked with looking after him, and tried to keep up with him by discussing his ideas with him. That was not a problem in itself, only it took some getting used to as due to being jetlagged, Claude was lying in a bathtub, and because of the bad acoustics and me sitting in the living room, he invited me to come to the bathroom – a memorable encounter, indeed! From the beginning, I liked his rather unconventional ways, though I know that this also led to some difficulties in certain circles, and, to be honest, it sometimes also unsettled me.

My own path, which, due to my history, often moved between the poles of adaptation and rebellion, led me to transactional analysis (TA) in the late 1970s. After several years of my own therapy, I decided to start my own training. The year Claude came to Berlin, I had just been to a four-week workshop with Bob and Mary Goulding in California. I had quit my permanent position as assistant doctor in the Jewish hospital in Berlin, which completely contradicted an adjusted attitude towards life. The work with the Gouldings had meant that I could finish my own therapy at once; I had gained much inner freedom through the nourishing and appreciative atmosphere. I felt strong and self-confident and responded to Claude's theories with a healthy dose of contradiction, and remember well that I called his concept of emotional literacy "old wine in new bottles". Amazingly, he did not contradict me, but agreed, with great serenity. While the individual elements of his theory were not new, the concept was, in its entirety, very coherent, practical and relatively easy to learn. In addition, I experienced Claude, both professionally and personally, as absolutely authentic and radically honest, which, in my experience of professional contexts, is not always the case.

My first participation in his Emotional Literacy Workshop has remained in my memory. Claude was brilliant at theoretical explanations, unflinching and unconventional in practical application, and what impressed me the most was that he was completely honest with his feelings and fantasies in the process. He dealt with the emotional and intuitive reactions of the participants just as authentically. The developmental history of the concept, its political background and the arguments in the International Transactional Analysis Association (ITAA) were not really clear to me at this time. In the workshops he reported only the beginning of the arguments, for instance that led to him not becoming President of the ITAA after Berne's death (see Chapter 16), and why emotional literacy was not recognised by the TA community – Claude never received an award for this contribution.

In the following years through until 1996 I invited him to do a workshop in Berlin every year. He became my teacher and my friend. Initially, I only organised the workshops, later I grew into co-directing them more and more. Claude lived with us and he became a friend of the family. For our wedding he gave my wife and me an article about omnigamy (Steiner, 1981c)! The reminiscence of earlier hippie times did not necessarily testify to a sensitive assessment of the situation – but this was Claude.

In 1988, my family and I visited Claude at his ranch in Ukiah, northern California. He was living apart from Darca, his then wife, who still lived in the main house. To make it as comfortable as possible for us and our little daughter, he left us his own house and slept outside in the sleeping bag – with the rattlesnakes. My

184   *Hartmut Oberdieck*

kids liked him a lot; he did not think much about rules. One unforgettable occasion was our visit to a pretty good, full Greek restaurant. After enjoying an ouzo, Claude – apparently drunk – slipped under the table, which caused considerable irritation for the other guests; my children, however, laughed so much, they had tears in their eyes.

Radical psychiatry, transactional analysis and emotional literacy

In 1984, an article by Claude on "Emotional literacy" appeared in the *Transactional Analysis Journal* (Steiner, 1984b). In it, he described how Eric Berne thought about dealing with feelings: "feelings, schmelings, the main thing is you should love your mother" (Berne, quoted in Steiner, 1984b, p. 162). Berne held groups that – mostly attended by women – had the goal of predominantly negative feelings (mostly anger), for what Berne referred to as "chicken soup therapy" (ibid., p. 162), and which he did not see as effective in curing patients. However, according to Claude, Berne was a thinker, was not very concerned with feelings and usually ignored them. He devoted most of his attention to distinguishing feelings and "rackets" which he saw as the cause of manipulation and extortion. Nevertheless, from Claude's point of view, Berne accepted the feelings of others, but without promoting the emotional aspect of relationships.

This history, including Berne's own attitude towards feelings and play, influenced the early TA movement, the result of which was that the focus was more on inauthentic feelings and feelings of substitution (e.g., English, 1971, 1972) than on authentic feelings and what feelings are. Here Claude saw, starting from a highly moral, orthodox TA standpoint, a glorification of what he referred to as "emotional illiteracy" (Steiner, 1984b, p. 163).

At the time, this attitude was consistent with other scientific directions. After initially great interest in emotional processes at the beginning of the 20th century, the establishment of behaviorism brought the research to a standstill. Emotions did not seem to be measurable in the lab; the introspective method was rejected as unscientific. In his article, Claude also points out that in the 11 years of his studies in psychology he never encountered the term "love" as the subject of discussion let alone as a research object. This also had an effect on his initial approach as a psychotherapist. If a patient had emotions or talked about love, he would steer the process to more "substantive" issues such as childhood, trauma, dreams and sibling rivalries. At that time, feelings were described as "free-floating fears, inappropriate affects, acting out or constraints that had to do with unresolved conflicts in childhood" (ibid., p. 164). Apart from as the subject of abstract scientific discussion, emotions had no value.

By describing the concept of strokes as units of social interaction, Berne made the quantification and scientific study of love (and hatred) possible (see Steiner, 1984). Claude saw this as the beginning of his own interest in love and other emotions, which, ultimately, led to the development of the concept of emotional literacy.

On emotional literacy 185

It is remarkable that Claude came to this point of view given his own history (as evidenced in his *Confessions* – here in Chapters 3, 5, 7, 10, 12, 14 and 16), which describes his yearning for parental love. He dedicated his book *Achieving Emotional Literacy* (Steiner & Perry, 1997) to his mother with the words: "To my mother Valery, whose heart I longed to touch" (p. v). Also, as he often mentions, his encounter with Hogie Wyckoff, his beloved associate from the radical psychiatry movement, also had a significant impact on his personal emotional development path.

Claude further describes in his article that, in the long run, the fundamental suppression of emotions is not possible. The alienation from our emotional nature makes people a kind of living dead. In his article, he could not resist a polemical swipe at the then American President Ronald Reagan and his wife Nancy, both of whom he described as emotionally incompetent. Here and in other places, the political side of Claude, which developed in the 1960s and 1970s, especially in the radical psychiatry movement, becomes clear again and again (see Chapters 7, 8 and 9), and many of the elements of emotional literacy were created and tested there.

For instance, cooperation, and especially the cooperative contract, is seen by Claude as the best prerequisite for learning emotional competence. Current and neurobiological research is concerned with the evidence that cooperative relationship patterns were developed and internalised very early in human history. Thus the humanistic view that humans are inherently good seems to be well-founded and proven. Likewise, families, collectives and groups of people are able to establish an openness for an emotionally competent relationship. Claude refers to the experiences of the radical psychiatry movement in problem-solving groups, work and life collectives, as well as intimate relationships. Moreover, even though the best time to learn such competence is in childhood, as an adult, one can improve one's emotional abilities.

Claude points to the power of emotion and the need for control so as not to hurt the boundaries of others. Unlike others, Claude pointed out that we can and do trigger feelings in others, just as they do in us, and both must bear responsibility for this – as an example he cites the well-known poem by Fritz Perls, which in his view is an invitation to emotional irresponsibility (see Steiner, 2003c; and Chapter 12). Moreover, if feelings were not understood, or spoken about, they would lead a life of their own in relationships, leading to confusion and misunderstandings.

In the rest of this chapter, I discuss Claude's initial ideas about emotional competency training as first described in his 1984 article. This is followed by the final training concept, as described in his 1997 book (with Paul Perry) *Achieving Emotional Literacy*, which was developed from nearly 15 years practice. I illustrate these ideas with regard to the integration of such training in the treatment concept of a drug treatment facility in Berlin and a psychosomatic clinic in Bad Grönenbach, Germany. I conclude with reviewing the emotional literacy movement in Germany and France and a short overview of the latest and further developments.

186   *Hartmut Oberdieck*

"Baby steps toward emotional literacy" (Steiner, 1984b)

The training programme for emotional literacy/competence as initially described by Claude comprises:

1. **Asking for permission**
   Here, the purpose is to prepare the other person for something emotionally important to come to terms with, and to give him the chance to say "No".

2. **Strokes**
   This exercise – involving giving, taking, asking for, rejecting unwanted, giving oneself strokes – emerged from the experiences of the late 1960s, when people attending the San Francisco Social Psychiatry Seminars tried different forms of positive and negative strokes in groups. Claude developed an exercise called "Stroke City", which violated the so-called "stroke economy" (Steiner, 1971f) by exchanging only clearly positive strokes. He also wrote about strokes and, specifically, the shortage of strokes in his world famous children's story, *The Warm Fuzzy Tale* (Steiner, 1977d).

3. **Making a feeling–action statement**
   On the one hand, this exercise was based on Berne's identification of negative feelings ("brown stamps"), which often coincided with the final release in psychological games. On the other hand, actions did not just trigger so-called "negative" feelings such as anger. In conversation, Claude told me that he was also inspired by Marshall Rosenberg's work (2016) on this point.
   The feeling–action statement (later the action–feeling statement) establishes in a simple sentence the connection between the action of one person and the resulting feeling in the other, without any evaluations, interpretations, attacks or confusion between intuitive assumptions (e.g., "I have the feeling that …") and feelings. When this method is adopted, it is clear when Adult transactions are contaminated by the content of the Parent and/or Child ego states.

4. **The reception of feeling–action statements**
   In this article Claude also attaches great importance to the exact reception and reproduction of the emotional information he considers necessary in order to avoid misunderstandings. For those who initially find this type of communication difficult, he writes with good humour in the words of an imaginary protagonist. His justification for this approach is that it allows emotions to cool down and adult (Adult), safe and productive communication about emotional processes.
   In reality, and also in workshops on emotional competence in which the participants agree to embrace this concept, there is always the difficulty of dealing with resistance to it, which requires a "loving suppleness" so that you do not end up in power games. Time and time again and with the development of the concept, I saw Claude being able to act with this suppleness and smoothness. Notwithstanding this, there were always fights about the right rules for emotional competence, which were expressed in the European–American "founding group" (described later in this chapter).

On emotional literacy 187

5. **Paranoid fantasies**

In his article, Claude emphasises that we constantly have what he called "paranoid fantasies" about other people, either because we have too little information about their thinking and feeling, or because we do not trust their statements. Although severe psychiatric delusions are pathogenic, they usually contain a grain of truth, and, according to Claude, paranoia has its source in an increased consciousness and may be translated as "heightened awareness". In his *Confessions*, Claude describes his experiences with his first wife Ursula, who later suffered from extreme paranoid ideas, though even here he saw that there was a grain of truth, albeit small and hidden. Claude was also influenced by the work of the British psychiatrist and therapist, R. D. Laing, the founder of the antipsychiatry movement, who argued that denying the perception of people can lead to madness – and hence the importance of identifying the grain of truth in the fantasy.

6. **Responding to a paranoid fantasy**

The goal here is to provide the most accurate validation of the paranoid fantasy by exploring and naming the "grain of truth", as a result of which the person can let go of or at least modify their fantasy, which, in turn, generally leads to relief all round and an emotionally closer and more productive relationship.

7. **Rescues**

As the last point of the "baby steps towards emotional literacy", Claude addresses the issue of Rescues in his article. What is meant by this is when we do something we don't really want to do and/or we do more than is appropriate in the situation, and Claude refers to the Rescuer role in the drama triangle (Karpman, 1968). Here, I suggest that there is a conceptual inaccuracy, as the roles of the drama triangle are, by definition, unconscious. However, in group process, the behavioural manifestations of the roles become more apparent, so it may be useful to refer to preconscious roles.

Whilst outlining these useful steps in emotional literacy, the article did not fully elaborate the complete concept which was still under development. For instance, Claude did not focus on taking responsibility by naming mistakes and negotiating redress (which he developed later, for a description of which, see p. 192 below).

Achieving emotional literacy (Steiner & Perry, 1997)

The final version of Claude's training programme in emotional literacy developed from the workshops he held all over the world. In terms of the development of emotional literacy/competence (or "EmLit" as it also became known) in Europe, I want to acknowledge Anne Kohlhaas, who had established contact with Claude in the mid-1970s. Later, she and her husband, Richard Reith, regularly invited Claude to workshops in Waldkirch, in Germany. Based on these international workshops, which took place over some 15 years, Claude wrote up a more developed version

Figure 13.1 Claude Steiner, 1997

of the original training programme in a book, *Achieving Emotional Literacy* which was first published in 1997 (co-authored with Paul Perry), and republished in 2003 (with Claude as sole author). Here I summarise the key aspects of the programme.

Contracts

TA is known for its contractual method. As Claude put it:

> Contracts are made to protect the participants from the fearsome possibilities of emotional work; being coerced into opening up, being judged, attacked, ridiculed or deceived, being made responsible for other people's actions, being gossiped about or shunned from the group. Safety facilitates honest and free communication essential for emotional literacy.
>
> (Steiner, 2003c, p. 242)

TA and EmLit identifies and uses three types of contracts: confidentially contracts, cooperative contracts, and treatment and training contracts.

Confidentiality contracts

Confidentiality contract, Type I: Nothing that happens at the meeting is discussed outside the meeting.

On emotional literacy   189

Confidentiality contract, Type II: When discussing the events of the meeting outside the meeting (i.e., their own participation in the meeting), the individual concerned takes responsibility to ensure that others at the meeting cannot be identified. Moreover, "anyone can impose a partial or total ban on being discussed outside ... the meeting by ... requesting it" (ibid., p. 242).

Cooperative contract

A cooperative contract is a voluntary agreement between people to renounce manipulative power plays and power plays in any form or situation without restriction. Power plays are manoeuvres that we do to make or prevent other people from doing something they do not want to do. These include mental and physical violence, but also other, subtler methods or coercion. Two types of subtle psychological powerplays are especially important in interpersonal relationships and should be especially avoided:

- Lies: these include those we say to others, but also embezzlement and concealment, including:

    (a)   lying about what we want; and
    (b)   lying about what we feel.

- Rescues: which, as described in Claude's earlier work, is when someone does something, either:

    (a)   that he or she does not want to do; or
    (b)   that he or she does more than his or her appropriate share.

Instead of engaging in lies and Rescues, we encourage people to ask for what they want until they are satisfied; not to do anything they don't want to do; and to negotiate every situation until they come to a voluntary, satisfactory consensus.

Treatment or training contract

As with any legal contract, a treatment or training contract is a reciprocity-based agreement between adult human beings in which a particular benefit is agreed between the therapist and the client or between the teacher and the student. Contracts can be long-term contracts (for instance, to treat depression) or short-term contracts (such as learning about and practising strokes).

Strokes

Strokes are units of interpersonal recognition.

190   *Hartmut Oberdieck*

Strokes can be good or bad, positive or negative

- Good, positive strokes (also called warm fuzzies, fluffies or gold tiles) are fully positive, heartfelt and honest recognition transactions.
- Bad, negative strokes (also called cold pricklies) are toxic recognition transactions, and take the form of:
    1. Open devaluations; and/or
    2. Covert devaluations, by means of:
        (a) unfavourable comparisons; and/or
        (b) insincere strokes (also called plastic fuzzies).

Strokes may be desirable or undesirable, that is, strokes of a positive nature are not necessarily desired by a particular person.

Strokes can be physical or verbal

- Physical strokes include forms of touching, hugging, being held, kissing, etc.
- Verbal strokes may be about a person's appearance, clothing, intelligence, generosity, elegance, wisdom, dignity, leadership qualities, tact, warmth, energy, honesty or any other attribute.

Strokes have power

- They have the power to calm down or stir up good or bad feelings, and can make people feel OK or not OK.
- Some strokes are more powerful than others, depending on how much they are wanted, who gives them and how much they are expressed or given.
- Stroke hunger and deficit (i.e., the absence of strokes) can lead to physical, mental or emotional illnesses such as depression.

Strokes involve a risk, that is, the risk of giving and then asking depends on how much they are wanted and if and how they are rejected.

The stroke economy

People need strokes, so why aren't they exchanged freely and generously? Because of the stroke economy (see Chapters 5 and 6), which is enforced by the Critical Parent. The rules of the stroke economy are:

- Don't give strokes – that is, if you have a stroke you want to give, don't give it;
- Don't ask for strokes – if you want a stroke, don't ask for it;
- Don't accept strokes – don't take a stroke that you want;
- Don't stroke back – don't refuse a stroke that you don't want;
- Don't give yourself strokes.

On emotional literacy 191

These rules are enforced by the Critical Parent self (also known as the Pig Parent, the Enemy, the Internalised Oppressor, the Prison Guard, the strict Superego, lack of self-esteem, the Electrode, etc.). The Critical Parent self is a coherent learned system of critical and controlling perspectives and is often, but not always, heard as an internal parental voice. The basic message of the Critical Parent Self is that you are not OK, specifically: you are bad (sinful, lazy, vile, etc.), you are ugly (having an ugly face, body, etc.), you are crazy (mentally, emotionally, irrationally, out of control, etc.), you are stupid (retarded, can't think clearly, are confused, etc.) and/or you are damned (sick, hopeless, self-destructive, etc.). When people follow some or all of these rules, there is a dramatic decrease in stroke exchange; however, as any stroke is better than no stroke, people are willing to accept negative, toxic strokes and, at worst, even crave them.

Three stages and ten steps to emotional competence

0. **Ask for permission** – to prepare for emotionally competent communication. We agree to precede every emotional communication with a request for permission to proceed. This gives the person addressed the choice to engage in or decline a potentially difficult transaction.

Stage one: open the heart

1. **Give strokes** – give full, positive, honest, non-comparative messages of recognition.
2. **Take strokes** – then ask, accept and give yourself strokes, and reject strokes you don't want.

Stage two: discover the emotional map

Part 1: action–feeling designation

3. **Name action(s)–feeling(s)** – "As you (action), I feel/felt (feeling)", with no judgements, accusations or theories.
4. **Accept the naming of action(s)–feeling(s)** – i.e., the acceptance of the emotional information without defending oneself.

Part 2: intuition

5. **Express intuition, empathic perceptions or paranoid fantasies** – the subjective presentation of an intuitive perception of the feelings, actions or intentions.
6. **Name the true portion of a paranoid fantasy or intuition** – seeking the true portion, however small (the "grain of truth") that acknowledges or confirms the intuitive impression of the other without defending oneself.

192 *Hartmut Oberdieck*

Stage three: take responsibility, expose and apologise

7. **Expose lies, Rescues, Persecutions and Victim behaviour** – "When I (action),

    (a) I have lied or not told the full truth; and/or
    (b) I have Rescued you, because, either:
        • I did something I didn't really want to do; or
        • In my opinion, I did more than my share; and/or
    (c) I have persecuted you with my anger, which did not belong to you at all; and/or
    (d) I have put myself in a Victim position because I assumed that you would Rescue me, or I pressed you to do it.

    This is followed by the statement "I apologise for that and will (or won't) do it next time", and the question: "Do you accept my apology?"

8. **Accept the disclosure** – a non-defensive acceptance of the given emotional information, followed by the acceptance or rejection of the apology. When rejecting the apology, it must either be changed, postponed or withdrawn.
9. **Apologise and ask for forgiveness** – "I apologise for (the action); it was wrong and I regret that I hurt you. Will you forgive me?"
10. **Accept the apology and grant or refuse forgiveness** – listen to the apology and after intense insomnia, either:

    (a) grant forgiveness; or
    (b) postpone forgiveness, or requesting other wording or additions.

Emotional competence in practice

At the end of 1984, at the same time as participating in my first workshop with Claude, I took over the medical and therapeutic management of a drug treatment facility in Berlin, which worked on the basis of a very consistent concept of a therapeutic community (TC) (whose roots were in the Synanon model of TC). Our clients lived out the opposite of cooperation and the team, half of which were ex-users, responded accordingly, with rigid limitations and often violent confrontation. Although, in the context of the sometimes unbelievable self-destructiveness of our predominantly heroin-dependent patients, I initially took part in this approach, inspired by Claude's work on EmLit, I began also to experiment in the community with the concept of emotional competence. I argued a lot with Claude about confrontation as a means of intervention. From my point of view, it was acceptable as an intervention in the context that clients were playing destructive psychological games; and, moreover, that it was even effective in order to prevent drug addicts from relapsing and suicide. But it was important that they did not experience the confrontation as being unfair. Claude, however, saw confrontation as a power game and said that in using such confrontations, I – and, indeed, the community – would pay a price for such power games. The introduction of the training initially met with resistance in the team, which heated up more and more over the years. Although, initially, our patients welcomed some of the EmLit techniques as increasing the possibility of trickery, interestingly, they quickly became excited about proving their lies to others through the use of expressing and checking out their paranoid fantasies. I remember one patient with a considerable criminal past who was sitting next to me in a group, beginning to sweat, because trying to be honest was costing him incredible effort, while the others in the group, and with some pleasure, immediately exposed his lies. When drug addicts first dared to exchange truly honest positive strokes, of which they were terrified because of their often desperate developmental stories, a change was evident, although relapse into old behaviours and patterns is always tempting. The efficacy of EmLit has been an integral part of the therapy over the years and has contributed significantly to a more humane approach to the overall concept.

The introduction of the training programme in the context of a psychosomatic clinic

From September 1996 I began work as a medical psychotherapist in a psychosomatic clinic in Bad Grönenbach, at which, after two years, I became a senior and the deputy chief physician. The clinic also worked on the principles of the TC, this time a development of the model of the Herrenalber Clinic, albeit in a much looser way than the TC described previously. Another difference between the two was that this clinic already had staff who were familiar with TA, which was a wonderful prerequisite for introducing the concept of emotional competence. Initially, there was great interest, especially as at that time Claude came to Bavaria regularly and presented his ideas in the clinic to the team – and to the patients. However, I had underestimated the resistance within the clinic, which, in the beginning, was epitomised by such sentences as: "Here you don't get what you want, but what you need!" Also, I did not really consider the consequences of my "missionary zeal" among the other members of the leadership, who were committed to their own theories. In the meantime, I was very convinced about emotional competence and its effects, and initially probably presented it with a lot of pressure.

The introduction of emotional competence was not without disputes and sometimes devaluation. With the strong support of Claude, with whom I talked for many nights during his visits, and also the colleagues from the original Emotional Literacy Group in Europe (see below), it gradually became possible to establish emotional competence training as an integral part of the therapy concept in our clinic. Especially after I took over the management of the department for predominantly depressive patients, I developed with my staff a depression-specific therapy concept with a central integration of the concept of emotional competence, which,

194 *Hartmut Oberdieck*

in many respects, was compatible with findings from contemporary research into depression and the brain. We moved away from the original workshop model and conducted ongoing weekly groups. In addition, there was a theory group led by advanced patients.

Depression can be understood as an illness based on a lack of support. Many people with depression have an insecure attachment style in childhood, due to violations of attachment needs. The first triggers of depression are often losses (of relationships, work, privileges of a phase of life, etc.). Once the depression is manifest, the lack of support, due to the attacks of the Critical Parent ego state, against which the person can hardly defend himself, is inevitable. The introduction of the concepts of emotional literacy/competence, coupled with neurobiological aspects of depression, provided patients with a plausible, easy-to-understand explanatory model with a training programme that worked immediately.

The cooperative contract provided security and protection. Depressed people often suffer greatly from the relentless attacks of the Critical Parent ego state (or, as our patients rightly called it, "The Inner Bastard") and, at the same time, have an extraordinary sensitivity to external criticism. Simply creating a "power play"-free situation in the group was a salutary experience for them. As soon as the client was able to accept good, positive attention, his or her depressive mood was reduced, and the resolution of conflicts stabilised his or her self-esteem. Because depressed people are much more suspicious of other people than are healthy people because of the activation of their Critical Parent self, the honest review and correction of their intuitive perceptions, their "paranoia" leads to significant relief. The identification of the "Inner Pig" ("Pig Parent") and its defusing by various techniques and by the cooperative group atmosphere led to the understanding of negative script messages and emotionally corrective experiences. Accepting appropriate responsibility has helped to correct real mistakes and undermine inappropriate guilt feelings which are also typical of depression.

In addition to the regular weekly training groups for the patients, there were training sessions for employees. Some were enthusiastic about the concept and received training. One of my highly valued employees, Maria Trageser, showed a very special talent and commitment and took over a large part of the work, and, apart from the conceptual content of the programme, it is thanks to her that the training in this clinic still exists. After my departure and the departure of the old leadership team, the concept of the TC was abolished; only the emotional skills training has survived, simply because it is highly appreciated by the patients.

Conferences and training for external clinics led to contact with the chief physician of two clinics, on Chiemsee (near Rosenheim in Bavaria), who hired me to supervise his teams. The multi-team project took over ten years and was conducted almost exclusively according to the rules and structure of emotional competence. Claude came to the opening lecture (wearing my old leather jacket!) and enjoyed the appreciation of his work very much.

On emotional literacy 195

Other projects and developments included:

- A (first) study on the effectiveness of emotional competence, conducted by researchers at the University of Bamberg, regarding which the final results of the doctoral thesis are still outstanding Vöhringer, n.d.).
- One of my former interns became a chief physician in another clinic and implanted emotional competence there.
- The same person has also conducted large-scale training sessions for executives at large companies.
- Another long-term employee, also now the chief physician at a large psycho-somatic clinic, regularly works with aspects of the training.
- We presented many lectures on the concept in companies, schools and for the public.

The "Origin Group" in Europe

The concept of emotional literacy has spread all over the world, partly as a result of Claude's own interest in travelling and presenting, and also due to the fact that Agustín Devós has translated all of Claude's books into Spanish. In 2002, Anne Kohlhaas-Reith and Richard Reith, two Teaching and Supervising Transactional Analysts, brought together an international group, which met, for the first time in Waldkirch, Germany. The Origin Group comprised: Marielle Debouverie (France), Elizabeth Edema (UK), Michael Epple (Germany), Marc Devos (France), Becky Jenkins (USA), Anne Kohlhaas-Reith and Richard Reith (Germany), Denton Roberts and Claude Steiner (USA), Heinz Urban (Germany), Marian Weisberg (USA) and me. Later came Sylvia Cavalie, Manfred Kiewal, Norbert Nagel and Petra Rieder (Germany), and Lily Roussel (France).

These meetings took place in Waldkirch and later at Lily and Marc's house in Ranrupt, France, until 2008, and were largely productive. We focused on the content development of the concept, structures and initial ideas for education and training. In addition, there was a lot of practical experience in training groups and living together for several days under the protection of the cooper-ative contract.

In 2009, a smaller circle met by invitation at Claude's Round Mountain Ranch, Ukiah, California. While this had the effect of splitting the original Ori-gin Group (as Claude had only invited some but not all of the group), this gath-ering did provide the initial spark for the founding of the Deutsche Gesellschaft für Emotionale Kompetenz e.V. (DGEK eV, the German Society for Emotional Competence, www.dgek.de), the non-profit association for the dissemination and development of the concept. With the start of the founding conference, in June 2010, in the psychosomatic clinic in Bad Grönenbach, a very productive time was initiated with the development of further education guidelines and certifications, regular conferences and topic-specific projects. As a member of the Origin Group, I have no objective standpoint about the split, but I do

196 *Hartmut Oberdieck*

know that some people were upset by Claude's rough style (which he him-self describes in his *Confessions*), others by his somewhat unorthodox style, in addition to which there were battles for the recognition of our charismatic teacher. For myself, I think that, in taking the attitude that he wanted to avoid Rescues at all costs, Claude could sometimes be quite ungracious – and, like any human being, he was not free of power games (see Chapter 15). On the other hand, you could talk to him about everything and he also dealt with his mistakes very honestly.

Some history and further developments

Claude was a charismatic, sometimes chaotic leader, who could quite deny his Mexican socialisation. I remember preparing for the first conference on EmLit at his ranch in Ukiah in the 1990s. In his *Confessions*, Claude writes that he observes things before he intervenes (Steiner, 2008a). For my taste, he had been observing or watching things at the ranch too long. With a basically affectionate humour we called each other a "Dirty Mexican" and a "Rigid German"! When we were done clearing up and cleaning, we went for a Mexican meal as a reward. Claude looked fine, including wearing an impressive Hawaiian shirt. Unfortunately, on the way to his car, he noticed a broken truck; he repaired the radiator expertly. With a now obviously blemished shirt we arrived at the Mexican restaurant, which did not bother anyone but me!

As far as the conference was concerned, we were about 12 people from different countries, who lived, learned and practised emotional literacy together for a week under the protection of the cooperative contract. In a short time, an unusually dense and intense atmosphere was created. Claude was awesome in facilitating groups, and brilliant as far as theory was concerned. However, as far as the implementa-tion of any professionalisation and structuring of the emotional literacy movement was concerned, he showed little interest, which was, perhaps, a reaction to the commercialisation of TA that he saw – and with which he disagreed – follow-ing Berne's death. In a conversation with Anne Kohlhaas-Reith recorded in 1991, Claude reflected on this part of TA history:

> When he [Berne] died, there was no guidance. All he said is I want us to be international. He did make it clear that he didn't want people to profit tremen-dously from T.A. But he never sat down and structured the future of T.A. The Institutes became money cows, courses, workshops, and training programs at high prices selling the T.A. fad. He never made any statements about that, so that there was nothing to stop people from being greedy. When he died I tried to introduce some socially conscious attitudes, tried to run for president but was rejected by the Board. But I took this as exile, and left the organization.
>
> (Steiner & Kohlhaas-Reith, 1991, p. 13)

Similarly, although he sought recognition for his work (and, indeed, recognition was a significant drive for him as may be seen from his *Confessions*), Claude was

On emotional literacy 197

not commercially minded. Alongside Daniel Goleman on emotional intelligence (Goleman, 1995) and Marshal Rosenberg on non-violent communication (Rosenberg, 2001/2016), Claude was one of several important trailblazers who paid attention to the importance of emotions in communication processes, and, in contrast to Goleman, he even developed an efficient, easy-to-learn training programme. However, unlike Goleman and Rosenberg, Claude failed to publish and market his conceptual ideas as successfully as they did and have. One reason for this may have been that Claude's work on EmLit was never recognised by the ITAA, for instance, with an award. In the TA world, the reaction to Claude is still divided, which certainly has to do with his unadjusted, rebellious and sometimes provocative perceived political position: Claude was never mainstream.

The term "emotional intelligence" was introduced in 1990 by Peter Salovey and John Meyer; in 1995, Goleman published his work on emotional intelligence, and the term gained worldwide popularity. Although Claude had first used the term "emotional literacy" 15 years earlier in 1979 (in *Healing Alcoholism*), Goleman did not cite Claude's work – and, as he told me, he had tried to contact Daniel Goleman after the publication of his book, but Goleman was not interested. By contrast, in his book on non-violent communication, Rosenberg does acknowledge Claude as a source. Claude (Steiner, 2003c) himself described the difference between emotional literacy/competence and emotional intelligence as follows: "Emotional competence is emotional intelligence with the heart, in other words, emotional intelligence, which refers to the basic emotion of love and the common good" (pp. 242–243).

Claude's as yet unpublished book on EmLit (Steiner, 2016) points out that emotional intelligence can be abused in many ways, be it through emotive advertising or as psychological coercion in dictatorships or other power structures. Many who would attach great importance to emotional intelligence have completely lost sight of the ethical dimensions of emotional education. It is not just about improving the emotional skills of a person or a group, but about making the lives of all people more liveable. As Claude put it: "It is my conviction that the only emotional abilities that empower people's lives in a long-lasting, humane manner are the skills that are organized around human affiliation; the true source of personal power, the love-centered skills" (Steiner, 2016, p. 10). It should be noted, however, that Goleman (1995) does have an ethical position regarding emotional education.

In 1997, Claude's first book on emotional literacy was published (Steiner & Perry, 1997). Claude wanted to write a bestseller and engaged in the collaboration with Paul Perry (as Perry had previously co-authored some other successful books), but, ultimately, Claude was not really satisfied with the book, so, in 2002, he completed a significantly revised version, which was published in 2003 by Personhood Press (Steiner, 2003c). In 2016, he finished his last (and to date unpublished) version of this, which has been translated into German by Christine Freund and Andrew Chaffin. Although much more mature in content, this book is not finished and remains unpublished. The influence of Claude's Parkinson's disease is palpable, and he wrote this important last work with incredible effort and

198   *Hartmut Oberdieck*

willpower. Shortly before his death he wanted to make further changes, but he was not able to do so.

In 2002, Claude encouraged me to respond to the request of the Herder Publishing House to write a small book on emotional competence. In collaboration with Gabriele Michel, a literary scholar and author of several books, this led in 2004 to a publication, which includes a German version of "The Warm Fuzzy Tale" (Steiner, Michel, & Oberdieck, 2004); a revised edition was published in 2007 (Michel & Oberdieck, 2007) by Junfermann-Verlag Paderborn.

In 2010 (as noted above), the German Society for Emotional Competence was established as part of a founding conference in the psychosomatic clinic in Bad Grönenbach. As a non-profit organisation, it aims to disseminate and further develop the concept of emotional competence according to Claude Steiner. Uniform standards of education and training were developed for the first time. Further education institutes were established or existing ones committed themselves to align their education according to these criteria. Although Claude was pleased with this development, it was initially very difficult for him to let go again and to entrust his "baby" to other hands, and to accept that his influence was limited. For instance, I remember very clearly my friend and colleague Michael Epple, with whom I run our training institute, explaining to Claude that, with regard to the DGEK eV, it would be the members of the Association who would decide what happened in the Association – and not Claude. In his *Confessions*, Claude describes his repeated experiences – and feelings – of being excluded (see Chapter 16), and it appears that he was afraid that this could or would happen again. However, the development in Germany showed him that he did not have to worry about it, and Claude was repeatedly celebrated and valued during his presentations at the conferences. Due to his deteriorating health, in 2013, Claude attended our conference in Germany for the last time. One unforgettable memory of this occasion was his anarchic sense of humour, when he was crowned with a lot of fun as the Emotional Literacy King.

What remains?

The interest in emotional processes and their meaning is undiminished, and, indeed, continues to increase. This applies to all areas of social life: basically, there is hardly any aspect of human existence that is not directly related to emotions. At the same time, with the rise of xenophobia and reactionary attitudes with regard to women, GLTBQI+ communities and others who are viewed as marginal and dissenting, we can also see there is a rise in emotional illiteracy, as well as in political power players who seem to understand how to play the keyboard of emotional manipulation. Heart-oriented emotional intelligence – emotional literacy, as conceived and conceptually developed by Claude – competes with such political, economic and social power plays and power players. I see in the dissemination and development of Claude's ideas the chance to strengthen the constructive aspect of human development and aspiration. Through cooperation that overcomes boundaries and enables us to understand what our existence is all

Figure 13.2 Claude and Hartmut, Ukiah, 2016

about – love – I see the opportunity for better relationships with ourselves and others, and a better world. Claude's life – in all its human aspects, his strengths and weaknesses – revolved around this theme. From his own life script as well as the encounters with important people in his life, he understood the question and found: "Love is the answer".

SIETE
Love

14 Confessions of a psychomechanic

Excerpts on love and sex

Claude Steiner

I was reputedly born with an erection and all I wanted, I presume, was to lie in my mother's arms and suck on her breasts. But according to the fashionable custom of the time, she did not breast-feed me. That may be one reason I have been genuinely obsessed with women's breasts all my life. I have been known to say that my mother did not love me but to be fair it would be more accurate to say that she loved me (actually a lot) but did not ever say so until she was near death, 62 years later. She had read all my books and my developing ideas on love and recognition and evidently decided that it would be important to finally make her feelings known. Smiling devilishly behind my father's back she whispered, "I love you," the last time I saw her alive.

What my mother never told me but I learned decades later from her sister Hedi is that at age 30 when I was born she was in the throes of a torrid romance. Her lover was a Jewish friend of my parents, an intellectual man living in another city. My father, age 32, a Protestant engineer of Polish peasant descent, whose one unfailing quality was that he was ever in love with my Jewish mother, stood by her side during the highly arduous and ambivalent event of my birth. My parentage was in doubt, it seems, and that uncertainty was never resolved in my parent's lifetime.

Sex, sex and more sex

During these years [1965–1970] of serious psychotherapeutic work in Berkeley, sexuality had suddenly taken a dramatic turn. In Berkeley and the San Francisco Bay Area the Sexual Freedom league, open marriage and homosexuality were in, monogamy and chastity were out. People were taking LSD and dancing topless (and bottomless at times) in the streets. Tim Leary was preaching "turn on, tune in, drop out" and the slogan of our anti-war marches was "sleep with a stranger tonight" (in the name of erasing class and race differences for the sake of solidarity in struggle). The majority of women were on the pill, there was no AIDS or herpes yet, and crabs [pubic lice] were still rare. Fuelled by the suddenly released libido and liberated by grass and acid, we became energized into the counterculture revolution.

204 *Claude Steiner*

Sex, Drugs and Rock and Roll were a serious triad of elemental issues that seriously affected me. After years of sexual frustration, I was plunged into unlimited, effortless sexual opportunities. Married against my better judgment I had pursued extramarital affairs and succeeded twice in the five years of my Ann Arbor studies and, when I returned to Berkeley in 1965, I was rearing to go, and so it seems was every other middle aged, single or married man. Spurred on by the Playboy philosophy, pot and the hippy movement, sexual promiscuity infected everyone, it seemed.

But not everyone experienced the situation as some of us – mostly men – did. Others, mostly women, felt compelled to participate but also felt tricked, abused, betrayed and/or sickened by it even though it took a while for that to become evident. While sexual liberation was eagerly welcome by most men it became a two-edged sword for women. On one hand women, with the pill and abortions widely available, were now supposedly free to have or not have sex, to demand orgasm equity, to choose their favorite method of enjoying sex. But men's dominance of sexuality was not challenged, and many women wound up being sexually oppressed anyway and lacking even the societal support to refuse sex. Instead they were exposed to pregnancy, STDs [sexually transmitted diseases], heartbreak and abandonment on a large scale.

After nine years of marriage I was desperately unhappy in the marriage with Ursula and, while pretending everything was OK, I had a number of relationships with other women. I had been oblivious of women's orgasms but now I learned about them with Z___, with whom I was briefly involved.

M____

After Z, I took out an ad in the *Berkeley Tribe* alternative magazine; "Terpsichore will you be my muse? I am a psychologist/writer trapped in the Berkeley hills" giving my telephone number at work. My plea was heard by M____.

...

I don't remember how long it was before we made love, but she quickly let me know that I wasn't very good at it. I was eager to learn. She insisted on extended foreplay and expected me to last until she came, instead of my habitual 20 seconds. Now that I had learned about women's orgasms from Z, I was an eager student; for about a year every Tuesday right after my work ended at the Center for Special Problems, we met at her apartment.

The relationship never expanded from those Tuesday meetings, though very occasionally, when Berne was out of town, I might skip the Seminar and go to the movies with M or also, very occasionally returned to her apartment and spent the night. We had one wonderful weekend together on the Santa Cruz Boardwalk, but I avoided being seen in public with her and I am ashamed to admit that, while my excuse was that as a married professional I could not be seen with a young lover, the real reason was that a birthmark on her face embarrassed me. When the relationship ended, I was surprised by the fact that she was ready to let go. From my experiences with Ursula I had expected a scene and was greatly relieved that we parted in good terms. She had been a spectacular lover who taught me the joys of pure, untrammeled, mutually satisfying sex.

Hogie

[Hogie's] rules were simple. We would not lie to each other and we would not start relationships with other people, which were not acceptable to the other. The implication of this is that we would be completely open about any attractions and potential or actual sexual involvements that we contemplated or got involved in. Her constant demand of me was that I be honest, that I ask for what I want, that I express my feelings openly and I give and receive love freely. I was a shamefaced illiterate in this respect; like a child who doesn't know how to read but fakes it by recognizing a word here and there, I mimicked some form of compliance by rote. The fact was that I did not acknowledge any feelings other than anger and that I was in constant panic about what it was that I felt and what it was that I wanted, and that I layered everything I did and said with a thick coat of half-lies. I was eager to be loved and pursued and tried to deserve that love by "'good deeds," hard work, leadership, cleverness and wit but I barely understood what it was that she wanted from me.

Hogie taught me to breathe, to move freely, to open my chest to the point that without gaining weight I eventually could not fit into my shirts. She talked to me about women's liberation, which I was aware of and sympathized with but did not understand. Little by little it all made sense to me. She spoke in personal as well as political terms; liberation was not just freedom to be but also freedom from oppression. For me freedom was to be free to be in love. For her it was freedom from sexist oppression, freedom to speak her mind and state her needs, freedom from the sexual expectations placed on women, freedom to demand parity of orgasms. Chief among the rewards that she preferred was making love and, I hope this bears repeating, our connection was short of amazing; we made spectacular exhausting love to the point that we could hardly walk a straight line for hours after.

Hogie however, was not satisfied. She wanted more and she was not going to settle for half measures. We had an almost constant struggle on these demands for all the years of our relationship. For my part I was mesmerized by Hogie's sexuality … In this I notice I have an affinity with Leonard Cohen … [and] his song "Light as a breeze" (Cohen, 1992): "She stands before you naked | you can see it, you can taste it," he rasps. "You can drink it or you can nurse | it don't matter how you worship | as long as you're | down on your knees." And, [as] if that weren't enough he continues: "So I knelt there at the delta | at the alpha and the omega | at the cradle of the river and the seas." Reflecting my own experience, he goes on: "And like a blessing come from heaven | for something like a second | I was healed, and my heart | was at ease."

…

In the Fall 1973 *IRT* [*Issues in Radical Therapy*] issue Carmen wrote a debunking article in response to two articles in praise of three-way intimate relationships

206   *Claude Steiner*

[Kerr, 1973]. The two articles had been written by Red Hawk Woman (Red for short) [1973] and Mano (1973) respectively; the primary couple. Carmen interviewed Libra, the third member of the threesome and in her article pointed out the coupleist problems (oppression of a single person by a couple) encountered by Libra. The article was a veiled rejection by Carmen of what had been a very similar situation between Hogie, her and myself. In the same issue, partially as a preemptive move, I wrote an article on Coupleism in which I elaborated on and was critical of that form of power abuse, which Carmen had clearly suffered in her relationship with Hogie and me [Steiner, 1973b].

We were learning about the liberation of sexuality but in hindsight all that sexual freedom while delightful to the men was more often than not fraught with problems (birth control, pregnancy, sexually transmitted diseases, broken hearts) for the women; something that was not immediately obvious because the women were interested in taking charge of their sexuality and seemingly very willing to take whatever freedom was available.

Carmen lost interest in Hogie who was devastated while Carmen and I continued our relationship. For a while Carmen and I got along very well and were in love with each other while I was simultaneously in love with Hogie. Carmen was jealous of Hogie while Hogie was jealous of me. Typically, I, the man in the threesome, was in the catbird seat. Eventually Carmen became dissatisfied and asked me the fatal question: "If you had to choose between me and Hogie who would you be with?" My response was: "I would not be willing to choose." She angrily insisted, and eventually I said, "If you are forcing me to choose, I have to choose Hogie."

...

The failure of this three-way relationship was, to me, a harbinger of all the other failures of free love that we pursued with such conviction and energy at great emotional costs over the years.

Omnigamy

The developments of the sixties and seventies gave us the confidence to champion a point of view which we called Omnigamy, a term coined by Darca Nicholson. Omnigamy was a system of non-monogamous, intimate relations involving three or more people. Basically, it espoused the possibility that people could have more than one intimate sexual relationship as long as all the participants entered into a cooperative agreement to eschew power plays, lies or rescues and to ask for everything they wanted 100% of the time.

We set out to try this approach with pedal to the metal and, for a while, as long as all involved stuck to the agreements it seemed to work for some people. Everything was done above board; no one started a relationship without informing and obtaining the approval of the other person(s); no one pushed for something the others didn't want; no one did anything they didn't want to do.

But we didn't anticipate that it was humanly impossible to stick to these agreements. Even if people refrained from openly power playing, they weren't necessarily able to be completely honest about how they felt, their jealousies, disappointments or anger, or to avoid doing what they didn't want to do. In addition, a basic premise of these arrangements was that there were endless supplies of strokes which, while theoretically true was not materially possible because stroking takes time and time is limited. Omnigamy became a full-time job, taking up the participants energy as they put out the constant fires that multiple relationships constantly caused. So, in the end, omnigamy didn't work and it hurt some people, some badly, usually women. We had to retreat from what was basically a command economy not unlike other unworkable command economies that were generated by socialist principles.

Omnigamy was a failed experiment. However, the idea derived from Stroke City and emotional literacy training – that one can learn to fully love and that strokes can be plentiful – has proven to be durably valid; the second original notion, after my ideas on paranoia that I have contributed to the knowledge of the human being.

...

Darca was also committed to non-monogamy. As I mentioned before she even coined the term "omnigamy," which became our codification of cooperative non-monogamous relationships, which we proceeded faithfully to pursue; we would not lie to each other about our outside relationships and we would not initiate relationships without the other's approval of the new lover that was being contemplated.

Here is an example of how serious we were about omnigamy: at a certain point in our relationship when I told Darca that a woman I was interested in questioned that Darca would be OK with it she volunteered to make me a wallet-sized "permission" card in which she wrote and signed in her own hand: "To my sisters: I love Claude and wish the best for him. If you desire to be good and loving to him, including sexually, I would be eternally thankful. Signed: Darca."

Darca and I got along famously; the last years of my relationship with Hogie had been punctuated by constant fights and competitive acrimony fueled by her dissatisfaction with me; my unwillingness to fully commit and have a child with her. In the first years of my relationship with Darca, to my great surprise and relief, we did not fight at all. But with all her attributes I was not persuaded into a commitment either.

Coda (2008): love of self, others and truth

Writing this book has been a surprisingly emotional enterprise; sadness as I saw where I missed human opportunities, guilt as I recognized things I should and should not have done, pride at my accomplishments, happiness and dread when I recovered long forgotten memories, and awe about how much has happened and had been forgotten in my life. I was fearful that what I was taking such pains to write could not be published or that, if I published it, I would suffer or make others suffer.

When Eric Berne passed away at the young age of 60 it seemed to me that he had died of a broken heart. This was literally true insofar as he died of a heart

208　*Claude Steiner*

attack, but his heart was broken in more ways than one, in that his relationships with women had been truncated by disappointment. I believe he disappointed the women he was with and they tried but could not take it any more. I saw a pattern that I resolved not to repeat and I promised myself to attempt to live one hundred years. Since then it has became clear to me that love is the answer, the engine of survival (novel thought) and that it is love we must focus on and nurture in whatever form, to the end.

Everyone wants to love and to be loved, knowing how good it feels when it happens. I want to write about love and the trajectory of that emotion in my own life. Even though I believe I was born with a normal capacity to love and empathize, I must have had it beaten out of me, for I came into adult life badly lacking in sympathy for other people, a narcissist unable to nurture or to be nurtured and unable to declare my love in the rare occasion that I felt it. Over the years, through many lessons, I developed what I would like to call a loving attitude: love of others but, just as importantly, love of self, and love of truth.

As far as loving myself I was imbued with a healthy dose of self-esteem. Because I love myself, I am able to stand my ground in defense of my personal uniqueness. Individuality keeps me firmly focused on what I want and makes me capable of deciding what will contribute or detract from my personal path. Love of self is a double-edged sword and can turn into narcissism, selfishness and obliviousness. But it has given me the strength to persevere in my decisions while everyone was losing faith in who I am or what I was doing and that strength is attractive to others so I have always found people to love me.

Loving myself, aided by obliviousness, at first came at the expense of loving others. To be sure, I felt love for others but not frequently and unreliably so. When I fell in love, as I did with Ursula, I was taken over by love and then love, in relatively short order, went away and only returned when I fell in love again with the next person; Bobby and then Micky and so on. I had to learn to reliably love others. Until I did, I compensated for my handicap with loyalty. Loyalty – different from love – kept me involved in the lives of those who I might have loved but proved insufficient for those who loved me. Often, after I stopped being in love I merely Rescued people as I grudgingly looked after them; those Rescues bringing on the inevitable, eventual Persecution and dissolution. Love of self without love of others is selfishness. Love of others without love of self turns us into potential Victims at the mercy of selfish others as we willingly give everything away.

But neither love of self or love of others can be sustained if one does not love the truth enough to represent it and defend it. Love of truth involves not lying overtly or by omission; being truthful about how we feel and what we want. Radical truthfulness – the vow never to tell a lie in our relationships – is the only practical long-term application for those who love truth themselves and others. I find that being truthful when I am angry, sad or afraid, being willing to express my wishes and refusing to go along with what I don't want, are essential aspects of a successful long-term loving relationship. In addition, love of truth keeps me actively involved in pursuing valid information, that is information that reflects the realities of the

Excerpts on love and sex 209

world upon which to build a life that is supportive of love. Again, at the risk of repeating myself, love of self or others is impossible without love of truth.

I am now 73 years old; that gives me another 27 years that is 9,800 days, and counting to enjoy, at an age in which many have folded their tents and are marking time waiting to face the grim reaper. Yet I am behaving as if I have a whole lifetime ahead of me in which I intend to apply the above lessons to the hilt. I try to live every day of my hoped for remaining days as if it was the last. And I am privileged to do this while I enjoy, what feels to me, like a perfect love with my wife Jude.

All the nastinesses have come home to roost. I believe I am continuing to confront my lack of empathy – even brutishness, my neglectful attitudes, my self-centered narcissism, my obliviousness, my critical attitudes, my lack of spirituality, my cynicism, my compulsive sexuality and need to control everything and everybody and my still imperfect capacity to love, in my relationship with Jude. My friends Becky, Charlie, David, Ron, Denton, have tried in their own way to bring me around with partial success. My daughter Mimi and my son Eric have struggled mightily but it was Jude that found the means to bring me up by the short hairs and broken my stubborn, nasty streak.

15 Love is the answer

Karen Minikin

> To the untrained eye love is a simple, highly elusive emotion, sought by some, feared by others, more or less free to exist in people's hearts depending on previous experience.
>
> (Steiner, 2009, p. 65)

The importance of love to Steiner underpins his theories and his life long quest to understand the meaning of life personally, philosophically, socially and politically. His thinking about love and the transactions expressing this emotion build on Eric Berne's (1966b) theory of hungers. From Steiner's earlier work, we have his development of stroke theory and especially the stroke economy (Steiner, 1971f).

Like all of us, Claude Steiner was a person of his time and place, in his case maturing as a man in 1960s California with the social and political backdrop of that era. His relationships with women were key, alongside the emerging social and sexual liberation that was beginning to happen in the West. In 1960, Britain saw the court case over Penguin's "scandalous" 1959 publication of *Lady Chatterley's Lover* (Lawrence, 1928/1959), whilst in California, the sun was shining, the beach inviting and the contraceptive pill was out. This was also the decade in which I was born, so it has pertinent meaning for me to have this opportunity to reflect on this time.

During the 1970s and 1980s, I imagine that Steiner had time to reflect on the decade of liberation and he seems to do this with an open mind motivated by an urge to speak truthfully about both social and his own personal developments. As evidenced by the previous chapter, excerpted from his *Confessions*, he is candid about his personal discoveries and struggles. Like his mentor, Eric Berne, he shared the challenge of how to establish, experience and stay connected in loving relationships with women. His developing interest in personal politics helped grow his thinking about social and sexual politics, and from these exciting times and vitalising relations, he shared his learning in his book *When a Man Loves a Woman* (Steiner, 1986).

Moving into the 1990s, this was a decade when research and knowledge about the brain developed and neuroscience shared findings profoundly helpful to the psychological professions. At last, it seemed there was scientific validation for what had already been known in psychotherapy for some time – that is, that relational experiences during infancy were of primary importance when it came to bonding, attachment and capacity to love. Significant publications on this included

Love is the answer   211

Affect Regulation and the Origin of the Self (Schore, 1994) and, a decade later, *Why Love Matters* (Gerhardt, 2004). Although Steiner does not reference these books, his thinking about love developed in what I see as a parallel direction. Between these years, he seemed particularly interested in the essential human quality of love and the capacity it has to fulfil human potential, as expressed in his paper, originally presented at a conference in 2000, "The meming of love".

Steiner's passion, connection and thinking about love seemed to develop further as he grew in age and also perhaps to some extent in response to his long-term battle with Parkinson's disease. His last writing on the subject of love was his book *The Heart of the Matter: Love, Information and Transactional Analysis* (Steiner, 2009), which includes additional reflections on the spiritual connection with love as a power to transcend an impulse to control and our capacity for hatred. Here, he offers a structure connecting love with the seven chakras and a more expansive connection with body, mind and spirit (see also Chapter 11).

In this chapter, I summarise the development of Steiner's thinking about love as it is related to these three areas: sexual politics linking to political power; human attachment, bonding and love; and, finally, his expressions of a longing for cosmic connection and transcendence of hatred.

When a Man Loves a Woman (Steiner, 1986): heterosexual politics

In the previous chapter we witness the open reflections of how Claude Steiner grew and struggled in his personal relationships, learning much from the influential women in his history. Starting with the lack of certainty about his identity accompanied by some insecurity about being loveable, he recognises how hungry he was to experience being loved and then, later, loving others. His writing conveys how deep hunger can leave a sense of insatiable longing that becomes confused with sexuality and sexual behaviour. The way he talks about this speaks particularly to heterosexual men. He offers explanations of how sex can become a compulsive hunt to experience something close to satisfaction. However, as he develops his consciousness, Steiner describes how limiting this was and that it never quite satisfied his hunger for physical intimacy. Through the important women in his life, he comes to yearn for and enjoy wider expressions and experiences of sexual love.

Steiner's honest account of his engagement with the mood, the pleasure-seeking experiences and sexual permissions of 1960s California reveals his then capacity for macho sexual behaviour, as well as, in contrast, his emerging willingness to listen and learn from women. In my view, he shares the Shadow side of this liberating time with some humility. For instance, in the previous chapter, he writes about how involved he was in experimenting with omnigamy. To work with and manage this, he and his partners lived and practised the transactional analysis (TA) principles of open communication, contracting and honesty. There was the hope that these communicative provisions could protect against the challenges of having multiple partners by being the necessary vehicles for autonomy, allowing for awareness, spontaneity, though, in particular, intimacy. His accounts of his relationships bear witness to how committed he and others around him were in their endeavour to find

212 *Karen Minikin*

something amongst themselves that represented freedom, honesty and respect. Yet, as he confesses, the experiment "failed" (p. 207). Having described their efforts and commitment, Steiner concludes that omnigamy benefitted men more than women and did little to help men like him encounter and process their struggles and resistance to commitment in longer-term loving relationships.

The 1960s and the following 1970s were a time of great experimental learning and Steiner's writing in *When a Man Loves a Woman* collects and amalgamates his learning about sexual love between a man and a woman.

This is a book that presents a challenge to both sexes, perhaps especially men. The book is subtitled "Sexual and emotional literacy for the modern man". Noting his awareness of his earlier limitations and the life changing learning he encountered, I can understand how crucial it may have felt for him to share this with other men, so I take this to be a heterosexual or heteronormative text of its time. Notwithstanding this, some themes remain relevant such as the polarities we are currently witnessing between liberalism and conservatism, and oppression and freedom, which continue to be part of our global experiences.

As a woman reading this book, it was interesting and at times challenging to be reminded of the aggression in sexual machismo, which was validated in the 1970s and the way these feelings were expressed and acted on between the sexes. For example, "When a man meets a woman who doesn't enjoy his advances, the combination of his tendency to be unaware of people's feelings and his drive to have intercourse results in a disregard for the annoyance he causes her" (Steiner, 1986, p. 12); and also: "As we evaluate women by the size of their breasts, we are likely to be evaluated by the size of our wallets" (ibid., p. 13).

Exposing crude expressions of how the sexes objectified each other and exposing oppressive social behaviours is very much a part of this book and clearly represents the values Claude and others in radical psychiatry held regarding honesty and the commitment to challenge oneself and others in the quest of personal and social liberation. The book maintains a tone of being both a social and a practical handbook as, in the early chapters, it goes into specific detail about heterosexual sex. The latter part of the book, however, is much more concerned with emotional literacy, especially for men, and here Claude seems to speak directly as a man who felt he had learnt so much from the women he loved.

Steiner's heartfelt passion comes through as this book progresses and he starts to bring together his learning from personal and political life, sometimes with a plea: "Our lives may appear to be orderly, productive, and well organised, but our emotions are in shambles ... We can compute megadeaths. But we cannot direct our loving energies at home, at the office, or across the negotiating table" (Steiner, 1986, pp. 115–116).

And, later, one that, sadly, continues to apply to our world in many contexts:

> when the living dead acquire power, as they so often do, they subject the rest of us to their control, power plays, and violence. When the emotionally illiterate inhabit the corridors of power and dominate whole governments, they threaten the citizenry with apocalypse, war, death, hunger, and disease.
>
> (ibid., p. 116)

Love is the answer 213

Although Steiner does not make reference to Crossman and her work on protection and permission (Crossman, 1966), it does seem relevant to refer to it here. Crossman had written about the relationship between the two, citing how the provision of protection makes it safe to experiment with new ways of being (i.e., permission). This was evident in the way Steiner lived his life and how he wrote about emancipation. However, he also added a third "P" (Steiner, 1968b), that of potency, which he develops in this book as he explores how, in sexual politics, power can be used to dominate and abuse people. He writes of learning how to hold his potency with greater genuine authority, as well as finding permission in himself and others to loosen oppressive sexual ties and have experiences that were liberating – such was the mood of the time, as well as Claude's own personal longings to be free, sexually. What may be missing from the previous chapter which excerpts from his *Confessions*, his writing on love and sex, is a sense of protection for the vulnerability we all face in our most intimate relations, protection that even the most robust cooperative contracting and honest sharing of feelings is hard to establish. In other words, the robust contracting, the vows of absolute openness and honesty did not protect Claude or his lovers from feelings of intense vulnerability, competition and jealousy. I would add that the primitive nature of sex and the feelings that go with it are sometimes hard to reach through words alone, so all the contracting in the world is no substitute for a felt sense of safety, trust and security that are essential for getting close to feelings of genuine emotional and physical love. Nonetheless, Claude's capacity to critique society, politics and social culture as well as himself is remarkable. In some ways this book reminds me of the feminist slogan that the personal is political (Hanisch, 1969/1970).

The meming of love (Steiner, 2000d)

This paper was presented at the Third Adolescence Health Conference, in London, in October 2000. This is contextually relevant as this was just a few years after Allan Schore's (1994) publication on *Affect Regulation and the Origin of the Self*, and a few years before the publication of Sue Gerhardt's (2004) *Why Love Matters*. Both Schore and Gerhardt spoke and wrote about the growing evidence from neuroscience about the essential requirement of relational contact in developing fluidity in the limbic system of the brain. This facilitates emotional literacy and a capacity for relating to self and others, leading to the security to love. Steiner's paper came 14 years after the publication of *When a Man Loves a Woman*; Claude was then 65, more reflective, and more generally emphasising love as a matter of the heart. Reading this paper, it seems that, alongside a certain change in knowledge in Western society, something had also changed for Claude himself.

In the paper, Steiner shares his interest in the general human condition and love. Drawing on ways of thinking about psychological evolution, he quotes from neuroscience and the different functions of the brain. He considers primitive processes with reference to: reptilian functions; the limbic system, associated with mammals and their care of their young; and, finally, the neo-cortical system. He describes how sophisticated variants of love have developed in connection with social and cultural development as well as scripting. With reference to the limbic brain, he

214   *Karen Minikin*

picks up on my previous point about protection and love by referring to the importance of protective love in creating safety which creates an environment allowing for contact and bonding:

> Protection of the young required affiliative behavior based on a drive for contact and mutual recognition. This hunger for contact maintained the bond between mother and offspring and generated closely knit, cooperative groupings ... The principal emotions associated with affiliation is love; sadness, hope and guilt are emotions that are generated when affiliation fails to repair the failure.
>
> (Steiner, 2000d)

Following the emerging paradigm of this era, Steiner considers love as part of our evolution and, in the paper, he specifically draws on the work of Dawkins (1989).

Dawkins claims that genetic evolution has slowed down, and yet our capacity to adapt and change has not. Dawkins talks about "memetic" evolution, which draws on guiding ideas or "memes" and acknowledges that these replicate horizontally rather than vertically. For instance, I began this section of writing by introducing neuroscience and the work of Schore and Gerhardt. I have no idea if Steiner read these works, but by then (2000) he is interested in Dawkins and in findings from neuroscience. This may be part of the professional and academic environment in which we live, though this common interest may also reflect the fact that core, influencing paradigms that frame knowledge, ways of thinking, society and culture get communicated horizontally. In other words, cognitively, conceptually, emotionally and philosophically, we are connected consciously and unconsciously across nations and landscapes. The idea of memes thus makes a bridge, as possible neuroscience does from the sciences into the social sciences.

In other words, we can begin to consider ancestral knowledge as our vertical inheritance and memes as communal knowledge that represents a horizontal inheritance. Steiner goes on to link the significance of Dawkins's work with key ideas in TA, especially those relating to love, namely, hungers which drive a need for: recognition and contact; strokes, which are the currency in which recognition and contact are offered (see Chapters 5 and 6); and injunctions, which are the learnt limiting inhibitions to free expression and security. As usual, Steiner identifies the Critical Parent as the enemy to freedom and intimacy as it inspires hate towards the self and others. Vengeance, criticism, jealousy, judgement evoke feelings of competition, insecurity and a dislike of the self and others which diminish, or, worse, destroy love. So, here, Steiner's exploration of love takes in a wider context. He acknowledges the findings from neuroscience confirming the significance of maternal love, and he addresses the intensity of adolescent sexual love, citing a powerful example of adolescent passion swinging between fantasised desire and obsession and then switching to hatred and murderous rage when such strong feelings are not reciprocated. He also speaks/writes movingly about the repression of love between men and boys, leading to suppression of expressions of affection between them.

Love is the answer 215

Steiner's expansion in his thinking about love and his reference to human nature seems to marry with his life stage and he demonstrates how he looks back with reflection on his life, as well as how he is reflecting on the troubles of current society. Whilst he does not refer directly to the holding, containing and regulating influence of love, he is recognising here how crucial it is personally, socially and culturally. In addition, we see the beginnings of spiritual reflections developing in Steiner, as he makes reference to Jesus of Nazareth and Christianity, thought of by some as the religion of love. In my view, in this paper, whilst drawing on TA and its attention to how psychology drives behaviour and relationships, Steiner takes a more expansive theoretical model of love. He also brings together some key elements from his philosophy and his own theories to offer four moral and behavioural guidelines for people and society:

- *Power parity*, which involves the powerful giving up power, and the powerless empowering themselves. Here we can see the influence of radical psychiatry and the importance of liberation on Claude's thinking, which shows that he maintained his political perspective throughout his life and that it continued to inform and guide his aspirations.
- *Honesty*, that is, no lies, either of commission or of omission. This echoes his embracing of directives from Hogie Wyckoff, Carmen Kerr and Darca Nicholson about which and whom Steiner writes about (in the previous chapter). It is clear that the ownership, openness and honesty about feelings contributed enormously to his own sense of liberation as he experienced it in previous decades.
- *Cooperation*, that is, no power plays, asking for 100 per cent of what we want, and negotiating. Cooperation also feeds into the method of seeking egalitarian and fair relationships where there is profound commitment to respect for oneself and the other. This also marries up with the fundamental philosophical principle in TA that people are OK. Being a lifelong advocate for radical psychiatry, Steiner embraced this philosophy and lived it, and wanted to see others doing the same.
- *Gentleness*, that is, an empathic response to other people's needs. The inclusion of gentleness touched me, as it seems like an antidote to the sort of man that Claude had started out to be in life. It leaves me reflecting on how deeply engaged he was in discovering love and expressions of affection and gentleness in his middle and later years. I imagine he suffered enormously from the deficit of this in his early life (see Chapters 3 and 14), and, in a sense, one might say that he spent a lifetime in recovery. My sense of Claude's loss and his longing for a more loving life and a more loving world seems validated by his proposal in this paper that adherence to these four moral and behavioural guidelines will enable humanity not only "to create helpful and fertile settings for love to flourish, but for a far more proactive approach which will actually rehabilitate love" (Steiner, 2000d).

Steiner goes on to describe how he activated the capacity for human love in his group workshops called *Stroke City*. Here, people were encouraged to share

216　*Karen Minikin*

appreciations (genuine positive strokes) with each other and, in so doing, their critical processes diminished in remarkable ways. Positive feelings were contagious, and defences laid to rest, allowing people to become infected with a kind of "love euphoria":

> At first I assumed that people were just cheered up by these activities in a manner similar to what happens at a ball game in which our side wins. But upon closer examination it became clear that these exercises had a profound effect on the participants' loving emotions. They spoke of loving feelings, of having an open heart and of transcendent experiences of affection and universal love.
>
> (Steiner, 2000d)

Steiner was very committed to the behavioural aspect of TA, that is, the philosophy that if we behave properly towards each other, the rest will follow. He was clearly very emotionally and intellectually stimulated by these "Stroke City" workshops and it led him to have great hope for humanity. So, I have taken it that, at this stage of his career and life, he was thinking in an increasingly expansive way about love. He considered the innate genetic drive, the aggressive and critical damage done by scripting and the destructive force of violence and domination, which I would link to "thanatos" (Freud, 1920/1984; Spielrein, 1912/1994). In the paper, Steiner presses us to practise the values of cooperation, honesty and gentleness, values and ideas that continued to dwell in him and were developed further in his later and last compendium on love, *The Heart of the Matter* (Steiner, 2009).

The Heart of the Matter (Steiner, 2009)

This book is an important attempt by Steiner to bring his ideas together – on power, politics, human hungers and needs, along with human potential. This reads as a text from the man who was facing his mortality and wanting to gather up the creative produce from his life, as well as to offer his contemplation on spiritual growth as he journeyed towards the end of his life on this planet. From earth to heaven, the book reads to me as if he is gathering himself together and attempting to apply wisdom to his past, his life as a man and his life as somebody very unwell and facing death. Overall, the book reads as something that seeks to capture his legacy.

The title of the book expresses Steiner's developing emphasis on love as the critical force for humanity. In addition to summarising his life works, there are a number of philosophical reflections and questions. For instance, "to the untrained eye love is a simple, highly elusive emotion, sought be some, feared by others, more or less free to exist in people's hearts depending on previous experience. Why should it be the target of focused suppression?" (ibid., p. 65). Then, "love is far more than a quotidian source of good or bad feelings. Love is a major motivating power, interacting in a complex, human power field" (ibid., p. 65).

Far from having romantic notions about the power of love, Steiner recognised the converse in the love of power and he positioned the suppression of love as a political manifestation. In other words, love can be a threat to those with power and so its suppression serves a political purpose in society. It facilitates a "power

Love is the answer   217

over" dynamic that allows those with power to retain it. Also, although he believed passionately in the value of romantic love, he did not support a romantic notion of love as a "cure all". My sense is that he would have been aligned with some of the messages offered in Cornell and Bonds-White (2001) who debated the truth of love or the love of truth, and, in doing so, critiqued the shift towards empathy, attunement and holding that had come about in the late 1990s. As I have suggested, this was an era of paying attention to maternal love and its function in affect regulation, and the concomitant shift in TA challenged the previous confrontation approach, with its potential shaming effect.

Yet, as we have seen with and from Steiner, he held fiercely on to truth – right up to and on his dying day it seems. Above all, he continued to be able to confront himself and to challenge his "nasty streak" as he referred to it (in the previous Chapter, p. 209), exposing it in his writing with admirable reflexivity, humility and resilience. This fits, of course, with his hunger for genuine contact and recognition and his antipathy to "plastic strokes" (Steiner, 1977d).

Having gathered my own thoughts and reflections on his writing and the three texts on which I have chosen to focus in this chapter, I think his model on love-centred power (Steiner, 2009) is particularly noteworthy. I have chosen to make specific reference to this given the stage of life Steiner had reached at this point, and my sense that his reflections on his work were taking a more transpersonal turn. These are taken from ideas central to Hindu tantrism, which perhaps suggests his need to reach beyond his own culture and scriptures and search for texts that spoke to his heart and soul. Linking his key thinking about love and power, he attributes the conducting power to the heart chakra, so that the feelings of love direct power as and when it is required or needed (see also Chapter 11). So, Steiner relates his learning about love with the seven chakras and the function these serve in personal, social and spiritual guidance. Here I summarise the key ideas from his model:

1.   The base (Muladhara) chakra.
     This is considered the foundation of energy, creating stability and stirring to untie both feminine and masculine energies. Steiner relates this to balance and stability and the need to be grounded. He also talks to this politically, bringing in gender scripting (Steiner, 2009) as he emphasises movement between positions, as opposed to getting stuck in a submissive or dominating place.

2.   The second (Svadhishthana) chakra.
     The second chakra is located in the area around our sexual organs. It is connected to our sensuality and sexuality and Steiner links this to the creative and destructive force of passion. Looking back at *When a Man Loves a Woman*, it seems that this was a profound source of his human experiences through his middle years and in relationships with women. In this last model, Steiner links passion with the speed of processing, recognising both the drive to live and the capacity to kill in the throws of passion.

3.   The third (Manipura) chakra.
     This third chakra, located at the navel, just below the solar plexus is thought to be connected with the process of transformation, with digestive functions

218   *Karen Minikin*

in the body and with willpower and dynamism. Steiner links this to the use of control, the capacity to make things happen and, in its deficit, to passivity. He also notes how important it is to be conscious of this energy source in order to direct control and regulation wisely.

4.   The heart (Anahata) chakra.
     This fourth chakra is able to experience a sense of being free-moving. It offers a capacity to suspend our position from our egos and consider apparently contradictory experiences to deliver fresh perspectives. In other words, it helps us to transcend script. Steiner links this chakra directly to love, the emotion of love, and sees this as pivotal in making use of our power. He cites specifically the love of self, the love of others and the love of truth, including "radical truth telling" (Steiner, 2009, p. 139).

5.   The throat (Vishuddi) chakra.
     This fifth chakra is linked to creativity and self-expression. It is considered the place where negative experiences are transformed into wisdom and learning. Thus, Steiner relates this to the function of communication and the ability to induce ideas or feelings. Throughout his descriptions of all these chakras he considers the importance of balancing assertion with reception to others by directing the heart-based energy to where it needs to be.

6.   The third eye (Ajna) chakra.
     This chakra is said to be located in the brain, close to the pineal gland and sits between the eyebrows. It is related to the subconscious mind and the capacity to have insight and also the sort of intuition that can receive implicit communication and see how the future will be laid out. Steiner calls this the place for information and to make decisions. He describes the importance of integrating information from worldly knowledge such as science and history and combining this with intuition and vision. As he himself puts it: "This book focuses on Information and Love. Love and Information have the power to change the world" (ibid., p. 141).

7.   The seventh (Sahasrara) chakra.
     This is also referred to as the crown chakra and as such "is thought to be related to pure consciousness, influencing all the other chakras" (ibid., p. 141). Steiner names this the place of transcendence, which allows us to see clearly amidst trauma and changes. His connection to his mortality is expressed as he states how short our lives are on earth, before returning to "cosmic dust" (ibid., p. 142), and goes on to say:

> The power of transcendence gives us hope and faith that there is a meaning to life even if our limited intelligence can't grasp it. With it we can "rise above" a particular situation and trust and feel our power in spite of material conditions.
>
> (ibid., p. 142)

Love is the answer 219

Steiner writes that he has presented these seven sources of power as an "alternative to the control-obsessed form that is so often seen as the ideal avenue to personal power. Heart centred power replaces Control with Love while giving control its due as one of the indispensable seven" (ibid., p. 143).

Conclusion

Claude Steiner's relationship with Eric Berne was clearly one of immense importance to him and a source of inspiration throughout his life. His respect and affection for Berne grew from a relationship as a mentor and colleague to that of a friend, though Claude always said that he was a "disciple" of Berne's.

Claude Steiner made many dear friends during his professional career in TA, radical psychiatry and emotional literacy. He also made some enemies, though he did on occasion have the courage to declare his faults, his mistakes, to acknowledge some of the damage he did in human relations and, on occasion, to apologise. I met Claude Steiner on a few occasions at conferences. My contact with him was brief, and mainly comprised a limited exchange about his ideas and my response to them. My experience was that he had an open, curious mind and even when he was weak in his body, he maintained a vitality expressed in debate and wit. Engaging in writing this chapter, and re-reading some of his work, has given me opportunity to appreciate him as a man, as a vulnerable human being, as a thoughtful person of advancing years and as someone who, although gone from this earth, lives on in many constellations in the minds and hearts of those still here. I conclude this chapter with some of his last words from his last book. Firstly, talking about therapists, he writes: "Her love of truth keeps her honest about the effects of her therapy – positive, negative or neutral. These are the elements that we must study and master to qualify as effective productive 21st century soul healers" (ibid., p. 236). And then, some words of wisdom:

> Valuable as time is becoming in the next years of my life, I hope to use it to investigate the new information age and how it may help redeem the urgently wretched situation human kind is facing; this is my emerging interest.
>
> Ever powerful in human affairs, love alone has not been equal to the redemptive task. Teamed with information, love, I believe, is still the answer.
>
> (ibid. p. 237)

OCHO
Reflecting on the legacy

16 A final confession from the psychomechanic

On games

Claude Steiner with Keith Tudor

Although Claude Steiner wrote a book on games – *Games Alcoholics Play* (Steiner, 1971b) – this book was more a development of Eric Berne's ideas about games than an original contribution to the literature; and, indeed, neither games nor his work on alcoholism (see Steiner, 1979b) appear in Claude's own list of his "10 Top Ideas" (see Chapter 1). Nevertheless, a significant theme of this book is the strand of Claude's own reflections from his *Confessions* (Steiner, 2008a), arranged with regard to theory including scripts (Chapter 3) and strokes (Chapter 5), and, like the rest of us, as Claude got caught and engaged in psychological games, I wanted to represent this strand of his autobiography and theory. Interestingly, as I read and re-read Claude's *Confessions* and the document *CS at 80* (Steiner, 2017), I found relatively few references to games and/or game theory, and so, when I last saw him (in July 2016), I asked him about it. Thus, this chapter comprises some (few) excerpts from his *Confessions* on the subject, and from that recorded conversation.

From "Confessions of a Psychomechanic: on games"

In addition, there was something clearly wrong with the way things went between myself and people in organizations that I belonged to. The ITAA [International Transactional Analysis Association], of which I was a founding member with Berne, had refused to allow me the Presidency after Berne died; the Berkeley Free Clinic expelled me and the rest of the Radical Psychiatry Collective from their building; and a few years later the Radical Psychiatry Collective had broken up and both sides proceeded to excluded me, in turn, from their meetings. I had a very unpleasant experience with the Abalone Alliance during our action against Diablo Canyon nuclear plant which I ended abruptly when I broke the discipline that required that we all be arrested together and had myself arrested in order to get away from the affinity group and join my friend Jackson Browne in jail.[1]

After Berne died, I began to see that I had repeatedly experienced what seemed like a betrayal by several groups of people who I had led and who I thought owed me recognition and had, instead, rejected me leaving me with a bitter taste and a desire for revenge and vindication closely paralleling the Pied Piper story.

224   *Claude Steiner*

I am not sure how I got interested in being a leader, but I remember that my first effort was organizing a social club – Club Aries – in my first University year in Mexico City the purpose of which was to throw parties and attract girls and eventually elect me president for even larger attractiveness. But it quickly became clear that I was not to be president and the presidency went instead to a rich, handsome boy instead. But leading groups of people was in my blood and I proceeded to organize parties for all the years of graduate school and my singular contribution at those parties was to supply dancing music.

The betrayals continued. In graduate school I thought I was leading a student revolt and got in trouble when my cohorts abandoned me. When after years of being maintenance manager at the Kingsley Street married coop in Ann Arbor, the sounds of bitter strife between Ursula and I became too much for the other tenants they tried, unsuccessfully, to evict us. When I tried to get elected as ITAA president, it was the Board of Trustees that made sure that I wasn't.

I felt from an early age that my parents betrayed me. I based that feeling on their increased lack of interest when my sister was born, being left alone in the evenings and abandoning me at the boarding home, sending me away in the summer to friends who seemed to dislike me probably because I walked in on them while they were fucking late one morning and who yelled at me for inexplicably unfair reasons. An example etched in my mind was when, at the breakfast table, I quite innocently asked if I could have some "stinkadorous" cheese, which is what my parents called gorgonzola cheese. I got yelled at mercilessly and accused of deliberate rudeness; obviously they were not fond of my presence. A small thing to be sure but it's strange how certain events, however minor, stick in one's mind. From early on I had a keenly developed sense of injustice and was shocked and felt betrayed when people behaved unfairly towards me.

Excerpts from a conversation between Claude Steiner and Keith Tudor, 17 July 2016

KEITH: Reading the *Confessions*, I was struck that, while you talk a lot about script, you don't say much about games, that is, the games you played. What was your part in the slights and offences that you feel, especially with regard to the TA community? I'm interested in this particularly as I think that … [with regard to a particular colleague] you're still wanting to fight the ITAA.

CLAUDE: Well, it's interesting cos I know I did power plays.[2] I know that my part in my problems with the ITAA may have to do with my sexual behaviour in the time that I was active, which was basically [that] I got laid whenever I could – and I wasn't hiding the fact. In fact, I got a phone call from some kind of committee [within the ITAA] saying they wanted me to stop going over[seas] to do workshops and hooking up with people. I said that if I couldn't hook up with grown up, consensual adults, I wouldn't even be interested to do the travelling. In some ways it [the hooking up] made the travelling worthwhile.

A final confession from the psychomechanic   225

[Also,] I literally saw it as a way of keeping myself physically healthy – and I still feel that way right now.

KEITH: That's very Reichian [of you]!

CLAUDE: It may be Reichian, it may be whatever it is, I feel it in my bones. So, it could be that that's the reason that they don't want to have anything to do with me, that I have this reputation even though that was many, many years ago. But maybe that's not it. I asked Gianpiero Petriglieri [President of the ITAA, 2006–2009] to do a little research and find out what was wrong, and why people were doing this, and his answer was there's a kind of cadre of old timers who are a big pain in the arse in the ITAA and I'm seen to be part of it even though really I'm not ... You know, people who just won't let go. My reaction [to that] is that if you don't want my stuff, then I don't want you.

KEITH: I think people see that there's a difference between you and your stuff. Also, when you're feeling particularly irritable or grumpy with the ITAA, [I think] you underestimate the influence of your work: every student of TA is taught your work, from day one.[3]

CLAUDE: Well, that's interesting ... [However,] I made a list of the evidence that there's something wrong. I happened to find this yesterday when I was working through my papers. Here's my evidence that there's something really wrong. I get the *TAJ* [the *Transactional Analysis Journal*], which I consider a kind of index of what's going on [in the] ITAA ...

Regarding emotional literacy

... [and] there's absolutely no references to emotional literacy: none, zero, ever.

KEITH: Since 1984?

CLAUDE: Since, lately, you know, in the last maybe three or four years.

KEITH: Okay. I'll check that out, and you know I'm academic enough to check this out, so I will![4]

Regarding recognition

CLAUDE: Just before Istanbul, I was offered a keynote speech, [an offer] which was later withdrawn: "Sorry, we don't really want that." Then I power-played [the organiser] ... I said, "You either give me a spot [doing] the keynote thing or I'll just be a tourist: I'll come, I'll do my workshop and I won't interact at all." And she said, "No, that's OK," and she put me on. ...

I applied for [the] Eric Berne Memorial Award three times ... three times I've done that, three times it didn't work.

KEITH: But you've won the Award twice?

CLAUDE: I have two already,[5] but I wanted to have a third one. It could be that that's why I don't get it! ... Anyway, it's bullshit, I don't care.

KEITH: ... You do care!

226 *Claude Steiner*

CLAUDE: Not really, I mean – I'm curious about what's wrong. Why is that? I was a Vice President of Research & Innovation for a number of years and I wrote a paper; my contribution was to look for any kind of research in the behavioural sciences that corroborated Eric's ideas. When I wrote the paper, Bill Cornell refused to print it in the *TAJ* and I was ready to get into a huge fight about it and Jude said, "Uh-uh. Don't get into a fight, let me talk to Bill about it," and they compromised in that the paper was going to be published in *The Script*, but it never got into the journal.

KEITH: Really? Was it published in *The Script*?

CLAUDE: It was published in *The Script* [Steiner, 2003b]. The fact that I did all that research and all of that … I never received a single request for information by any further Vice Presidents of Research & Innovation. You'd think that they would try to at least figure out what I did. There were never any questions, ever. And then – and this is probably what happens to everybody who writes for the *TAJ*, because nobody reads it – I've written a number of papers, because if I write a paper it gets published in the *TAJ*, if it's a simple paper, just because it's well-written and it's usually interesting. So, I have papers on apology [Steiner, 2000a], … on writing styles [Steiner, 2006b], I have a stack of papers – [but] never, ever [get] any feedback: No comment that this was a good paper.

 So, I think that this is my list. Not that interesting but … I'm being paranoid, but I'm not being *that* paranoid.

KEITH: Going back to games … you're saying, yes, you have played games but, you've also stimulated [or initiated] games?

CLAUDE: I don't know, I probably play games that I'm not aware of, I'd be very interested in figuring out what they are. I know I power-play. Like I power-played [about] the conference in Istanbul.

KEITH: The other thing I would add to that list [about recognition] is that when there was an ITAA conference in San Francisco [in 2007] and it was on the theme of "Cooperation and Power", you weren't invited. [Personally] that led me to do something to honour you, three years ago [in 2014]. So, I'm curious, does that make a difference? Does that experience three years ago, when we did the workshop together, you drew quarter of the conference …

CLAUDE: Oh yeah, but I'm used to putting up a subject matter for a conference and having everybody come to it. That's nothing new. That's what makes it so shocking: all I have to do is say "I want to present this" and it's approved immediately … which makes sense because having my name on the programme is probably helpful to a conference. Not having my name on a programme is probably not very helpful at all.

KEITH: They get kudos from having your name.

CLAUDE: But they don't initiate, I have to do the initiating.

KEITH: Except three years ago, I did the initiating! Was that good?

CLAUDE: Yeah, it was great … So, back to the more interesting part: what games? Was I being punished for previous bad behaviour? Was I just promoting my script?

KEITH: That's a good question.

CLAUDE: I think most of my games are power plays.

[A long pause, which included Claude going to the bathroom.]

CLAUDE: You got me thinking about my games and, you know, I suddenly realised that it's true: most of my games are power plays, and the fact is that one of the ideas that I had is that all games are power plays. Some are played/power plays for stokes which is the Bernean idea of games played for strokes [Berne 1964/1966a], and the rest are played for other things: for money, for position, for status. So my power plays are: "I'm poor", "I'm only trying to help", "Rescuing" … [pause, then, talking about a personal situation] I think there's a Rescuing game … I could work it out that she's betrayed me, but I don't think that's true.

KEITH: And, as you say, that would be the payoff of your original script. You've spent so much of your life promoting honesty … so …

CLAUDE: [Referring to the situation] It's hard.

KEITH: It's hard, but it's not a betrayal.

CLAUDE: Interesting [pause]. So, for me, the script had to do with betrayal, with reaching the Promised Land but being shot down before I do. And I think that's, kind of, the way I could see it. So, if the *Confessions* are going to be published, I'd like that to be included.

Notes

1 This is likely to have been in 1979.

2 In an interview conducted by Anne Kohlhaas-Reith with Claude in 1989 and 1990, Claude acknowledged that, in the period when he had left the ITAA and was concentrating on radical psychiatry, he would still attend TA conferences: "I was always showing up and making trouble and dramatic political gesture[s]" (Kohlhaas-Reith & Steiner, 1991, p. 13). He continued: "The large membership liked me because I'd written a book, *Scripts People Live*. But the small leadership didn't because I had grown over their heads and I kept picking on them" (ibid., p. 14), though he did acknowledge that "I took pleasure in that" (ibid., p. 14).

3 The syllabus of the standard TA introductory "101" course (see ITAA, 2018) includes the script matrix (Steiner, 1966) and the stroke economy (Steiner, 1971f).

4 I did and found that, since the publication of Claude's article on emotional literacy in 1984, the concept had been cited 43 times in peer-reviewed articles in the *TAJ* (and a further 15 times in editorials, book reviews, and letters). The term "emotional literacy" had been cited once in each of the four years preceeding our conversation – which is neither "none, zero, ever" nor very much – and, in both 2017 and 2018, it was cited three times.

5 In 1971 and 1980, for the script matrix and the stroke economy, respectively (see note 2 above).

17 Claude Michel Steiner

Death, life, and legacy

Keith Tudor

As I noted in the Introduction, Claude Steiner's last words were "Love is the answer", a phrase to which Hartmut Oberdiek refers at the end of his chapter on emotional literacy (Chapter 13), and which Karen Minikin takes, appropriately enough, as the title of her chapter on Claude's work on love (Chapter 15). In his "Last word" to his book *The Heart of the Matter* (Steiner, 2009), the subtitle of which is "Love, Information, and Transactional Analysis", as Karen also notes, Claude himself reflected that "love alone has not been a redemptive task. Teamed with information, love, I believe, is [nevertheless] still the answer" (p. 237). Given that Claude chose to die with dignity[1] and surrounded by the love of his close family, it seems appropriate to end this book, firstly, with some information and comments on Claude's illness and death. This part also incorporates the obituary I wrote for *The Script*, the newsletter/magazine of the International Transactional Analysis Association (ITAA) (Tudor, 2017), and acknowledges various events which have focused on remembering Claude's life and work since his death. Secondly and finally, I offer some thoughts on Claude's legacy, including a summary and map of his various contributions in and to transactional analysis (TA), radical psychiatry (RP), and emotional literacy (EmLit), and on the man himself.

Death with dignity

Everyone who knew Claude was aware of his declining health over the last 12 years of his life as he battled with prostate cancer and with Parkinson's disease (what he referred to as "P"). In April 2015 he started a second autobiographical document, which he titled *CS at 80*, in which he reflected on certain crises he was facing. The first one he describes as "ME and my Body":

> Parkinson's – after two years following prostate surgery, hospitalization with septicemia, hernia surgery, two trips to Europe, 41 radiation sessions while chemically castrated and months of chilling out to find my bottom line, it has become evident that the treatments have left me with no libido, no erections and [being] mildly incontinent and that I do indeed suffer from P. which is slowly but methodically, starting at least ten years ago, progressing as it robs

Death, life, and legacy 229

me of my former powers of balance, dexterity, sexuality and mastery, most notably the capacity to move about with energy and grace.

I suffer from mild urinary incontinence; two hours max[imum] between pisses, subtle leaking requiring that I wear a pad and change it daily and stay near a bathroom 24/7 to avoid an occasional accident that requires that I change underwear and pants.

My hands have lost the nimble use that I had, and tremble. I have trouble buttoning and putting on shirts, pants and jackets, getting in and out of socks and shoes, chairs and bed. I have very limited energy left over for physical tasks. Walking is an insecure step-by-step shuffle. I feel like I am inside a clumsy leaking robot which is unable to execute my commands, requiring instead exhausting and exhaustive efforts to carry out my wishes. I clearly know what I want but my robot won't execute. And all of this is getting relentlessly though almost imperceptibly worse every day so that I am getting adapted and accepting my increasingly disabled condition. No wonder I am depressed.[2]

Still, all of this is manageable so far, I recently stopped attending a physical therapy group with an excellent teacher who is a former actor who teaches that for P sufferers every action is performance requiring mindfulness, grace and completion ending with a taraaa! I have also stopped my steady attendance to the health club and its machines.

But I cope. I have to reduce my maintenance fixit man responsibilities and I am doing that little by little. It helps to have able-bodied persons around (Matt, Eric, Kelvin, and Jude sometimes). I am badly affected by the unpredictably of the outcome and only know that I will not see 100 and that if I wind [up] in a wheelchair I am checking out.

(Steiner, 2017)

In April 2015, "checking out" meant some form of suicide. However, in June 2016, and after some 25 years of lobbying, California's End of Life Option Act came into effect, which allowed for physician-assisted dying, more commonly referred to as "death with dignity". I refer to this here as I had some conversations with Claude about being open about (t)his decision and choice. Some years ago, in 2006, Petrūska Clarkson, another elder in the international TA community, had committed suicide, following which there had been a lot of rumours and speculation about her state of mind, motivation, and so on – and what it meant about her life and work, including some aspects of her theoretical contributions, not least about suicide (Clarkson, 1992). I didn't want this to happen to Claude or his legacy and so counselled him to be open in his communication about this and his decision, a philosophy which, of course, was consistent with the cooperative contract of radical psychiatry: "No lies, no Rescues, no power plays" (see Chapter 10). When I visited Claude in 2016, I was also able to discuss this with him and his daughter Mimi, and both he and Mimi agreed that he and we should be open about the nature and manner of his death.

230   *Keith Tudor*

On 26 September of that year, Claude sent an email to himself containing the following:

VIVA LA MUERTE; a modest proposal regarding the end of life
By Claude Steiner
The end of life; death is the last taboo. We know when a taboo is being invalidated when we see it treated as normal on television. In the last half century taboos relating to sexuality, speech, bodily functions have been graphically programed in serials while we are exposed to commercials about urination, defecation [and] constipation. Only death it seems is still not to be freely discussed or practiced.
There are reasons for this, some understandable and reasonable. Early death is to be genuinely dreaded when measured against missed opportunities. Death after unspeakable sufferings clearly an uncomfortable subject; but death to prevent suffering, suicide is an ugly word not to be considered.
Why is that? Why is voluntary self-determined end of life a taboo subject and disallowed choice?
The answer is that it is yet another area of, in fact a principal illegitimate exertion of, patriarchal power abuse, deeply embedded in the dogma of organized religions. All three [major monotheistic] religions sternly disapprove of extra-marital sex, homosexuality, a woman's rights over her own body, female priesthood, and has fought long and hard to preserve these prohibitions, each with its own dogma and punishment. Each religion has its own myths all of which require belief in the ultimate myth; life after death. Without the afterlife belief there is nothing to stop one from ending one's life at will. Whether hell or eternal damnation or reincarnation: these myths are aimed at keeping us alive and distracting us from the only true disadvantage of death whether natural or self-inflicted; the suffering that our death may cause to other people – our loved ones.

Re-reading this, I love the fact that Claude links the prohibition on the ending of one's life to power abuse, an analysis that demonstrates the ease and depth of his RP to the end! Finally, as he prepared to travel from Berkeley to Ukiah, he wrote the last entry in *CS at 80*:

Final thoughts: Jan 6 2017
After a wonderful Fiesta de Despedida, 25 intimates; family, students, friends [with] Mexican food paid by Denali [and] hot tub by Eric; speeches, poetry, songs, two poems about me from Jude. I am ready to travel to Ukiah and make my final exit.

(Steiner, 2017)

Re-reading Claude's *Confessions* as I completed the editing of this book, I found a short passage on working with suicidal clients:

Ken Everts and I practiced psychotherapy and trained transactional analysts at the Berkeley TA Institute. We routinely worked with clients that were

Death, life, and legacy 231

potentially suicidal and in 1967 Ken, a psychiatrist, had two suicides in his practice three months apart. He was devastated by the experience.

The usual approach to suicide was, unbelievably today, to not bring it up, with the rationale that bringing it up may exacerbate the likelihood of it. Of course, if the client brought it up we would discuss it but in a detached, objective way, again not to "stimulate" the suicidal impulse. The notion that the therapist should make an emphatic argument against suicide was considered mistaken. Surely, the thinking went, the deranged suicidal client would be all the more motivated to commit the deed if we weighed in against it.

As a psychologist, in a profession that was not yet considered to be legitimately in the practice of psychotherapy I could not, I told myself, afford to have a suicide among my clients. So I decided to seek out potential suicidal tendencies and bring them out in the open. Whenever I had the slightest hint of suicidal ideation, I asked my clients about it and if they confirmed my suspicions I inquired whether they had a suicide plan formulated and what it was. I told my clients that I expected them to agree not to kill themselves while in therapy with me and asked them to make a contract to that effect. If pills or a gun or some other objects were involved I asked that they bring them to the office where I locked them up and agreed to return them when they discontinued therapy if they still wanted them back.

This was considered quite a radical if not wrong-headed approach. It went against the general psychoanalytic strictures against intervention and personal involvement that were the accepted approach of the day. But it seemed "Martian" common sense[3] to me and most clients were thankful and none I asked refused in the long run; I never had a suicide occur in my practice. Today such a contract is a requirement of professional psychotherapists working with a suicidal client, and the failure to do so is considered malpractice and vulnerable to a lawsuit for negligence.

(Steiner, 2008a)

I quote this here as it highlights not only what I would call Claude's humanity and radical care (also with an eye to the social and professional context at the time), but also his commitment to common sense (Martian or otherwise) and straight-talking, qualities he maintained to the end of his life.

Claude Michel Steiner: an obituary[4]

It is with a heavy heart that I write this contribution to *The Script* as it marks the passing of a great elder in our community, a passionate exponent and proponent of TA, and a personal friend.

I was first introduced to Claude Steiner's work in the late 1970s when I was studying social work, and, as a radical social worker, I particularly appreciated his work in developing radical psychiatry. My next point of contact with his ideas was in the mid-1980s and specifically his work on EmLit, which I applied both in my work with clients and in my personal life. It was only when I began training

232   Keith Tudor

in TA in 1987 that I realised what a huge contribution he had made to it, which he continued to make until his death. Claude's bibliography stands at over 150 contributions, including 13 books – from *TA Made Simple* (in 1969) to *The Heart of the Matter* 40 years later (in 2009). In a conversation I had with him last July (2016), in which we were clearly talking about his legacy, he himself listed his "10 Top Ideas" as:

1. Paranoia, that is, the emphasis on this as "heightened awareness".
2. Stroke hunger – for his work on the stroke economy he won the Eric Berne Memorial Scientific Award (EBMSA) in 1980.
3. The "Pig Parent", which was one of the key concepts in RP.
4. Radical truth – which he often framed in terms of one of the rules of cooperative contracts, that is "no lies".
5. That lies are absolute, while truth is relative.
6. The concept of the psychomechanic, that is, that psychologists and therapists actually *do* things. Claude himself was a mechanic, and, by all accounts, a great one. As a teenager living in Mexico he taught himself English by reading popular mechanics' magazines from the USA and his first job as an immigrant in Los Angeles in the 1950s was as a mechanic in a gas station.
7. Power – about which he wrote a number of articles in the magazines he co-founded and helped produce, namely *Issues in Radical Psychiatry* and *Issues in Cooperation and Power*, and later in his book *The Other Side of Power* (1981e).
8. Cooperation – often expressed as another rule of cooperative contracts, that is "no power plays".
9. Emotional literacy, a concept which preceded other people's work on this and emotional intelligence.
10. Cyborgs – in what is perhaps the least known aspects of his work, he argued that we are all cyborgs or information-processing beings. Following his interest in mechanics, he adapted early and enthusiastically to new technology. He had a personal computer from their earliest availability and he continuously mastered this evolving technology. He was a news junky and, as technology evolved, his reflections on propaganda evolved as well. Trump was elected three months before Claude died and, according to his daughter, Mimi, Claude spoke often about having optimism about democracy in the United States and that Trump was a manifestation of new technology and authoritarianism. Claude was fascinated by the millennial generation and their inter-digitation with technology.

To this list, I would add his work on the script matrix, for which he was awarded the first Eric Berne Memorial Scientific Award in 1971 (see Chapters 3 and 4); on RP, about which he was enormously influenced by his partner Hogie Wyckoff and other radicals in the San Francisco Bay Area, including Becky Jenkins, Beth Roy, and Bob Schweibel, (an approach or movement) which, in 1978, Stan Woollams and Michael Brown recognised as one of the "Schools" of TA (Woollams &

Death, life, and legacy 233

Brown, 1978; see Chapters 7, 8, and 9); and, finally, his more recent work on love (see Chapters 14 and 15).

This is a remarkable legacy, and, whilst he was honoured by the ITAA, there were times when he was passed over and/or ignored. That said, most of his books were translated into a number of languages and he had quite a following especially in the Spanish speaking world. I remember him at the ITAA World Conference in Bilbao in 2011 at which he was somewhat of a fringe figure, but where a book launch, organised by his Spanish publisher, attracted over 300 people. (Some may not realise that, as a Viennese Jew born in Paris and raised in Madrid and then Mexico, English was Claude's fourth language!) In the context of his relationship with TA, it was particularly good for him – and for us – that he presented a workshop (on TA and Politics) at the ITAA World Conference held in San Francisco in 2014, a workshop that attracted a quarter of the conference delegates, and boosted him for some time.

Claude often introduced himself by saying "I am a disciple of Eric Berne", and he was certainly a fierce defender of Berne's legacy. A number of us can attest to some scars from arguments with Claude as he would defend his mentor from what he regarded as unwarranted re- or misinterpretations of Berne's work. At times this led him into fierce fights with colleagues, and a concern (perhaps overly) about defining core concepts of TA (see Steiner & Tilney, 2003).

Claude was a controversial figure. For many years he led what could be reasonably described as a bohemian lifestyle – which upset a number of people in TA. He got into fights with people, and, as he admitted to me in one of our last conversations (in July 2016), he played games which he later identified as "power plays" (see previous chapter) – but, as this comment also demonstrates, he was committed to honest self-reflection and cooperative collaboration. He and I had many differences and disagreements (see Introduction), but in all this, and, indeed, in large part precisely *because* we could and did disagree robustly about all of this, we got on. If we got upset with each other, we used the method of EmLit to sort this out. I experienced the power of this; I saw him teach this to others; and I also saw him live this with others. Whatever people thought about him, he walked his talk and lived this to the end.

In his obituary notice, the majority of which Claude dictated the night before he died to his daughter, Mimi, he wrote:

> Claude Michel Steiner, PhD, Clinical Psychologist, was born a Jew in Paris, France, 6 January 1935. He died, on 9 January 2017, in comfort and with dignity, on the shore of Pennyroyal Lake on his Round Mountain Ranch in Ukiah, California, surrounded by family and nature's beauty. For over a decade he struggled with the subtle and brutally relentless disability of Parkinson's disease. His final words before dying peacefully were "I'm so lucky" and "Love is the answer". He is the author of *The Warm Fuzzy Tale* and *Achieving Emotional Literacy*, among numerous other books. These two books embody his theories of emotional intelligence, about which he lectured and gave workshops around the world. He is survived by his children Noemi Mimi Doohan,

Eric Steiner, and Denali Nicholson Lumma; his wife Jude Steiner Hall; his grandchildren Matthew Doohan, Bella Doohan, Alex Steiner, Mariel Steiner, Adric Lumma, and Dylan Lumma; his siblings Miguel Steiner and Kati Quibell; and his nieces Allyson Quibell Wilinsky, Valeska Steiner, Cecilia Steiner, and nephew Julian Quibell. His ashes will be buried in a private ceremony at Pennyroyal Lake.

Most readers of *The Script* will be aware of Claude's declining health over the past ten years as he battled with prostate cancer and with Parkinson's disease – and with the debilitating treatment of both of these. Being fiercely stoic and independent, very few people knew how sick he was and for how long. Despite this, he still managed to conduct workshops, including one at his ranch in Ukiah last July, which he referred to as "my last hurrah" in which, albeit for short periods, due to debilitating exhaustion and physical weakness, he was as sharp as ever. In the last year of his life he talked more about wanting to die with dignity, and thanks to Californian state law, he was able to do so with medically prescribed and self-administered liquid oral medication. He died as he lived: with self-awareness, honesty, bravery, and "no lies". After he had fearlessly drunk the "Aid in Dying" medicine, followed by a shot of tequila, and in the embrace of his family, his final words, uttered while he gazed over the water of his country lake, were "I'm so lucky", followed by "Love is the answer."[5]

Mimi reports that in Claude's last day, he gave the gift of some teachings to his family. These included:

1. No rescues – that, at the end of life, the person dying must not engage in Rescues, albeit that the Rescue triangle can be like a sticky trap and can feel impossible to escape. Nevertheless, one must free oneself from these sticky traps in order to die in peace.
2. Humility – he was genuinely bemused and incredulous that people seemed to care so much for him, his ideas and ideals. He said repeatedly "I can't stop wondering if they are really meaning me." We [his family] had no idea how widely influential and significant his professional work was because he rarely spoke of his world connections in this way. He presented his position in the psychology world as being equal to all around him. In his dying days he had no ego, and was extremely humble, and this was a teaching for his children.
3. Apologies – he asked to have private time with each family member and asked to be forgiven for the specific and unique injury he felt he caused each of his family members (about which he was right and spot on), and he asked for us to share our feelings with him. He did emotional literacy therapy for the family on his last day with us.
4. Music – Claude loved music, and we had a lot of music on his last day. He cried and sang the words. He reminded us that the sweetest beauty of life is right in front of us: just listen.

On 29 January, Claude's ashes were buried beside the lake at his ranch in Ukiah, California.

Death, life, and legacy 235

Remembering Claude

Various memorial events have already taken place to celebrate Claude's life and work – in Berkeley, where he lived for most of his life; in Ukiah, where he had a ranch; in San Francisco; at the ITAA World Conference in Berlin, Germany in 2017; and again in Berkeley a year after his death.

Following his death, a small group of us who had met at Claude's final workshop in 2016 – Luigi (Gino) Althöfer, Hartmut Oberdieck, and myself – had the idea of celebrating Claude's life and work at the ITAA World Conference in Berlin. In consultation with his family, and with the agreement of the Berlin Conference Organising Committee, we organised a workshop to remember and celebrate Claude. The three of us were joined by his daughter Mimi Doohan (née Steiner), his son Eric Steiner, his grandson Matthew Doohan, and Eric's partner, Rebecca Verdon. We welcomed over 50 participants and enjoyed a lovely and moving time together.

We began by introducing our own connections with Claude, in the chronological order in which we'd met him, that is, Mimi, Eric, Hartmut, Matthew, Keith, Rebecca, and Gino. We then opened up the workshop to the audience, a number of whom shared their connections with and experiences of Claude, a process that offered everyone an opportunity to hear about his life and work. People talked about his enormous influence, how much he had helped them, and the different ways in which he had profoundly touched their lives. Some of us also acknowledged that he was a somewhat controversial figure; that he could be quite curmudgeonly, especially when defending Eric Berne's legacy as he saw it; and that, over the years, he had managed to upset some people in TA. At the same time, we acknowledged that his behaviour was motivated by his passion for TA and, as a result, he had made an enormous contribution to it, which I summarised by presenting what Claude himself described as his "10 Top Ideas" (see above and the Introduction), as well as to RP and EmLit. The workshop ended with Matthew singing the song he had composed for his grandfather, which he had sung to Claude in the last days of his life.

Look deep into my eyes

> Look deep into my eyes
> Tell me what do you see?
> Wondrous child of mine
> Do you know what it means to be?
> Your mother taught you well
> Daddy was there for you
> I'm here to break the spell
> Guide you out of your youth
> I will tell you the truth.
> I'll let you know about the ways a woman can steal a heart from you
> I will break down the walls they build up around the greater truths
> And I will trust you to be the man that I know you'll be someday
> And the one thing I won't do is be afraid.

236   *Keith Tudor*

My time has come and past
Your journey's just begun
I don't think I want to last
I've seen more than enough my son.
Nations have come and gone
Battles I fought for truth
So long ago now you
Take for granted the trees we grew.
And now I see you beautiful and strong under the sun
Raising banners and fighting for a peace I thought we'd won
And though my heart aches to see you struggle I know you'll be free someday
And the one thing I won't do is be afraid.
Now will you take my hand?
I want to see your face
In these remaining hours
I'm so happy to have this place.
I know my soul lives on
You feel it in every breath
In every strong ideal
And in every certain step.
Look deep into my eyes
Tell me what do you see?
Wondrous child of mine
Do you know what it means to be?
Grandfather I think I see.

(Doohan, 2016)

There wasn't a dry eye in the workshop.

The following day there was another celebration, this time in the form of a Festive Evening, hosted by Mimi and Eric, Gino and Hartmut, to which a number of people came – from EmLit and radical therapy, as well as TA. We enjoyed good food, told stories about Claude, and were entertained with lovely music, and again heard Matthew's song.

On Saturday 6 January 2018, a year after Claude's death, a private memorial celebration of his life was held, organised by his children (Mimi, Eric, and Denali), comprising about 50 people who represented various parts of his life. It took place in the Brazilian Room on Tilden Park in the hills above Berkeley. The event began at 11.00 a.m. in the morning and lasted until 4.00 p.m. in the afternoon, and was a beautiful representation of Claude's life, personally and professionally.[6]

A legacy with honesty

In this second part of the chapter and by way of ending this book about Claude, I discuss the man and his work or, rather, his work and the man.

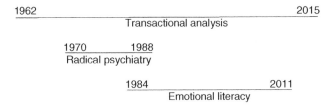

Figure 17.1 Timelines of Claude Steiner's involvement in TA, RP, and EmLit (in terms of publications)

Spheres of influence

As I indicated in my Introduction, and elaborated in Chapter 1, Claude was hugely influential in three fields: TA, RP, and EmLit. As is clear from the book, he lived and breathed all three: more so, TA, as he was involved in it for most of his professional life; RP earlier in his life (from his mid-30s to early 50s), and EmLit (from his late 40s) (see Figure 17.1).

In the interview conducted by Anne Kohlhaas-Reith in 1990, Claude described the relationship between these different fields in terms of the development of his ideas and, to some extent, his transition between these fields:

> Every time I get interested in something it's like, taking something I've said before and looking into and amplifying it. Scripts People Live got me into power. So then I wrote The Other Side of Power. And that got me into emotional literacy and then I did When a Man Loves a Woman, and then I got interested in subtle psychological power-plays, [and] propaganda.
>
> (Kohlhaas-Reith & Steiner, 1991, p. 23)

While this describes a personal – and, I would say, logical – progression of ideas, it appears that, in order to achieve this, Claude had to break away from previous or preceding certainties. In what I think is a particularly interesting passage in the same interview, Claude made a point about the problem of developing theory within an organisation:

> I agree the theory should be brought forward and refined. [However] I don't think that can ever be done from within T.A., you know, systems like that have a way of becoming encapsulated and can't work their way out of themselves. Anybody who really changes the system is seen as an outsider and is pushed away, actually rejected. There's something conservative about a system; it can't really assimilate change.
>
> (ibid., p. 21)

Claude's point about organisational and institutional dynamics is well-made; it is also personal in that, despite two awards from the ITAA (for his work on the script matrix and the stroke economy), he also felt hurt and rejected, and not least because the ITAA didn't recognise (with an award) his work on emotional literacy. I think this is partly why he saw EmLit as somewhat separate from TA (see also Chapter 13).

There is, however, a certain irony about Claude's comment in that, when he re-engaged with TA in the early 2000s, he reprised his "grumbling sourpuss watchdog" role (which he had acknowledged as far back as 1975 – see Chapter 2, note 16), and enacted it by promoting the identification of certain "core concepts" of TA (Steiner et al., 2003; Steiner & Tilney, 2003) – the logic of which was that other concepts or thinking about TA would be rejected from the core and become peripheral and even excluded! A number of people within TA (including me) viewed this as problematic, in addition to which I considered it deeply conservative and conservatising, a point I made to Claude on a number of occasions, for instance, in our last workshop (Steiner & Tudor, 2014). In owning this role (in a letter published in 1975; Steiner, 1975c), Claude had referred to what Berne (1972/1975b) called "the evangelical position" (p. 91), that is, "I'm OK, You're OK, They?" – and it was precisely this that I regarded as problematic: that Claude, as the evangelist, was not only questioning the "They" – in particular those he referred to as "the integrationists" (namely Richard Erskine, Janet Moursund, Rebecca Trautmann, and me) as well as colleagues who were informed by psychoanalytic thinking (principally Bill

Figure 17.2 Claude, evangelist, "grumbling soupus",[7] and "perspicacious bad dog", c.2003

Cornell, Helena Hargaden, and Michelle Novellino) – but also wanting to exclude them/us. These and other colleagues responded to Claude in various ways (see Cornell, 2009; Erskine & Trautmann, 1998; Hargaden, 2003a; Steiner & Novellino, 2005). My own response to this was to engage with Claude personally (see Introduction) and to re-present what Berne had written about the nature of ego states, the Adult ego state, and integration, especially in *Transactional Analysis in Psychotherapy* (Berne, 1961/1975a), for a commentary on which see Tudor (2010), and about the nature of games in *Games People Play* (Berne, 1964/1966a).

Although, as he himself acknowledged on a number of occasions, for instance, in the interview with Anne Kohlhaas-Reith (Kohlhaas-Reith & Steiner, 1991), Claude moved away from TA and, from the mid-1980s onwards, certainly focused more on EmLit, he still wrote about subjects across all three fields, and revised and reprinted earlier work, both of which demonstrate his continued interest in and concern about subjects and fields in and about which he had written earlier in his life (see Figure 17.3).[8]

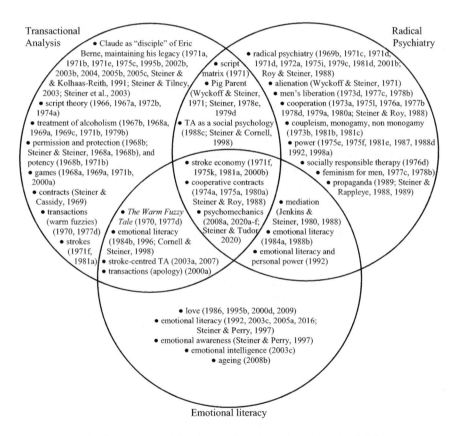

Figure 17.3 Claude Steiner's publications and writing (1962–2019) by field[9]

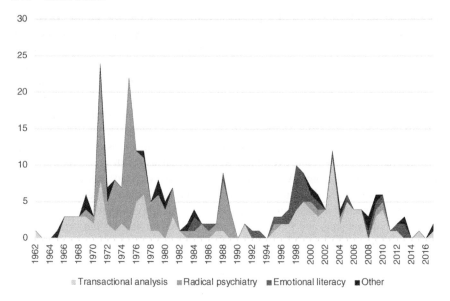

Figure 17.4 Claude Steiner's publications in TA, RP, and EmLit: A comparative, chronological view

Nevertheless, these three fields remain somewhat separate. In TA training, the "School" or tradition of radical psychiatry is rarely mentioned, and the TA concepts, such as the script matrix (Steiner, 1966) and the stroke economy (Steiner, 1971f), are often presented without reference to the political analysis from which they grew (see Kohlhaas-Reith & Steiner, 1991; and Chapter 8). RP and, more broadly, radical therapy (RT), or at least those informed by TA, hardly exist, and many of those colleagues that do practise RT do not appear to have kept up with more recent developments in TA. Whilst EmLit came from TA (Steiner, 1984b), it has developed as a separate movement – and indeed, in his Introduction to *The Heart of the Matter* (Steiner, 2009), Claude himself refers to this as a "movement" – with the result that most practitioners of EmLit are neither radical therapists or transactional analysts (see Chapter 8). Interestingly, in that same Introduction, Claude acknowledges three sets of colleagues – in RP (six), in TA (six), and in the EmLit movement (14) – only one of whom, Becky Jenkins, appears in more than one of the fields (RP and EmLit). Thus, it appears that Claude himself held these three fields and his close colleagues in them somewhat separately – which made his last workshop in Ukiah even more significant as he invited colleagues from all three fields to it (see Introduction).

In terms of his own development of and relationship with these different fields, in 1991, he framed his contributions in terms of TA:

> power is certainly a completely transactional concept; it's a development of T.A. The script matrix is a transactional idea. It contains the Pig Parent. The

Death, life, and legacy 241

next idea was the stroke economy which is wholly connected to the script matrix and the Pig and it is a transactional idea. Power plays ... [are] totally connected to transactions, the Pig Parent, and to the script matrix. Emotional literacy begins to perhaps not be a transactional idea. It becomes transactional because the way to develop emotional literacy is through transactions.

(Kohlhaas-Reith & Steiner, 1991, p. 19)

By 2008 (in his *Confessions*), he was putting this somewhat differently:

In time I combined all of the transactional analysis and radical psychiatry insights into an Emotional Literacy Training program. The theory and practice of Emotional Literacy Training incorporates under one roof contracts, the analysis of transactions, strokes and the drama triangle stemming from TA on one hand, and on the other hand my theory of paranoia and intuition, *The Warm Fuzzy Tale* [Steiner, 1977d] and the stroke economy [1971f], the Critical Parent, power plays and cooperation. (Chapter 12, p. 180)

From this, we can see that how Claude reflected on his own contributions as well as the development of his ideas – and, indeed, how others may subsequently analyse and assess his contributions – depends on where you stand and in which house you feel more at home, and perhaps under which roof you might feel more protected.

Notwithstanding the differences between these three fields and the different perspectives from which they may be viewed, it is clear that they are related, not only by and through the central figure of Claude himself, but also through underlying and related ideas and concepts, some of which inform and overlap with others, interrelationships I represent in Figure 17.3.

What this Venn diagram in Figure 17.3 represents is not only Claude's contributions to these different fields but, importantly (at least for my present purpose), the overlap between them. Claude himself spoke and wrote about the relationship between these different aspects of his life, especially about TA and emotional literacy: in an article published in the *Transactional Analysis Journal* (Steiner, 1996); in an interview with Bill Cornell, published in *The Script* (Cornell & Steiner, 1998); and in *The Heart of the Matter* (Steiner, 2009). He described the relationship between TA and RP both in some early writing (Steiner, 1973c, 1973e) and some 20 years later (Kohlhaas-Reith & Steiner, 1991) in an interview in which he also reflected on the relationship between them, a relationship that was clearly stronger in the early years of RP and during the development of EmLit in the early 1980s than in more recent times (see Chapters 8 and 11). In his last book, *The Heart of the Matter* (Steiner, 2009), Claude drew on all three fields in defining what we might view as his own basic – and final – "thesis":

Humanity's full potential for love, joy and productive thought has been selectively suppressed for centuries by an authoritarian abusive social system with

242   *Keith Tudor*

the active collaboration of the Critical Parent in each person. This suppressed potential can find release through heart-centered, information based, democratic corporation, free of power plays, facilitated by transactional analysis.

(p. 5, original emphasis)

In terms of analysing and mapping Claude's work and, with regard to the Venn diagram (Figure 17.3), working from the outside inwards, I was particularly interested to consider the overlap between all three fields, which I identify as the stroke economy, cooperative contracts, and, appropriately enough, Claude's own approach, that of psychomechanics.

The stroke economy

Claude himself wrote a lot about this (Steiner, 1971f, 1975k, 1981a, 2000b), and, in doing so, clearly linked the concept to its root metaphor, that of an oppressive, exploitative, and restrictive, capitalist economy (see Chapter 3), based on a Marxist critique of the political economy, and a Reichian analysis about the impact of this on the body and human, personal, and sexual relations (see Reich, 1933/1975; and also Chapters 3, 4, 5, and 6). As Claude himself put it: "If you take my theory seriously you have to, at the very least, attempt to deal with sexism, racism and crude capitalism" (Kohlhaas-Reith & Steiner, 1991, p. 21). Unfortunately, the stroke economy is, in my experience, often taught (as a set of rules), without reference to its origins and, thereby, divorced from its radical roots, and in this sense, some transactional analysts are not taking Claude's theory (or at least this theory) seriously. Also, and as Deepak Dhananjaya points out in his contribution (in Chapter 6), contemporary TA tends not to acknowledge the somatic basis of stroke theory. Indeed, I consider that an appreciation of the somatic is a central, though implicit, part of Claude's contribution.[10]

Part of the problem of what I view as a conservatisation of theory is Claude's own move away from radical theory and politics (see Chapters 8 and 9). Thus, while he elaborated the radical origins of the stroke economy most clearly in *Scripts People Live* (Steiner, 1974a) and returned to it in his last book *The Heart of the Matter* (Steiner, 2009), in neither *Achieving Emotional Literacy* (Steiner & Perry, 1997) or *Emotional Literacy* (Steiner, 2003c) does he refer to Marx or Reich, which bears out the criticism made by Ellen Morrison (in Chapter 8).

Nevertheless, and despite contemporary misrepresentations of the theory, the concept of the stroke economy both draws on and contributes to: TA, in terms of the theory of strokes, including how to "trash" the original, restrictive stroke economy, based on Critical (or Pig) Parent injunctions, in favour of a stroke economy that supports liberation through the free exchange of strokes (see Steiner, 1977d); RP, in terms of the praxis of Marxist and Reichian analysis, not least as a manifestation of alienation, transmitted by the Pig Parent; and EmLit, in which the restrictive stroke economy leads to emotional illiteracy which is challenged through the practice of EmLit.

Death, life, and legacy 243

Cooperative contracts

In terms of Claude's approach to cooperative contracts, this developed over time:

- In *Scripts People Live* (Steiner, 1974a) he defined the "rules" of cooperation as: (1) no scarcity, (2) equal rights, (3) no power plays, (4) no secrets, and (5) no Rescues.
- Similarly, in a chapter on the subject (Steiner, 1976a), he identified five requirements for cooperative relationships or situations, i.e., no scarcity, equal rights, no power plays, asking (for what one wants) (presumably as the practice of having no secrets), and no Rescue.
- In an article reporting on the launch of the Cooperative Survival Project at the Round Mountain ranch in Ukiah (1978a), he wrote about cooperation as involving an assumption of equality, followed by guidelines (in effect prohibitions) of certain behaviours, i.e., no power plays, no lies, and no Rescues. In order to avoid inequality in relationships between men and women, this was to be a feminist community, and in order to pursue "harmony with the Earth", one based on an "ecological morality" (p. 19). The assumption (of equality) and these guidelines also appeared in *A Manual on Cooperation* (Steiner, 1980a).
- In *Achieving Emotional Literacy*, Steiner and Perry (1997) emphasised equality and honesty as the basis of a cooperative contract.
- In *Emotional Literacy: Intelligence with a Heart* (Steiner, 2003c), he wrote about the cooperative (non-coercive) contract", which

  > promised that the participants and the leader would never engage in any attempts to manipulate or power play anyone. It also specifically required the participants would never do anything they did not honestly want to do. The contract further promised that the leader would take responsibility to oversee the safety agreements would not permit any transactions that came from the Critical Parent.
  >
  > (p. xxiv)

- This, together with a contract of confidentiality, constituted what Claude referred to as "calming, trust-enhancing agreements" that formed – and still form – the basis of emotional literacy training (see Chapter 13).

To this, and inspired by what Mimi Doohan (née Steiner) reports about Claude's last day (see pp. 234), I would add humility as a prerequite of or necessary attitude for any cooperative contract as, I suggest, this is the basis for an interest in the other/Other (see Levinas, 1961/1969; Orange, 2012) and, informed by person-centred psychology, even putting the other before I or me (see Schmid, 2006).[11]

In any case, it is clear that the concept of cooperative contracts both draws on and contributes to: TA, in terms of the bilateral nature of such agreeements, as well as the underlying principle of clear, open, and Adult communication (with no Rescues or Rescuing); RP, in terms of the praxis of cooperation, based on an analysis

244   *Keith Tudor*

of power and equality, if not equity, and the practice of open communication in terms of honesty, no secrets, no lies, etc.; EmLit, based on honesty and informed by practice (see Steiner, 1984a; and Chapter 13).

Psychomechanics

For those who have read the book thus far, it will be clear that Claude was not an easy man. In the last page of his original *Confessions* (Steiner, 2008a), in a passage that echoes the ancient proverb "Physician, heal thyself", Claude offers this self-appraisal:

> **Fixer, fix thyself.**
> I am notorious in my family for my fixing and the pursuit of "fixers." Like Joey Lewis says, in the last line of the movie "Some like it Hot", when Jack Lemmon reveals that he is not a woman: "Nobody's perfect." This is the basis for one of my mottoes "most everything can be fixed" when it comes to dealing with the imperfections of life to which I would add my other life rule: "practice controlled neglect". [Together,] "nobody is perfect" and "practice controlled neglect", while potentially workable can also result in a scandalously shabby, if marginally effective way of life. On that basis, I am in constant pursuit of the fixer, that diamond in the rough: that car, home computer, clothes washer, house or person that though somewhat dysfunctional and shop-worn can be made to provide long and satisfactory service, sometimes even better than a brand-new model. ("They don't make them like they useta.")
> And since no one is perfect and there is no point in pursuing perfection I will allow things to deteriorate under my watchful eye until something really needs to be done and, in this way, save myself the unnecessary expense and work of keeping everything squeaky-clean and in shipshape. Whether letting tires wear down, failing to empty the trash, sweep the floor, fix the gutters or confront a conflict, I will keep things in a state of functionality which, to me, looks perfectly safe and sound and to others may look like I am skating on the edge of disgusting catastrophe.
> In personal relations, that approach has the advantage of avoiding Rescuing people, (aka: codependency) wherein one rushes to help or fix someone else rather than letting them do it for themselves. Meanwhile I always keep an eye on the situation in case it needs serious attention in which case I am likely to swoop in and take care of business. Letting the apple ripen on the tree rather than plucking it while it's still green has its risks but the advantage is that the fruit will fall effortlessly into your hand and what you eat will be sweet and luscious.
> I learned this approach from my parents' neglect and have practiced a sanitized and improved version of it over the years. In the first fifty years of my life I was close to being oblivious and even cruel in my studied neglect but in time

Death, life, and legacy   245

I have developed into a sophisticate of the art of thinking and living out of the box a fact that my grandson Matthew seems to relish if one is to believe him when he says, with stars in his eyes: "Abuelo, I admire your life style." I have applied this approach to my houses, cars, friends, clients, family and intimate relationships and most importantly to myself. The reviews are mixed, to be sure, and I am imperfectly satisfied. I have some time still to further improve my dubious self and I shall, to the best of my ability, while I reconcile with the irreducible aspects of my imperfection.

(Steiner, 2008a)

His son Eric concurred:

I saw him as a frontiersman, self-sufficient, confident and resourceful. He took anything on with tenacity and enthusiasm, whether solving the mechanical issues of a stranded car or delving into the complexities of human psychology. His approach was simple, yet his method was sophisticated: take it apart, look at it; then throw all your intelligence, experience and energy at the problem.

(Eric Steiner, personal [email] communication, 14 March 2019)

Over the years I knew him and saw him both professionally and personally, I think that Claude did improve his "dubious self", though, no doubt, there will be other views and, in time, other reviews of his work and his life.

I quote this self-appraisal partly as this is one of the elements of the book (the autobiographical, see Chapter 1) by which it presents Claude's reflections, including those about himself in his own voice; and partly as it synthesises something of his personal style. For instance, in his acceptance statement on receiving the 1980 Eric Berne Memorial Scientific Award, he acknowledged that:

Neither Eric Berne nor myself were in the 60's famous for our capacities to be loving. I, for myself, have struggled long and hard in my personal life to undo the crippling effects that the Stroke economy has had on me.

(Steiner, 1981a, p. 9)

Thus, I would say that Claude's psychomechanics describe his particular integration of TA, whence comes open communication, simplicity, and analysis of script and the restrictive stroke economy, and subsequent stroke hunger, and working with permission, protection, and potency, with a clear, bilateral contract; RP, and its analysis of alienation, oppression, mystification, and power, and the practice of "offing" the Pig (Parent); and EmLit, with its emphasis on radical truth and plain talk, its analysis of paranoia, and its commitment to no lies, no power plays, and no Rescues – all mixed and manifested through his own particular personality, "warts 'n' all", not least as evidenced in this present volume.

246 *Keith Tudor*

Final thoughts

In the interview with Anne Kohlhaas-Reith, Claude made an interesting and significant comment:

> I see that the apple doesn't fall far from the tree in the case of scripts either. People can only go so far away from where they started and I think that's also what happened with Eric [Berne]. He started as a psychoanalyst and didn't end up so far away from that. He got as far as he could, and somebody else had to go further. And I can't go so far away from where I started either. That's how it is. But in the process you can make some tremendous changes and improvements.
>
> (Steiner & Kohlhaas-Reith, 1991, p. 7)

I think this is a significant statement from Claude in a number of respects as, in it:

1. He acknowledges both the limitations of scripts and the limits of change, as well as the significance of changes we can make in our lives.
2. He suggests something about his own motivation, role, and work in going "further" than Berne, including, and perhaps specifically, taking TA further away from psychoanalysis; and, thus, offers a clue as to why he was so critical of TA colleagues who were (and are) informed by psychodynamic and psychoanalytic thinking, and who elaborate this in TA (see Steiner, 2003e, 2003f, 2006d).
3. He offers an insight into his own limitations, and the impact of his own personality, proclivites, and vulnerabilities – and, if this book reveals anything, it is that Claude had feet of clay, but that, for the most part, he was honest about the impact that his "clay" had both on himself and others. Reading and re-reading Claude's *Confessions*, I think there is a certain rawness to his transparency and a certain naivety to the rawness. As Jackson Browne expressed it in a song titled "I Thought I was a Child": "It's such a clever innocence with which you show myself to me | As if you know how it feels to never be who you wanted to be" (Browne, 1973b).
4. He points to the fact that someone else has to go further – which is why, in addition to looking backwards on Claude's work, the contributions to this book (and, I hope, other contributions to other publications will) also look forward. While Claude was quite controlling about Berne's legacy, I didn't experience him as at all controlling about his own legacy.

At the end of the Festive Evening in Berlin, a TA colleague and friend of mine, Giles Barrow, said to me: "It seems to me that you are freeing the man from his work" (G. Barrow, personal communication, 29 July 2017). At the time, I was very touched by that comment, although I'm not sure that I knew quite why, but, during the planning and editing of this book, and the writing of my own contributions to it, I have held those words in mind.

In some ways, I disagree with the analysis (or ontology) inherent in the statement: just as the personal is political and the political is personal – the feminist

Death, life, and legacy 247

slogan that influenced and informed much of Claude's work, especially in RP, as well as his life – so, too, I would say that the man is his work and the work is the man, and, in that sense, the two are inextricable and inseparable. Indeed, it is the very struggle, with his parents (and his own Pig Parent), and with regard to love, sex, power, recognition, betrayal, and so on, that informed Claude's life and infuses his *Confessions*, that made him the man he was and influenced his work – and, herein, lies his greatest contribution: that he was willing to disclose, declare, and, to a certain extent, decontaminate and deconfuse that. In this, I find Claude's approach echoes Carl Rogers's (1953/1967) perspective that *"What is most personal is most general"* (p. 26, original emphasis). Rogers continued:

> when in talking with students or staff, or in my writing, I have expressed myself in ways so personal[ly] that I have felt I was expressing an attitude which it was probable no one else could understand, because it was so uniquely my own ... In these instances I have almost invariably found that the very feeling which has seemed to me most private, most personal, and hence most incomprehensible by others, has turned out to be an expression for which there is a resonance in many other people. It has led me to believe that what is most personal and unique in each one of us is probably the very element which would, if it were shared or expressed, speak most deeply to others.
>
> (ibid., p. 26)

That said (or written), some of what constituted and represented "the man", that is, some of his bad behaviour (as he himself describes it throughout his *Confessions*), has got in the way of his work, of the appreciation of his work, and of what we – the contributors to this book as well as others – might take forward. At one point in her interview with Claude, Anne Kohlhaas-Reith asked him what he thought about Jacqui Schiff's work.[12] Claude responded: **"**I don't have a very kind opinion. I think that in the process of taking in people who are extremely disturbed, and applying a method, she sometimes abused them" (Steiner & Kohlhaas-Reith, 1991, p. 13), though he did go on to say that "I think that some of her theories are very good" (ibid., p. 13).

Some – even many – may not have "a kind opinion" about Claude; nonetheless, and as I hope this book reflects, his theories are not only "very good", but, I suggest, are inspired and inspiring, profound and practical, radical and even revolutionary. Whether this book has helped to distinguish the man from his work, à la Rimbaud (see Chapter 1), or even to free the man from his work, à la Barrow (above), I am not sure; ultimately, only you, the reader, can and will decide.

In his conclusion to *Beyond Scripts and Games*, Claude wrote about Berne, that

> His work could possibly in the future change the face of psychiatry all over the world. His views, which are becoming more and more accepted, have established in the minds of people the possibility that all emotional disturbance can be cured because everyone is basically OK. His contribution along with the contributions of other of his contemporaries ... Have humanised the practice of psychotherapy and advanced towards being truly a service to people.
>
> (Steiner, 1977a, p. 371)

Figure 17.5 Pennyroyal Lake, Round Mountain Ranch, Ukiah, California

The same might be said of Claude himself. Moreover I think that his life and work, not least as represented in these pages, also humanises the person of the psychotherapist, the radical psychiatrist/therapist, and emotional activist/warrior. In this respect, I think that Giles's reflection is a fitting ending to this book and to this contribution to the project of honouring Claude's own contributions as well as his legacy, with openness and honesty.

I hope that this book sings some of Claude's dreams to him as well as others, reflecting back and moving forward, and, in this sense, that the book does free the man – and may he rest in peace by his beloved Pennyroyal Lake – from his work, which lives on in the articles and books he wrote, as well as in the hearts and minds of those whose lives his work and life touched.

Notes

1 Legal in California since 2016.
2 See Claude's comment about depression and strokes (Chapter 5, p. 88).
3 According to Berne (1962), who coined the expression, "the 'Martian' approach" (p. 32) represents a way of thinking without preconceived ideas.
4 I was – and am – grateful to Noemi Mimi Doohan (neé Steiner) for her cooperation in writing the obituary.
5 In the obituary, these phrases were reversed; this is the correct version.
6 I am grateful to Marielle Coeytaux for her report of this event.
7 See Chapter 2, note 12.
8 In an article published in 1978 about being "Back at the Ranch" in Ukiah, Claude wrote:

"I have moved to the ranch and spend ten days out of every fourteen on the land. The practice and teaching of Radical Psychiatry, which was a full-time involvement for

Death, life, and legacy 249

me until recently, now occupies approximately one-third of my time and attention. To my still very active Radical Psychiatry concerns, I have added an interest in other matters which are reflected in the Cooperative Survival Project" (Steiner, 1978a, p. 29).

9 For the purposes of clarity and this figure, I have allocated all Claude's publications to only one category, i.e., transactional analysis, radical psychiatry, emotional literacy, or others, despite the fact that some of his areas of interest overlapped (see Figure 17.3).

10 The somatic does not appear in the central vector of Figure 17.3 because Claude did not write much specifically about the body. In 1973 and 1974, he contributed as part of the Issues in Radical Therapy Collective (IRTC) to two special issues of *Issues in Radical Therapy* on "Radical Therapy and Body Politics" (IRTC, 1973/1974, 1974), and published an article on Wilhelm Reich (Steiner, 1974c). Although his ontological view of human beings would have been that we are somatic beings, and he credits especially Hogie Wyckoff for (re)introducing him to his own body (see Chapter 7), he only began to write about the body and his own body in his *Confessions* (Steiner, 2008a) and *CS at 80* (Steiner, 2017), and in his work on ageing (2008b).

11 Though far from person-centred in the Rogerian sense of the term, Claude did cite the work of Carl Rogers approvingly (e.g., Steiner, 1977a, 2009).

12 Jacqui Schiff was a social worker and early transactional analyst who advocated reparenting and, specifically undertook total regression reparenting with schizophrenic patients. Her work and that of others associated with her led to major theoretical contributions to TA (discounting, frames of references, and passivity) but also to controversies (see Jacobs, 1994; Schiff et al., 1975).

References

Legal statute

End of life, Cal., Assemb. B. 15 (2015-2016), Chapter 1. (Cal. Stat. 2015).

References

Ainsworth, M. D. S. (1973). *The development of infant-mother attachment*. Chicago, IL: University of Chicago Press.

Aldebaran. (1976). Fat liberation. In H. Wyckoff (Ed.), *Love, therapy and politics. Issues in radical therapy – The first year* (pp. 197–212). New York, NY: Grove Press.

Allen, J. R., & Allen, B. A. (1997). A new type of transactional analysis and one version of script work. *Transactional Analysis Journal, 27*(2), 89–98.

Althöfer, L. (2017). Die Radikale Therapie [Radical therapy]. *Zeitschrift Für Transaktionsanalyse [Journal for Transactional analysis], 34*(1), 44–64.

Aptheker, H. (Ed.). (1965). *Marxism and alienation*. New York, NY: Humanities Press.

Barnes, G. (2004). Homosexuality in the first three decades of transactional analysis. *Transactional Analysis Journal, 34*(2), 126–155.

Baruch, J., Frühling, C., & Mono, N. (2015). Das Persönliche ist politisch! [The personal is political]. *Oya - Anders Denken, Anders Leben [To Think Differently, to Live differently], 31*, 78–79.

Berger, K. (1996). *Co-Counseling: Die Therapie ohne Therapeut. Übungen und Anleitungen [Co-Counseling: Therapy without the therapist. Exercises and Guidance]*. Reinbek, Germany: Rowohlt.

Berne, E. (1962). The classifications of positions. *Transactional Analysis Bulletin, 1*(3), 23.

Berne, E. (1966a). *Games people play: The psychology of human relationships*. (Original work published 1964). New York, NY: Grove Press.

Berne, E. (1966b). *Principles of group treatment*. New York, NY: Grove Press.

Berne, E. (1968). *The happy valley*. New York, NY: Grove Press.

Berne, E. (1971). Foreword. In C. Steiner, *Games alcoholics play* (pp. ix–xi). New York, NY: Ballantine Books.

Berne, E. (1973). *Sex in human loving*. (Original work published 1970). Harmondsworth, UK: Penguin.

Berne, E. (1975a). *Transactional analysis in psychotherapy*. (Original work published 1961). New York, NY: Grove Press.

Berne, E. (1975b). *What do you say after you say hello? The psychology of human destiny*. (Original work published 1972). London, UK: Corgi.

References 251

Berne, E., Karpman, S., Dusay, J., Steiner, C., Callaghan, V., Boyce, M., ... Kline, A. (2017). Eric Berne's San Francisco seminar: A transcript (B. Cornell with M. Landaiche, Transcribers & Eds.) (Original work transcribed 1970). *The Script*, *47*(4), 7–18.

Beveridge, A. (2011). *Portrait of the psychiatrist as a young man: The early writing and work of R. D. Laing, 1927-1960*. Oxford, UK: Oxford University Press.

Boss, M. (1963). *Psychoanalysis and daseinanalysis*. New York, NY: Basic Books.

Boss, M. (1979). *Existential foundation of medicine and psychology*. New York, NY: Jason Aronson.

Boyer, R. (1971). *R. D. Laing and anti-psychiatry*. New York, NY: Perennial Library.

Breitenbürger, W., & Faber, A. (1996). Männer-Radikale-Therapie [Mens-Radical-Therapy]. In H. Brandes & H. Bullinger (Eds.), *Handbuch Männerarbeit [Handbook of men's work]* (pp. 154–164). Weinheim and Germany: Beltz.

Browne, J. (1973a). I thought I was a child. In *On For everyman*. Hollywood, CA: Asylum.

Browne, J. (1973b). Sings my songs to me. (Original work published 1967). In *On For everyman*. Hollywood, CA: Asylum.

Browne, J. (1989). Lights and virtues. In *On World in motion*. Hollywood, CA: Electra.

Brownmiller, S. (1975). *Against our will: Men, women and rape*. New York, NY: Simon & Schuster.

Cassius, J. (1980). Bodyscript release: How to use bioenergetics and transactional analysis. In J. Cassius (Ed.), *Horizons in bioenergetics* (pp. 212–244). Memphis, TN: Prometheus.

Childs-Gowell, E., & Kinnaman, P. (1978). *Body-script blockbusting*. San Francisco, CA: TA Pubs.

Chinnock, K., & Minikin, K. (2015). Multiple contemporary views on therapeutic relating in transactional analysis game theory. *Transactional Analysis Journal*, *45*(2), 141–152.

Clarkson, P. (1992). *Transactional analysis psychotherapy: An integrated approach*. London, UK: Routledge.

Cohen, L. (1992). Light as the breeze. In *On The future [Album]*. New York, NY: Columbia.

Cooper, D. (Ed.). (1968). *To free a generation: The dialectics of liberation*. New York, NY: Collier Books.

Cornell, B. (2009). Further thoughts on research project. *The Script*, *39*(4), May-June, 1, 6.

Cornell, B., & Steiner, C. (1998). Transactional analysis and emotional literacy. *The Script*, *28*(2), March, 1–6.

Cornell, W. (1975). Wake up "Sleepy": Reichian techniques and script intervention. *Transactional Analysis Journal*, *5*(2), 144–147.

Cornell, W. F. (2016). Failing to do the job: When the client pays the price for the therapist's countertransference. *Transactional Analysis Journal*, *46*(4), 266–276.

Cornell, W. F. (2019). *Self-examination in psychoanalysis and psychotherapy: Subjectivity and countertransference in clinical practice*. New York, NY: Routledge.

Cornell, W. F., & Bonds-White, F. (2001). Therapeutic relatedness in transactional analysis: The truth of love or the love of truth. *Transactional Analysis Journal*, *31*(1), 71–83.

Cornell, W. F., de Graaf, A., Newton, T., & Thunnissen, M. (2016). *Into TA: A comprehensive textbook on transactional analysis*. London, UK: Karnac.

Cornell, W. F., Hargaden, H., Allen, J. R., Erskine, R., Moiso, C., Sills, C., ... Tudor, K. (2006). Roundtable on the ethics of relational transactional analysis. *Transactional Analysis Journal*, *36*(2), 105–119.

Cornell, W. F., & Landaiche, N. M. (2006). Impasse and intimacy: Applying Berne's concept of script protocol. *Transactional Analysis Journal*, *36*(3), 196–213.

Corsini, R. J. (Ed.). (1981). *Handbook of innovative psychotherapies*. New York, NY: Wiley.

252 *References*

Crossman, P. (1966). Permission and protection. *Transactional Analysis Bulletin, 5*(19), 152–154.

D'Amore, I. (1997). The source of motivation and stroke theory. *Transactional Analysis Journal, 27*(3), 181–191.

Dawkins, R. (1989). *The selfish gene.* (2nd ed.). Oxford, UK: Oxford University Press.

Dhananjaya, D. (2018, November 9). *The journey that continues* [Blog post]. Retrieved from https://cwlsc.wordpress.com/2018/10/31/the-journey-that-continues/.

Green, S., & Tudor, K. (Eds.), & Dillon, G., Duncan, A., Fay, J., Land, C., Morice, M. P., & Woodard, W. (2014). Ngā Ao e Rua | The two worlds: Psychotherapy, biculturalism, and professional development in Aotearoa New Zealand. *Psychotherapy & Politics International, 12*(2), 129–150.

Doohan, M. (2016). *Look deep into my eyes.* [Song]. Unpublished.

Drego, P. (1983). The Cultural Parent. *Transactional Analysis Journal, 13*(4), 224–227.

Dworkin, A. (1987). *Intercourse.* New York, NY: Free Press.

Dylan, B. (2004). *Chronicles: Volume one.* New York, NY: Simon & Schuster.

Ernst, S., & Goodison, L. (1981). *In our own hands: A book of self-help therapy.* London, UK: The Women's Press.

Erskine, R. G. (1988). Ego structure, intrapsychic function, and defence mechanisms: A commentary on Eric Berne's original theoretical concepts. *Transactional Analysis Journal, 18*(1), 15–19.

Erskine, R. (1998). [Letter to the editor (Members' Forum: Steiner and Erskine/Trautmann dialogue continues).]. *The Script, 28*(8), November, 6–7.

Erskine, R., & Trautmann, R. (1998). [Letter to the editor (Members' Forum).]. *The Script, 28*(4), May-June, 6–7.

Evison, R., & Horobin, R. (1990). Co-counselling. In W. Dryden & J. Rowan (Eds.), *Neue Entwicklungen der Psychotherapie [New developments in psychotherapy]* (pp. 98–125). Oldenburg and Germany: Transform Verlag.

Foucault, M. (2006). *Madness and civilization: A history of insanity in the age of reason.* (J. Khalfa Ed. J. Murphy, Trans.). New York, NY: Routledge.

Fowlie, H., & Sills, C. (Eds). (2011). *Relational transactional analysis: Principles in practice.* London, UK: Karnac.

Freud, S. (1984). Beyond the pleasure principle. In J. Strachey Ed., *The Penguin Freud library* (Trans.), (11; pp. 269–337). London, UK: Penguin. (Original work published 1920).

Fromm, E. (1955). *The sane society.* New York, NY: Holt.

Fromm, E. (2010). *The pathology of normalcy.* (Original work published 1953). Riverdale, NY: American Mental Health Foundation Books.

Gerhardt, S. (2004). *Why love matters: How affection shapes a baby's brain.* Hove, UK: Routledge.

Goleman, D. (1995). *Emotional intelligence: Why it can matter more than IQ.* New York, NY: Bantam Books.

Goulding, M. M., & Goulding, R. L. (1976). Injunctions, decisions, and redecisions. *Transactional Analysis Journal, 6*(1), 41–48.

Groder, M. (1977). Asklepieion: An integration of psychotherapies. In G. Barnes (Ed.), *Transactional analysis after Eric Berne* (pp. 134–137). New York, NY: Harper's College Press.

Guggenbühl-Craig, A. (1971). *Power in the helping professions.* (M. Gubitz, Trans.). Woodstock, CT: Spring Publications.

References 253

Hanisch, C. (1970). The personal is the political. In S. Firestone & A. Koedt (Eds.), *Notes from the second year: Women's liberation* (pp. 76–77). New York, NY: Radical Feminism. Retrieved from: www.carolhanisch.org/CHwritings/PersonalIsPol.pdf. (Original work published 1969).

Hargaden, H. (2003a). [Letter to the Editor (Members' Forum: Response to Hargaden's speech about Berne).]. *The Script, 33*(6), August, 5–6.

Hargaden, H. (2003b). Then we'll come from the shadows. *The Script, 33*(x), July, xxx.

Hargaden, H. (2005). Letter from the guest editor: All that jazz ... Transactional analysis and psychoanalysis [Special theme issue]. *Transactional Analysis Journal, 35*(2), 106–109.

Hargaden, H., & Sills, C. (2002). *Transactional analysis: A relational perspective*. Hove, UK: Brunner-Routledge.

Hill, D. (2015). *Affect regulation theory: A clinical model*. New York, NY: Norton.

Hillar, T., & Frick, D. (1996). Von Groll-, Schmuse- und Gespinsterunde: Einführung in das Konzept der "Radikalen Therapie" in der Kommune Feuerland [About resentments, fantasies and strokes: An introduction to the concept of "Radical Therapy" in the Feuerland Community]. In K. Kommunebuch, *Das Kommunebuch: Alltag zwischen Widerstand, Anpassung und gelebter Utopie [The community book: Everyday life between resistance, adaptation and lived Utopia]* (pp. 276–289). Göttingen and Germany: Verlag Die Werkstatt.

International Transactional Analysis Association. (2018). The TA101 introductory course. In *ITAA training and examinations handbook* (Section 4). San Francisco, CA: Author.

Issues in Radical Therapy Collective. (1973/1974). Radical therapy and body politics [Editorial]. Wilhelm Reich and body politics, Part I [Special issue]. *Issues in Radical Therapy, 2*(1), 3, Winter.

Issues in Radical Therapy Collective. (1974). Editorial. Wilhelm Reich and body politics, Part II [Special issue]. *Issues in Radical Therapy, 2*(2), 3, Spring.

Jackins, H. (1982). *Fundamentals of co-counseling manual (Elementary counselors manual): For beginning classes in re-evaluation co-counseling*. (3rd ed.). Seattle, WA: Rational Island.

Jackins, H. (1994). *The human side of human beings: The theory of re-evaluation counseling* (3rd ed.). Seattle, WA: Rational Island.

Jacobs, A. (1994). Theory as ideology: Reparenting and thought reform. *Transactional Analysis Journal, 24*(1), 39–55.

Jenkins, B., & Steiner, C. M. (1980). Mediations. *Issues in Cooperation and Power, 3*, 4–11. Fall.

Jenkins, B., & Steiner, C. M. (1988). Mediation. In B. Roy & C. M. Steiner (Eds.), *Radical psychiatry: The second decade* (pp. 107–120). Self-published manuscript available from www.radikale-therapie.de/DL/TSD.pdf

Johnson, F. (Ed.). (1973). *Alienation: Concept, term, and meanings*. New York, NY: Seminar Press.

Karakashian, S. (1976). Staright men are in drag. In H. Wyckoff (Ed.), *Love, therapy and politics. Issues in radical therapy – The first year* (pp. 136–144). New York, NY: Grove Press.

Karpman, S. (1968). Fairy tales and script drama analysis. *Transactional Analysis Bulletin, 7*(26), 39–43.

Kaufman, K., & New, C. (2004). *Co-counselling: The theory and practice of re-evaluation counselling*. London, UK: Routledge.

Kerr, C. (1973). Up against monogamy. Part III – An interview. *Issues in Radical Therapy, 1*(4), 28–29.

254 References

Kolhaas-Reith, A., & Steiner, C. M. (1991). On the early years of transactional analysis: Eric Berne and his disciple Claude Steiner. Unpublished manuscript retrieved from www.ta-kohlhaas-reith.de/institut_publikationen.htm

Laing, R. D. (1960). *The divided self.* London, UK: Tavistock.

Laing, R. D. (1969). *The politics of experience.* New York, NY: Pantheon Books.

Laing, R. D. (1972). *The politics of the family.* (Original work published 1969). New York, NY: Vintage Books.

Laing, R. D., & Cooper, D. G. (1964). *Reason and violence.* London, UK: Tavistock.

Lawrence, D. H. (1959). *Lady Chatterley's lover.* (Original work published 1928). Harmondsworth, UK: Penguin.

Levinas, E. (1969). *Totality and infinity: An essay on exteriority.* (Original work published 1961). Pittsburgh, PA: Duquesne University Press.

Ligabue, S. (1991). The somatic component of the script in early development. *Transactional Analysis Journal, 21*(1), 21–30.

Mailer, N. (1968). *The armies of the night.* New York, NY: New American Library.

Männerrundbrief [Men's Newsletter]. (2000). *No. 14. Schwerpunkt: Männer und Therapie (Special issue: Mens and Therapy).* Münster: Selfpublishing. (http://maennerrundbrief. blogsport.de/).

Mano. (1973). Up against monogamy: A personal account – Part II. *Issues in Radical Therapy, 1*(3), 22, Summer.

Marcus, J., LaRiviere, P., & Goldstine, D. (1971). Community organizing and radical psychiatry. Berkeley [Special issue]. *The Radical Therapist, 3*(2), (Work also published 1975).

Marcus, J., LaRiviere, P., & Goldstine, D. (1975). Community organizing and radical psychiatry. In C. Steiner (Original work published 1971) Ed., *Readings in radical psychiatry* (pp. 123–141). New York, NY: Grove Press.

Marcuse, H. (1962). *Eros and civilization.* New York, NY: Vintage Books.

Marcuse, H. (1991) (Original work published 1964). *One dimensional man: Studies in the ideology of advanced industrial society* (2nd Ed.). London, UK: Routledge.

May, R. (1967). *Psychology and the human dilemma.* New York, NY: Norton.

May, R., Angel, E., & Ellenberg, H. F. (Eds.). (1958). *Existence.* New York, NY: Basic Books.

Members of the Radical Psychiatry Center. (1975). An analysis of the political values of the Berkeley Radical Psychiatry Center. In C. Steiner (Ed.), *Readings in radical psychiatry* (pp. 159–161). New York, NY: Grove Press.

Meulenbelt, A. (1983). *Weiter als die Wut [Further than anger].* Munich and Germany: Women's Offensive.

Michel, G., & Oberdieck, H. (2007). *Die Kunst, sich Miteinander wohl zu Fühlen [The art of feeling good together]* Paderborn and Germany: Junfermann-Verlag.

Nicholson, D. L. (2007). *Body matters.* Ukiah, CA: Overhead Press.

Orange, D. (2012). Clinical hospitality: Welcoming the face of the devastated other. *Ata: Journal of Psychotherapy Aotearoa New Zealand, 16*(2), 165–178.

Perls, F. (1969). *Gestalt therapy verbatim.* Layfayette, CA: Real People's Press.

Pheterson, G. (1978). Co-counseling and problem solving. *Issues in Radical Therapy, 21*, 20–22.

Rabenold, D. (1988). Appendix A: The Pig lexicon. In B. Roy & C. M. Steiner (Eds.), *Radical psychiatry: The second decade* (pp. 197–198). Self-published manuscript available from www.radikale-therapie.de/DL/TSD.pdf.

References 255

The Radical Therapist Collective. (1971). *The radical therapist.* (J. Agel, Producer.). New York, NY: Ballantine Books.

Rauch, A., Detlefsen, U., & Stoebbener, K. (1996). *Das FORT-Skript* [The FORT Script]. Privately circulated manual.

Reich, W. (1948). *Listen, little man.* New York, NY: Orgone Institute Press.

Reich, W. (1961). *The function of the orgasm.* (Original work published 1942). New York, NY: Farrar, Straus and Giroux.

Reich, W. (1962). *The sexual revolution.* (Original work published 1945). New York, NY: Noonday Press.

Reich, W. (1971). *The invasion of compulsory sex-morality.* (Original work published 1951). New York, NY: Farrar, Straus and Giroux.

Reich, W. (1972). *Sex-pol essays, 1929-1934.* (L. Baxandall, Ed.). New York, NY: Random House.

Reich, W. (1975). *The mass psychology of fascism* 3rd rev. ed.. T. P. Woolfe Trans.. (Original work published 1933). New York, NY: Orgone Press Institute.

Rimbaud, A. (1958). Letter [to G. Izamard]. In P. Harmann (Original work published 1871) Ed., *Oeuvres* (pp. 305–306). Paris and France: Aulard.

Risse, J., & Willms, S. (2011). *Zum Frieden befreien - Selbsthilfe durch Co-Counselling: Fühlen, Denken und Handeln versöhnen.* [Liberate to peace – Self-help through counselling: To reconcile feeling, thinking, and action]. Osnabrück and Germany: Sozio-Publishing.

Rogers, C. R. (1967). This is me. In *On becoming a person: A therapist's view of psychotherapy* (Original work published 1953) (pp. 3–27). London, UK: Constable.

Rosenberg, M. (2016). *Gewaltfreie Kommunikation: Eine Sprache des Lebens.* [Nonviolent communication: A language of life]. Paderborn and Germany: Junfermann-Verlag. (Original work published 2001).

The Rough Times Staff (1973a). Introduction. In J. Agel (Producer), *Rough times* (ix–xiii). New York, NY: Ballantine Books.

The Rough Times Staff. (1973b). *Rough times.* (J. Agel, Producer). New York, NY: Ballantine Books.

Rousseau, -J.-J. (2017). *Confessions.* Retrieved from www.gutenberg.org/files/3913/3913-h/3913-h.htm. (Original work published 1782).

Rowan, J. (1987). *The horned god: Feminism and men as wounding and healing.* London, UK: Routledge.

Roy, B. (1988a). Combatting racism. In B. Roy & C. M. Steiner (Eds.), *Radical psychiatry: The second decade* (pp. 185–188). Self-published manuscript available from www.radikale-therapie.de/DL/TSD.pdf.

Roy, B. (1988b). Introduction. In B. Roy & C. M. Steiner (Eds.), *Radical psychiatry: The second decade* (pp. 1–7). Self-published manuscript available from www.radikale-therapie.de/DL/TSD.pdf

Roy, B. (1988c). Loss of power – Alienation. In B. Roy & C. M. Steiner (Eds.), *Radical psychiatry: The second decade* Self-published manuscript available from www.radikale-therapie.de/DL/TSD.pdf. (Original work published 1980) (pp. 25–31).

Roy, B. (2014). *The Bernal story: Mediating class and race in a multicultural community.* San Francisco, CA: Syracuse University Press.

Roy, B., & Steiner, C. M. (Eds.). (1988). *Radical psychiatry: The second decade.* Self-published manuscript available from www.radikale-therapie.de/DL/TSD.pdf. (Original work published 1980).

256   *References*

Rush, A. K. (1973). *Getting clear: Body work for women*. New York, NY: Random House.

Salovey, P., & Meyer, J. D. (1990). Emotional intelligence. *Imagination, Cognition, and Personality, 9*(3), 185–211.

Schiff, J. L., Schiff, A. W., Mellor, K., Schiff, E., Schiff, S., Richman, D., … Momb, D. (1975). *Cathexis reader: Transactional analysis treatment of psychosis*. New York, NY: Harper & Row.

Schmid, P. (2006). The challenge of the other: Towards dialogical person-centered psychotherapy. *Person-Centered & Experiential Psychotherapies, 5*(4), 240–254.

Schore, A. N. (1994). *Affect regulation and the origin of the self: The neurobiology of emotional development*. Mahwah, NJ: Erlbaum.

Schore, A. N. (2012). *The science of the art of psychotherapy*. New York, NY: Norton.

Schultz, W. T. (Ed.). (2005). *Handbook of psychobiography*. New York, NY: Oxford University Press.

Schwebel, R. (1975a). Radical psychiatry and the Vietnam veteran. In C. Steiner (Original work published 1972) Ed., *Readings in radical psychiatry* (pp. 162–171). New York, NY: Grove Press.

Schwebel, R. (1975b). Trashing the stroke economy. *Issues in Radical Therapy, 3*(3), 13–15.

Schwebel, R. (2018). *Leap of power*. Tucson, AZ: Viva Press.

Schwebel, R. S., Schwebel, A. I., & Schwebel, M. (1985). The psychological/mediation intervention model. *Professional Psychology, 16*(1), 86–97.

Shlien, J. (2003). Theory as autobiography: The man and the movement. In J. Shlien (Ed.), (Original work published 1989), *To lead an honourable life* (pp. 212–216). Ross-on-Wye, UK: PCCS Books.

Slochower, J. A. (1996). *Holding and psychoanalysis*. Hillsdale, NJ: Analytic Press.

Smith, E. (1988). Disability. In B. Roy & C. M. Steiner (Eds.), *Radical psychiatry: The second decade* (pp. 179–184) Self-published manuscript available from www.radikale-therapie.de/DL/TSD.pdf (Original work published 1980).

Spielrein, S. (1994). Destruction as the cause of coming into being. *Journal of Analytical Psychology, 39*(2), (Original work published 1912), 155–186.

Spitz, R. A. (1945). Hospitalism. *The Psychoanalytic Study of the Child, 1*(1), 53–74.

Stark, M. (1999). *Modes of therapeutic action*. Northvale, NJ: Jason Aronson.

Steiner, C. M. (1965). *An investigation of Freud's attention cathexis theory in the context of a concept formation task*. Ann Arbour and Michigan, USA: A dissertation submitted in partial requirement for the degree of Doctor of Philosophy, University of Michigan.

Steiner, C. M. (1966). Script and counterscript. *Transactional Analysis Bulletin, 5*(18), 133–135.

Steiner, C. M. (1967a). A script checklist. *Transactional Analysis Bulletin, 6*(22), 38–39, 56.

Steiner, C. M. (1967b). The treatment of alcoholism. *Transactional Analysis Bulletin, 6*(23), 69–71.

Steiner, C. M. (1968a). The alcoholic game. *Transactional Analysis Bulletin, 7*(25), 6–16.

Steiner, C. M. (1968b). Transactional analysis as a treatment philosophy. *Transactional Analysis Bulletin, 7*(27), 61–64.

Steiner, C. M. (1969a). Alcoholism. *Transactional Analysis Bulletin, 8*(32), 96–97.

Steiner, C. (1969b). Manifesto. Unpublished manuscript.

Steiner, C. M. (1969c). The alcoholic game. *Quarterly Journal of Studies on Alcohol, 30*(4), 920–938.

Steiner, C. M. (1970). A fairytale. *Transactional Analysis Bulletin, 9*(36), 146–149.

Steiner, C. M. (1971a). A little boy's dream. *Transactional Analysis Journal, 1*(1), 46–48.

Steiner, C. M. (1971b). *Games alcoholics play*. New York, NY: Grove Press.

References 257

Steiner, C. M. (1971c). Radical psychiatry manifesto. In J. Agel Producer, *The radical therapy collective, the radical therapist* (pp. 280–282). New York, NY: Ballantine.

Steiner, C. M. (1971d). Radical psychiatry: Principles. In J. Agel Producer, *The radical therapy collective, the radical therapist* (pp. 3–7). New York, NY: Ballantine.

Steiner, C. (1971e). *TA made simple: Ego states, games, scripts and "The fuzzy tale"*. Berkeley, CA: TA Simple.

Steiner, C. M. (1971f). The stroke economy. *Transactional Analysis Journal*, *1*(3), 9–15.

Steiner, C. M. (1972a). Radical psychiatry. In H. M. Ruitenbeek (Ed.), *Going crazy: The radical therapy of R. D. Laing and others* (pp. span). New York, NY: Bantam Books.

Steiner, C. M. (1972b). Scripts revisited. *Transactional Analysis Journal*, *2*(2), 83–86.

Steiner, C. M. (1972c). Two love poems. In J. Marcus (Ed.), *Poem-maker soul-healer* (pp. 18). Berkeley, CA: Radical Psychiatry Community Press.

Steiner, C. M. (1973a). Cooperation. *Issues in Radical Therapy*, *1*(3), Summer, 7.

Steiner, C. (1973b). Coupleism. *Issues in Radical Therapy*, *1*(4), Autumn, 31–32.

Steiner, C. (1973c). Inside TA or I'm OK, you're OK (but what about them?). *Issues in Radical Therapy*, *1*(2), Spring, 3–7.

Steiner, C. (1973d). [Open] Letter to a brother: Reflections on men's liberation. *Issues in Radical Therapy*, *1*(1), January, 15–18.

Steiner, C. M. (1973e). The rescue triangle. *Issues in Radical Therapy*, *1*(4), Autumn, 20–24.

Steiner, C. M. (1974a). *Scripts people live: Transactional analysis of life scripts*. New York, NY: Grove Press.

Steiner, C. M. (1974b). We are all outlaws. *Issues in Radical Therapy*, *2*(3), Summer, 26–28.

Steiner, C. (1974c). Wilhelm Reich: A defeated revolutionary. *Issues in Radical Therapy*, *2*(2), Spring, 10–11.

Steiner, C. M. (1975a). Contractual problem-solving groups. In C. M. Steiner (Ed.), *Readings in radical psychiatry* (pp. 73–79). New York, NY: Grove Press.

Steiner, C. M. (1975b). Editorial. *Issues in Radical Therapy*, *4*(1), Winter, 3.

Steiner, C. (1975c). Letter to the editor. *The Script*, *4*, 7. June.

Steiner, C. (1975d). Manifesto. In C. M. Steiner (Ed.), *Readings in radical psychiatry* (pp. 3–6). New York, NY: Grove Press.

Steiner, C. M. (1975e). Power: Part I. *Issues in Radical Therapy*, *3*(3), Summer, 7–12.

Steiner, C. M. (1975f). Power: Part II. *Issues in Radical Therapy*, *4*(1), Winter, 20–22.

Steiner, C. (1975g). Radical psychiatry history. In C. M. Steiner (Ed.), *Readings in radical psychiatry* (pp. 142–147). New York, NY: Grove Press.

Steiner, C. (1975h). Radical psychiatry: Principles. In C. Steiner (Ed.), *Readings in radical psychiatry* (pp. 9–16). New York, NY: Grove Press.

Steiner, C. M. (Ed.). (1975i). *Readings in radical psychiatry*. New York, NY: Grove Press.

Steiner, C. M. (1975j). Teaching radical psychiatry. In C. M. Steiner (Ed.), *Readings in radical psychiatry* (pp. 55–70). New York, NY: Grove Press.

Steiner, C. M. (1975k). The stroke economy. In C. M. Steiner (Ed.), *Readings in radical psychiatry* (pp. 28–43). New York, NY: Grove Press.

Steiner, C. M. (1975l). Working cooperatively. *Issues in Radical Therapy*, *3*(4), Fall, 22–25.

Steiner, C. M. (1976a). Cooperation. In H. Wyckoff (Ed.), *Love, therapy and politics: Issues in radical therapy – The first year* (pp. 28–42). New York, NY: Grove Press.

Steiner, C. M. (1976b). Coupleism. In H. Wyckoff (Ed.), *Love, therapy and politics: Issues in radical therapy – The first year* (pp. 127–135). New York, NY: Grove Press.

Steiner, C. M. (1976c). Rescue. In H. Wyckoff (Ed.), *Love, therapy and politics: Issues in radical therapy – The first year* (pp. 43–63). New York, NY: Grove Press.

258   References

Steiner, C. M. (1976d). Socially responsible therapy: Reflections on "The female juvenile delinquent". *Transactional Analysis Journal, 6*(1), 11–14.

Steiner, C. (1977a). Conclusion. In C. M. Steiner & C. Kerr (Eds.), *Beyond games and scripts by Eric Berne: Selections from his major writings* (p. 371). New York, NY: Grove Press.

Steiner, C. M. (1977b). Cooperative meetings. *Issues in Radical Therapy, 17*, 11. Winter.

Steiner, C. M. (1977c). Feminism for men. *Issues in Radical Therapy, 20*, 3–10. Fall.

Steiner, C. (1977d). *The original warm fuzzy tale: A fairytale* J.-A. Dick. Rolling Hills Estate, CA: Jalmar Press. Illustrator.

Steiner, C. M. (1977e). The principles revised. *Issues in Radical Therapy, 19*, 12. Spring.

Steiner, C. (1978a). Back at the Ranch. *Issues in Radical Therapy, 21*, 28–29. Winter.

Steiner, C. M. (1978b). Feminism for men, part II. *Issues in Radical Therapy, 22*, 3–9. Spring.

Steiner, C. (1978c). Letter to the editor. *The Script, 7*(4), April, 4.

Steiner, C. M. (1978d). Living visions: The Cooperative Healing Center. *Issues in Radical Therapy, 24*, 9. Fall.

Steiner, C. M. (1978e). The Pig Parent. *Issues in Radical Therapy, 23*, 5–11. Summer.

Steiner, C. M. (1979a). Cooperation. *Issues in Radical Therapy, 27*, 3. Fall.

Steiner, C. M. (1979b). *Healing alcoholism.* New York, NY: Grove Press.

Steiner, C. M. (1979c). Radical psychiatry: Once again with feeling. *Issues in Radical Therapy, 25*, 26–30. Spring.

Steiner, C. M. (1979d). The Pig Parent. *Transactional Analysis Journal, 9*(1), 26–37.

Steiner, C. M. (1980a). *A manual on cooperation.* Berkeley, CA: Issues in Cooperation and Power.

Steiner, C. M. (1980b). Editorial. *Issues in Cooperation and Power, 4*, 3. Winter.

Steiner, C. M. (1981a). Acceptance statement from Claude Steiner on co-winning the Eric Berne Memorial Scientific Award for the stroke economy. *Transactional Analysis Journal, 11*(1), 6–9.

Steiner, C. M. (1981b). Monogamy, non-monogamy, and omnigamy. *Issues in Cooperation and Power, 5*, 4–6, 8–11, 13–15, 18–19, 21–23. Spring.

Steiner, C. M. (1981c). Omnigamy in Iowa. *Issues in Cooperation and Power, 7*, 18–25. Fall.

Steiner, C. M. (1981d). Radical psychiatry. In R. J. Corsini (Ed.), *Handbook of innovative psychotherapies* (pp. 724–735). New York, NY: Wiley.

Steiner, C. M. (1981e). *The other side of power.* New York, NY: Grove Press.

Steiner, C. M. (1984a). Creating an ecology for emotional literacy. *Issues in Radical Therapy, 11*(2), 6–9, 49–52.

Steiner, C. M. (1984b). Emotional literacy. *Transactional Analysis Journal, 14*(3), 162–173.

Steiner, C. (1985). *Principles of radical psychiatry (1985 revision).* Retrieved from www. emotional-literacy.org/principles-radical-psychiatry-1985-revision/.

Steiner, C. M. (1986). *When a man loves a woman.* New York, NY: Grove Press.

Steiner, C. M. (1987). The seven sources of power: An alternative to authority. *Transactional Analysis Journal, 17*(3), 102–104.

Steiner, C. (1988a). Brave New World Revisited, revisited. *Propaganda Review, 3*, 32–35. Winter.

Steiner, C. M. (1988b). Emotional literacy. In B. Roy & C. M. Steiner (Eds.), *Radical psychiatry: The second decade* Self-published manuscript available from www.radikale-therapie.de/DL/TSD.pdf. (Original work published 1980) (pp. 77–90).

References 259

Steiner, C. (1988c). Global TA action projects encouraged. *The Script, 18*(9), December, 1–7.

Steiner, C. M. (1988d). Power. In B. Roy & C. M. Steiner (Eds.), *Radical psychiatry: The second decade* Self-published manuscript available from www.radikale-therapie.de/DL/TSD.pdf. (Original work published 1980) (pp. 11–23).

Steiner, C. M. (1988e). The Pig Parent. In B. Roy & C. M. Steiner (Eds.), *Radical psychiatry: The second decade* Self-published manuscript available from www.radikale-therapie.de/DL/TSD.pdf. (Original work published 1980) (pp. 47–58).

Steiner, C. (1989). Editorial. *Propaganda Review, 5*, 1. Summer.

Steiner, C. M. (1992). *Surfing the info-wave: Emotional literacy and personal power in the information age. How to live in the information-driven years without giving up your heart to the new machines.* Unpublished manuscript.

Steiner, C. (1995a). The liberation of love and the emotions. *The Script, 25*(9), December, 1–7.

Steiner, C. M. (1995b). Thirty years of psychotherapy and transactional analysis in 1,500 words or less. *Transactional Analysis Journal, 25*(1), 83–86.

Steiner, C. M. (1996). Emotional literacy training: The application of transactional analysis to the study of emotions. *Transactional Analysis Journal, 26*(1), 31–39.

Steiner, C. M. (1997). Transactional analysis in the information age. *Transactional Analysis Journal, 27*(1), 15–23.

Steiner, C. (1998a). *Cyber-psychology: Love, power and redemption in the age of information machines.* Unpublished manuscript.

Steiner, C. M. (1998b). [Letter to the editor (Members' Forum).]. *The Script, 28*(4), May-June, 5, 6.

Steiner, C. M. (1998c). [Letter to the editor (Members' Forum: Steiner and Erskine/Trautmann dialogue continues).]. *The Script, 28*(8), November, 6.

Steiner, C. (1999a). (September-October). Emotional excess on the internet. *The Script, 29*(7), 2.

Steiner, C. (1999b). E-style: The emotional wasteland. *The Script, 29*(6), August, 3.

Steiner, C. M. (2000a). Apology: The transactional analysis of a fundamental exchange. *Transactional Analysis Journal, 30*(2), 145–149.

Steiner, C. M. (2000b). Games and the stroke economy. *The Script, 30*(5), July, 1–2.

Steiner, C. M. (2000c). Letter to the editor. *Transactional Analysis Journal, 30*(4), 305.

Steiner, C. M. (2000d). *The meming of love: Invention of the human heart.* Keynote lecture given at the 3rd Adolescence Health Conference at the Royal College of Physicians, London, October 2000. Unpublished paper available from www.emotional-literacy.org/meming-love-invention-human-heart/.

Steiner, C. (2000e). Transactional analysis in the information age. *The Script, 30*(1), January-February, 1, 7.

Steiner, C. M. (2001a). Nowhere to hide: Feelings on the internet. *The Script, 31*(4), May-June, 3.

Steiner, C. M. (2001b). Radical psychiatry. In R. Corsini (Ed.), *Handbook of innovative psychotherapies* (2nd ed., pp. 578–586). New York, NY: Wiley.

Steiner, C. M. (2002a). The adult: Once again, with feeling. *Transactional Analysis Journal, 32*(1), 62–65.

Steiner, C. M. (2002b). The development of transactional analysis theory and practice: A brief history. *The Script, 32*(9), December, 3.

Steiner, C. M. (2003a). Core concepts of a stroke-centered transactional analysis. *Transactional Analysis Journal, 33*(2), 178–181.

260   *References*

Steiner, C. M. (2003b). Corroborating research sought [Research file]. *The Script, 33*(4), May-June, 3.

Steiner, C. (2003c). *Emotional literacy: Intelligence with a heart.* Fawnskin, CA: Personhood Press.

Steiner, C. M. (2003d). [Letter from the guest editor.]. *Transactional Analysis Journal, 33*(2), 111–114.

Steiner, C. (2003e). [Letter to the Editor (Members' Forum).]. *The Script, 33*(7), September-October, 6.

Steiner, C. (2003f). [Letter to the Editor (Members' Forum: Response to Hargaden's speech about Berne).]. *The Script, 33*(6), August, 5.

Steiner, C. M. (2004). Understanding the enigma of Eric Berne [After He Said Hello (P. Levin, Ed.)]. *The Script, 34*(4), May-June, 2.

Steiner, C. M. (2005a). *Emotional literacy.* [DVD and booklet files]. London, UK: Visions of Psychotherapy.

Steiner, C. (2005b). Introducing members of the ITAA Board of Trustees: Claude Steiner, Vice President of Internet. *The Script, 35*(3), April, 4.

Steiner, C. M. (2005c). Transactional analysis: An elegant theory and practice. *The Script, 35*(2), March, 4–5.

Steiner, C. M. (2005d). Letter: Steiner to Berne [Members' Forum]. *The Script, 35*(8), November, 5.

Steiner, C. (2006a). Games and lovelessness. *The Script, 36*(5), July, 1–2.

Steiner, C. M. (2006b). Transactional analysis and psychoanalysis: Writing styles. *Transactional Analysis Journal, 36*(4), 330–334.

Steiner, C. M. (2006c). Quo vadis transactional analysis? Change and trust. *The Script, 36*(9), December, 6–7.

Steiner, C. M. (2006d). [Letter to the Editor: Response to editorial comments by Helen Hargaden in *Transactional Analysis Journal* April 2005]. *Transactional Analysis Journal, 36*(1), 70.

Steiner, C. M. (2007). Stroking: What's love got to do with it?. *Transactional Analysis Journal, 37*(4), 307–310.

Steiner, C. M. (2008a). *Confessions of a psycho-mechanic.* Unpublished manuscript.

Steiner, C. M. (2008b). *Excellence in aging for men: Twelve strategies.* Privately circulated publication.

Steiner, C. M. (2008c). Honesty and respect. *Greater Good, 4*(3), Winter, xx-yy.

Steiner, C. M. (2008d). People's power plays [text file]. In C. M. Steiner (Eds.), *Claude Steiner's emotional literacy.* London, UK: Visions of Psychotherapy, [DVD and text files].

Steiner, C. (2009). *The heart of the matter. Love, information and transactional analysis.* Pleasanton, CA: TA Press.

Steiner, C. (2010). Eric Berne's politics: "The great pyramid". *Transactional Analysis Journal, 40*(3-4), 212–216.

Steiner, C. M. (2011). *Pleased to meet you, hope you guess my name: The inner critic.* Retrieved from www.emotional-literacy.org/pleased-meet-hope-guess-name-inner-critic/.

Steiner, C. (2012). The OK position: Freedom, equality, and the pursuit of happiness. *Transactional Analysis Journal, 42*(4), 294–297.

Steiner, C. M. (2013). Becoming a writer. *The Script, 43*(3), March, 6–7.

Steiner, C. (2015). Lima's conference honors Berne's legacy. *The Script, 45*(12), December, 1–3.

References 261

Steiner, C. (2016). *Emotionale Komptence: Der Weg zur Befreiung des Menschen. Eine Grundierung* [Emotional literacy: The path to human liberation. A primer] (C. Freud & A. Chaffin, Trans.). Unpublished manuscript.

Steiner, C. M. (2017). *CS at 80*. Unpublished manuscript.

Steiner, C. M. (2020a). Confessions of a psychomechanic: Excerpts on emotional literacy. In K. Tudor (Ed.), *Claude Steiner, emotional activist: The life and work of Claude Michel Steiner* (pp. **175–181**). London, UK: Routledge.

Steiner, C. M. (2020b). Confessions of a psychomechanic: Excerpts on love and sex. In K. Tudor (Ed.), *Claude Steiner, emotional activist: The life and work of Claude Michel Steiner* (pp. **203–209**). London, UK: Routledge.

Steiner, C. M. (2020c). Confessions of a psychomechanic: Excerpts on power. In K. Tudor (Ed.), *Claude Steiner, emotional activist: The life and work of Claude Michel Steiner* (pp. **147–154**). London, UK: Routledge.

Steiner, C. M. (2020d). Confessions of a psychomechanic: Excerpts on radical psychiatry. In K. Tudor (Ed.), *Claude Steiner, emotional activist: The life and work of Claude Michel Steiner* (pp. **105–115**). London, UK: Routledge.

Steiner, C. M. (2020e). Confessions of a psychomechanic: Excerpts on script. In K. Tudor (Ed.), *Claude Steiner, emotional activist: The life and work of Claude Michel Steiner* (pp. **57–65**). London, UK: Routledge.

Steiner, C. M. (2020f). Confessions of a psychomechanic: Excerpts on strokes. In K. Tudor (Ed.), *Claude Steiner, emotional activist: The life and work of Claude Michel Steiner* (pp. **83–88**). London, UK: Routledge.

Steiner, C. M., Campos, L., Drego, P., Joines, V., Ligabue, S., Noriega, G., … Said, E. (2003). A compilation of core concepts. *Transactional Analysis Journal, 33*(2), 182–191.

Steiner, C. M., & Cassidy, W. (1969). Therapeutic contracts in group treatment. *Transactional Analysis Bulletin, 8*(30), 29–31.

Steiner, C., & Cornell, B. (1998). Transactional analysis and emotional literacy. *The Script, 28*(2), March, 1, 6.

Steiner, C. M., & Kerr, C. (Eds.). (1977). *Beyond games and scripts by Eric Berne: Selections from his major writings*. New York, NY: Grove Press.

Steiner, C. M., & Meigham, S. (1975). An interview with R. D. Laing. *Issues in Radical Therapy, 3*(4), Autumn, 3–9.

Steiner, C., Michel, G., & Oberdieck, H. (2004). *Die Kunst, sich Miteinander wohl zu fühlen.* [The art of feeling good together]. Freiburg im Breisgau and Germany: Verlag Herder.

Steiner, C. M., & Novellino, M. (2005). Theoretical diversity: A debate about TA and psychoanalysis. *Transactional Analysis Journal, 35*(2), 110–118.

Steiner, C. M., & Perry, P. (1997). *Achieving emotional literacy: A personal program to increase your emotional intelligence*. New York, NY: Avon Books.

Steiner, C., & Rappleye, C. (1988). Jacques Ellul: Quirky trailblazer of propaganda theory. *Propaganda Review, 2*, 29–33. Summer.

Steiner, C., & Rappleye, C. (1989). Propaganda is a conscious conspiracy, period. *Propaganda Review, 5*, 7, 10–11, 46. Summer.

Steiner, C. M., & Roy, B. (1988). Cooperation. In B. Roy & C. M. Steiner (Eds.), *Radical psychiatry: The second decade* Self-published manuscript available from www.radikale-therapie.de/DL/TSD.pdf. (Original work published 1980) (pp. 44–46).

Steiner, C., & Steiner, U. (1968a). Claude and Ursula Steiner: Permission classes. *Transactional Analysis Bulletin, 7*(25), 2.

262   References

Steiner, C., & Steiner, U. (1968b). Permission classes. *Transactional Analysis Bulletin, 7*(28), 89.

Steiner, C. M., & Tilney, T. (Eds.). (2003). Core concepts [Special Issue]. *Transactional Analysis Journal, 33*(2).

Steiner, C., & Tudor, K. (2014, August 7). *Still radical after all these years: TA and politics.* Workshop presented at the International Transactional Analysis Association World Conference, San Francisco, CA. Available from www.youtube.com/watch?v=0m5zzQyAe_M.

Steiner, C., & Wyckoff, H. (1975). Alienation. In C. M. Steiner (Ed.), *Readings in radical psychiatry* (pp. 17–27). New York, NY: Grove Press.

Strauss Clay, J. (2003, June 7). The real Leo Strauss. *The New York Times.* Retrieved from www.nytimes.com/2003/06/07/opinion/the-real-leo-strauss.html.

Summers, G., & Tudor, K. (2000). Cocreative transactional analysis. *Transactional Analysis Journal, 30*(1), 23–40.

Tarcov, N. (1986, September-October). Will the real Leo Strauss please stand up? *The American Interest.* Retrieved from: www.the-american-interest.com/2006/09/01/will-the-real-leo-strauss-please-stand-up/.

Tha'sa. (2000). Geliebt werden. Ein MRT-Wochenende zu sexualisierter Gewalt [To be loved. An MRT weekend on sexual violence]. *Männerrundbrief [Men's Newsletter], 14,* 9–10.

Thomas, R. (2017). *Why Dylan matters.* London, UK: William Collins.

Totton, N. (2000). *Psychotherapy and politics.* London, UK: Sage.

Tubbs, W. (1972). Beyond Perls. *Journal of Humanistic Psychology, 12*(2), 5.

Tudor, K. (2003). The neopsyche: The integrating Adult ego state. In C. Sills & H. Hargaden (Eds.), *Ego states* (pp. 201–231). London, UK: Worth Reading.

Tudor, K. (2010). The state of the ego: Then and now. *Transactional Analysis Journal, 40*(3&4), 261–277.

Tudor, K. (2016). Permission, protection, and potency: The three Ps reconsidered. *Transactional Analysis Journal, 46*(1), 50–62.

Tudor, K. (2017). Alienation and psychotherapy. (Original work published 1997). In K. Tudor (Ed.), *Conscience and Critic: The selected works of Keith Tudor.* London, UK: Routledge.

Tudor, K. (2020). *Transactional analysis proper – And improper: Selected and new papers by Keith Tudor.* in press. London, UK: Routledge.

Tudor, K., & Summers, G. (2014). *Co-creative transactional analysis: Papers, responses, dialogues, and developments.* London, UK: Karnac.

Valéry, P. (1957). *Oeuvres Vol. 1* (J. Hyties, Ed.). Paris, France: Gallimard.

Van Mens-Verhulst, J., & Waaldijk, B. (Eds.). (2008). *Vrouwenhulpverlening 1975-2000. Beweging in en rond de gezondheidszorg [Women's help 1975-2000. Movement in and around the healthcare system].* Houten and The Netherlands: Bohn Stafleu van Loghum.

Van Velden, F., & Severijnen, F. (1985). *MRT-Anleitung [MRT training guide].* Utrecht and The Netherlands: Author.

Vöhringer, M. (n.d.). *Training of emotional competence: Scientific basis and evaluation of the application in a stationary setting.* Bamberg and Germany: University of Bamberg, Germany.

Wilson, M., Lavis, J., & Guta, A. (2012). Community-based organizations in the health sector: A scoping review. *Health Research Policy and Systems, 10*(36).

Woollams, S., & Brown, M. (1978). *Transactional analysis.* Dexter, MI: Huron Valley Institute Press.

References 263

Woman, R. H. (1973). Up against monogamy: A personal account – Part I. *Issues in Radical Therapy, 1*(2), Spring, 8–10.

Woods, K. (2007). The stroking school of transactional analysis. *Transactional Analysis Journal, 37*(1), 32–34.

Woollams, S., & Brown, M. (1978). *Transactional analysis*. Dexter, MI: Huron Valley Institute Press.

Wyckoff, H. (1970). Radical psychiatry and transactional analysis in women's groups. *Transactional Analysis Bulletin, 9*(36), 127–133.

Wyckoff, H. (1971). The stroke economy in women's scripts. *Transactional Analysis Journal, 1*(3), 16–20.

Wyckoff, H. (1974). Sex role scripting in men and women. In C. M. Steiner (Ed.), *Scripts people live: Transactional analysis of life scripts* (pp. 165–205). New York, NY: Grove Press.

Wyckoff, H. (1975a). Permission. In C. M. Steiner (Ed.), *Readings in radical psychiatry* (pp. 106–120). New York, NY: Grove Press.

Wyckoff, H. (1975b). Problem solving groups for women. In C. M. Steiner (Ed.), *Readings in radical psychiatry* (pp. 80–105). New York, NY: Grove Press.

Wyckoff, H. (1975c). Women's scripts and the stroke economy. In C. M. Steiner (Ed.), *Readings in radical psychiatry* (pp. 44–54). New York, NY: Grove Press.

Wyckoff, H. (Ed.). (1976). *Love, therapy and politics. Issues in radical therapy – The first year*. New York, NY: Grove Press.

Wyckoff, H. (1977). *Solving women's problems: Through awareness, action and contact*. New York, NY: Grove Press.

Wyckoff, H. (1979). *Vrouwenpraatgroepen. Feminist Oefengroepen Radicale Therapy [Women Self-Help Groups: Feminist Exercise Groups in Radical Therapy]*. Amsterdam and The Netherlands: Bert Bakker.

Wyckoff, H. (1980). *Solving problems together*. New York, NY: Grove Press.

Wyckoff, H., & Steiner, C. (1971). Alienation. Berkeley [Special issue]. *The Radical Therapist, 2*(3), 4.

Young, M. L. (2008b). A handbook on bears. *Qualitative Inquiry, 14*(6), 999–1009.

Young, M. L. (2008a). Death comes. *Qualitative Inquiry, 14*(6), 990–998.

Index

Achieving Emotional Literacy **11**, 53, 185, 187–188, 242, 243

action 75, 101, 101–102, 111–112, 130n1, 131, 132, 138, 156; –feeling designation 191; /feeling statements 140, 186; *see also* feeling–action statements; political 87, 223; social *see* stroke: as unit of social

ageing 149, 228–229, *239*, 249n10

Ainsworth, M.D.S. 92

alcohol studies 14

alcoholism, the treatment of **17**, *239*

Aldebaran 168

alienation 74–77, 86, 97, 116, 131–132, 159–161, 242, *239*, 245; from body and emotions **161**, 185; forms of 160–161, **161**; gender 86; from hands 160; from the heart 142; impact of 75–76, 77, 114–115; from love **161**; from (the) mind 140, **161**; and power 160–163; theory of 110–115, 156, 159, 160, 169; from society 100; from work **161**; *see also* powerlessness

Allen, B.A. 78

Allen, J.R. 78

Althöfer, L. 115, 136, 139

Angel, E. 75

apology **18**, 65, 192, 226, 234, *239*

Aptheker, H. 76

attention 138; cathexis (attention deficit disorder) 14; *see also* groups; radical therapy

attribution 70–74

autobiography 16, 223; confession and editing 19–22

awareness 61, 75, 87, 101, 111, 114, 116, 130n1, 132, 139; emotional *see* emotional awareness; heightened *see* paranoia; of internal dialogue 159; of oppression 143, 156; of privilege 134; of socialization 134; *see also* action; contact

Barrow, Giles 246, 247

Baruch, J. 136

Berger, K. 132

Berne, E. 13, 51n16, 61, 62, 67, 68, 69, 72, 83, 84, 89, 113, 166, 210, 227, 238, 239, 248n3

Berne, Eric **10**, **11**, 14, 25–26, 26n15, 63; Archives 27; a Beta psychiatrist 168; death 62–63, 67, 196, 207–208; and feelings 184, 186; and politics 105, 168; script 67; working attitude 67

Beveridge, A. 72, 74, 76

Beyond Scripts and Games 27, 247

body 92–95, 112, 133, 137, 160–161, 179–180, 249n10; -centred work 90; culture 58; politics 249n10; reference to the 137; physical strokes 100; therapies 84; work 106 107, 124; *see also* groups; radical therapy; somatic

Bonds-White, F. 217

Boss, M. 75, 76

Boyer, R. 72

Breitenbürger, W. 136

Brown, M. 88n1, 232–233

Browne, J. 20, 246

Browne, Jackson 223, 246

Brownmiller, S. 114

Index   265

Cassius, J. 92, 93
chakras 162, 163, 211, 217–219
Childs-Gowell, E. 92
Chinnock, K. 78
Clarkson, P. 229
clients 64, 71, 73, 75, 77, 91, 95; suicidal 230–231
co-counselling 132–133
Cohen, L. 205
Confession (the nature of) 16, 19–22
contact 101, 111, 214; + awareness + action (formula) 101, 111, 116, 132; hunger for contact 214, 217; raps 87; *see also* action; awareness
contracts **17**, 117, 132, 138, 188–189, 211, 231, *239*; confidentiality 188–189; cooperative 13, 21, 132, 138, 152, 164, 165, 179, 185, 189, 194, 195, 196, 229, 232, *239*, 243–244; treatment/training 189; *see also* groups; radical therapy
Cooper, D. 70
Cooper, D.G. 72
cooperation 13, **18**, 23, 91, 119, 122, 123, 138, 151, 177, 185, 198, 215, 232, *239*, 241; as collective power 163–164; components of 149; guidelines for 243; 243; rules of 243; as a value 216; *see also* cooperative contract(s); *Issues in Cooperation and Power*; *Issues in Radical Therapy & Cooperative Power*; *A Manual on Cooperation*
Cooperative Survival Project 243, 248n8
Cornell, B. 239, 241
Cornell, W. 92
Cornell, W.F. 70, 78, 217
Corsini, R.J. 160
coupleism 151, 158, 167, 206, *239*
Critical Parent 96, 113, 132, 148, 149, 180, 190–191, 194, 214, 241–242, 243; basic message 148; and the Pig Parent 158–159; *see also* Pig Parent
Crossman, P. 213
Cultural Parent 22, 95, 97–100, 101, 102; and the "dark" self *97*, 99–101, *99*; and the stroke economy 95–96
cyberpsychology **18**
cyborgs, 13, **18**, 232

Dawkins, R. 214
death 4, 62–63, 230; with dignity 228–229
deception 75, 178; self- 177; *see also* mystification
de Graaf, A. 70
depression 66, 64, 77, 86, 88, 112, 114, **161**, 180–181, 193–194
Detlefsen, U. 134
Dhananjaya, D. 97, 101
Doohan, Matthew (grandson) **11**, 235–236, 245
Doohan, Noemi (Mimi) (née Steiner) (daughter) *10*, **10**, 21, 23, 61, 64–65, 209, 229, 232, 233–234, 235, 236, 243
the drama triangle 137, 156, 161, 187; as a political tool 161
Drego, P. 22, 95, 96, 97
Dworkin, A. 114
Dylan, B. 20

editing (approach to) 21–22
Ellenberg, H.F. 75
EmLit *see* emotional literacy
emotional: awareness 16, *239*; competence 182, 185, 186, 191–193, 194, 195, 197, 198; intelligence 16, **18**, 197, 198, 232, 233, *239*
emotional literacy (EmLit) **18**, 175–181, 182–200, 212, 213, 225, 227n4, 232, 233, 234, 237–243, *239*; in the context of a psychosomatic clinic 193–195; and TA and RP **17–18**, 184–185, 237–245, *239*, **240**
Emotional Literacy: Intelligence with a Heart 6n1, **11**, 154n3, 243
Ernst, S. 133
Erskine, R. 239
Erskine, R.G. 15
Evison, R. 133
Excellence in Ageing for Men **11**

Faber, A. 136
feeling–action statements 186
FORT (Feminist Oefengroepen Radicale Therapy) (feminist radical therapy exercise groups) *see* groups
Foucault, M. 152
Fowlie, H. 78

266 *Index*

Freud, S. 216
Frick, D. 136, 143
Fromm, E. 75, 76
Frühling, C. 136
F*ORT (Frauen* Organisieren Radicale Therapie) (women*-organised radical therapy groups) *see* groups

game 105; playing 121; theory 14, 72, 78
games **17**, *239 see also* power plays; Claude Steiner games and game-playing
Games Alcoholics Play **11**, 52n27, 112, 113, 127, 166, 182, 223
gentleness 215, 216
Gerhardt, S. 211, 213
Goldstine, D. 112
Goleman, D. 197
Goodison, L. 133
Goulding, M.M. 100
Goulding, R.L. 100
Green, S. 169
Groder, M. 120
Groder, Martin 114
group: -centered movements 77; encounter 84; phase of psychotherapy 75; *see also* Stroke City
groups 111, 125, 132, 193; Claude's therapy 116–118; feminist radical therapy exercise (FORT) 133–135; process 119, 143, 187; men's radical therapy (M*RT) 134–135, 136, 141; open-ended discussion 87; problem-solving 132, 133, 138, 140, 185; radical psychiatry (RP) 131; radical therapy (RT) 132, 136–142; training 118–123, 128–130, 195; wild therapy 105–107; women*-organised radical therapy (F*ORT) 134–135, 136, 141
Guggenbühl-Craig, A. 155
Guta, A. 19

Hanisch, C. 213
Hargaden, H. 25n15, 53n54, 53n57, 78, 92, 93, 239
Healing Alcoholism **11**, *52n27*, 127, 197
The Heart of the Matter 9, **11**, 26n22, 161, 168, 211, 216–219, 228, 240, 241, 242
Hill, D. 92
Hillar, T. 136, 143

honesty 20, 21, 24, 164, 176–177, 180, 211, 212, 215, 216, 227, 234, 236, 243, 244, 248; radical 177, 178
Horobin, R. 133
hunger: information 14, 91; recognition 13; stroke *see* stroke hunger; *see also* contact hunger for

India, colonisation of, 96
information; Age 14, 15, 219; hunger 14, 91; scarcity 14
International Transactional Analysis Association (ITAA) **10**, 14, 132, 183, 223
isolation 86, 87, 89, 90, 97, 98–100, 111, 131, 139, 160, 162, 169; *see also* mystification; oppression
Issues in Cooperation and Power 14, 123, 232
Issues in Radical Therapy 14, 27, 113, 115, 124, 125, 155, 169, 205, 249n10
Issues in Radical Therapy & Cooperative Power 14, 27

Jackins, H. 133
Jenkins, B. 123, 165
Jenkins, Becky 113, 116–117, 195, 209, 240
Johnson, F. 76

Karakashian, S. 168
Karpman, S. 62, 132, 137, 156, 161, 187
Kerr, C. 27, 206
Kerr, Carmen **11**, 150, 205–206, 215
Kaufman, K. 133
Kinnaman, P. 92
Kohlhaas-Reith, A. 14–15, 196, 227n2, 237, 239, 240, 241, 242, 246, 247
Kohlhaas-Reith, Anne 187, 195

Laing, R.D. 13, 70, 72–76, 176
LaRiviere, P. 112
Lavis, J. 19
Lawrence, D.H. 210
Levinas, E. 243
liberation 75, 101, 106, 116, 130n1, 131–132, 139, 151, 159, 168, 205, 215, 242; movements 77, 167, 168; sexual 204, 206, 210; women's 205

Index 267

lies 13, **17**, 88, 111, 115, 153, 178, 179, 189, 192, 193, 232; no 13, 21, 132, 138, 149, 165, 176, 178, 206 215, 229, 232, 234, 243, 244, 245; "noble" 179; *see also* cooperative contracts; lying; radical truth

life scripts 61–62, 160; basic 160, **161**; *see also* script

Ligabue, S. 92

love **18**, 59, 62, 77, 86–88, 112, **161**, 162–164, 184–185, 197, 199, 210–219, *239*; is the answer xiv, 23, 26n22, 210–219; and cooperation 215; and depression 114, 161; free 164, 206; and gentleness 215; and honesty 215; hunger 87, 210; and information 218; and power 215, 216–217 *see also* power; and recognition 203; of self, others and truth 207–209; and sex 59, 203–209; unequal exchange of 86; *see also* The meming of love; omnigamy; Stroke City

lying 151, 176–179, 189

Mailer, N. 117

Männerrundbrief [Men's Newsletter] 136

Mano 206

A Manual on Cooperation **11**, 164, 165 243

Marcus, J. 112, 115n4

Marcus, Joy 110, 113, 116, 118, 125, 127

Marcuse, H. 71, 74, 112

Marxism/Marxist 71, 74, 75, 76, 110, 131, 153, 242

May, R. 75, 76

mediation 123–124, 127, 128, 129, *239*

Meigham, S. 13

The meming of love 211–216

men's liberation 167, *239*

Meulenbelt, A. 133

Meyer, J.D. 197

Michel, G. 198

Minikin, K. 78

Mono, N. 136

monogamy 203, *239*

mutual support 137, 143; *see also* groups; radical therapy

mystification 51n17, 78, 97–98, 111, 131–132, 160

M*RT (Mannen* Radicale Therapy/ Männer* Radicale Therapie) (men's radical therapy) groups *see* groups

New, C. 133

Nicholson, Darca (partner) *10*, **11**, 61, 120, 124, 183, 206–207, 215, 234

Nicholson, D.L. 124, 128

Newton, T. 70

non-monogamy 207, *239*

Novellino, M. 239

Oberdieck, H. 198

omnigamy 183, 206–207, 211, 212

open communication 16, 211, 244, 245

oppression 72, 74–75, 86–87, 97–98, 101, 111–112, 131–133, 139, 143, 151–152, 156, 159, 205–206; and activism 77–78; internalised 101, 131, 139, 147–148, 158–159; + mystification + isolation (formula) 97, 111, 116, 131, 160; and power 158, 160; sexual 90–91; *see also* isolation; mystification; power oppressive

Orange, D. 243

The Origin Group 195–196

The Other Side of Power **11**, 126, 149–152, 155, 170, 182, 232, 237

paranoid fantasies: 25n8, 132, **140**, 187, 191, 193; round of 140–141

paranoia 12–13, **17**, 121, 140, 176, 179, 194, 207, 245; and its grain/kernel of truth 121, 175–176; as heightened awareness 12, 121, 187, 232; and intuition 121, 129, 176, 180, 194, 241

Perls, F. 151

Perls, Fritz, 185

permission 5, **17**, 117, 120, 137, 147, 207, *239*; asking for 186, 191; classes 83–84; protection and potency 132, 165, 166, 213, 245

Perry, P. 13, 132, 162, 185, 187–188, 197, 142, 243

Pheterson, G. 133, 134

philosophy 6n1, 16, 215, 216; treatment 165

Pig Parent 13, **17**, 70, 132, 147–149, 155, 158–159, 191, 194, 232, *239*, 240–241, 242, 247

plain talk 16, **17**, 245

268 *Index*

politics 113–114, 149, 152, 157–158, 214; heterosexual *see When a Man Loves a Woman*; personal 149, 158, 210; power 166–170; sexual 210, 211–213

life position(s) 62, 149; evangelical 51n16, 238

potency **17**, 147; 155, 165-166, 213, *239*; internal (P_0) 93; political 136

power **18**, 147–154, 155–171, *239*; collective 163–164; as control 155, 156; oppressive 155, 158–159; parity 215; plays **18**, 90–91, 109, 123, 149–150, 152, 156, 164–165, 180, 189, 206, 224, 227, 241–242; relational 157–158; and responsibility 155, 164–166; social imbalances of 158; sources of 150, 155, 159–163, **161**, 219

propaganda 14–15, **18**, 152–153, *167*, *239*

Propaganda Review **11**, 52n37, 152, 153, 166

psychomechanics **18**, 232, *239*, 244–245

Quibell, Julian (nephew) *10*, **10**, 234

Quibell (née Steiner), Kati (sister) *10*, **10**, 234

Rabenold, D. 159

radical psychiatry (RP) **17**, 105–115, *239*; formula 116, 117–118, *239*; *see also* action, alienation, awareness, contact, isolation, liberation, mystification, oppression; and Radikale Therapie *140*; and TA and EmLit **17–18**, 184–185; 237–245, *239*, **240**; as wild therapy 105–107; *see also* theory of alienation

The Radical Psychiatry Collective 109– 110, *114*, 116, 118, 121, 123, 132, 223

The Radical Therapist 14, 27, 125

The Radical Therapist Collective 69, 70, 168

radical therapy (RT): and attention 133, 138, 139, 142; and co-counselling 133; and contracts 138; dispersion and differences 126–128; and emotional literacy in the 2000s 128–130; the fifth decade of 131–144; the first decade onwards 116–130; and individual responsibility 137; influence of 123–126; learning it by observation and participation 118–123; meeting structure in 138–142; movement in Germany 142–143; and radical psychiatry (RP)

131–132; and the body 124, 137, 160, **161**; as a self-help therapy 133–135; structure of meetings in 138–142; theory, practice and influence of 123–126; *see also* groups

radical: truth 16, **17**, 178, 180, 218, 245; truthfulness 176–179; 208

Rainer, Adriane (partner) **11**, 61

Rappleye, C. 152, 153, 166

Rauch, A. 134, 135, 136, 138, 141

Readings in Radical Psychiatry **11**, 113

recognition hunger 13, 214; *see also* strokes

Reich, W. 71, 74, 77, 86, 242

Rescues 152, 179–180, 187, 189, 192, 208; free from 164; no 21, 149, 229, 234, 243, 245

Rescuing 151, 163, 165, 179–180, 227; avoiding 244

research 14, **18**, 59, 63, 84, 89, 105, 108, 178, 185, 194, 210, 225–226, *239*

resentments 120, 123, 125; round of **140**, 141–142

responsibility 76; in emotional literacy 185, 187, 189, 192, 194, 243; individual 137 *see also* radical therapy groups; mutual 149; power and 155, 164–166; in radical psychiatry and radical therapy 111, 133, 135, 136–137, 138, 143; shared 138

Rimbaud, A. 20

Risse, J. 133

Rogers, C.R. 247, 249n11

Rosenberg, M. 197

Round Mountain Ranch, Ukiah, California 3, **11**, 195, 233, 243, *248*

Rousseau, J.-J. 19

Rowan, J. 133

Roy, B. 124, 159, 164, 166, 168

RP *see* radical psychiatry

RT *see* radical therapy

Rush, A.K. 124

Salovey, P. 197

San Francisco Social Psychiatry Seminars 14, 67, 68, 105, 186

scarcity 71, **161**; information 14; no 243; of sex 87, 90; stroke 14, 84, 91

Schiff, J.L. 249n12

Schmid, P. 243

Schore, A.N. 94, 211

Schultz, W.T. 16
Schwebel, A.I. 124
Schwebel, M. 124
Schwebel, R. 96, 118, 121, 127, 168
Schwebel, Robert 113, 116, 117–118, 122, 130n1
Schwebel, R.S. 124
scoping review 24
script: matrix **11**, 66–68, *66*, *68*, 157, *157*, 232, *239*, 240–241; no love 142; Steiner's early writings on 69–70; theory 66–68, 70, 72, 160–162, *239*
The Script (newsletter/magazine of the ITAA), 68, 226, 228, 231, 241
scripting 93, 160–161, 213, 216, 217
Scripts People Live **11**, 63, *63*, 66, 70, 85, 182, 237, 242, 243
Severijnen, F. 134, 135, 136, 138, 141
sex 203–205; economy *see* scarcity of sex; /gender 132, 134, 135, 141, 144n1
sexuality 86–87, 112, 203–204, 206, 209, 211, 217; *see also* stroke economy and sexual minorities
Shlien, J. 20
Sills, C. 78, 92, 93
Slochower, J.A.,
Smith, E. 168
socially responsible therapy *239*
somatic, 92, 242, 249n10
Spielrein, S. 216
Spitz, R.A. 84
Stark, M. 22, 94
Steiner, Claude: 10 top ideas 11–13, *12*, 223, 232, 235; ageing and growing old 149, 228–229; attitude to alcohol and drugs 52n27; bibliography 24, 27–50; and Becky Jenkins *126*; and Bill Cornell *79*, 226, 241; and his body 228–229; childhood 15, 57–58, 107; concreteness 71–72, 76; *Confessions* 19–21, 57–65, 83–88, 105–115, 147–154, 175–181, 203–209; death 216, 229, 230, 234; a disciple of Eric Berne 14, 219, 233; and Eric Berne **17**, 25–26n15, 27–28, 61, 66–67, 68–69, 83, 86, 116, *239*, 245; on Eric Berne 62–63, 246, 247; and Eric Berne's legacy 233, 235, 246; and the Eric Berne Scientific Award 11, 13, *66*, *68*, *85*; father's aversion to 58, 63, 64;

father's influence on 59, 60, 67; as fixer 15, *15*, 244–245; final thesis 241–242; games and game-playing 24, 149, 223–225, 226–227; and Gino Althöfer 169, *170*; and Hartmut Oberdieck 182–184, *199*; humility 129, 211, 217; and Keith Tudor 1–2, *2*, 4, 5, 13, 19; legacy 9–53, 171, 216, 232–233, 236–245; life script 57–65, 199; love of self, others and truth 207–209; and love and sex 203–207; love and sex addiction 59; and need for recognition 64, 67, 196, 217, 223, 225–226, 247; mother's influence on 59, 107, 147, 175, 177, 235; in Nicaragua 152–153; obituary 231–234; Parkinson's 182, 197, 211, 228–229, 233, 234; and politics 168–169, 151, 152–153; and power plays 227; relationship with Carmen Kerr (partner), 206; relationship with Darca Nicholson (partner) 207; relationship with Hogie Wyckoff (partner) 61, 64, 86–87, 109–110, 111–112, 149–150, 164, 168, 176–177, 205–206, 207; relationship with mother 57, 64, 185, 203; relationship with transactional analysis 3, 51n16, 69, 90–91, 196, 197, 224–225, 233, 235, 238; relationship with Ursula Steiner (née Cohen) (wife) 58–59, 60, 110, 175, 204, 208, 224; and Robert Schwebel *118*; spheres of influence 237–245; as a teacher/trainer 117, 118–120, 124–125, 129–130, 183, 196; *see also* transactional analysis Claude Steiner's contribution to
Steiner, Eric (son) *10*, 230, 235, 245
Steiner, Hedi (aunt) 57–58, 60, 203
Steiner, Miguel (brother) *11*, **11**, 153, 234
Steiner, U. 83
Steiner-Hall, Jude (wife) **11**, 61, 65, 88, 169, 209, 226, 229, 230, 234
Stoebbener, K. 134
Strauss Clay, J. 181n2
stroke: -centred TA **17**, 90–91, *239*; City 5, 6n4, 84, 87, 90, 186, 207, 215–216; hunger 13, 14–15, **17**, 87, 88, 91, 142, 190; relational completion *94*, 94, 102 theory 22, 89–90, 242; as unit of social action 89

270   *Index*

stroke economy **11**, **17**, 59, 67, 71, *85*, 86–87, 90–91, 93, 95, 112, 121, 132, 190–191, *239*, 240–241, 242, 245; messages 149; radical (economics) 87–88; and sexual minorities 96–102; rules of 142, 190; trashing the 84, 90, 95–96, 121, 122, 124; *see also* stroke City; in women's scripts 86, 112

strokes: brain and body 92–95; round of **140**, 142; as a unit of recognition 83, 84, 89, 96, 142, 189–190, 191

suicidal clients 230–231

Summers, G. 1, 78

Surfing the info-wave 14

TA *see* transactional analysis

TA Made Simple **11**, 132

technology 15, 232

therapeutic slogans 26n18

therapy, self-organised 136–138; *see also* body reference to; radical therapy and attention, and contracts, and individual responsibility; mutual support; time

Thomas, R. 20

Thunnissen, M. 70

Tilney, T., 233, 238, *239*

time 136–137; working 138 *see also* radical therapy groups

Totton, N. 155

transactional analysis (TA): Claude Steiner's contribution to 13–14, **17–18**, 67, 69–70, 72, 90–91, 121, 158, 165, 170, 232, 238 *239*, 241, 242–244, 249n9; commercialisation of 196; and RP and EmLit **17–18**, 184–185, 237–245, *239*, **240**; as a social psychology *239*; stroke-centred **17**, 90–91, *239*

transactions 13, 94, 132, 149–150, 210, *239*, 243; dilemma 78; and emotional literacy 180, 186, 190, 241; power and 155, 158, 166, 241

Transactional Analysis Journal (the journal of the ITAA), 69, 225

Trautmann, R., 239

Tubbs, W. 154

Tudor, K. 1, 2, 3, 76–77, 78, 165, 169, 228, 238, 239

Van Mens-Verhulst, J. 133, 134

Van Velden, F. 134, 135, 136, 138, 141

Vöhringer, M. 198

Waaldijk, B. 133, 134

warm fuzzies **17**, 85, 190, *239*

The Warm Fuzzy Tale **11**, 90, 107, 180, 241

When a Man Loves a Woman **11**, 210, 211–213, 217, 237

wild (body) therapy 105–107

Wilinsky, Allyson Quibell (niece) *10*, **11**, 234

Willms, S. 133

Wilson, M. 19

Woman, R.H. 206

Woollams, S. 88n1, 232–233

working time 137, 138, 139

Wyckoff, H. 13, **17**, **18**, 23, 74, 86, 96, 97, 112, 121, 123, 132, 134, 138, 159, 160, **161**, 168, *239*

Wyckoff, Hogie **11**, 61, 64, 86–87, 90, 109–110, 111–112, 116, 118, 120, 122, 123, 124, 125, 131, 134, 149–150, 151, 164, 168, 176–177, 185, 205–206, 207, 215, 232, 249

Young, M. L. 16